Army Wives

Army Wives

From Crimea to Afghanistan: the Real Lives of the Women Behind the Men in Uniform

Midge Gillies

Aurum Press

Quarto is the authority on a wide range of topics.
Quarto educates, entertains and enriches the lives of our readers—enthusiasts and lovers of hands-on living.
www.QuartoKnows.com

First published in Great Britain 2016 by Aurum Press Ltd
74–77 White Lion Street
London N1 9PF

A catalogue record for this book is available from the British Library.

ISBN 978 1 78131 289 6

eISBN 978 1 84513 551 4

10 9 8 7 6 5 4 3 2 1
2020 2019 2018 2017 2016

Typeset in Dante MT Std by SX Composing DTP, Rayleigh, Essex

Printed and bound in Great Britain by
CPI Group (UK) Ltd, Croydon, CR0 4YY

This book is dedicated to the memory of Renee Winifred Gillies (1922–2013), with love

Contents

Cast List of Army Wives 1

Prologue 4

1: Getting There: Packet ships, palanquins and ponies 15

2: Accommodation: Barracks, bungalows and bivouacs 29

PART ONE: THE IMPERIAL ARMY WIFE

3: The Early Anglo-Indian Army Wife: Margaret Campbell Hannay 51

4: The Crimean Wife: Fanny Duberly, Nell Butler and Elizabeth Evans 63

5: The Changing Image of the Soldier And His Wife 79

6: The 'Great Sepoy Mutiny': Harriet Tytler, Fanny Wells and Lady Julia Inglis 90

7: The 'Career Wife': Lady Elizabeth Butler 111

PART TWO: LOSS AND THE GREAT WAR

8: The Army Widow: Clare Sheridan and Hazel Macnaghten 135

9: The Letter: Lena Leland, Clementine Churchill and Ethel Cove 157

10: The Damaged Husband 176

11: The Changed Husband 193

PART THREE: WORLD WAR TWO

12: Life on the Home Front: Diana Carnegie, 1940 215

13: Life on the Home Front: Rachel Dhonau, Summer 1941 to December 1942 226

14: The Prisoner of War's Wife: Renee Boardman, 1942–44 247

15: The End of the War: Surviving the Peace, 1943–45 261

PART FOUR: THE MODERN ARMY WIFE

16: The Cold War Wife 281

17: The Modern Army Wife 301

Epilogue: Life after the Army 318

Bibliography 337

Endnotes 350

Acknowledgements and Permissions 377

Index 382

Cast List of Army Wives

(in alphabetical order)

Armstrong, Carol. Women's Royal Army Corps officer and wife of Richard, Major Royal Signals, who served in West Germany during the Cold War.

Baker, Phyllis. Wife of Captain 'Barry' Custance, of the Royal Corps of Signals, 27 Line Section, who served in the Far East during the Second World War.

Boardman, Irene ('Renee'). Wife of Tom, Royal Army Ordnance Corps (RAOC), who served in the Far East during the Second World War.

Booty, Dolly. Wife of Ernest, private in the Durham Light Infantry held as prisoner of war in Europe during the Second World War.

Butler, Lady Elizabeth. Painter and wife of William, Brigadier-General and career soldier, who served around the world.

Butler, Ellen (or 'Nell'). Wife of Michael, a private in the 95th Derbyshire, who served in Crimea.

Carnegie, Diana. Wife of James, Second Lieutenant in the 352 Search Light Battery, Royal Artillery during the Second World War .

Churchill, Clementine. Wife of Winston, served 1915–16, Western front with Grenadier Guards, appointed Lieutenant-Colonel, commanding 6th Battalion Royal Scots Fusiliers.

Cove, Ethel. Wife of Gunner Wilfrid, Royal Garrison Artillery, who served in the First World War.

Cresswell, Adelaide. Married to captain in the 8th Hussars, who served in Crimea.

Dhonau, Rachel. Mass Observation diarist living in Norfolk and wife of Ernest, 'Jakob', a private in the Intelligence Service during World War Two.

Duberly, Fanny. Diarist and wife of Henry, Paymaster to the 8th Royal Irish Hussars, who served in Crimea, India and other parts of Britain.

Duffield, Daisy. Wife who passed on messages from German radio during the Second World War to relatives of soldiers held as prisoners of war.

Erroll, Lady Eliza. Wife of officer in the 60th Rifles, served in Crimea.

Evans, Elizabeth. Wife of William, who served in Crimea and India with the 4th (King's Own) Regiment of Foot.

Forrest, Annie. Wife of Major William of the 4th Dragoon Guards, who served in Crimea.

Gillies, Agnes. Wife of Alec, driver in B company, 17th Division, Royal Field Artillery in the First World War.

Gillies, Rebecca. Wife of Donald, 1st Dunbartonshire Rifle Volunteer Corps and, later, sergeant in the 72nd Field Ambulance in the First World War; father of Alec.

Gillies, Renee. Wife of Donald, Sergeant Major in the Scots Guard during the Second World War; son of Alec.

Hannay, Margaret Campbell. Wife of Lieutenant Simon Fraser of the 50th Regiment Native Infantry, who spent his career in India.

Inglis, Lady Julia. Wife of Brigadier John, who commanded the garrison at Lucknow in India.

Kaye, Mollie. Novelist and wife of Goff Hamilton, an officer in Queen Victoria's Own Corps of Guides; daughter of Sir Cecil Kaye.

Kelly, Peggy. Wife of Brian, a commando in the Second World War, and later, a police officer.

Leland, Lena. Wife of Captain Herbert John Collett, 1st South Staffordshire Regiment, who served in the First World War.

Macnaghten, Hazel. Wife of Angus, an officer in the Black Watch in the First World War.

Middleton, Sue. Wife of Richard, Captain in the Royal Artillery, who served in Cold War Germany and elsewhere.

Sheridan, Clare. Sculptor and wife of William Frederick 'Wilfred', captain in the Rifle Brigade during the First World War.

Speller, Elizabeth. Novelist and wife of Roger Bolter, Second Lieutenant who served in Cold War West Germany.

Stephens, Eleanore. Wife of Lieutenant-Colonel Reginald of the 2nd battalion of Rifle Brigade, who served in the First World War.

Tolkien, Edith. Wife of John Ronald Reuel, 2nd lieutenant in the Lancashire Fusiliers, served in the First World War.

Tytler, Harriet. Diarist and wife of Robert, officer in 38th Native Infantry, who served in India and the Andaman Islands.

Wells, Frances Janet or 'Fanny'. Wife of Walter, who was a doctor in the 48th Native Infantry, who served in India.

Wilton, Barbara. Wife of Chris, an officer in the Army Air Corps (AAC), who served in Northern Ireland, Cold War Germany, Canada, the Middle East and Africa.

Wright, Ada. Wife of Robert Thomas, 23rd battalion, Lance Corporal, County of London, who served in the First World War.

Prologue

There's something about a soldier
There's something about a soldier
That is fine fine fine
He may be a great big general
He may be a sergeant major
He may be a simple private of the line line line
But there's something about his bearing, something about his wearing
Something about his buttons all a-shine shine shine
O a military gent seems to suit the ladies best
There's something about a soldier that is fine fine fine.

(composed by Noel Gay, performed by Cicely Courtneidge in the film *Soldiers of the King*, 1933)

Barbara Wilton's spice rack is over forty years old. But she has no intention of replacing it. While the jars promise a now slightly jaded taste of the exotic through ginger, pepper and paprika, the foreign names scribbled on the back still vividly conjure up the wandering life of an army wife. The list also represents an alternative narrative of recent British foreign policy, through the Troubles in

Northern Ireland and the Cold War to a new world of diplomacy.

Lisburn Road, Belfast	1972
Marlborough Gardens, Belfast	1973
Lavenham, Salisbury	1974
Auckland Rd, Bulford Camp	1975
Cheshire Close, Salisbury	1976
Stresseman Strasse, Detmold	1977
Bliefterningwig, Minden	1978
Anrochte, Germany	1979
Korbecke	1980
Melfa Ave., Canada	1981
Nelson Close, Bulford Camp	1984
Neuengeseke, Germany	1986
Dennington, Suffolk	1988
Wildhern, Hampshire	1991
Middle Wallop, Hampshire	1993
Rome	1994
Dennington, Suffolk	1995
Beirut	1996
Docklands, London	1999
Brussels	1999
Fulbourne, Cambridge	2001
Nakasero, Kampala Uganda	2002
Flat 111, Kampala	2005
Suffolk on Retirement	2005

The ability to establish a new home, to make friends quickly and to embrace the support network offered by other army wives has always been key to a successful military marriage. Being able to endure long periods of time away from your husband also helps. In the Victorian era the list on the spice rack would have been shorter but still varied and, depending on the husband's rank and the luck of the draw, might well have included Indian military bases. For most wives in the two world wars there would have been no spice rack; their job was solely to wait.

But, despite the many challenges of being married to one, as Cicely Courtneidge trilled in the 1930s, there definitely is *something* about a soldier. The song's composer, Noel Gay, unencumbered by modern feminist sensibilities, tried to explain the essence of that attraction. *His bearing*, stressed in the words, *a great big general*, acknowledges that – aside from professional athletes – the armed forces are among the fittest members of any community. *His wearing* (of a uniform) both sets him apart from other, civilian, men, but also marks him as belonging to a way of life governed by uniformity. The *fine, fine, fine* is never actually spelt out, but many modern army wives would say that they were partly attracted to a soldier because he is trained to react in a crisis and to live by a certain code of conduct.

These attributes may seem outmoded in the twenty-first century but today, in Britain alone, more than 68,000 women are married to, or in civil partnerships with, soldiers. Some married when their fiancé was already 'in'; others faced the much harder task of joining an army life that was equally new to their husbands. Either way, being married to a soldier is not easy – as the figures for divorce show. Most research suggests the rate is twice as high in the army as in civilian life. Many reasons have been put forward for this. In a survey divorcées who had been married to soldiers suggested that many young military couples rush into marriage faster than their civilian counterparts because the army does not allow girlfriends to share married quarters. It is therefore convenient to marry and many do so before they have tried living together under one roof.

The very facts of army life that can make the role of wife so appealing can also place an intolerable strain on a marriage. Army wives have the chance to make new friends in different parts of the UK and abroad, but the upheaval of frequent house moves also means it is difficult for a wife to further her own career. Her partner's job may still be more secure than other industries, though the British Army is shrinking, but at the same time, few positions carry such risks. There are not many jobs where going to work involves passing through a checkpoint surrounded by barbed wire and security cameras. The uniform that can seem so appealing also makes its wearer a target. Being part of the 'army family', with the mess dinners, coffee mornings and reunions, can feel either suffocating or supportive and, at the end of that career, looking in on that family from a civilian world – as a widow or the wife of a retired soldier – can feel lonely.

Today, someone in the armed services is just as likely to be a 'geographic terrain specialist', helping to plan the next move on the battlefield as the infantry soldier belly-crawling across it. Soldiers, male and female, perform all sorts of jobs, and have joined for all sorts of reasons. In 2015, 7,790 women served in the army, representing about 9 per cent of the total force – a proportion that has changed little in the last five years. About 1,500 women are officers. But, despite the diversity of roles, the army can seem like an eccentric career choice. This was not always the case. Scratch the surface of any family and you are likely to find a soldier – and usually his wife – lurking in the foliage of a genealogical tree. They may have signed up looking for excitement, escape, or simply to earn a living. Or they may have had no choice and, like millions of men in the First and Second World Wars, been conscripted into the forces, their wives and sweethearts compelled to wait at home.

Even if they do not consider themselves 'army', most families in Britain have a military wife loitering in their past. My family is no exception. We are certainly not 'army', and without looking too hard, I can find three generational layers of army wives. My paternal great-grandfather, Donald Gillies, served in the 1st Dunbartonshire Rifle Volunteer Corps in late nineteenth-century Scotland, probably as a way of finding companionship after his parents died when he was a teenager and his three younger siblings moved to the other side of the country to live with their maternal grandfather, leaving him to eke out a living from the precarious Clyde shipbuilding industry. Donald and his son, Alexander, both served in the First World War and my father, another Donald, was a sergeant major in the Second World War. He met my mother at a Scots Guards' dance and married her in 1946 when he returned home from Stalag IVB and Stalag 357, where he was a POW. My mother's father had served in the First World War and suffered all his life from the effects of being gassed. The lives of four wives were profoundly affected by their husbands' wartime service, although none was a career soldier.

On my husband's side, age and disability intervened to limit the tally of army wives. My mother-in-law Peggy's father was saved from the trenches by his age: he was sixty-seven in 1914. Peggy's future father-in-law, Bernard Kelly, a commercial clerk, also avoided serving in the First World War, but in his case it was disability, rather than age, that kept him at home. When Bernard Kelly reported to the recruiting officer he was quickly dismissed. His profound deafness, a result of a childhood accident or illness, meant he would never hear the 'curious singing noise' of shells being fired in a foreign field. Instead, he married Kathleen, who had lost her hearing after a bout of measles when she was a young child. She fell pregnant in what was to be the final year of the war and Brian was born on 17 August 1918. Brian Kelly grew up in a strange house of flashing lights and a cat's cradle of string that sent a ping-pong ball whizzing above his deaf parents to pierce their peripheral vision and let them know someone was at the door. He met Peggy when buying flowers at a stall near a hospital, where both were visiting sick friends. They married in January 1942 and he left the police force a few months later to join the Commandos. Peggy and Brian faced their first long separation after they had been married for seven months when he was sent abroad and she was left to look after her aged mother and his disabled parents.

But the story of the army wife has not always been set against a loving family background. The image of the soldier and his waiting wife has gone through many transformations since Penelope in Homer's *Odyssey*, who keeps suitors at bay for the twenty years that her husband is away at war. There is also a long narrative tradition of soldiers who seduce and then abandon their sweethearts. George Farquhar's Restoration play *The Recruiting Officer* (1706) is built around two womanising officers. Jane Austen understood leaves of absence, garrisons and the newly introduced barracks: in *Pride and Prejudice* (1813), George Wickham, a duplicitous officer in the militia, tries to elope with Georgiana Darcy. In *Far From the Madding Crowd* (1874), Thomas Hardy creates the dashing Sergeant Francis 'Frank' Troy, who shuns the servant woman he was betrothed to and uses his swordcraft to woo Bathsheba. The traditional nursery rhyme, 'O soldier, soldier, won't you marry me', focuses on the fear that soldiers were out to manipulate innocent young women. The first verse hints at the soldier's cunning ways:

O soldier, soldier, won't you marry me
With your musket fife and drum?
O no sweet maid I cannot marry you
For I have no coat to put on.
So up she went to her grandfather's chest
And she got him a coat of the very, very best
And the soldier put it on.

From the evidence it seems that my great-grandfather, Donald, may have been part of that same strain of unreliable soldier. In March 1892 the volunteers held their annual soirée, a concert and dance. Scottish airs were played and there were female violinists, as well as a 'very interesting display of Indian club exercises'. I have no proof, but I like to think that Donald was there that night – I even allow myself to imagine that my grandfather, Alexander, was conceived after the celebration. What is certain is that Alexander was born nine months later at 214 High Street, Dumbarton. On the handwritten birth certificate Donald is shown as living at number 235. Alexander's mother, Rebecca Davenport, is a domestic servant and, at twenty-one, a year older than Donald.

It seems likely that Rebecca fell for the romantic image of the soldier. Rebecca is not remembered as being a keen reader of novels and her impression of soldiers would have come from the ones she met, local newspapers, collective memory and songs. Since she was born in Ireland, she probably knew the Irish tune 'The Girl I Left Behind Me' (also known as 'Brighton Camp'), which, in 1893, was transformed into a balletic version performed at London's Drury Lane. In the stage production the hero is ruined by gambling on horses and enlists in the Highland regiment to sail for Burma (Myanmar). He later wins a Victoria Cross and marries the sweetheart who has remained faithful to him. The melodrama ran for fifty-three weeks. The American artist Eastman Johnson used the song title for his painting of a young, girl-like wife, completed in about 1872. He imagines her standing on a hill in front of a glowering sky, where she has parted from her soldier. The wind whips her blonde hair up behind her and lifts her cape to reveal a passionate crimson dress and several inches of ankle, but despite the sensuous undertones, the woman's wedding ring provides the focus of the painting.

The evidence of Rebecca's passionate romance with her soldier is there for all to see in the word 'illegitimate' written under the baby's name. A later note has been added in the column next to the entry: 'Paternity of child found by Dec. of Court'. Donald and Rebecca's wedding did not take place until March 1898 and then not in a church, but in Helenslee Arms Coffee House, the same establishment that had supplied the 'excellent tea' at the volunteers' soirée. Was Donald one of those dashing soldiers Victorian parents were so worried about? Did he follow the drum abroad, or simply leave to find work elsewhere? The year 1892 was particularly difficult for the shipyards: in June the carpenters went on strike and then in September hours were severely reduced. Once Rebecca and Donald had finally married, they settled down to a life of respectable breeding in which they produced another two sons and one daughter. The reason they were slow to marry remains a mystery while their reputation as a loving couple has been handed down untarnished to subsequent generations.

The image of the soldier and his wife was transformed during the Victorian period but has undergone an even more dramatic sea change within the last few years. Say the words 'army wife' to most people in Britain today and they are likely to respond by mentioning Gareth Malone's BBC TV programme *The Choir: Military Wives* (2011). Malone a choirmaster who appeared as young and care-free as the women in his choir looked tense and careworn, chose a group of singers from the wives and partners of men based at Chivenor Barracks in Devon. All were serving in Afghanistan. The programme adapted extracts from the women's letters to their men and produced 'Wherever You Are', which the choir performed at the Royal British Legion's Festival of Remembrance at the Royal Albert Hall. Dressed in black and representing wives of men from across the ranks, the ensemble performed in front of giant screens showing soldiers patrolling foreign fields in helmets and camouflage gear and chatting to Afghan children. The song, whose lyrics refer to the soldier as 'my prince of peace', reached Number One in the 2011 Christmas music charts.

The army wife no longer has to rely solely on an unofficial female support network – although she may still find this resource the most sympathetic. A plethora of organisations – both charitable and official – are now ready to catch the army family should they falter at any of the major hurdles in an army marriage: deployment, accommodation, childcare and education, divorce, injury, bereavement and retirement.

Groups such as the military charity SSAFA, which started life in the Victorian period and used to be known as the Soldiers', Sailors' and Airmen's Families Association, and the more recent Army Families Federation are there to guide wives through both the mundane and the life-changing. They advise on issues such as childcare, overseas deployments and financial matters, but also provide concrete solutions – for example, in SSAFA's refuges for women and children who need help when a relationship with someone in the Forces breaks down. Other organisations support veterans and their families who have been mentally or physically damaged by their job. Names such as Combat Stress and Help for Heroes appeal directly to the public and assume a level of awareness and empathy with their cause.

Television and social media have brought us closer to the lives of army families. We watch soldiers leaving Britain to serve in war zones, and participate in their reunions when they return home. Though we may not actually be on the coach when it pulls into the army base, TV cameras ensure that we are observing from a polite distance. The battlefield has moved and, as in the shocking case of Fusilier Lee Rigby, who was killed in Woolwich, southeast London on 22 May 2013, we may even be privy to the intimate details of a soldier's final moments in images flashed around the world. Many of us identify closely with the loss suffered by members of the armed forces; the town of Wootton Bassett in Wiltshire earned the addition of 'Royal' for the way it honoured the returning army dead. Some of us also wear rubber wristbands and display stickers in our cars in support of 'heroes'. Poppies are no longer just paper-thin flowers that curl up and are lost as soon as (or even before) 'The Last Post' has been played on Remembrance Sunday, but may now be more permanent brooches of metal, wool and ceramic. In 2014 a crimson tide of poppies engulfed the Tower of London in an art installation created to mark the centenary of the outbreak of the First World War.

In the Victorian period the voice of the ordinary soldier's wife or sweetheart was muted by her limited education; she lacked the time, skill or inclination to keep a journal or to write letters. If she appeared at all, it was as a walk-on part in someone else's story; and if she did write, it was much later, in retirement when she had the leisure to reflect on her time 'following the drum'. By the twentieth century, army wives of all classes were writing more, but all too often their voices, at least in letters, were lost in the continual upheaval of their husbands' war. Letters from home, no matter how much they were cherished at the time of reading, are easily lost and left behind in the turmoil of conflict. Only the wife can fold correspondence away carefully, maybe even cosset it in tissue paper to be buried in her bottom drawer. Husbands on the move, or at the front, have no such luxury.

By the start of the new millennium, army wives were making themselves heard via social media or through the homogenous voice of choirs. Much of their communication with their husbands, though, was again ephemeral, this time lost in the cybersphere of emails and text messages.

The modern image of the soldier and his relationship to women has shifted dramatically from the traditional nursery rhyme whose final verse reads:

O soldier, soldier, won't you marry me
With your musket fife and drum?
O no sweet maid I cannot marry you
For I have a wife of my own.

The terror threat of the early twenty-first century has given the relationship between soldier and wife a further twist. While the modern wives interviewed in this book were fiercely proud of their husbands' work, they were also keenly aware of the public role that they, as members of the army family, played. The killings in Paris cafés and streets of 2015 blurred the line between battlefield and civilian life, and made army wives once again keen for their profile to slide back into anonymity. No doubt they will emerge once again, but it is the nature of their role that they will always be the women behind the men in uniform.

1

Getting There:
Packet ships, palanquins and ponies

Army wives are good at packing – they have to be. The frequency with which they move house is probably why an army wife's home – even if her husband has retired – is stripped of the detritus that normally silts up a typical family house. Surfaces remain clear of magazines and post, plants are chosen for their ability to travel, and knick-knacks are carefully selected to reflect army life: a regimental trinket – usually some kind of weapon or figurine, a carefully posed madcap photo from a passing out parade, a lamp bought on a particularly exotic posting.

Mollie Kaye – better known as M.M. Kaye, author of *The Far Pavilions* (1978), an epic story of a British officer serving in nineteenth-century India – was steeped in army life. Her grandfather, father and brother all served in India. She was born in Simla, that most British of Indian towns, and after marrying Goff Hamilton, an officer in Queen Victoria's Own Corps of Guides, she moved twenty-two times in seventeen years, living in places such as Kenya, Zanzibar, Egypt, Cyprus and Berlin. She wrote in her memoir, *The Sun in the Morning*:

> Tin-lined packing-cases, their contents redolent of the dried leaves of neem or tobacco, were among the more familiar

hallmarks of the Sikrar – the old Raj that vanished shortly after the end of the Great War of 1914–18. One of them stands, a forlorn, empty, rusting relic of Empire, in our garage in Sussex.

Likewise, for other retired army wives the words 'Wanted on Voyage' conjure up a flurry of packing and forward planning or, possibly, of sea air, illicit assignations and strange rituals such as crossing the line and communal games of 'Housey-Housey'. They remember taking special soap that would lather when combined with salt water and how newly washed hankies could be pressed flat on the metal top that closed over the wash basin, thus reducing the need for ironing.

Mollie's father, Sir Cecil Kaye, whom she called Tacklow, was an intelligence officer in the Indian Army and one of the first people in India to know that an armistice had been signed to mark the end of the First World War. However, he was such a stickler for protocol that he managed to keep the news a secret from his wife – much to her indignation. Mollie recalls the pain of saying goodbye to him at Bombay when she, her sister and her mother returned to Britain.

> I remember clinging to him like a frenzied octopus as we said our farewells in a cramped cabin on the SS *Ormond*, striving to express without words how much I loved him; and when the ship's hooter blew to warn all visitors to go ashore and he had to leave, watching him walk down the gangplank and turn to wave to us from the crowded dockside.

Her father had not seen his son, who had been sent home to a British boarding school, for six years and now he would be separated from his wife and two daughters for two years. Mollie was ten when she left for an English boarding school.

Her parents met when Tacklow was serving in North China with the 21st Punjabis. He spotted Daisy Bryson on the up-platform of Tientsin's railway station when he was seeing a friend off to Peking (now Beijing) but, despite accepting every invitation that was going, he failed to bump into her again. Her parents were Scottish missionaries and did not agree with such frivolities. They were finally reunited when he joined the 74th Sikhs in Tientsin and the band played her favourite song, 'Marching Through Georgia', to flush her out. He was thirty-eight when they were wed, nearly twice her age, and the fact that he persuaded her parents to agree to the marriage remained one of the achievements of which he was most proud. Daisy spent much of her married life in India engaged in a round of parties, leaving the children to run wild and play with the servants. As a result, Mollie spoke Hindustani (the Hind-Urdu amalgamation common in North India) before she was fluent in English.

Daisy had her work cut out on the journey. Mollie was a skinny child and grew thinner because she refused to eat the 'children's meals' that included preserved eggs and strange-tasting milk. There was also the danger of floating mines that had drifted off course during the recently ended world war. The journey to and from Britain was one of the most daunting aspects of marrying a soldier in Asia. As the daughter of a missionary, Daisy knew what to expect; it was much harder for others who had no experience of travel.

Frances Janet Wells, or 'Fanny' as her husband called her, was in a melancholy frame of mind when *The Lady Jocelyn*, a modern, three-decked iron steamship, set off for India with sixty-nine passengers in October 1853. The ship's band played polkas and waltzes, but the music was 'much at variance' with her mood. She wrote to her father, Dr Francis Ker Fox, who had seen her off at Plymouth, that she knelt by the cabin window looking at the moon's reflection on the sea and felt glad that they at least shared the same sight. This image of the universality of the moon as a way of linking loved ones reoccurs throughout the First World War and even in today's army families.

She told him how grateful she was that her husband, Walter, who was a doctor in the 48th N.I. (Native Infantry), had secured a three-berth cabin for just the two of them and how it was already beginning to feel a little like home. She had stowed her provisions under her berth, but when the door burst open in the middle of the night walnuts scattered over the floor. She found the constant noise and the people 'disagreeable'. The screw (ship's propeller) made a 'dreadful noise', as did the songs and chatter of the crew and passengers. But her ordeal soon became much worse when the ship entered the Bay of Biscay. On 23 October 1853 she wrote how for four days and nights they encountered 'such a gale of wind as you landsmen have little idea of: the vessel rolled and groaned fearfully and one night even the steam was useless'.

Plates and glasses had to be secured in frames but, even with these precautions, 'the crashes that take place are terrible'. She noted that, 'the ship seems to take a malicious pleasure in rolling worse at dinner time' and that a plate of soup and a bottle of claret had landed in her lap during one meal. She was grateful, though, that she was one of the few women out of eighteen ladies who had escaped seasickness; and added that the waiter had been in 'a most doleful state'. The food was appalling: the bread mouldy, the butter disgusting, the meat underdone and the poultry 'like an old shoe', forcing her to live off curry and cold water. Another army wife, Harriet Tytler, wrote of 'sea pie', a dish cooked when it was too rough to prepare anything else, and which consisted of meat, potatoes and pasta boiled in a cauldron and which they ate sitting on the floor with one arm clinging to the table leg. On another occasion a companion sent her food back because it contained three one-inch nails.

Fanny was upset by the poor standards of cleanliness. The washing water was 'condensed steam' and the colour of 'red earth'. She admitted to her father that she was 'never intended for a traveller as I find the dirt so very trying, especially the knives, which have never been cleaned since we left England: dear old country, how I have envied every homeward bound ship that we have seen'.

As the journey progressed she gave her father an account of a typical day on board:

5.00 a.m. – the crew starts 'holystoning the horror' (cleaning the deck).
7.30 a.m. – getting dressed takes an hour and a half 'as one is obliged to wash while the other retires behind a curtain'.
9.00 a.m. – breakfast, then prayers in their cabin, followed by mending and writing to her father before she goes out on deck to talk, read and walk.
Noon – tiffin: bread and cheese, biscuits, sardines and anchovy paste and 'one of our dear home apples'.
Afternoon – on deck again, where they talk to the captain, watch the observation of the sun being taken and hear any ship's news. 'Everything is here a matter of interest, a ship in sight, a little bird, in short things almost too trivial to mention.' The young men fill time by shooting at a bottle placed on deck.
2–4 p.m. – she plays her guitar in her cabin until they dress for dinner at 4 p.m. and walk the decks until teatime.
Evenings – this is the 'worst time' as there is too little light to read or work. There is plenty of music, but she dreads playing in front of strangers because the piano is next to the 'screw'. She is often asked to sing, but her husband will not let her as he considers it would make her 'cheap'. (Walter wrote to his father-in-law to say he thought Fanny should have a piano in India and had obtained an estimate for the cost of shipping one out.)
10.30 p.m. – A crewman goes round shouting, 'Lights out'.

In the early days of British rule in India, soldiers had no alternative but to sail round the Cape of Good Hope at the tip of South Africa and across the Indian Ocean. The treacherous seas made rounding the Cape a nerve-wracking enterprise, and, during the Napoleonic

War, passengers also risked attack from a French warship or pirates. If this happened, the women and children would be sent below deck, where they could only guess at the progress of the battle above. Troops were usually transported in 'East Indiamen' sailing ships; paddle ships made the voyage faster and less hazardous, and were introduced in the 1830s. When the Suez Canal was opened in November 1869 it provided a more direct route to Asia, reducing the journey time to Bombay to weeks. Even before then there was the chance to use the Red Sea Route, which shaved days off the longer voyage via South Africa. Passengers disembarked at Alexandria in Egypt and switched to a Nile boat that took them to Cairo. From here they transferred to horse-drawn wagons that bumped their way along primitive desert roads to Suez, where they joined a steamship to Bombay. Harriet Tytler, who made the journey in the mid-nineteenth century, remembered that it took 18–20 hours to cover 80 miles. By the time they reached Suez she was thoroughly bruised from the narrow seats and severe jolting and her feet were so swollen that she could not walk for three days.

Ordinary soldiers were not allowed ashore in case they deserted, but when they reached the Cape of Good Hope in November, Fanny visited a mission church and mailed bulbs and seeds back to England; in return, she asked for baby clothes to be sent out, as she was now pregnant. They stopped at Mauritius in December and landed in Calcutta in January 1854, where she was to live in Spencers Hotel, while her husband was posted to Barrackpore. Despite the poor quality food it was usual for passengers to have gained weight during the voyage, probably due to the lack of exercise.

The most dramatic example of the dangers faced by a wife and family sailing on a troop ship came on 1 March 1825, when the East India Company's ship *Kent* was, 'beating through a heavy swell' one Sunday afternoon in the Bay of Biscay. She had left England a fortnight previously on her long journey to Bengal and China, carrying more than 300 members of the 31st Regiment of Foot, as well as around fifty wives and a similar number of children. Colonel Fearon was travelling with his wife and her five daughters. The heaving waves (or perhaps a thirsty sailor) caused a barrel of spirits to break free and when an officer went down to secure it a sudden lurch of the ship jolted the candle out of a lantern and set fire to the spilt liquid. The flames spread throughout the hold, filling it with smoke.

Luckily for the *Kent*, another ship was also battling through the Bay of Biscay. Her passengers and destination provide an insight into the reach and diversity of Britain's trading interest; she was on her way from London to Mexico and her passengers were primarily Cornish miners. The occupants of the *Kent* waited anxiously to see whether the *Cambria* had spotted the distress flag and would come to her rescue. As the *Cambria* approached, the flames forced her to position her landing boats at the head and stern of the *Kent*, rather than alongside. Some passengers reached the boats by clambering through cabin windows but most slid down ropes; the soldiers' wives, slung together in threes like some particularly awkward livestock, were lowered into the boats. Over the next five hours the boats ferried soldiers, sailors and families from the stricken ship to the *Cambria*, where the miners gave up their clothes and beds for the women and children. The *Cambria*'s captain, Cook, in a letter to a Lloyd's insurance agent, later criticised the *Kent*'s crew for their reluctance to help save the passengers. One sailor was reported to have tied 400 sovereigns in a handkerchief round his waist before leaping towards one of the rescue boats; it was said that the weight of his treasure caused him to misjudge his jump and he drowned.

The rescue continued until the heat became too fierce and Cook feared the *Kent* might explode – which it did at 2 a.m., after the entire vessel had become engulfed in flames. Cook reckoned they had managed to save 554 people: 301 soldiers, forty-six wives and forty-eight children, nineteen private passengers, Captain Cobb and his crew. Sixty-four soldiers, one woman, twenty-one children and four members of the crew died. Cook added, 'It may not be amiss to state, that two hours after the ship blew up, a soldier's wife was delivered of a fine boy on board the *Cambria*, and both mother and child are doing well.' The pair, along with the other survivors, had to endure three days on an overcrowded ship and arrived in Falmouth having 'scarce a rag to cover them'. The local citizens provided them with clothing and raised a relief fund. Cook had his health drunk 'nine times nine' at the mess dinner held by the 31st Regiment.

It was difficult to forget the loss of the *Kent*. The disaster was recorded in several oil paintings and the anniversary marked in a variety of ways – from the production of a 'Turkey-red' fabric (named after a Turkish method of dyeing) in the 1860s, which showed the boat's sinking stern as passengers scrambled for the rescue boats, to a contribution from the famously bad poet William McGonagall. The first verse of 'The Burning of the Ship *Kent*' provides a taste of his style:

Good people of high and low degree,
I pray ye all to list to me,
And I'll relate a harrowing tale of the sea
Concerning the burning of the ship *Kent* in the Bay of Biscay,
Which is the most appalling tale of the present century.

The tragedy may have been one reason why, in 1851, Benjamin Taylor & Sons produced a 'patent cork floating bed' that claimed to save the occupant from drowning.

The heroic struggle against the elements in which ordinary men joined forces to save women and children was just the sort of tragedy Victorians enjoyed celebrating and the disaster had a long life. But it was not an isolated example of how treacherous travelling by sea could be. The troopship *Birkenhead* a modern, iron-built steamer, sank off the coast of South Africa in February 1852 when it hit a submerged rock. Most of the soldiers drowned – mainly due to their adherence to the order to allow women and children to leave the ship first. The loss of the steamer *Ava*, off the coast of Ceylon (modern-day Sri Lanka) in February 1858, provided an example of the extreme trials an unlucky army wife often had to endure. The passengers included Lady Julia Inglis and her three children who, with other wives, youngsters and injured soldiers, had joined the ship at Calcutta, having only recently been rescued from the Siege of Lucknow.

In February 1858 many of the survivors were on their way back to Britain. It was 8 p.m. on a beautiful evening when Julia, finding it too hot in the saloon after tea, was sitting on deck. She had only recently heard that her husband had been made a major-general, following his command during the siege. She wrote later, 'Suddenly we were startled by a loud grating sound something like the letting down of an anchor, and just then saw a large rock close to us.' Several men rushed to the wheel; they heard the sound again, only louder, and the whole ship started to quiver. Julia and her companion ran below and found the saloon filled with women and children, who had been hurled from their beds. Captain Lawrence, of the 32nd, seized her hand and said, '"Don't be afraid, Mrs. Inglis." This decided me that there was some cause for fear. . .' she wrote later.

She left the ship in a boat steered by one of the officers and accompanied by five other women, five children, an Irish nurse (whose 'absurd remarks' made her laugh), Julia's nurse, and her daughter; and three children. They spent the entire night rowing between the rocks and ship, hoping that as it sank it would not swamp their boats. When day broke the captain ordered them to row the ten miles to shore for help, while he waited on a raft. By now the weather had deteriorated and the men were despondent. Julia tried to lift their spirits by baling out the water, while her son, Johnny, appeared enchanted by the waves that broke over the boat – 'His merry laugh sounded sadly in my ears, for I quite thought that a watery grave awaited each one of us.'

Even when a ship approached, their captain told them to hide their valuables, in case their rescuers were pirates. They were hoisted aboard, 'The nurse, an immense woman, hung for some time midway, and I really thought the men would drop her.' The crew ordered them below deck, but they initially refused, believing this to be a trick. When they realised they had no choice, they were lowered through the hatchway ('another difficult operation') and then realised they had misjudged the crew, who spread sails for them to sit on and gave them boiled eggs and curry to eat. The children devoured the food 'ravenously'. When they finally arrived at Trincomalee, on the mainland, an officer of the 50th came on board and introduced himself as Colonel Weare, adding he had been subaltern to Lord Inglis in the 32nd. He took Julia and the other ladies to his home, where his wife looked after them. Very few possessions were recovered and those that did survive were damaged by water; the families who had been helped by a relief fund in Calcutta had now lost even these donations; Julia's missing possessions included a 'beautiful deckchair' and toys for her children. For many, the worst blow was the disappearance of the journals they had kept during the siege.

A small, overcrowded steamer took them to Alexandria, where Julia parted from her friend Mrs Case and her sister. She found the separation 'a great loss' as they had lived together, 'upon the most intimate terms of friendship, cemented . . . by mutual kindness'. She added, 'I was enabled during that sad time of bereavement to be of some comfort to them' and they, in turn, showed 'unvarying kindness' to her and her children – 'They are, and ever will be, two of my best and truest friends.'

For wives and mothers travelling out from Britain to be with their menfolk during the Crimean War of 1853–56, the voyage gave them a foretaste of conditions to come. The journey to Gallipoli in Greece was an uncomfortable two to three weeks in which the wives of ordinary soldiers were segregated from their husbands. Most had to bed down like animals (although the horses were, in fact, on a higher deck) and slept on blankets or pallets stuffed with cowhair. The ceiling was too low for them to stand up and the air was heavy with the stench of stagnating water, vomit, rotting vegetables and animal waste from the horses, who whinnied and strained against the slings that held them. The women were below the water line, and had no portholes to offer a gasp of fresh air. It was rare for females to be allowed on deck. In such confined conditions it was hardly surprising that typhus and lice took hold.

As an officer's wife, Fanny Duberly was much more comfortable in the large cabin she shared with her husband, but she was 'weakened almost to delirium' by seasickness a few days after leaving Plymouth. She was thrown into a depression by the death of several horses – including one of her own – and a terrible injury to a crewman when a gale brought masts, ropes and spars crashing onto the deck. Fanny was to spend several weeks living on ships in Crimea and would come to loath the 'creaking of that windlass! the convulsive shivering of the ship! the grinding of the hawsers!'. Living on board, even when not at sea, was still risky – as Fanny discovered in January 1855, when the vessel she was staying on, packed with around 1,000 tons of powder and ammunition and nestling close to two other powder ships, caught fire. The cause turned out to be the familiar scenario of a crewmember using a lighted candle down below – in this instance in a hold filled with sacking and dry oakum. The ship's own pumps, with help from a neighbouring vessel, managed to douse the flames.

When the army wife emerged from the lower deck, blinking into the sunlight of her port of arrival, she faced the next ordeal – marching with the regiment. In India, 'marching' could mean transport by horse, elephant or bearers. Margaret Campbell Hannay was four thousand miles, and at least six months, away from her birthplace in Scotland when she arrived in India in the

1820s. As an officer's wife she would spend days being transported by palanquin, a large, covered box carried by bearers on two long poles. She wrote:

> It blew and rained all last night – but I slept so sound I did not hear it – it rained during a good part of the March and all the officers envied me my comfortable palanquin – in consequence of the rain the air was so cool – indeed cold after breakfast – that I persuaded Hannay [her husband] to walk out with me – this has once been a very large and a very fine city [Camp Futtehpoor Sekrie, or Fatehpur Sikri, in the Agra district and once the capital of the Mughal Empire].

The railway did not arrive in India until the 1850s and until then communication – both the movement of men and commands – was painfully slow. The smoothness of Margaret's journey depended on the state of the roads, the weather and the strength and ability of those carrying the palanquin, who usually managed to cover around four miles an hour.

On one march she had ten bearers and 'they really almost shook me to pieces – this time I have only eight and they carry me so nicely I scarcely feel the motion of the palanquin.' But Hannay paid them well and delays were usually only due to extreme weather.

> My Bearers were frightened at the hail stones – (which when they do fall in this Country are sometimes so large as to be dangerous) and the first tree they came to they put me down under it – neither persuasion nor threats were of any avail – and as I was very nervous I thought it best to bribe them – this had the desired effect . . .

They arrived at the camp very wet and very late.

She grew anxious if they failed to keep up with the main body of the march, especially when they were travelling through terrain she knew to be the home of leopards, wolves, hyenas and other wild beasts.

> I was a great way behind the Regt. so you may suppose dear Mama that I was a little afraid knowing that had my Bearers seen a tiger a mile off they would have put down my palanquin and ran away . . .

Harriet Tytler's particular fear was 'Thugs' who struck up a conversation with lone travellers before strangling them with a rope and throwing their bodies down a well.

Even within the comparative comfort of a palanquin, marching was an arduous endeavour. Sometimes Margaret Campbell would be on the road by 1.30 in the morning. Once, even though they were only due to cover four miles, she had to rise at four so that the servants could strike camp.

> I began to think of home – and fancied – what would my dearest Mama think could she only see me at this moment – sitting in the middle of a camp in the centre of India warming myself at a fire of rushes, wrapped up in a large Tartan silk cloak and surrounded by natives, camels and elephants . . .

Occasionally, the bearers would take the wrong turn. This type of setback was most irritating when they were travelling in intense heat: 'I took or rather my Bearers took such a roundabout road this morning that I literally almost stewed when I got to Camp.' A few days earlier, she wrote, the noon-day heat had been 'so dreadful I could hardly bear my clothes.'

The arrival of the train made the palanquin seem like an uncomfortable remnant of Georgian England. Army wives transferred from ship to train, or travelled by rail from one cantonment to the next or to the summer retreat of Simla. In the early twentieth century first-class rail passengers boarded what felt like a mobile sitting room, complete with leather furniture and adjoining bathrooms. A servant brought cool drinks and hot water in which to wash. At around five feet, six inches, the track's wide gauge, as well as the absence of a corridor, made the first-class carriage feel roomier than its British equivalent, but the compartments were sweltering and the night-time stops in big stations produced glaring lights, a cacophony of voices from expectant passengers, guards announcing station names and street sellers peddling water, sweets and tea.

It was far too expensive, and took too long, to allow visits back to Britain to be anything other than rare treats. The first direct Air Mail service from London to Karachi (now in Pakistan) started in 1933. On the eve of the Second World War Karachi was still five days from Southampton. Before then the route involved long stretches when passengers had to leave their aeroplane for a train carriage to take them to the next aerodrome.

By the second half of the twentieth century getting to and from an overseas posting was much more comfortable and faster, but for most army wives the journey was still an ordeal. They often travelled without their husbands – especially if they were going back to Britain for a holiday or to collect children from school or relatives. Before the advent of cheap, fast air travel they faced ferry crossings to and from mainland Europe with fractious offspring and too much luggage or, if they were heading for somewhere like Africa, had to contend with foreign airport lounges and changing flights in the sweltering heat. They had more chance of a safe arrival than their Victorian counterparts, but the journey itself, and the days of preparation for it, were still a major feat of organisation.

2

Accommodation: Barracks, bungalows and bivouacs

Deciding to put up wallpaper is a significant moment for a modern army wife. It is a clear acknowledgement that the moving is over, that this is home – for good. Usually, she will only go to the effort of hanging wallpaper when her husband has left the army. Why would she if she might have to scrape it off in the next 18 months to three years?

Most army homes or, more properly, 'quarters' are in solid, purpose-built army blocks or 'patches'. The author of a satirical book, *Gumboots and Pearls: The Life of a Wife of . . .* (1990), advised that it was possible to tell the age of a quarter by its name: 'Beware Balaclava Road and Khartoum Crescent – they probably rate as archaeological sites. Ypres Avenue and Somme Street should be avoided but you are getting onto fairly safe ground once you see Dunkirk Row or Mulberry Way. I see Goose Green is cropping up now; isn't it nice to see traditions carrying on?' The anonymity of army quarters is also acknowledged in an anecdote about a soldier who returned home in a drunken state and fumbled to fit the key in the lock of his front door without switching the light on and alerting his wife to the state he was in. He collapsed on the sofa and woke in the morning to discover he had, in fact, been dozing in his neighbour's front room.

Moving into army accommodation involves a painful ritual called a 'march in', in which the new occupant haggles with the previous tenant about which dents and discolorations are their responsibility. The procedure is repeated at the end of their stay when the army wife suffers the, often humiliating, 'march out', during which the house or flat is inspected for breakages and cleanliness. It is then that a desperate or unscrupulous wife might resort to Snowpaque correction fluid or toothpaste to hide a crack in the washbasin, or talcum powder to cover an embarrassing stain on a mattress.

The frequency of moves also explains why army gardens can look so barren. Just as committing to wallpaper can seem decadent, so many army families can be reluctant to lavish care and expense on a garden they may never see in full bloom. Flowers like marigolds bring instant colour, but if an army wife digs up her treasured 'established' plants to transfer to her next posting she is viewed as 'not very officer like'. Inside the house, spider plants hold sway: they are cheap and it is less of a wrench to leave them behind. In the days when it was traditionally a husband's job to mow the lawn – and before lightweight, electrical machines or strimmers – the grass would be allowed to grow to jungle proportions if the soldier was away for several weeks. Barbara Wilton, owner of the spice rack (pages 6–7), recalls that their small house on an army estate in 1970s Germany was previously occupied by a cavalry officer who tethered his horse in the front garden. Having the horse nearby allowed him to ride at every opportunity, while also keeping the grass down.

In the early twentieth-first century some army quarters have started to look tired and battered: cutting back on repairs is an easy way for a government to save money. Newspaper headlines such as 'The Scandal of Shoddy Homes for Heroes' point to reports in which about one in thirty service families is said to live in properties with leaking roofs, broken boilers, faulty wiring, cracked windows and damp. Some wives prefer to escape the hothouse atmosphere of the patch by living 'out' and others have bought their own homes as a way of preparing for life after the army. Whichever option they choose, today's married quarters are luxurious compared to what was on offer for a Victorian army wife.

In the eighteenth century soldiers were mostly billeted in taverns, but by the following century they were starting to move into barracks or being posted overseas. One of the first purpose-built barracks appeared at Berwick, close to the Scottish border, in 1717; it was designed by Nicholas Hawksmoor, now better known for his Baroque London churches, and could hold 600 men. Barracks grew up in places where troops were so unpopular that they could not be boarded locally, such as the Curragh in Ireland, or near ports, like Southampton, to make it easier to ship them abroad. This new type of accommodation separated soldiers from the rest of the population and made it easier for the army to control who came in and out of living quarters. The main barracks, which housed more than 1,000 men, were built at twenty locations in Britain and names such as Aldershot, Colchester and Woolwich still carry a military echo. Each took a different attitude to wives living there; within the cavalry, for example, the number might hover around fourteen women to permission for all wives to 'live in'.

The first half of the nineteenth century saw the development of a more paternalistic approach in which the army ethos of 'looking after its own' began to take hold. The Crimean War, often described as the first 'media war', brought home the appalling conditions under which soldiers lived, while the model villages of Saltaire, Port Sunlight and Bournville, and the practices among a few landowners of providing living quarters for their workers, suggested another way. Gradually, the rigid separation between army and home began to break down and wives were allowed to live in the corner of a barrack – although this raised moral concerns. Was it right that a woman should sleep in the same room as other men, separated, if she were lucky, by a curtain, where she would be exposed to ribald conversation, nightly nakedness and practices such as the doubling up of a latrine tub which was scrubbed out and converted to a washbasin? The overcrowding, poor hygiene and lack of anywhere to dry clothes properly meant that diseases such as typhoid and tuberculosis were rife.

In 1864 there was an outbreak of scarlet fever among army children at Aldershot and between July 1865 and December 1874, 120 children living in huts on Woolwich Common died of the same disease or diphtheria – a far higher rate than in the civilian population. Soldiers were not always keen on sharing their dormitories either, as the washing and cooking carried out by the wives created a fetid atmosphere. In 1858 the House of Lords pointed out that a convict had 1,000 cubic feet to himself, whereas the soldier enjoyed only 400. Gradually, some regiments started to introduce married quarters, although they were, to begin with, also overcrowded.

Whether they were stationed in a damp English port or a sweltering outpost of empire, officers were encouraged to find a wife, whereas many obstacles were put in the way of an ordinary soldier who wished to marry. He needed his commanding officer's permission and only a small percentage was allowed to have their wife by their side, living with them 'on the strength' of the regiment. Wives received half-rations and children quarter-rations, depending on their age.

As the odds were stacked against marriage for so many soldiers, a high proportion turned to prostitutes. In addition, soldiers were seen to have heightened sexual needs, compared to other men. As a result of these factors, prostitution flourished and became an accepted part of army life. At the Curragh, the permanent camp for the British Army, just outside Dublin, soldiers referred to 'wrens' – young prostitutes who lived in gorse bushes and ditches outside the camp – and in parts of India whole communities existed to cater for soldiers' sexual appetites. But this ready supply of women led to disease and, according to one estimate, in the middle of the nineteenth century about one quarter of the British Army had VD. This double standard also lay behind the Contagious Diseases Acts of 1864, 1866, and 1869, which were introduced to protect soldiers from VD. Under the Contagious Diseases Act any woman in certain garrison towns or ports suspected of being a prostitute could be arrested and forcibly examined. If infected, she would be held until cured, then given a certificate and made to return for periodic check-ups. However, the rates for infection remained high in India, and rose to 438 admissions per 1,000 men in 1890–93 – double the rate for the British Army at home and almost six times the German Army. This was partly why more wives were allowed to follow their husbands to the subcontinent. The Act was eventually repealed in 1886 after a national campaign led by women such as the feminist and social reformer Josephine Butler.

When a regiment was ordered abroad a certain number of places were allocated for the wives of ordinary soldiers. In 1800 six women per hundred-men company were allowed to go with their husbands. When soldiers began to travel further afield this rose to twelve per hundred men in India, China and New South Wales, and by the 1870s it was one in eight soldiers. The wives drew lots to determine who would accompany their husbands in a tense, and very public, ritual that was usually left to the very last minute to avoid the risk of desertion if a man found his wife would be left behind. This most cruel of lucky dips took place either in a room into which the wives filed in order of their husbands' rank – the most senior first – or in a more public gathering. Sometimes the process took place at the very docks where the soldiers' ship was waiting and led to harrowing scenes in which distraught wives hoped for a white pebble among six black ones, or plucked scraps of paper from a hat or ballot box placed on top of the regimental drumhead. Their family's fate rested on whether the words before them read: 'To go' or 'Not to go' (or, alternatively, 'to be left'). The wrong message meant they might not see their husband again for several years – if ever. The news could be devastating for soldiers too, and one man is said to have cut his throat on hearing that his wife would not be able to accompany him. The outcome of the ballot affected the whole regiment – married and unmarried – because it determined whether they would share their quarters with a cheerful, useful wife, who would be a boon to the regiment, or whether they would be defending a part of the empire side-by-side with a grumpy troublemaker. In the latter case, the husband occasionally failed to disguise his disappointment that he was not leaving his wife behind.

There were even instances of stowaways. The wife of a Rifleman went so far as cutting her hair and putting on her husband's regimental uniform to impersonate a soldier. Her ruse worked until she was safely on board the *Himalaya* troopship on its way to Crimea. At this point several ladies – that is, officers' wives, including the wife of the Rifle Brigade's commander, Lady Erroll – successfully lobbied for her to be allowed to stay.

Those who were left behind found themselves washed up in an area where they knew no one and had few places to go for help. In 1854, around 200 wives threw themselves on the mercy of the city of Portsmouth after the 2nd Battalion of the Rifle Brigade left for Crimea. They had met their future husbands on a previous posting to Canada and were now abandoned in England, far from home and unable to ask their local parish for financial help. In this instance the good people of Portsmouth stepped forward to assist.

Although some commanders resented the need to feed and shelter army wives, most recognised the important service they offered cooking, cleaning, laundering, sewing and nursing for a little extra money. Some became *sutlers*: buying and selling food and drink – although this role became less important as the army's professionalism increased in the late Victorian period. Other practices declined as the well-publicised horrors of Crimea finally settled the question of whether a wife's place was at the front. Until then, some officers' wives still viewed battle as a spectator sport – taking picnics to good vantage points from which to observe the Charge of the Light Brigade, for example – while the wives of ordinary soldiers were getting closer still. Some wives would rush to their fallen husband's side to protect them from body-strippers, who would ransack the body for anything of value (including teeth, which made prized dentures). Other, less scrupulous women, particularly in the Peninsular War (1808–14) between Napoleonic France and the combined forces of Britain, Spain and Portugal, joined local people and other soldiers to scour the battlefield for buckles, buttons and other trinkets to sell. When Lieutenant Mathew Anderson, of the 52nd (Oxfordshire) Regiment of Foot, was badly injured at the Battle of Waterloo, he lay on the field for around four hours, during which time, according to his obituary in *The Gentleman's Magazine*, June 1844, a soldier's wife took his watch, sword and 'everything of value'. Clothing was highly prized and was sometimes collected to replace a soldier's tattered uniform, but often proved to be the hidden carrier of disease.

Mrs Elizabeth Evans, who considered herself part of the 4th (King's Own) Regiment of Foot and went with her husband to both Crimea and India, shared a barrack room with twenty-four men shortly after her marriage in 1851. She maintained that the other men always showed her respect. Later, three women joined her and it became the place where they gave birth and at least one died, but Elizabeth was happiest when she was the only woman there. Her first meal in the barracks was a large bowl of soup, but she was more troubled by the lack of a tablecloth. The food was of poor quality and the rations meagre. In order to supplement their diet she took in washing, twice weekly; at times she had as many as twelve men 'on her books'. 'What would some of your Army women of today think of doing a soldier's washing for a halfpenny a day, and sometimes fight to get the work even at that price, because the extra pay meant so many more little luxuries for the soldier and his wife?' she wrote in 1908.

There was more room, but fewer comforts, when the army was on the move. This was a frequent occurrence in the early nineteenth century when three-quarters of the infantry was patrolling the British Empire overseas. 'It was tramp, tramp, tramp, for woman as well as man, and I held up to it with a stout heart,' Elizabeth remembered of her time in Crimea. 'I was young and strong, and I loved my husband.'

Those women who 'followed the drum' took what accommodation they could during the long marches between outposts or at the bases themselves. They were given half rations and those who were 'on the strength' were allowed to pitch their tent behind the main army camp, although many shared their husband's tent or hut, or simply slept outside with him under a blanket. In Crimea Elizabeth and her husband dug out a trench to sleep in and covered themselves with a blanket of twigs and branches, but when the bad weather arrived, their wood was taken for fuel. Later, she found some warmth under a plaid shawl or her husband's trench coat when he was not there; when he returned, she would rub his feet and plead with him to feign illness so that he did not have to return to the fighting.

Fanny Wells moved from Spencers Hotel in Calcutta to a thatched bungalow at nearby Barrackpore, a cantonment she believed to be the most beautiful in India and which would be her home for the rest of 1854. Troops in India had originally lived in forts such as Fort William in Calcutta, but as the Honourable East India Company extended its reach, it built barracks within cantonments outside strategic towns. The Company's roots went back to 1600, when Elizabeth I granted a charter to 'The Company of Merchants of London trading into the East Indies'. By the eighteenth century its commercial interests had expanded to the Indian subcontinent, where it needed a military arm to overpower and control the territory it sought. In an attempt to retain independence from the British government, it recruited, trained and equipped its own armed forces and occasionally hit the military jackpot through leaders like Robert Clive, a clerk from Madras who secured the position of military commissary and conquered Bengal for the Company. British officers held their commissions from the Company's court of directors and could command British troops, if they were east of Suez. By the time Victoria took the throne in 1837 it ruled directly, or through local alliances, an area of 1.6 million square miles and acted more like an agent of imperial rule than a company with commerce at its heart.

Officers and their families lived in bungalows like Fanny's, while unmarried officers often shared bungalows or 'chummeries'. The situation was quite different for the ordinary soldier and in 1859 only about a quarter of Indian barracks had separate rooms for married couples. These consisted of small, two- or three-bedroom bungalows; however, most families lived in special barrack rooms or rooms off the main barracks. A few had to endure living in the barrack itself, shielded, as in Britain, from the soldiers by a blanket or screen.

Fanny wrote to her father of Barrackpore's exotic trees: the 'magnificent' banyan that grows to 'an enormous size' and the elegant tamarind. She enjoyed riding in the park with its aviary and menagerie of wild beasts and the ornamental bridges over streams 'thickly strewn' with 'scarlet water lilies'. The prickly heat she had suffered in Calcutta disappeared and the place appeared free from mosquitos. She knew her father was keen to hear about the bungalow and wrote to him on 26 January 1854 in a letter she expected he would receive in the middle of March:

> Picture to yourself then a square white house entirely surrounded with a veranda, all on one floor and consisting almost entirely of doors and windows. The room in which I am sitting has two doors in front of me, two behind and one at each side, those in front and behind have no wooden doors but mats called chics which roll up when there is no glare: we pass through these chics into empty rooms answering to halls in each of which there are three French windows or front and back doors which ever you may like to call them.

Their sitting room has no windows but is 'exactly' in the middle of the bungalow and, therefore, 'very cool'. A side door opens into their bedroom that has nothing but a bed and *punkah*, a cloth fan on a string pulled by a *punkah-wallah* (manual fan operator), over it. There is a window above the bed and two other doors open into her dressing room, which has a picture from home of Brislington church hanging by the dressing table, and the bathroom, 'where I have the most splendid ablutions possible, for the supply of water is unlimited'. Walter's dressing room and bathroom are on the other side of the house. They have little furniture, and most of this is hired; but they are content with what they have. They store their plate and glass in its own room.

Bathing was one of the practices that set Anglo-Indians apart from other Victorians. Cleanliness was a virtue observed by the high caste Brahmins and the colonial rulers adopted it as a way of establishing their authority. At home taking a bath was a rare occurrence; in India it became a daily ritual. From the 1830s bathrooms were attached to most bungalows; they were not common in well-to-do British homes until the end of the century. There was also a practical consideration to keeping clean. Rats and cockroaches enjoyed the various substances used to dress hair and it made sense to abandon this habit in favour of frequent hair washing. In *The Complete Indian Housekeeper and Cook* (1888), authors Flora Steel and Grace Gardiner, who were both married to members of the Indian Civil Service, included a recipe for shampoo – a word derived from the Hindi *campo*, to massage, and Anglo-Indians brought the tradition back with them in the 1920s.

Fanny's bungalow was in the centre of the compound and surrounded by the servants' houses, the stables and kitchen and they were close to the hospital. She had little to do with the servants, who sat on the veranda all day. She listed them for her father, next to what she considered to be their English equivalent:

Khausamah – butler
Khitmagar – footman
Bearer – valet
Ayah – lady's maid
Bawencher – cook
Mansolgy – scullion
Mater – sweeper
Bheestie – water carrier
Dhoby – washerman
Mallee – gardener
Chowkydar – watchman

In addition to the above there was always a 'Sikh' waiting to take a message.

Fanny admitted that she found it difficult to remember the role of each servant, especially as their caste prevented them from taking on certain jobs: the *khitmagar* would not light the lamps or candles because that was the bearer's duty; another servant would not empty the 'chamber utensil' because that was up to the *mater.* But she was 'getting on fast with the language': 'I must say on the whole I like the native servants, there is no impudence, no finery with them and I think ours will soon get into order as they see that we are very punctual in our meals and that I am very particular about having all things in proper order . . .'

She found the birds 'much too tame to be pleasant' and became annoyed that they used the house as a garden and the *punkahs* as trees. At night, she faced a barrage of noise as frogs croaked and packs of jackals kept up an 'incessant screeching'. The cantonment was also crowded with pariah dogs, bats, squirrels, carrion crows and chestnut and white Brahminy kites – that were 'dreadful thieves'. She could contend with most creatures that 'have no wings' [her underlining]. In late January 1854 a snake appeared, the first she had seen, and Walter was cross with her for watching as the servants beat it to death. She wrote calmly of a 'rat hunt' in the drawing room.

Fanny spent her days reading, singing, writing and working. They rose at 7 a.m. and had breakfast two hours later, after Walter had returned from the hospital. Dressing took a long time because after her bath the *ayah* washed her feet and took care to arrange her hair in a 'beautiful manner'. After breakfast they read a chapter and prayed; she ordered dinner and tended to numerous domestic tasks. They enjoyed 'tiff' at 1 p.m. when, following her father's advice, they ate nothing but bread, butter, ginger or cake. Visitors called between noon and 2 p.m., although this changed in the hot season. She and her husband walked between 5 and 6 p.m. After dinner they talked or slept until 8 p.m., followed by coffee, after which she worked while Walter read to her, in return for which she sang.

She was sorry when they had to leave Barrackpore for Allahabad in December 1854, partly because of the expense of buying tents for the journey, although she looked forward to the march. When they reached their stop the regiment marched in and out as the band played and bayonets flashed in the sun. A dozen elephants, including one that was just a few weeks old and 'so full of mischief', followed, carrying the sepoys' tents.

At the turn of the nineteenth century a tent was still considered a luxury and its size depended on rank: a captain could expect one that was 10½ feet wide, 14 feet deep and 8 feet high; whereas a private would share a tent that was 6½ feet square and 5 feet high with four other soldiers. By the time of the Crimean War in 1854, canvas was an important way of protecting both soldier and wife from the elements. In India it was even possible to make the tent a home, despite the wild fluctuations in weather. During the day it could be sweltering under canvas, but at night, and during the winter months, temperatures plummeted.

In 1829, Margaret Hannay wrote in her journal from a remote camp in India, 'the wind roaring above our heads sounds very awful'. But inside the tent, every effort had been made to ensure the officer and his family were as comfortable in the field as possible. In fact, a whole industry had sprung up with that object in mind. An officer's canvas home was closer to modern-day 'glamping' than the bell-tent so often associated with army life. A Commanding Officer in India, for example, might have a double-poled tent measuring about 30 feet by 16 feet, as well as one or two smaller tents.

The key to creating this illusion of an English front room was due, in great part, to 'campaign' or 'knock-down' furniture. The latter term refers to the ingenious way in which each piece was designed so that it could be easily taken to bits, transported thousands of miles by ship (where it could fit snugly under the bunk shared by husband and wife) and then by horse or mule, and then be reassembled in a tent or bungalow. These items were the forerunners of modern-day 'flat pack' furniture – but with the important difference that the late Georgian and Victorian versions were not mass-produced, factory goods, but carefully engineered objects created by craftsmen – and occasionally women – in long-lasting materials such as oak, mahogany, walnut, teak and brass. Their purpose was as much about the maintenance of social standing abroad as comfort.

The need for campaign furniture started in the eighteenth century when Britain's soldiers and traders travelled further afield – and stayed away for longer. Furniture makers like Chippendale, Hepplewhite, Thomas Shearer, William Ince, John Mayhew and Thomas Sheraton all recognised the need to include camp furniture in their ranges and Chippendale designed a 'field bed' as early as 1762. As the number of campaigns waged abroad increased so did the ingenuity and scope of the furniture available. An officer's luggage might include a writing desk, baby's crib, a bookcase with a metal grille to stop books escaping in transit, games table, sofa bed, washstand, bidet for ladies and dining table with six oak dining chairs (each leg stamped with the appropriate number to make assembly easier – no poring over a baffling instruction manual, Allen key in hand, for the colonial home-maker).

Pieces of camp furniture were ingenious shape-shifters. A mahogany washbasin could be miraculously transformed into a dining table (which could be extended further by inserting flaps) or a writing desk; sofas could become four-poster beds. On unpacking, luggage was found to have Russian doll-like layers. A *chiffonier*, a hybrid piece combining a cupboard and sideboard, might hold a whole suite of furniture including four chairs, a sofa and a centre table. It is no wonder that the instructions urged, 'care should be taken to screw all *very tightly home*'.

Margaret, bent over her journal, may have been leaning on a writing box with a detachable drawer for pens and other small compartments. Secret drawers were a popular feature in the Victorian period and a dispatch box belonging to an officer in the 19th Bengal Lancers was found to have a locked compartment containing two envelopes: one with strands of blonde hair; the other with a brunette alternative.

A piece of camp furniture was a long-lasting investment that became a common wedding present for army couples who were expected to go abroad – as most officers were in the nineteenth century. The National Army Museum in London has among its collection a suite of walnut, oak and metal chiffonier, four chairs, a table and a day bed made for Lieutenant Edward August Carter of the 45th (Sherwood Foresters) Regiment of Foot and his wife Mary Hemphill on the occasion of their marriage in Dublin, 1875. The ensemble was made by Ross and Co, the Victorian Army's 'manufacturer of choice', which began trading in 1821. Captain Benjamin Simner, of the 76th Regiment, and his new wife, Mary Bolton, received an extensive set of carved furniture made by Ross as a wedding present from trees growing in the family estate in Bective. They took the furniture with them to India in 1865 and it came back with them in 1877 after the couple had travelled to Burma in 1869 and then to various parts of India. Sydney J. Maiden, writing in *The Connoisseur* (May 1957), mused: 'It is pleasant to think that Captain and Mrs Simner had their changing quarters furnished in a way that must have alleviated the discomforts of life in the East in the days before modern comforts such as electric fans and refrigerators. It is easy to picture the scene as the Simners sat under a punkah in a tent furnished with these pieces so reminiscent of Ireland. Mrs Simner's thoughts must often have returned to the woods of Ireland as she entertained her husband's brother officers at little dinner parties, far from the home she left to go on service with her husband.'

Shops recognised an important market for this furniture. Heal's in London's Tottenham Court Road included campaign furniture in its catalogue and Harrods boasted that it packed for 'Head, Mule or Camel Loads'. The Army and Navy Stores, which in the twentieth century grew into a landmark department store, was started in 1871 by a small group of officers who needed a wine club and then expanded into a co-operative to provide items of furniture and clothing to its members at the lowest possible price. By 1887 it employed 5,000 workers – many of whom were paid to service its vast mail order trade: it received 4,000 letters a day from some of its 50,000 members looking for items in its 1,000-page catalogue. Its staff could also be prevailed upon to fulfil a number of chores for the busy defender of empire, from decanting wine, tuning pianos, winding clocks at regular intervals and arranging removals and funerals. Initially, membership of 'The Stores' was restricted to the higher ranks, widows of officers and representatives of regimental messes and canteens, although a breakaway junior Army and Navy Stores appeared in 1879. The original became a corporation in 1871 and opened a store in Victoria Street, London, the following year. In 1890, an agency was set up in Plymouth to supply military messes and, in the same year, a depot was established in Bombay (modern-day Mumbai) for members in India. Further depots followed in

Karachi and Calcutta (Kolkata). In the 1930s, smaller stores sprang up in New Delhi, Simla and Ranchi. By this time the Society was issuing an enormous illustrated price list each year and had introduced a telephone ordering service.

The British were less well prepared for the extreme range of temperatures in the unfamiliar terrain of the Crimean campaign (1853–56). Their main ally, France, had superior accommodation and their tents in particular were bigger and better, protected by wooden palisades and snow screens. The English soldier spent the day freezing and returned to a cold and waterlogged tent. When the rain was particularly heavy he endured a night standing around the tent pole – from which weapons and other equipment were suspended and which was often secured in a barrel – rather than lie on the sopping ground. Officers had a slightly easier time and ordered their servants to fit a wooden floor in the tent or to line the shallow pit that had been dug below with stones. Unlike French officers, whose custom was to live cheek by jowl with their men, the high-ranking British officer escaped most of the privations those under him endured. They were allowed to find their own accommodation or spend the winter in Constantinople. But not even the French's superior tent skills could protect them from the violent storm that tore through the Allies' camps on 14 November 1854. The wind snatched up canvas and hurled luggage, clothes and tent poles, javelin-like, through the air. Horses bolted and soldiers found themselves soaked and roofless in the early hours of the morning. When the storm finally subsided the rain turned to snow.

The French army did not allow wives to accompany their men – except in the case of a few officers – but each French regiment included paid women who prepared food and drink for the soldiers and organised laundry and nursing. *Vivandières* and *cantinières* sold food and alcohol from mobile field canteens and often wore baggy trousers and tightly fitting military jackets. In battle they sometimes handed out brandy and cartridges and helped the wounded. The British troops envied the French system of cooking in which each regiment had its own kitchen and chefs and often the smell of freshly baked bread could be too much to bear. Although the British soldier had more meat and larger rations they were, at least at the start of the war, left to prepare it themselves and the result was not as appetising or nutritious. The French, by comparison, supplied their troops via efficient wagon trains and paved roads that allowed for a more reliable supply of dried food. This came in the form of hard biscuits that were activated by boiling hot water, a sort of early Pot Noodle for the front line. The French base at Kamiesh became a bustling town in itself, where shops sold Paris perfumes and hats for the *cantinières*. It took the arrival of a French cook, Alexis Soyer, to improve the British cuisine.

As usual in the British Army, a husband's rank reflected the accommodation a wife could expect, which led to tent envy. Fanny Duberly particularly admired the tent where Captain Portal of the 4th Light Dragoons lived. It was paved with flints, had hen coops holding nine birds and a mud kitchen built by his servant. Lady Eliza Erroll, eldest daughter of General the Hon. Charles Gore and sister to three soldiers, gained notoriety at Scutari, the port opposite Constantinople, at the entrance to the Black Sea, because she and her husband lived in a green, canvas marquee outside the barracks and next to the Commander-in-chief. It was slightly more comfortable than the standard issue bell tent, although Lady Erroll later told a grandchild that she had slept on the ground while her husband had taken the bed. Despite being bigger than most tents, it collapsed during a rainstorm and Lady Erroll emerged from under the canvas splattered with mud. (She also discovered later that she had become famous for the unintentional strip-tease shadow show she performed when getting ready for bed by the light of a lantern.)

At the other extreme, wives of ordinary soldiers suffered appalling privations. Some lived in caves hollowed out by medieval monks.

A corporal in 23rd (Royal Welsh Fusiliers) and his wife lived in a 'dog-kennel tent' (named for its size), where she gave birth to a daughter in the snow. When Lord Raglan, Commander-in-Chief of the British Expeditionary Army, heard about her plight he sent his aide-de-camp to investigate and later visited the woman himself. He made sure his doctor attended to her and that she received hot food and clothing, as well as his own rubber sleeping bag that was lined with flannel and which had been sent from home.

Compared to a tent, a hut offered greater protection against the Crimean winter. The British were never as efficient as the French at collecting firewood and, as a result, wood was at a premium and other materials were used to supplement it. Many huts were semi-subterranean and their occupants seemed like strange, Neanderthal creatures who went to ground. A typical hut was built over a pit of three or four feet; one or two poles supported the roof that might be formed from brushwood and waterproofed using animal hides from the ever-increasing supply of dead horses and bullocks. Stones, earth and mud blocked either end and a chimney of tin pots and clay completed the Hobbit-like cosiness. The huts became more sophisticated when Joseph Paxton, architect of Crystal Palace and head gardener at Chatsworth stately home, sent navvies out to Crimea to build wooden huts during the second winter on the Sevastopol Heights. Some were clapperboard and looked like large garden sheds.

Most soldiers saw these huts as places of retreat, where they could create a semblance of domestic life. For Lieutenant-Colonel Edward Hodge, though, the fact that he had to share his with a married couple made that home life a torture. Fanny Duberly described Hodge's new roommate, Annie Forrest, wife of Major William Forrest of the 4th Dragoon Guards, as 'very dowdy'. William himself had joined the army at the age of sixteen, in India, and became well-known for standing up to Cardigan, who refused to allow him to escort Annie to friends when she was seriously ill just before the birth of their first child. By contrast, Hodge was forty-five and single, and strongly disapproved of women at the front. He worried that Annie's presence would prove a further distraction for her husband, who was not a 'very active officer' at the best of times.

Hodge was also concerned that sharing his hut with the couple might become a permanent arrangement. He refused to allow Annie into the mess and had food and a jam pot full of rum sent to her. She screamed 'in her vulgar way' for the cook to bring her food and Hodge was driven out of the hut by the sound of the couple washing, dressing and chatting. He was disgusted by the way she 'sponged' off the regiment by eating their rations and felt that Major Forrest had demeaned himself by allowing his wife to become the focus of camp gossip. He was relieved when they stopped using the officers' mess, but disappointed that she still did not have a female attendant and that Private Denis Shine had become her lady's maid and had to empty her leather bucket (toilet). The smell of the 'greasy concoction' the couple cooked made Hodge feel sick and he asked them to stop using the hut as a kitchen, but Forrest said he could not possibly switch to his marquee. The final straw was when the batman was spotted picking fleas out of Mrs F's drawers before hanging them out to air.

By the end of November Hodge was complaining that the rain poured into his side of the hut because the Forrests had done nothing to waterproof theirs and he was forced to read out loud to drown Annie's 'chatter'. However, Hodge seems to have had impossibly high standards of housekeeping: he refused to invite his friends over to play whist because they smoked and brought too much mud into the hut.

By contrast, Fanny Duberly described her hut with great affection. On her way to Crimea she had spent several days on various 'cursed ships' and shared a cabin with her husband, Henry, on board *Star of the South*. During the harsh winter of 1854 it was moored at Balaklava, where they entertained officers, although the ship swung violently from side to side and she noticed other vessels 'crashing and crowding together'. Fanny was unable to find a house in which to live when Henry went ashore, but Captain Lushington arranged for a hut of about 12 feet square to be erected for her in the spring of 1855. Here they ate, slept, read and received company. By April the hut was supplemented with a large, hexagonal Turkish tent that served as a drawing room, and then dining room. It was double-lined in dark blue material, which she had requested from home, and open at both ends; it was carpeted and furnished with a table and armchair. In the months to come the bottles and glasses would shake on their shelves from the reverberations of the guns; but nothing ever fell. As her stay in the wooden hut continued she papered the walls with pages from the *Illustrated London News* and coloured in some of the pictures as a way of brightening up the interior. She asked her sister to send Charles Dickens's periodical, *Household Words* or Thackeray's *The Newcomes*, 'anything clever with a lot of reading in it or I shall cut my throat this winter'. By September she and Henry confessed that they would both be sad to leave the hut that looked so welcoming in the stove light.

Modern army wives no longer have to face the hardships of making a temporary home in a hostile environment, but service accommodation and the frequency with which their husbands move remains one of the most testing aspects of being married to someone in the armed services. Wives are not as willing to move unquestioningly to wherever their husband has been posted, but the dilemma of whether or not to follow them to a new posting – at least in Britain – remains as keen as ever.

Part One:

The Imperial Army Wife

3

The Early Anglo-Indian Army Wife: Margaret Campbell Hannay

I find the thorns and briers great enemies to my dresses – I seldom bring home the whole gown with me – sometimes a piece of petticoat is left behind – and my stockings are in a sad plight – I suspect Hannay is afraid of losing me altogether among these nasty thorns – for when we come to a very bad place he carries me through it.

Margaret Campbell Hannay wrote this description of the sorry state of her clothes at the end of February 1829 from Camp Himrah, on the way to the cantonment town of Mhow in Madhya Pradesh, central India. It had been a trying day, as the bearers who were carrying her palanquin had taken the wrong path and they had been forced to retrace their steps. Margaret, in her twenties and originally from Scotland, was accompanying her husband, Lieutenant Simon Fraser Hannay, of the Fiftieth Regiment Native Infantry. They had married a year-and-a-half earlier, at Saint Andrew's Church in Calcutta, when he was twenty-six. Hannay's family was already well known in northeast India, where his maternal grandfather, Captain Simon Fraser, had played a key part in furthering the interests of the Honourable East India Company. The Company was keen to tame the thickly forested and hilly area of Orissa province, some two hundred miles to the southwest of

Calcutta. In May 1817 it instructed Fraser to raise the Cuttack Legion, a local force to keep order in a region in which local tribes and maharajas vied for power. He spent the rest of his career defending the area, and Assam, in the extreme northeast India, against tribal attacks and invasions from Burma.

It is not known how Margaret and Simon met, but as both their families had their roots in southwest Scotland, their courtship may have originated there. A wife was an important commodity for an officer in India who, in the nineteenth century at least, could expect to spend years abroad – if not his entire career – with little opportunity of finding a British mate. From the late seventeenth century, the East India Company did its best to meet this need by paying the one-way ticket for European women prepared to make the sixth-month sea journey to the subcontinent. These would-be brides became known as the 'Fishing Fleet' and the young women who made the journey back to Britain unattached as 'returned empties'. The arrival of the 'cargo', as the women were sometimes referred to, at the start of the cold season always caused great excitement. Not only did the females provide a frisson of sexual anticipation for the men, they also brought with them news from home and the latest European fashions. Mollie Kaye remembers her mother making friends with Miss Beatrice Lewis at their first home in Jhelum, a garrison town on the borders of the North-West Frontier province. She had ventured to India in the early twentieth century as a 'hopeful member of what Anglo-Indians [here meaning the British who served in India, rather than mixed-race] chose to call the "Fishing Fleet".'

As India's economic importance grew in the nineteenth century, so did its attractiveness as a source of husbands. According to one estimate, in 1837, about 41,000 Europeans lived in India – of these, some 37,000 were soldiers. The East India Company was no longer prepared to pay a potential wife's fare and instead charged a hefty premium. For some historians, the increasing number of *memsahibs*

– European wives – played a direct part in the social unrest that coalesced in the Indian Mutiny of 1857–58. At the beginning of the nineteenth century it was not unusual for British soldiers to form relationships with local women, *bibis*, or even to run two separate households: one Indian, one European. The men who took local 'wives', regardless of whether they were officially recognised, often had a better understanding of local customs and languages and, if they were officers, could be more sympathetic to the men under their command. But as the century progressed, East India Company officials were less likely to experience close relationships with local women. Between 1780 and 1785 Indian women appear in one in every four wills written by officials; however, by the middle of the century a mention of a *bibi* was rare and any reference to local wives or mixed-race children had been edited out of the memoirs of prominent eighteenth-century officials in India. For some ordinary soldiers, though, the presence of a local wife persuaded them to stay on in India after their period of service had ended. Inter-racial marriages continued for longer in Burma, where caste and purdah were not observed as strictly. In parts of Assam, where Margaret and Simon Hannay were eventually posted, liaisons with local women persisted until the Second World War because the area was remote and tribal and, in some ways, apart from India.

Margaret recorded her experiences as an extended letter to her mother, writing in a black-bound journal, slightly larger than a chequebook, in elegant, sloping handwriting. The notebook provides an intimate account of her time as an officer's wife in India, but her thoughts turn regularly to her family at home. Amid the new and exotic experiences – 'the beautiful little mosque of purest white relieved by a clump of dark green trees', the 'celebrated Taj [Mahal]', the 'immense number [of] Alligators' and a tiger in a cage that she fled from when it roared until her husband led her back and persuaded her to pat its back – her points of reference remained Scottish. The roads reminded her of the approach to a harbour in the Kintyre Peninsular in southwest Scotland: 'I could not help crying – you dearest Mama will say this feeling is excusable – for you know how often with yourself and with my Brothers and Sisters I have gone along that road – with light and happy hearts . . .'

Officers' wives, like Margaret, were expected to pay for their own food and accommodation and in India it was normal for them to join their husband on long and often gruelling marches, while wives of ordinary soldiers stayed behind in barracks. 'I enjoy a March so much that I must have been cut out for an Officer's wife . . .' she wrote in her journal after they had struck camp on the bed of the River Gumber. She received visitors in the large tent, where she passed the time by embroidering and making clothes, reading the Bible, history books and novels by Sir Walter Scott, and running a school for young orphan 'band boys'. She tried to keep them as close as possible to the teachings of the Church of England and if her 'little scholars' were attentive she gave them a glass of wine after dinner.

Like a twenty-first century army wife, she learnt how to add touches to a temporary home to help make it her own before she was forced to abandon it. She spent nine 'happy' months at Mysopoorie, where she cultivated her garden. 'Every tree and shrub – I felt some attachment to – they were all planted and arranged by myself – but it has not been my fate to see them come to perfection – and my beautiful flowers will now in all probability go to ruin . . .' Her regret at having to move from the country to a large station like Mhow will also sound familiar to a modern army wife: '– at Mysopoorie I did just as I pleased – I could look after the garden and the farmyard – and never was intruded on – but at a large station such as Mhow if you associate with the people you must in some measure conform to them – to their habits and customs and a young woman requires some strength of mind to withstand mixing with the gay and thoughtless crowd . . .'

As they marched from station to station a routine emerged. Sometimes, when the men stopped for a drink she would indulge her passion for collecting pebbles. Often they camped on, or near, dried-up riverbanks where, if she were lucky, she might find black agates or deep red cornelions. On other occasions she made them pause so that she could pick blossom from the trees. She was as curious about the people and places she glimpsed from her curtained viewpoint as the locals were of her. A crowd of old men, women and children followed her when she visited a mosque with her husband and stared at the British 'as if we were beings from a different world'. In January 1829 she acknowledged it was 'not proper for a lady to go into these large towns where the greater proportion of the inhabitants are Musselmen, as you are almost always liable to insult by being crowded by faquers or Holy beggars who scruple not at abusing the Europeans whenever they can'. However, a few weeks later she was feeling more daring and left the doors of her palanquin open as they passed through a town or village – 'I like to see everything that is to be seen and as it does no harm – the natives staring at me – the curiosity of both parties is satisfied'. When the bearers tried to take a shortcut over a deep ravine she was forced to get out of the carriage and walk in her worsted stockings, but she was 'now so accustomed to these little incidents that I take it all very quietly . . .'

Margaret divided her time when they were not on the march between sedate activities such as sewing, reading and teaching the young boys – and more physical pursuits. Her scholars were 'so ignorant poor little fellows that I am obliged to explain everything I read to them so that nimble as my tongue may be I feel a little tired sometimes . . .' She took them with her when she went in search of pebbles that she later ground into different shapes.

She and Hannay seem to have had a warm, companionable relationship. They often went on walks together in the evening; or, on a rest day, she would read while he, 'lazy man', would doze with an open book in his hand. When she admired the local women's dress he promised to buy her a silk equivalent. She was sympathetic when he was unwell – no matter what the reason: 'The truth is

Hannay dined with some old school fellows of his – at the European Mess the night before – and drunk too many bumpers to "Auld Lang Syne" and as he never transgresses in this way – he could not indulge even once with impunity.' She even stood in for him as adjutant when the colonel was very cross because he had been out too long fishing. She gave the parole and countersign and then 'sent about the orders – fortunately it was all right and no one knew that my husband was not at home . . .'

Their longer walks were often intrepid – one trek was six miles and took them close to a very dangerous, steep river edge so that she wrote in her journal: 'I shudder at the very thought of it . . .' They scrambled through 'frightful ravines' and jungle and arrived home late to discover that the servants were 'all tipsy' from the strong liquor they had brewed from the babul tree, a sort of tropical acacia. The same plant had embedded thorns in her feet that were so sore that she could barely stand the following day.

Once the heat set in, though, excursions became rarer: 'I am obliged to have recourse to my light muslin gowns already – poor Hannay is so tired . . .' When it grew chilly she slept wrapped in a thick dressing gown and two blankets. Although she complained at how close the tents were to each other in one camp, and that theirs was near to a ravine, she was dismissive of officers and wives who demanded extra luxuries:

> . . . the Officers are all quite disconcerted at hearing that the Mess wines are out – people in this country cannot bear to want any comfort and I do think unless a man marries young – he is apt to [be] very selfish – you would be quite astonished dearest Mama could you see or know how selfish ladies are in India – they would not give up <u>one comfort</u> which they have been used to for anyone . . . I always dress myself – brush and dress my own hair – and take care of my own clothes – I am not praising myself dear Mama but only wish to show that it is quite possible

> for a Lady to exert herself in this Country – I keep no Ayah (Lady's Maid) which diminishes the expenses of our establishment not a little. Hannay often insists on my having one but I will not indulge in such laziness unless obliged by bad health.

She was popular with the other officers and 'the old Colonel' called her, 'My dear old girl' and – when he was in a bad mood – 'Ma'am'. The officers invited her to dine in their Mess, where they were 'so attentive and so anxious to please', and she received other visitors, some of whom may have been missionaries, civil servants or employees of the East India Company. Margaret was proud of her position as a seasoned traveller and described how one visitor, Maggy, 'chatters and makes such a noise calling out O Hannay look at this and O Hannay look at that I am obliged to call her to order. She is as much pleased to look at an Olde Tomb or Temple as if it was a Palace. The fact is if you see one of either Hindu or Musselman, you see the whole . . .'

At the end of January 1829 she had been ill with a bad headache but later managed to walk with Hannay to see a 'curious Temple in the middle of a large piece of water', which was reached by a bridge of twenty arches. A Mr Shuckburgh, who accompanied them on many of these excursions and proved an attentive companion, cut her name in 'one of the prettiest pillars and there it remains as long as the building stands'. When they visited the Taj Mahal and he overhead her saying she would like some prints to remember it by he arranged for some to be sent to her; later he taught her chess. Then they went to the 'finest Native garden I have ever seen – it was very large and kept in fine order but the stiffness of everything must strike a European'. She saw elephant bulls and peacocks cut into the Myrtle hedges but found she could not 'have helped laughing at them'.

On the whole, she made light of the dangers she faced. When she was living in a tent in Camp Bianah she wrote on 1 February 1829:

'There are a great many wolves here – but I am happy to say no children have as yet been carried off which is a very common occurrence in this part of India.' The next day she noted, matter-of-factly, the threat from robbers: 'We have had no robbers in Camp yet except three old women* who were making off with some things during a gale . . . but they were caught and put into the guard – the Colonel would have them beat, their heads were shaved and their faces painted white – a terrible disgrace – and they were sent off to their village again – crying with all their might.' In a footnote she added: '*Old women are generally the worst of thieves'.

But of all the perils of the Indian subcontinent the range of tropical illnesses, which could snatch a European away overnight, was the most deadly. Margaret's journal is peppered with regular complaints of ill heath. She wrote from Camp Shackohabad on 21 January 1829: 'I have been very unwell and very lazy this morning – I lay down to read after breakfast and did not get up till it was time to dress for dinner. It has been very cold all day – if I am spared to go back once more to dear dear Scotland – I know my beloved Mama will never get me from the fireside – I really cannot bear the cold and strange to say I always feel in better health when others are suffering from extreme heat of weather.'

She was ill again at the end of the month, when the only thing she could bear to consume was camomile tea. When she had recovered she wrote to her mother: 'Mama you know not how sad a thing it is to be sick and helpless on the line of March – on you must go – in spite of everything and when one is sick the shaking of a palanquin is not pleasant for 15 or 16 miles in the morning.'

One of the first entries in her new journal, which she began in August 1839 when Hannay was posted to Sadiya (also written as 'Suduja' or 'Sudiya') in the North East Frontier of Upper Assam, mentions a letter from a missionary friend at Jaipore (Jaipur) telling her how twenty people had died of cholera. The illness killed more soldiers in India than the enemy: in 1853 the 70th Foot lost two officers, 344 men, thirty-seven wives and ninety-nine children to it. The classic children's novel *The Secret Garden* (1911), by Frances Hodgson Burnett, begins with a chapter called 'There is no one left' and describes how soldiers arrive at a bungalow in India to discover that only a young girl, Mary Lennox, has been spared after cholera swept through her home, killing her father, her beautiful mother and all their servants.

Hannay joined the Assam Light Infantry (today's 6th Queen Elizabeth's Own Gurkha Rifles) on 14 May 1838 and embarked on what a military historian of the late twentieth century has described as: 'jungle warfare of the most testing kind fought by small detachments at the end of long and primitive lines of communication . . . [and] incredibly long marches through some of the toughest country in the world'. Correspondence between Hannay in his spidery writing, which has become faint with the passage of time, and representatives of the East India Company gives the impression that European rule over these 'rude' tribes was at best shaky and that no responsibility could be assumed for a European's safety. 'I think it right to caution you,' the Resident at Ava wrote to Hannay, 'to be always on your Guard . . . with the wild tribes you are about to Visit particularly the S[?] who bear among the Burmese a character for [C?] treachery . . .'

Confirmation of the danger came in 1839, when members of the kamti tribe (also written as Hkamti or Khamti) launched a surprise attack on the garrison at Sadiya. The Political Agent in Upper Assam, Colonel Adam White, whom the Hannays knew well, and several other men, women and children were killed, and the fort was retaken only after a 'stiff hand-to-hand fight'. Another wife sent Margaret 'beautiful verses' about the attack. The tragedy meant that Hannay was promoted to Commanding Office – a post that he would hold for twenty-two years.

Despite the dangers they faced as a couple, Hannay's physical appearance, however, was not typical of a rugged soldier used to jungle warfare. A miniature sketch of him is more suggestive of a comic character from Dickens than a great military leader. It shows a baby-faced man with a delicate mouth and small but piercing eyes. His high forehead and high collar accentuate the impression of a child's face drawn on a hardboiled egg. By the time photography was available for his image to be captured on film he has become an old man. In the Reverend Edward Higgs' photo, taken the year before Hannay's death in 1861, he is seated and wearing a smoking jacket and baggy trousers; he looks much older than his fifty-nine years. But, although he has lost much of his vigour, he has the same pointed nose, thin lips and small jawline. No photo of Margaret exists.

In Assam, the couple found themselves in the remotest of remote colonial outposts: an area dominated by two great rivers, the Brahmaputra and the Surma, thick forests and imposing mountains. At one cantonment they were warned that there were four tigers in the area and Hannay, in fact, shot a tigress. The tea trade had yet to provide the impetus to open up the country and travel was by river or the 'roughest of roads, bridlepaths or tracks'. In 1844 the journey from Gauhati to Sadiya along the River Brahmaputra (about 267 miles) took six weeks. There were few brick houses; most were wattle and daub with thatched roofs and no windows. Some travellers fell into the habit of carrying window frames, which they could fix into rest houses when they stopped. Burmese rebels were still making raids over the border to snatch local people into slavery. Hannay led two expeditions against the 'insurgent khamtis' and other forays into Singpho, the Mishmi Hills and the Sadiya Frontier. He was sent on an intelligent-gathering mission to the Naga Country and led negotiations over the disputed Ava area.

Margaret found it difficult to adapt to her new role as wife of the Commanding Officer and continued to spend time with her twenty-one 'scholars', some of whom may have been Ghurkas because the regiment now included two companies of them. On 20 August 1839 she wrote: 'Walked out, and ran about with my scholars till I was tired – Such conduct would I suppose be thought very undignified in the Commanding Officer's Wife – still more determined than ever to be guided by the dictates of my own conscience – in all my conduct, and not be swayed by the rules laid down by a selfish, hollow-hearted world.'

Hannay told her off for lounging away the morning and she was upset, with a 'sore heart' about the 'harshness' of his language. A few weeks later there was another tiff and she became drawn into army gossip. She worried about the prospect of another war with Burma and became anxious that Hannay would send her alone to Rungpore: '...I have a horror of going alone amongst strangers – more particularly, as I know that Mr Marshall has tried to prejudice everyone at the station both against me, and my beloved husband. . . . [at dinner] I can't bear to be obliged to think of what I must say next; or in short to be obliged to make conversation . . .'

Many modern army wives would identify with this social unease. She was wretched when Hannay left by himself to go to Rungpore, but the other officers consoled her and six of her little boys slept in the bungalow with her. Her servant proved to be an unexpected comfort. 'She makes me laugh talking of the Hill Sepoys, and the Hindostani men – and her satirical remarks are capital. She says my husband is a perfect Love – that his eyes and countenance shew his disposition – in short that I am a lucky woman to have such a Husband – She says I am not so generally liked as Hannay – by the Hindostani men, but that every Porbutia in the Regt. says they would fight to the last for me, that I am worth all the Sahibs put together . . .'

While Hannay was away she worked on the gown she was sewing and continued to teach her scholars. She was given a parrot and an otter as pets, but could not stop worrying about her husband; she had heard a rumour that the rebel who killed Colonel White was in the neighbourhood. It was while they were in Assam that a son, Henry Sutherland Hannay, was born although her diary does not mention this event. Instead, there are regular references to her health and at times a note of desperation creeps in: 'It seems impossible to live without beer, and wine in India; I wonder what we shall do, when we go home, should God spare us to go home.'

She strolled on the veranda for exercise but complained of pains in her side and of headaches, which meant she had to cancel school. She witnessed at first hand the speed with which an illness like cholera could dispatch its victim: 'one of the poor Sepoys is dead, and a few short hours ago, he was well, and on duty.'

On 17 June 1841 she was in Gowattie (Gauhati): 'At intervals as freedom from pain will admit of, I shall write down daily events, my thoughts, feelings, and the state of health I am in, knowing that to my beloved Hannay it will all be interesting . . . Oh! How dearly would I now prize even the slightest indication of returning health. Alas! . . . The rain has been pouring in torrents all day, – and we have seen no one. – Darling Henry is well and very good – No news.'

She died two weeks later, aged thirty-five, and is buried in Gauhati. Her husband added a final entry to her journal:

> These are the last heartfelt
> Expressions of my beloved and
> deeply Lamented Maggie, put to
> paper by her previous to her
> death.
> 5 July 1841

The pains in her side and headaches make it seem unlikely that she was carried away by cholera. The illness was usually marked by abdominal cramp and the speed with which it took hold of its victims. Perhaps her health had been weakened by childbirth or she had contracted some other illness. In India, at the time, there were plenty to choose from.

4

The Crimean Wife: Fanny Duberly, Nell Butler and Elizabeth Evans

The night before, in Portsmouth, heavy clouds had obscured the eclipse of the moon. When the morning of 5 June 1909 dawned it was unseasonably cold and the *Hampshire Telegraph* commented that, given the weather and the age of the men – most of whom were in their seventies – the number of Crimean veterans who attended the funeral was 'considerable'. Perhaps the cold and damp brought back, for some, memories of the mud and ice of that winter of 1854, of conditions so grim that their enemy, Tsar Nicholas, described the months of January and February as his 'two generals who will not fail me'.

The chief mourners – Staff-Sergeant Major Ramsden, who represented the local Veterans' Fund, and a party from the Dorset Regiment – met the coffin, covered in a Union flag and bearing the brass plate stating 'Crimean Veteran', at Fratton Station, from where they accompanied it to the Catholic section of Kingston Cemetery. The site had been opened in 1856 to ease the congestion of dead at a time when victims of the cholera epidemic, which had killed so many in Crimea, were putting pressure on the city's other graveyards.

Old soldiers, some of whom remembered the deceased from the

war, joined the procession as khaki-clad soldiers bore the coffin to its grave. Although the funeral of a Crimean veteran was not particularly rare, this farewell was covered in newspapers ranging from the *Teesdale Mercury* to the *Derby Daily Telegraph* and the *Hull Daily Mail*. The reason why the ceremony attracted so much attention was that the person being honoured was a woman. The body inside the coffin still carried the scars of that time: a withered right hand attacked by frostbite half a century before and never restored to full working order.

Five years later, and a similar funeral attracted even more attention – and two photos in the *Daily Mirror*, 2 February 1914. One shows a detachment of the 1st Battalion, King's own, who had travelled from Dover to walk behind the hearse in Richmond, southwest London; the other photo reveals a woman wearing the Crimean Medals, above the quote, 'I got used to dodging shells'.

The women being mourned in each case – Ellen (or 'Nell') Butler in Portsmouth and Elizabeth Evans in Richmond – had both accompanied their husbands to Crimea in what was to be the last war in which women were allowed at the front. Both were married to ordinary soldiers and had shared their privations, but some aristocratic wives, from each side of the conflict, had viewed fighting as a spectator sport. After the Battle of Alma, for example, the victorious Allied troops discovered the debris of a hastily abandoned picnic, including field glasses, shawls, bonnets, a petticoat and parasols, left behind by fleeing spectators from Sevastopol urged to attend by an over-confident Prince Menshikov, Commander-in-Chief of the Russian forces in Crimea.

The Crimean War (1853–56) was initially sparked by France and Russia's tussle for Ottoman Turkey, but it also reflected wider concerns about the Tsar's ambitions to expand south and west. Britain and France each sent an army of around 28,000 to Varna, a west coast port on the Black Sea (now in modern-day Bulgaria), and when the Russian threat failed to appear, Allied troops were transferred to the

Crimean Peninsular, north of the main Russian naval base of Sevastopol on 14 September 1854. Victory at Alma, six days later, allowed them to continue south to Balaklava and to besiege Sevastopol. Through the autumn the Russians tried to break the siege by attacks on Balaklava in October and Inkerman in November. The Russians finally abandoned Sevastopol in September 1855 and peace terms were agreed in the Treaty of Paris, March 1856.

In Britain, politicians, Queen Victoria, the Church and ordinary people alike viewed Russia as a country intent, not just on swallowing up Turkey, but on stomping on further to India, where it would uproot Britain's trading network in the sub-continent. The bestselling travelogue *Journey to the North of India*, by Lieutenant Arthur Connolly (1834), appeared to support this fear and cartoons in *Punch* reinforced the image. John Tenniel, the illustrator of *Alice in Wonderland*, depicted Russia as a giant, crown-wearing bear hugging a squawking turkey with a fez on its head (*Punch*, 9 April 1853). The cartoon highlighted Russia's designs for the Ottoman-controlled Holy places such as Jerusalem and Bethlehem. In another Tenniel cartoon an even fiercer bear demands honey from bees; the hives resemble Turkish minarets and the insects retaliate by stinging the aggressor (*Punch*, 16 July 1853).

It is impossible to say how many women joined the British Army as it travelled east in the spring of 1854. Estimates range from 750 to 1,200 and Helen Rappaport in *No Place for Ladies* believes that a 'good three-quarters of the army wives never returned.' The British Army permitted six wives of ordinary soldiers per company to tag along. The rule did not apply to officers and some even brought their mothers.

Many women only went as far as Malta or Gallipoli; others stayed behind at Scutari. A dwindling number of wives continued with the fleet across the Black Sea to Varna on the next leg of the journey. Some 400 ships, carrying 60,000 men and an uncountable number of women, left the port on 7 September 1854 for the Crimean peninsular and the real war. Towards the end of the campaign, a further 250 travelled to Turkey and Crimea as nurses. Russian wives also joined the conflict and served in similar roles. Those who journeyed deep into the war zone appear in photos, wearing aprons and holding pots, or striking poses with soldiers.

Nell Butler married her Irish husband, Michael, a private in the 95th Derbyshire, in Portsmouth in 1851. She was twenty-four and from Twyford, Winchester. She landed at Gallipoli in Greece with her husband and then, wrapping her belongings in her bedding – a single Army blanket – made the journey to Crimea via 20-mile-a-day marches, the occasional lift on a bullock cart and a troop ship that took her across the Black Sea. She and Elizabeth Evans were among the wives who waited onboard ship while the troops, horses and provisions were ferried ashore by smaller boats to Kalamita Bay, a sandy beach about 30 miles north of Sevastopol, and close to the town of Evpatoria.

When the Russians opened fire on the British troops, Nell borrowed a telescope to try to establish if her husband had been hit and was ordered below decks with the other women. Only a personal plea from her husband to Lord Raglan, Commander-in-Chief of the British Expeditionary Army to the East, gave Elizabeth the chance to join the men marching towards Sevastapol. Raglan was sixty-five and occasionally referred to the French, rather than the Russians, as the enemy. However, he brought with him a reputation for bravery based on his fortitude at Waterloo when he underwent the amputation of his right arm without crying out and then had the presence of mind to ask the surgeon to retrieve from the defunct limb a ring his wife had given him.

Once Nell was allowed ashore she trudged to Balaklava, where she searched the hospital ships for her husband. A doctor assumed she was a nurse and called for her to hold a man's hand while he sawed off his leg. Unlike the Russians, the British were unenthusiastic about the use of chloroform and believed the 'smart of the knife' acted as a stimulant to the soldier, who was widely thought not to experience pain in the same way as other patients. Although Nell fainted during the operation – for which the doctor chastised her – the ordeal was a rite of passage that earned her a nursing role. As supplies ran short she tore up her petticoats for bandages and made poultices out of old sacking. Often the mortar blasts lifted the poles out of the hospital tents and the canvas came crashing down on patients and medical staff, sometimes while they were in the middle of an operation.

Eventually she found Michael, who was badly injured, and accompanied him on the 300-mile journey back to the hospital barracks at Scutari, where the two sides of Constantinople (Istanbul) almost meet on the Bosphorus. Here she found a different kind of hell and one that Florence Nightingale was struggling to contain. Although no records exist of Nell's role, it was not unusual for army wives to nurse in this unofficial capacity and, on her death, *The British Journal of Nursing*, 19 June 1909, stated that she had served as a nurse in Scutari Hospital under Miss Florence Nightingale. A photo taken in her later years shows a gaunt and lined woman, her hair scraped back into a bun, Michael's medals pinned to her chest. She is wearing the sort of plain dress you would expect to see in a Victorian prison or poor house and, indeed, there is evidence that her years as a widow were so impoverished that she existed on two pennies a week in 'out-relief' and by taking in sewing. Michael eventually found work at Portsmouth dock but died aged fifty-eight. Accounts suggest that he continued to suffer from his wounds and the effort of finding a job.

In its coverage of Elizabeth Evans' funeral in 1914, the *Daily Mirror* declared that she was one of three women to go through the war with their husbands. Although, in reality, the figure was far higher, she witnessed more fighting than most army wives who travelled to Turkey. After a week of hard marching from Kalamita Bay, during which the women struggled to keep up with their husbands,

Elizabeth could only watch from a safe distance as her husband in the 4th (King's Own) fought in the Battle of Alma (20 September 1854). Other wives followed the fighting from the decks of ships. The image of that dreadful battle – in which 2,000 British, 1,600 French and around 5,000 Russians died – remained with Elizabeth for the rest of her life. She wrote later that she suffered 'many agonies in the Crimea, but none so poignant as that pain which I endured when I watched my husband march across the far-stretched field, which was being ploughed by the merciless cannon-balls and pitted with the rifle bullets.'

While the soldiers were out fighting she mended the regimental flag, or 'colour', which had been shot through, and received ½d for taking in washing – a profession she pursued in her latter years. She became a favourite among the soldiers and was allowed to join her husband at the picket (a small group of soldiers sent out to watch for the enemy), dangerously close to the Russian lines. When the British troops were besieging Sevastopol, she watched the firing with some of the drummer boys. She wrote later that 'it was wonderful to look down into that marvellous fortress and see the big guns bursting into lurid fire and hear their solemn booming in the gloomy hills.'

Elizabeth stayed with her husband until she fell ill with fever in late 1854. If anyone came near her she would scream, fearing that if she did not she would be taken for dead and buried alive. Eventually, she was strapped to a mule and then loaded on to a ship to be evacuated home. She was reunited with her husband after the end of the war. In a photo of her as a widow, she is seated among Chelsea Pensioners and appears to have fared better than Nell Butler. She is regal in her lavish dress, her right arm, as thin and straight as a swagger stick, stretched out to grasp the hand of the veteran sitting next to her. Like Nell, she was given permission to wear her husband's medals after his death: the clasps of Alma, Inkerman and Sebastopol. Her burial with full military honours marked the only time the regiment had honoured a woman in this way.

Fanny Duberly always claimed to be the only *lady* to witness the Crimea War at first hand. She was in her mid-twenties when she arrived in Varna, the youngest of nine children born to a well-placed Wiltshire banker and politician. Both her parents died before her tenth birthday and she probably met her future husband, Henry, who was seven years her senior, when his brother, Major George Duberly of the 64th Regiment, married her sister, Katherine. At a time when promotion to the higher levels of the army had to be paid for, their older half-brother, James, who inherited most of their father's wealth, bought George a commission. In 1839 he paid for Henry to become an ensign in the 32nd regiment, and then, two years later, a lieutenant. When the regiment was ordered to India in 1846, Henry left on half-pay and studied to become a Paymaster, a non-combatant role which involved ensuring the men and bills were paid and that the books balanced. The salary was higher and there was no need, up to the rank of colonel, to buy promotion. It was not a prestigious position, but the 8th Royal Irish Hussars provided some compensation: a light cavalry regiment appealed to his horse-minded wife and carried a glamorous veneer. The couple were often short of money, as they had no other way of supplementing their income – and this may have been part of the motivation for the 1855 publication of Fanny's journal of her experiences in Crimea. In some ways, the war gave them an entrée into society. The straitened circumstances of life at the front meant there were few luxuries to set one officer apart from another.

Fanny was a vivacious, blonde-haired young woman who loved horses, music and attention. She spoke French well enough to be able to chat with the Allied generals and the French impresario and composer Louis Julien created the polka *L'Amazone* in her honour; the sheet music shows a lively woman riding side-saddle on a leaping horse. Many ordinary soldiers kept her photo in their tent and officers gathered wild flowers for her and feathers to trim her hat. Lord George Paget, who was said to miss the much-younger wife he had married in 1854, promised to get her a little dog and she took part in picnics and race meetings at the beginning and end of the campaign. When she was trapped on board ship at Balaklava, Captain Howard sent her a white horse for her forays ashore. Others rode with her, took her on excursions or joined her for dinner. Not all soldiers, however, approved of her behaviour. Captain Robert Beaufoy Hawley described her in a letter to his father as a 'pushing, vulgar woman' and said she treated her husband more as a servant. She was known in some quarters as the 'Vulture' because of the enjoyment she seemed to take in wandering battlefields once the action was over.

There is no evidence that her friendships with officers went further than dinner party flirtations or a mutual interest in horses. Jill Bennett's portrayal of her in the 1968 film *The Charge of the Light Brigade*, which shows Fanny in a sexual dalliance with Trevor Howard's Lord Cardigan, is pure fiction. She also appears in two of George MacDonald Fraser's Flashman novels, in which the bully from *Tom Brown's Schooldays* plays the anti-hero. In *Flash for Freedom!* and *Flashman at the Charge* she is again the subject of amorous attentions but, in these versions, that passion remains unconsummated. In reality, Fanny's husband, Henry, was a docile creature who seemed unworried by his position on the backseat of their marriage. Fanny's letters to her sister, Selina, reveal her devotion to him and her genuine concern about his safety. She enjoyed their riding excursions together; in August 1854 they trotted over the stubble near Varna to shoot quail. On other occasions they went sightseeing or simply read in companionable silence. At times she felt frustrated by his subservience.

Generally, Fanny viewed females of a similar social standing as rivals. She was particularly severe in her judgement of Adelaide Cresswell, wife of a captain in the 8th Hussars, whom she had heard was a '"tremendous woman", a dead shot, a brilliant rider & very fast'. Fanny may also have been intimidated by the fact that Adelaide's brother was the famous lion hunter Roualeyn Gordon-Cumming. Fanny dressed up in her best clothes to call on her in July 1854, but the meeting produced a catty response: 'after waiting some time a woman came from among the troop horses – so dirty – with such uncombed scurfy hair – such black nails – such a dirty cotton linen sleeve – oh you never had a kitchen maid so dreadful.' Adelaide called the officers 'the boys' and addressed them by their first names. Fanny disapproved of her tendency to talk too much about horses and then to have the audacity to criticise Fanny's saddle, of which she was rather proud. Adelaide had not ridden for nine years and cried when her horse did anything unexpected; she was unwise enough to offer Fanny advice about tents and to urge her to cook for Henry. She took Fanny's breath away so completely that she thought she might be 'broken-winded' all her life.

To begin with, Fanny was equally wary of – if not jealous of – Lady Eliza Erroll, whom she saw as her closest rival. In a letter home, in September 1854, she said how annoyed she was that the *United Services Gazette* had misspelt her name as 'Jubilee' and made more of Eliza's presence in Crimea. However, once they became friends, Fanny viewed her as the only other lady present. Eliza was famous for carrying a brace of loaded pistols on her belt and Christine Kelly, the modern editor of Fanny's journal and letters, speculates that she may have been keeping them away from her husband – who could be unpredictable and was often in trouble with his commanding officer. It was even suggested that, had his wife not been by his side, he would have been sent home. She was with the troops as they marched towards Sevastapol in September 1854 and the mules she had secured for her and her maid quickly became laden with the rifles sick men were too ill to carry.

Eliza was a rare female friend and Fanny admitted that she generally despised women – with a few exceptions, such as her sister, Selina; Becky Sharpe from Thackeray's *Vanity Fair*; and Madame Roland, a hero of the French Revolution who was guillotined in

1793. In many cases, this individual antipathy may have been sparked by social rivalry and an instinct for self-preservation; there were certainly few signs that Fanny enjoyed the close support network that so many modern army wives rely on. When Lord George Paget's wife, Agnes, who was well-known for her good looks, visited him in the summer of 1855 she failed to welcome Fanny into her circle, although – or perhaps *because* – Paget had been a regular at Fanny's picnic parties. Fanny was irritated by the tourists, many of whom were female, who started to visit in the summer of 1855 in guided tours of Malta, Athens and Constantinople. By then she had witnessed at first hand the suffering that soldiers and their wives had endured from the first days of the conflict.

Indeed, she saw just how hazardous everyday life in the army could be, long before the fighting started in earnest. And, like many other commentators, she was ignorant of the true reasons for the suffering. Heavy drinking was one of the many misguided theories thought to be behind the rise of cholera, an illness as deadly as it was misunderstood. In Varna the hot weather, boredom and cheap and potent *raki* produced riotous behaviour among the ordinary soldiers. Brothels did a brisk trade and Muslim café owners were offended by demands for something stronger than coffee. Just as Florence Nightingale believed cholera was spread by miasmas rising up from the sea, so the outbreak in Varna was blamed on vapours from nearby lakes – either that, or too much alcohol or soft fruit, but not overflowing latrines or carcasses left to rot in the water supply. In August 1854 Fanny wrote to Selina, marked 'Private & Confidential' of how 'the moans of a poor wretch now dying in the hospital marquee not twenty yards from me stab my ear'. She tried to distract herself by riding and writing.

The meagre rations of salted meat and a lack of fresh vegetables, combined with poor sanitation caused by the common use of streams for washing, laundering, drinking, cooking and disposing of dead animals, led to dysentery, scurvy and what Fanny described as 'this vile diarrhoea'. There were cases of jaundice and smallpox and less severe, but just as irritating, body lice. Her maid, 'poor Mrs Blaydes' relapsed into fever at Varna and Fanny blamed the illness on her servant's efforts to look after her mistress. The woman became unconscious and died two days later.

In the camp outside Varna in June 1854 Fanny wrote of the 'broiling' conditions, unalleviated by a tree or other shelter. When Captain Fraser arrived with some bottles of beer she downed one like a 'thirsty horse'. A few days later they marched 19 miles to the village of Devna. The reveille woke her at 2.30 a.m. She packed, ate a 'stale egg and a mouthful of brandy' and was in the saddle by 5.30 a.m. They marched for eight hours and, although she found the heat and fatigue overwhelming, could still appreciate the 'verdant hills . . . noble lake, luxuriant woodland and deep bosquets of brushwood.' When they finally rested, Captain Tomkinson made her a bed from his cloak and sheepskin. She pulled her hat over her eyes and slept under a bush close to her horse, Bob.

In August 1854, the troops were due to leave Varna, and so many wives wanted to join their husbands that Raglan made it a rule that only those with special permission could accompany their men. Fanny disguised herself as a poor woman by borrowing an old hat, shawl and boa and slipped unchallenged onto the *Himalaya*. The British vessels were so overcrowded that hundreds of soldiers' wives were left on the quayside as the last of the horses and luggage were winched on board. Other officers' wives went to even great lengths. Adelaide Cresswell was reported to have stowed away in a beer barrel and used the bunghole to breathe through. Most of the men on board the flotilla did not know where they were heading and some imagined the ships were taking them to a wild Russian land of bears and lions, rather than Kalamita Bay.

While wives including Nell Butler and Elizabeth Evans followed their men ashore, Fanny transferred to another ship, *Shooting Star*, where Captain Fraser watched over her and she shadowed the troops from the sea. It was during her time on the previous ship, the *Himalaya*, that Fanny adopted the look that would make her so recognisable. The ship's master, Mr Lane, gave her a pair of 'inexpressibles', or trousers, that she wore instead of petticoats. Until then she had restricted herself to brown-coloured dresses that were easy to wash; she kept petticoats to the minimum and wore linen drawers. She abandoned bonnets in favour of a white felt hat wrapped in white muslin and wore the trousers under a long skirt that she was not afraid to hitch daringly high to reveal her stout boots. The self-portrait she sent home shows a strange, hermaphrodite creature, but her outfit was ideal for clambering up and down gangplanks, tumbling in and out of boats and wading, knee-deep, through mud. She declared she would never again be able to wear a bonnet and when she finally returned home, she was stunned by her first sight of a crinoline.

As the months away from England lengthened, it became harder to keep up appearances. She told Selina that she despaired of the box she had asked for ever arriving. She was in 'terrible distress' for the many things in it: a decent gown, bandoline (a kind of gel for keeping hair in place) and gloves. Her agitation was compounded in June 1855 when a box sent by the army packers Hayter and Howell, containing her summer clothes, failed to arrive in Balaklava but, because it had been wrongly addressed, went to Scutari instead. Fearing it lost, she commissioned a tailor from the Zouave (France's elite infantry, created during the Algerian War) to make her a 'body' and breeches. It was based on the uniform of the French cavalrymen, the *Chasseurs d'Afrique*, and was sky blue with black military braiding on the sleeve. She sent her sister long lists of items she needed, such as a 'wide-awake', or soft-brimmed hat that would not crush en route; it had to have a low crown and be pretty. She also wanted three yards of black velvet and a black ostrich feather as trimming and enclosed a thread to denote the circumference of her head.

Fanny was at Evpatoria when she heard that Captain Cresswell, husband to Adelaide who boarded the ship at Varna by barrel, had died of cholera during the march from Kalamita Bay towards Sevastapol. Despite the scorn she had once poured on her, Fanny was shocked. 'God help and support her under a blow that would crush me to my grave!' A few months later another wife's 'fine healthy strong man' went down with the same illness and died within six hours. The woman displayed a 'frantic frenzy of grief' and Fanny had never encountered anything so 'frightfully extravagant' before. Her 'poor servant', too, heard rumours that her husband, a private in the 8th, had fallen off his horse and was wounded, but later discovered that he had been killed, 'Alas, poor woman!' Fanny wrote home: 'It is a novel office for me to be comforter to the poor broken-hearted little woman who is with me. She will not leave me for a moment "Oh ma'am it's my heart that's bad you seem to give me strength." Fancy me – from my weakness dealing out strength . . .' On another occasion she visited a soldier's wife who was suffering from fever. She had been lying on the wet ground in rain, wind and snow for twelve days. There was a ration of biscuit, a scrap of salt pork, some cheese, and a tin pot with some rum by her side. The woman was unpopular with the other wives and now it was left to her husband and his friend to look after her.

The role of the officer's wife had yet to assume the First World War dimension of comforter to families, but Fanny, nevertheless, wrote at least one consoling letter home to the bereaved. In another instance, it was her job to break the news to a wife that her husband was *only* wounded. When she wrote to the mother of Deane, a young officer shot through the brain while jumping on to the parapet of the Redan, one of the large fortifications that encircled Sevastopol, she had hoped to enclose a lock of his hair. This proved to be too clotted with blood and, instead, she sent his buttons and epaulettes.

In March 1855, Fanny recorded how her maid, Letitia, had recovered from the death of her husband, Private Francis Finnegan, who was killed in the Charge of the Light Brigade, and was making a lot of money from washing. She commented that the maid talked about her husband as if he were an old shoe, but added, kindly, that she was 'a very good woman nevertheless'.

Taking in washing was just one skill that helped wives to survive. They also cooked, sewed and mended. Women like Mrs Rogers, the wife of a non-commissioned officer in the 4th Dragoon Guards in 1855, were also admired for their bravery. In a letter of June 1855, Colonel Edward Cooper Hodge wrote that she deserved the Crimean Medal ten times more than half the men who would receive it. He felt so sorry for her that he gave her a pair of flannel trousers to help keep her warm.

When, in October 1854, Turkish soldiers retreating from a Russian attack ran through the settlement of Kadikoi, they were harangued by a group of British army wives, and a brawny washerwoman called Mrs Smith took hold of one of them and set about him for trampling over the laundry she had laid out in the sun to dry. Her wrath increased when she discovered that they had abandoned her husband's regiment, the 93rd. The Turkish soldiers retaliated by calling her *Kokana*, a term that suggests an improperly dressed woman, perhaps even a prostitute or a madam. Although she cannot have known what it meant, the name-calling enraged her further and she chased them down the hill, brandishing a stick. She survived the war and was known for the rest of her army life as 'Kokana Smith'.

On several occasions Fanny had a ringside view of the fighting. She watched the battle of Balaklava (25 October 1854) through her lorgnettes, seated on her horse, Bob. She and other wives also saw what became known as the Charge of the Light Brigade, from a vantage point of the North Valley. It was only when she returned to the safety of her ship and tried to sleep that it proved impossible to erase the day's bloody images. In June 1855 she told her sister that she wished she could expunge the image of 25,000 men running up a hill and charging with muskets when she fainted in her saddle from 'fatigue, illness and excitement'. A few days later she wrote of the attack in a way that made it sound like the start of a night-time theatrical extravaganza. They drank coffee at 2 a.m. and an hour later were at the front, seated on the ground as far forward as the Light Cavalry would permit. 'We were a few minutes late for the opening fire, but in time for such a storm of shot, grape, shell, and musketry as had never before annoyed the ears of Heaven.' By 18 June the British Army was preparing to storm the Redan and Fanny was inundated with officer friends visiting to say goodbye and telling her their wishes, should they be killed. She then rode up to the front, where she saw how badly the battle was going for the British. She returned home, where she lay on her bed, fully clothed, 'booted & spurred', before returning to watch more of the battle. She wrote to her sister of how soldiers had lost legs and arms and that one soldier's arm had flown 'clean over the parapet of a trench'.

The most testing time for Fanny came at the end of the eleven-month siege of Sevastopol in September 1855. Around 50,000 British and French troops surrounded, and finally, captured Russia's main Black Sea naval base, but only after heavy Allied losses brought on by a lack of preparation for the harsh winter. It took the victors three days to remove all the bodies from the town and in her journal Fanny describes the terrible sights she saw. She was horrified by the stench from the decomposing bodies of men, cattle and horses and described nearly being thrown from her pony as he shied away from two Russian cadavers and how she momentarily believed that a soldier sitting upright, hands in his lap, eyes looking straight at them was merely wounded, rather than long dead. The Allies were alerted to a hospital in the barracks by the sound of the dead and dying. Most horrific, a badly injured English officer from the 90th Regiment was discovered under a pile of corpses, where his captors had left him to die. He had had no food for three days and was found naked and raving.

> I think the impression made upon me by the sight of that foul heap of green and black, glazed and shrivelled flesh I never shall be able to throw entirely away. To think that each individual portion of that corruption was once perhaps the life and world of some loving woman's heart – that human living hands had touched, and living lips had pressed with clinging and tenderest affection, forms which in a week could become, oh, so loathsome, so putrescent!

Fanny reserved her frankest thoughts for her sister; she worried that she would be a 'sort of Bashi-Basouk' when she got home and said that she thanked God that she had no children – or, at least, no daughters.

Crimea was the last time wives accompanied their men to the front line. They had filled a number of roles: as cooks, laundry women, nurses and companions. Attempts in the second half of the century, however, to make the army more professional pushed women firmly back into a domestic setting. But, while the army wife would no longer follow her husband to war, she could still find herself in a position in which the battle came to her and her family. This state of affairs was to be at its most perilous in what was known as the Indian Mutiny of 1857.

5

The Changing Image of the Soldier and His Wife

One of many Russian cannons captured at the siege of Sevastapol still sits on its ornate iron carriage in Ely, Cambridgeshire. It points discreetly away from the Bishop's Palace and Norman cathedral to provide a favourite backdrop for tourist photos, its cold metal kept polished by the bottoms of hundreds of young children who have been plonked astride it. The cannon is so tall that the children need an adult, guiding hand to stop them tumbling off. Today the cannon's neck is stuffed with crisp and cigarette packets, whereas it was once capable of hurling deadly missiles at Russia's enemies. In the nineteenth century it was one of many such monuments that helped to make soldiers and their suffering more visible. The Crimean War, and the way it was depicted in newspapers, journals, letters and art, played a key part in shifting the perception of the ordinary soldier from a drunken ne'er-do-well and seducer of young women to a more 'muscular' Christian warrior.

Queen Victoria gave the cannon to the people of Ely in 1860 to mark the creation of the Ely Rifle Volunteers. It arrived by rail in June 1860 and was dragged up Ely's only hill by a team of six horses before being installed in the mud of Palace Green. As the century progressed few English towns and cities were without their reminder of Crimea: in street names; pub signs such as Balaklava, Raglan and

Cardigan; and the hundreds of memorials to some of the 20,813 men (one in five) who died. The French, by comparison, were quick to forget Crimea even though their war dead numbered one in three, or 100,000. In Britain, parents continued to call their daughters Florence and Alma and their sons Inkerman for decades after the end of the war. These three battles, together with Sevastopol, also gave their name to places in Australia, New Zealand, Canada and the United States.

In London, yet more captured Russian cannon was recycled to fashion the austere Guards Memorial in London's Piccadilly. The female figure of Honour, her arms outstretched, holding a wreath in each hand, gazes down on a Coldstream, Fusilier and Grenadier guard standing grimly beneath. The group did not immediately find universal favour. Some passers-by thought Honour's wreaths made her look as though she was engaged in a game of quoits, while another commentator muttered that the monument was best seen in the fog. However, despite these jibes, the war memorial was the first to feature the ordinary soldier and represented a distinct shift in attitude away from the notion that honour and courage were the preserve of the high-born officer. The Other Ranker could play his part – and often did despite the incompetence of his superiors.

Three years before the Crimean cannon arrived in Ely, Roger Fenton took a photo of the cathedral in one of a series of pastoral scenes in which he endeavoured to show that the new technique of photography could be the equal of art. The stately, bucolic image presents a sharp contrast to the photographs Fenton is best remembered for and which support the claim that he was an early prototype of the modern 'war photographer'.

Fenton helped to make Crimea the first war that was widely followed by citizens at home as he roamed the battle zone with his cameras, two assistants and a converted wine merchant's van. The horse-drawn wagon – which made an easy target, once had its roof blown off and was also mistaken for a secret weapon – housed a portable dark room containing unusually large glass negatives. Fenton was the son of a mill owner and banker who began his career as an artist but turned to law and then photography when his paintings failed to sell. He was commissioned by art publisher Thomas Agnew & Son, and carried letters of introduction from Prince Albert to the Allied military commanders. He was also a pioneer of 'salt prints', an early technique in which chemicals were used to 'fix a shadow' on light-sensitive paper coated in silver salts. His photos instil in his subjects an uncanny luminosity.

While the images present a partisan and positive view of the campaign, they are also strikingly intimate snapshots of life at the front: Balaklava Harbour cluttered with allied sailing ships; soldiers relaxing over a pipe or a drink; Lord Raglan; Omar Pasha, leader of the Ottoman Empire; and the French general Aimable-Jean-Jacques Pélissier discussing tactics seated at a small table covered with what looks like a tartan picnic rug. Although he was not a war photographer in the modern sense of the word – there are no corpses or casualties, as there would be ten years later in the American Civil War, and his photos look staged because an exposure time of twenty seconds ruled out spontaneity – he nevertheless managed to convey a sense of the desolation of the battlefield, most notably in *The Valley of the Shadow of Death*, which is strewn with the debris of war, but empty of human form. While Fenton did not have to worry about competing press 'snappers', he has still been accused in *The Valley of the Shadow of Death* of grouping cannonballs in clusters to deliver a greater visual punch. His photos also sometimes played into government hands, as when he showed soldiers wearing sturdy boots and thick sheepskin coats in a scene that gave the impression the soldiers had been kept warm throughout the cold months; whereas in reality, the photo was taken in April 1855, by which time the men had endured a harsh winter in tattered uniforms and were more concerned about the sweltering heat.

His photo of Fanny Duberly on her horse, Bob, with her heavily bearded husband Henry standing nearby, provided one of the lasting images of the war. She is prim and erect in her riding habit; her skirt covers most of the horse's withers and front body and gives the impression that she has been grafted onto the animal – although the real purpose of the skirt was to cover an outbreak of mange near the saddle. Henry stands casually in front, his jacket unbuttoned, his hat slightly crushed, making him look like a forerunner of the Confederate soldier. Fanny complained that he had adopted such a relaxed way to spite her and objected to the fact that the angle of the photograph made it look as though Bob had only one foreleg. Fenton took the photo in April 1855 and it proved so popular that he waived his fee for the sitting.

Photographs, as well as paintings, engravings and regular reports from the front, created a magic lantern show that fanned interest in the war and, for the first time, shaped a powerful public voice. A leader column in *The Times* of 5 May 1854 called the conflict, 'The people's War'. In the past a citizen's main concern had been whether war would lead to a hike in tax or prices; now readers wanted to know about the plight of their soldiers and families. Whereas conflict had previously been at arm's length now it arrived, for many people, every morning at the breakfast table. During the Napoleonic Wars the pamphlet had held sway but, by the middle of the nineteenth century, newspapers had found a keen audience, helped by the abolition of the newspaper stamp duty in 1855, which put newspapers within the grasp of the working man, who was now more likely to be able to read. The foreign correspondent had found his niche and war news no longer arrived through the filter of diplomats or army officers.

William Russell of *The Times* became a 'first person everyman of a narrator/hero' and, by the end of the war, a household name. His Anglo-Irish background placed him outside the Military Establishment, but inside the wagon circle of the rank and file of soldiers – a third of whom, like Nell Butler's husband, were Irish.

From February 1854, he sent dispatches home almost daily and was not afraid to tell his readers of the poor planning behind the deprivations encountered by the British soldier. Their suffering appeared all the more shameful compared to the slick French apparatus of hospitals, bread and biscuit bakeries and ample wagon trains. Newspapers, such as *The Times*, also printed uncensored accounts from the men and officers themselves. Sketches and photographs in other publications, like the weekly *Illustrated London News*, which saw its sales jump during this period, gave a clear impression of the danger and misery that British soldiers were experiencing.

The coverage of the war also injected, for the first time, a domestic note into the way soldiers and their sufferings were perceived. The image of Florence Nightingale as the 'lady with the lamp' appeared in the *Illustrated London News* of 24 February 1855, although the lamp shown was not the type she would have used at the hospital in Scutari, but a Grecian version that seemed to suggest magical qualities. The *ILN* which, by the summer of 1855 was selling more copies than *The Times* – 130,700 a week to a mainly middle- and upper-class readership – played a key part in altering the perception of war, partly through the illustrations produced by the artists it sent to Crimea. As Nightingale's modern biographer, Mark Bostridge, argues, the middle classes portrayed her as a symbol of efficient, housewifely virtue, opposed to the aristocratic and male mismanagement of the war and, while conditions may not have been worse than in previous wars, 'a principle of accountability had been established'. Funds flooded in for the wives and families suffering at home and Nightingale used money raised by *The Times* to buy a house at Scutari, which she converted into a washhouse. She then recruited wives and widows from the Barrack Hospital to work in it.

Advances in technology also made the – often shocking – experience of the soldier and his family more immediately available to the public. The invention of telegraphy meant intimate details of two major campaigns – the Crimean War and the Indian Mutiny – arrived with a startling immediacy into households throughout Britain. Paul Julius Reuters' news agency, which opened in London in 1851, adopted the new system, although telegraphs were designed to convey military reports and reporters were not supposed to use them for anything other than short headlines. And, while the mail boats were still slow, they were much faster than they had been in the Napoleonic Wars. News could now reach London in five days: two days by steamship from Balaklava to Varna, followed by a three-day horse ride to the nearest telegraphic link, at Bucharest. The French construction of a telegraph link to Varna meant that, by the winter of 1854, news arrived within two days; an underwater cable between Balaklava and Varna reduced this to a few hours by the end of April 1855.

The British press, unlike its counterpart in France, remained uncensored. Soldiers, too, were free to write home unfettered by the censor's pencil and felt able to tell their loved ones what was going wrong – whether the slow arrival of uniform or the fact that their new boots were the wrong size. Many of these letters were published in local and national newspapers and, in addition, ordinary people felt compelled to write to the letters' page in a way that had not been seen in earlier wars. A *Times* editorial of 30 December 1854 commented: 'Now the whole army rushes into print. Parents, wives, brothers, the whole family circle, as if they no longer cared for promotion and had forgotten the Horse Guards, urge us to publish, and tell the whole truth.' Letter writers conducted heated discussions about how soldiers could cope with the bitter winter (the hard frost in Britain made it easier for readers to empathise with troops exposed to the elements), what they should eat, how they should cook their food, what to wear and how to build the most insulated huts. Just as social media today allows everyone to comment on a public event, so these letters to the editor provided a forum for opinion.

A Mrs M. Walker, from Edgware Road in London, explained her plight in the same paper, on 2 March 1854:

> As a soldier's wife, I shall feel deeply grateful if you will allow this letter to appear in your paper. My husband has sailed with his fellow-soldiers, and I have nothing but my needle to depend on to provide for myself, one child and another unborn. I have neither the money nor the necessaries for my confinement, nor can I spare the time to walk about to make inquiries …

Fanny Duberly produced a stream of letters in which she revealed the dire conditions under which the troops were living; she sent them directly to newspapers or to her brother-in-law, Francis Marx, to forward, where they were published anonymously. Other women offered practical advice in their letters to newspapers, such as the pros and cons of crocheting versus knitting when sending 'comforts' to the troops. Their comments were welcome at a time when a whole army of knitters picked up their needles to defend the British soldier against the Crimean weather; Queen Victoria herself brandished a pair and recruited the female staff at Windsor to join her ranks. It was a moment that gave birth to that now most feared item of knitwear, the Balaclava helmet, a piece of clothing still guaranteed to make its wearer – whether terrorist or toddler – appear terrifying.

The growing concern for the ordinary soldier and his family indicated the extent to which the image of Tommy Atkins, the Everyman private, was changing. This was driven largely by evidence of his suffering and the idea that he was a Christian soldier marching, just as the plodding hymn first published in 1869 states, as to war. 'Tommy Atkins' first appeared in print as a generic term for a private in the British Army around 1850; by the Great War it had been shortened to 'Tommy.' The Crimean conflict raised the status of Tommy. As Orlando Figes, historian of the Crimean War, points out: 'Before the war the respectable middle and upper classes had viewed the rank and file of the British Army as little more than a dissolute rabble – heavy-drinking and ill-disciplined, brutal and profane – drawn from the poorest sections of society. But the agonies of the soldiers in the Crimea had revealed their Christian souls and turned them into objects of "good works" and Evangelical devotion.'

Writers and poets, too, helped to change the image of the soldier. Alfred Tennyson's 'The Charge of the Light Brigade' was published just two months after the event and Rudyard Kipling (1865–1936) later championed the lowly private in poems such as 'Arithmetic on the Frontier' and short stories like *Soldiers Three* (1890). From a Russian perspective, Leo Tolstoy, who was a second lieutenant in the 3rd Light Battery of the 14th Artillery Brigade, based *Sevastopol Sketches* on his experience of the town and of the ordinary soldier.

Despite this shift among the middle and upper classes, there remained considerable mistrust of the army among sections of the lower classes. Soldiers were still used to break up strikes and disturbances and there was still residual fear of the recruiting officer who might trick a poor man into signing his life away. In the period 1815–49 this meant enlisting for at least twenty-one years at a time when a man's life expectancy, if he came from a poor background, was not much above the age of forty. It took legislation to make the army more inviting to the lower classes. Cardwell's army reforms of 1870–71 cut the period of enlistment to 12 years and abolished the selling and buying of commissions.

Fanny Duberly's journal was first published in December 1855, to mixed reviews and easy parody. She was also disappointed that she failed to secure permission to dedicate it to Queen Victoria. *Punch* magazine was particularly effective in deriding the characteristics that some readers of her journal and journalism found most offensive. On 2 February 1856 it printed a satirical extract from her diary, poking fun at the nonchalant way she recounted moments of extreme danger, her masculine tropes and her belief that her time in the Crimea entitled her to the Balaklava clasp – an award she hoped to be buried with.

> *Saturday 10th.* Woke up by a loud explosion [sic] that made all the glasses in the tent rattle again, like the chandelier-drops during a maddening gallopade. Sky burning red, just as on a Vauxhall night. The flames seemed so close that I fancied I could have lit my cigar by them.
> *Monday 12th.* Walked over the battle-field to collect "charms" for my watch-chain.
> *Tuesday 13th.* A French trumpeter being killed by my side, I seized his trumpet, and kept up with his regiment during the remainder of the *melee.* Played all the tunes every bit as well as VIVIER. CANROBERT [who commanded a division at the Battle of Alma] sent me the Legion of Honour, which I put round the neck of my dear old 'BOBBY'.

Visual artists zoomed in on the military hero and his struggle against evil. As the art historian Joan Hichberger says: 'The army, the officers, the ranks and the women associated with it, were transformed in the art of the middle and upper classes. An organisation whose relation to the civilian state had always been equivocal was domesticated and incorporated into the belief system of the ruling classes . . .' Advances in lithography helped to answer the call for images, but when women were depicted, they were usually shown dealing with the aftershocks of the struggle – often as the recipient or purveyor of news both good and bad – in heavily upholstered Victorian drawing rooms or, occasionally, in tense siege conditions. John Millais' *News from Home* shows a Scottish Highlander, in elaborate dress, complete with a lavish sporran, reading a letter with a wry smile on his face as he stands next to a barricade in Crimea. John Ruskin queried, dryly, whether the artist imagined that soldiers at the front carried such elaborate uniforms and chose to wear them when reading a letter. It should be remembered that Millais was married to Ruskin's first wife, Effie Gray.

Images from the Indian uprising and the Crimean War stayed in the public's imagination for decades after the actual events and contributed to the shifting image of the soldier and his wife or sweetheart. He was no longer exclusively the blackguard of Washington Irving's short story *The Pride of the Village* (1820), whose suggestion that a maid should live with him unmarried led to her death from a broken heart, nor the seducer of 'Returning from the Fair' by Thomas Webster (1837), whose discarded dragoon's helmet led an elderly couple to fear the worst for their granddaughter, whom they glimpse through the window looking flushed as she flirts with a handsome soldier. After the Crimean War soldiers were more likely to be respectable husbands and fathers, mourned by, or reunited with, their dutiful wives. In John Noel Paton's 'Home' (ca. 1855–56), a wife has thrown her mending to the floor as she falls to her knees to embrace her injured husband with his heavily bandaged head; behind him an older woman – presumably one of their mothers – weeps on his shoulder. The room is cosily lit in muted browns and a child sleeps in a cradle; the artist has clearly taken pains to place the soldier at the centre of a domestic scene.

As well as the homecoming, wives and sweethearts were also shown seeing their menfolk off to war in tearful and dramatic scenes at dockside and railway station. Mostly they came from the lower ranks; farewells between officers and wives were more rare and usually took place inside. In Millais' 'The Black Brunswicker', the sweetheart seems to be imploring him to stay by blocking his exit through the half-opened door. Millais used Charles Dickens' daughter, Kate, as the model for the girl and a private in the Life Guards for the soldier. To protect their modesty, each had to model separately and a mannequin replaced the figure that the artist would paint them cleaving to. It was not until the Boer War that women were shown actively encouraging their men to leave.

These different representations supported the idea that it was not just the officer who was capable of noble acts. As Figes points out, the Crimea provided the opening chapter in a long-running drama in which the humble soldier assumed the role of hero amid the blunders of the ranks above him. The introduction of a new medal, the Victoria Cross, which was awarded regardless of rank, confirmed that the Queen herself felt Tommy Atkins was capable of heroic acts. The twentieth anniversary of the Crimea provided another opportunity to celebrate his heroic deeds. He became a staple of music hall songs, in which he was often depicted with affection but still someone capable of breaking hearts or of having his own heart broken.

6

The 'Great Sepoy Mutiny': Harriet Tytler, Fanny Wells and Lady Julia Inglis

Harriet Tytler's anxiety began on Sunday evening, 10 May 1857, when she heard the 'tootooing' of a *dak gharree* bugle, which she described as 'a very unusual thing' because native soldiers never used this type of wagon in Delhi. Days before, officials had noticed broken pieces of *chapatties* starting mysteriously to pass from village to village – it later emerged that this was a sign that the rebellion was about to begin.

She was right to be concerned. That same day the 3rd Light Cavalry and 11th and 20th Native Infantry at Meerut (Mirath), only 40 miles from Delhi, had opened fire on their officers at church parade. They massacred British families and set out for Delhi, where they arrived at about six in the morning and began the process of restoring to power the aged and bemused Mughal emperor, Bahadur Shah. On Sunday evening the local regiments, still apparently loyal to the British, were told that they must be on parade at dawn the following morning, when the punishment for the soldiers who had mutinied at the end of March at Barrackpore would be read. Harriet's husband, Robert, agreed to carry out this task in place of the quartermaster, who was ill. 'Little did we expect what the 11th May would mean to every Christian, man, woman and child, in Delhi,' Harriet wrote later. When Robert read the proclamation his men hissed and shuffled their feet.

Monday started as usual. The servants sealed the doors to keep out the 'raging hot wind' and watered the 'tatties', the grass screens over the windows, which were believed to reduce the temperature by as much as twenty degrees Fahrenheit. Everyone had their baths and the children – Frank, now four, and Edith, two – had eaten when Harriet, who was eight months pregnant, settled down to breakfast with Robert at about 8 a.m. They were in the middle of their final course of melons when the tailor, who usually sat sewing on the veranda, burst in, clasping his hands and saying, 'Sahib, Sahib, the *fauj* (army) has come.' Robert leapt up, put on his boots and hat and went to see the brigadier.

When he returned he told his wife he had been ordered to go with two companies to an army building to the northeast of the cantonments known as the White House. Here he was to guard the ferries that crossed the Yamuna River and stop the mutineers from entering the cantonments and blowing up the powder magazine. On his way there he called in again. Harriet could see servants running in the street, oxen lugging guns and Mrs Hutchinson, the judge's wife, without a hat, her hair flowing freely to her shoulders, a child in her arms and the bearer carrying a second. Harriet's Breton maid, Marie, said ominously: 'Madame, this is a *revolution*, I know what a revolution is', and began to lock everything away – even the clean clothes the washerman had brought that morning.

Lieutenant Holland's wife sent a letter suggesting Harriet join them at their house, but she refused as Robert had told them to stay put. Another letter arrived, together with the Hollands' phaeton (a big-wheeled but fragile-looking carriage familiar to readers of Jane Austen) and a message from the brigadier saying they must meet at the sergeant-major's bungalow. Here his wife made them comfortable, until they were told to move on to the Flag Staff Tower.

But all the carriages were full and Harriet began to cry at the thought of the distance she would have to travel on foot and without any relief from the sun. Her advanced pregnancy must have made everything seem so much worse. Mrs de Tessier, who was the last to leave the bungalow, took pity on her and asked her to join her, her baby and her *ayah* in the carriage. Their long cavalcade moved slowly to allow others to join it on its way to Flag Staff Tower, a short, isolated round tower perched on a ridge outside the city wall and close to the British cantonments. Harriet noted that it was more like a funeral march. The brigadier, soldiers and four guns were waiting for them.

The tower was some 18 feet in diameter and the squash of women, children and servants drove the already broiling temperature (38°C/100°F in the shade) still higher. Some women, due to the heat and the tension, fainted. Harriet remembered later how Dr Stewart sidled up to her to confide that he had found officers of the 54th lying dead; the Colonel, who had been bayoneted in nine places, was the only survivor. Although there was general confusion about the extent of the mutiny, many of the women had been told that their husbands, sons and brothers had been killed. As they waited in the tower Harriet's little boy, Frank, asked: 'Mamma, will these naughty *sepoys* kill my papa and will they kill me too?' Edith begged to be taken home. Harriet remembered gazing at Frank's white throat and saying to herself, 'My poor child, that little throat will be cut ere long, without any power on my part to save you.'

Robert was three miles away at the White House and she considered running over to tell him what had happened, but was too scared to leave her children. She had not seen Marie for hours.

The soldiers went to the roof to prepare for an attack. Harriet and some of the other women helped to pass muskets and arms up to them. The females took it in turns to share the two chairs and *charpoy*, a low Indian bed with knotted rope in place of a mattress. Eventually 'dear Mrs Peile' gave Harriet her chair and, after hours of standing or sitting on the floor, it was a relief to perch on one of the stone steps leading to the roof. Frank clung to her side and she held Edith in her arms. There was a sudden explosion and everyone ran to the door to look out on the city as a large cloud rose over the skyline; it looked like a very long sheet before turning into a 'thick brown mass'.

Eventually Robert appeared and the Brigadier and officers decided it was too dangerous to stay there. As if to confirm their worst fears, a cart containing the bodies of British officers who had been killed that morning appeared. The occupants of the tower viewed its arrival as a threatening gesture from the *sepoys*, whereas it had, in fact, been sent by accident by a British officer. There was a stampede for the carriages. Robert ordered the *palkee gharree* he used for hunting. Captain Gardner's wife, who was also pregnant, and her little boy joined them in a carriage designed for two and which already contained Marie, Emily sitting on her mother's lap and Frank cowering at her feet. Harriet's servant, Thakoor Singh, begged to join them but there was simply no room. She later discovered that he had been killed.

The reasons for what Harriet, fifty years later, referred to as the 'Great Sepoy Mutiny' are multifarious, although some retellings reduce the causes to one issue: the enforced use of greased cartridges in Enfield rifles. While this is a simplistic explanation, the cartridges are emblematic of the unrest that led to the uprising. New cartridges were introduced in 1856 and were rumoured to be lubricated with fat (wax would have been a more accurate description) taken from cows or pigs. Although unfounded, the rumour managed to offend both Muslims and Hindus: Hindus because they viewed cows as sacred and Muslims because they believed pigs to be unclean. In fact, the revolt was driven by a complex wave of social, administrative and technological reforms, which, collectively, were seen as attacks on the Hindu caste system and as symptomatic of a less sympathetic approach to India's customs. The General Service Enlistment Act of 1856, for example, forced Indian soldiers to serve abroad and in so doing to live in close proximity to men of a lower caste. Significantly, the Bengal Army, which formed the core of the Indian Army, was mainly manned by soldiers from the Brahmin class. On top of this, the 'doctrine of lapse', in which any kingdom dominated by the British and without a natural heir would be annexed to the crown, naturally infuriated local leaders and many Indian soldiers.

Of the many accounts of the ordeals endured by women in India, perhaps the most astonishing was not published until the twentieth century. Harriet Earle was born on 3 October 1828 in Secrora, a small army station in Oude (Awadh) in the middle of the modern state of Uttar Pradesh, where her father was a captain. Bathing her for the first time, her Indian nurse noticed a mole on the sole of her left foot and predicted that the child would spend her life travelling. In later years Harriet considered having the mole removed to put a stop to her wanderings.

Her first journey began when she was thirteen days old and she joined her father's regiment on their march to Nusserabad (Nasirabad). He had arrived in India in 1807, at the age of sixteen, when he served as an ensign for the East India Company. As was the custom, Harriet was sent back to England with her sister when she was eleven to receive a proper education and to avoid the enervating Indian climate. The girls lived with their uncle, Captain Raine of the 96th Regiment, and his wife in lodgings in Birmingham, while their younger brother went to boarding school. It was not a happy time for the sisters. Her aunt's idea of childcare was to make them wander round the cemetery for two hours every day. She fed them bread and water they had to earn by running the equivalent of four-and-a-half miles round the garden.

Harriet returned to India when she was sixteen, but on the way received a letter telling her that her father had died. On being reunited, her mother told her that she planned to go back to England with the younger children, leaving Harriet to join her uncle in northwest India, where he was serving in the 24th NI. To be eligible for her father's pension, Harriet was forced to stay in India.

She was often compared in appearance to a young Queen Victoria. Even if the comparison was based on a *young* Queen Victoria, it may not seem flattering today, and yet she attracted considerable attention from officers whom, it must be said, were starved of female company. At Allahabad one officer proposed and when she turned him down, he trotted after her palanquin for several miles in an attempt to persuade her to change her mind. She met her husband when the regiment, the 38th NI, in which he was captain, arrived at Lucknow. Robert Tytler was twenty-nine and Harriet nineteen when they married in March 1848. This was not an unusually large age gap for the time in India and in Robert's case was explained by the fact that his first wife, Isabella, had died in 1847, a few days short of their fourth wedding anniversary. She was seventeen when they married and they went on to have two sons. Robert had served in the 1st Afghan War (1840–42) and in the Gwalior Campaign (a region south of Agra, in the north of modern India). Although tall, he was not as obviously heroic as his cousin, Lieutenant John Adams Tytler, who was to win the Victoria Cross in February 1858 after driving back mutineers in hand-to-hand fighting. Robert climbed slowly up the army career ladder and took the unglamorous role of Baggage Master to the Field Force in Kandahar, a place that has earned a new resonance in the twenty-first century. He was known for his even temper, knowledge of local languages (both he and Harriet were fluent in Hindustani), and the fairness with which he treated his men, rather than his derring-do. He was also interested in birds and reptiles, and the couple became pioneering photographers who took some of the first images of Delhi.

From the very start, Harriet's married life was dogged by the sort of misfortune that was common to many army wives in India. Their first child, a son, was born in 1849 and they spent the summer in a cottage in the relative coolness of Mussoorie. From here they moved to Barrackpore, about 16 miles from Calcutta. 'The first year of our stay in Barrackpore was a very sad one altogether,' Harriet wrote later. First, her brother-in-law died and 'Then my dear little baby was born and died . . .' The baby suffered a series of fits and, Harriet believed, died of lockjaw.

From Barrackpore they were posted to the heat of Dacca in Bengal; their luggage went by river, while they marched for fourteen days. Less than five months after their arrival, Harriet and most of the other members of the cantonment were struck down with fever; her son, Frank, was born during this illness and her mother-in-law died from it. Frank survived, but when they were in Mussoorie their only daughter, Edith, started to have convulsions. The station doctor insisted she was simply teething, but a second doctor diagnosed an abscess on the liver. Treatment and the warmer air of Delhi, where Robert's regiment, the 38th NI, moved in 1856, helped her to recover.

Fanny Wells, the army doctor's wife who had sent her father regular reports of life on board *The Lady Jocelyn*, was also beginning to experience signs of the unrest at the heart of the Indian Army. She was in Lucknow with her husband and their baby, Georgy, and his brother, Dickey, when, in April 1857, their bungalow was destroyed by a fire started by *sepoys*. Lucknow was the capital of Awadh and had been annexed by the British in 1856. She had heard of the violence in Delhi and Meerut, although the insurgents had stopped the post and news was reduced to scraps that arrived by telegraph. On 17 May she wrote to her father:

> Dear Papa I am so horribly afraid; that if I could only get to England but that is impossible, as we are six hundred miles from Calcutta: the worst of it is there is no place of refuge here, not a shadow of a fort as at most places . . . I think so much of my

> children if anything were to happen, my poor little helpless darlings what should I do with them: we keep loaded pistols close to our bed; and the slightest noise arouses us.

It was thought unsafe even to go to church and Fanny was too worried to settle at anything. Her anxiety assumed a physical form: she suffered a 'nervous affection of the right breast' and had to wean Georgy.

Her next letter was written from Lucknow's official Residency, where she described sharing the space with seventy 'ladies', 150 children and 'gentlemen innumerable'. The numbers are difficult to pin down, but there were probably about 800 officers and men at the garrison, including some Indians who remained loyal to the British and 153 civilian volunteers. They were part of a group that Lady Julia Inglis estimated at around 800 women and children defended by 1,800 soldiers against a native force of some 15,000. Families were given only an hour's notice before being bundled into the Residency, an elegant, colonnaded building with large windows protected by awnings and views over the town's many minarets. Fanny wrote to her father: 'Oh dear Papa if I could have dreamt of this nothing should have tempted me to India; we are crammed like sheep in a pen, 8 in a room and the heat is awful: the vaults are filled with the wives and children of soldiers; and the noise is beyond description.'

At the start of the siege Lady Julia Inglis, who was to survive the sinking of the *Ava* off Ceylon on her way home to Britain, slept on the Residency's roof with her children. She wrote in her diary on 13 June: 'The nights were very pleasant in the open air, and the view of the city and country round very beautiful. Everything used to look so calm and peaceful, it was difficult to think it could ever be a scene of war; but looking down into the Residency garden, we could see the guns placed in position ready to be used at a moment's notice, and the soldiers sleeping among them.'

They could see great fires burning in the distance and imagined they represented the enemy signalling to each other. Her husband, Brigadier John Inglis, who commanded the garrison, had his bed moved out of the Residency so that he could be near his troops and stop false alarms. By the end of June, Julia and her children abandoned the upper storeys of the house and 'took refuge in a small, almost underground, room where the artillery women were quartered'. The windows were barricaded and they spent the day listening to the battle going on outside. Every so often a soldier would look in on them and tell them they were doing well. John managed to pop in once or twice, for ten minutes.

They seem later to have moved to another part of the Residency, a 'native gaol' with no windows or doors, but archways. It was 'hardly more than a verandah', 12 by 6 feet. They put up screens and curtains to offer some privacy and used an outhouse as a bathroom, 'a great luxury'. By this stage Julia had contracted smallpox and was worried that the children might catch it.

By the beginning of July, John warned them that they would hear 'heavy firing' and Julia wrote that many ladies had poison ready: 'We felt sure that the enemy must get in, when the most terrible death awaited us'. A few days later they heard 'dreadful shouting and screaming'. By the end of the month a Mrs Bird had detected the sound of mining directly under the room where most of the women lived; fortunately, the 32nd Regiment, which included many Cornish soldiers, was adept at digging defences.

Fanny and her children moved into the guardroom with fourteen others and felt lucky to have a cupboard in which to store her few belongings. Although the room was meant to be exclusively for women, men popped in and out all day, filling it with 'such a Babel' and 'such a smell of smoke'. They had rations for six months and lived off a sort of unseasoned *chapatti* made from coarse beef and flour and a little rice and dried peas. Supplies dwindled as the siege wore on and led to scurvy that caused loose teeth, boils and swollen heads and earned the name 'garrison disease'. A 'light infantry' of head lice added to the discomfort. Cholera began to move through the building and took a heavy toll. The soldiers suffered from a lack of tobacco and many were taken ill from smoking green leaves. There were several suicides among the men; Captain Graham shot himself in his bed, leaving a young widow. The flies proved a 'torment' and covered the tables, cups and dishes and bothered the children. Julia wrote: 'Every kind of insect, fleas, etc., abounded, and rats and mice ran about the room in broad daylight, the former of an immense size.'

Julia and John appear to have had a frank relationship in which, over the coming weeks, he shared his fears. She was also privy to the secret messages that arrived from outside, smuggled in by spies, and the notes that went out. One missive consisted of 283 words written on a tiny piece of paper about half a thumb in size and hidden in a quill; for added security the vital words were in Greek. Unlike many of the army wives she knew exactly how grim their prospects were. She also saw her husband weeping after Colonel Case had been killed and he had to break the news to his widow.

In August, six men died as part of the Residency collapsed, and the prospects seemed dire. Julia knew that her husband had made up his mind that every man should die at his post, but she worried about what would happen to the sick and wounded, the women and helpless children – 'The contemplation seemed too dreadful.' At one time he talked about blowing everyone up at the last minute, and showed her a letter from General Havelock at Cawnpore that ended, 'Do not negotiate, but rather perish sword in hand.' She later dwelt on how strange it was that they were able to talk calmly about such dreadful subjects.

Since many of the servants had escaped, Fanny had to learn new household skills. Astonishingly, under such conditions she still felt the need to wash, starch and iron clothes. Her *ayah* stayed behind but was wounded in the stomach and also had a baby, two events that Fanny dismissed with the comment, 'so she has not been of much use to me.' Julia noted that, given the lack of washermen, it was fortunate that the troops' white clothing had been dyed khaki or mud colour before the siege. She added that some of the refugees from the neighbouring stations presented 'a most ragged appearance'. One officer, whose clothes had been torn in the jungle, made himself a Lincoln green suit from the baize of the Residency's billiard table. J.G. Farrell incorporated this, and many other surreal details, in his novel *The Siege of Krishnapur*, the second in his Empire Trilogy. In the fictional version, the women made the suit as a birthday present for a civilian who was helping to defend the Residency.

Fanny's boys, Georgy and Dickey, were fractious from the heat and being trapped in a small space; many of the little ones, too, must surely have picked up the fear oozing from the adults. Dickey kept falling out with the other children and was so feverish that he cried constantly. Fanny was anxious that Georgie was sickening for measles, which had broken out in the Residency. She had already lost a son, her second child, who lived a matter of days after his birth in September 1855.

Julia wrote of the swing on the tree near the door which caused 'great amusement' for the children and that they did not seem to 'feel the confinement very much'. However, as the months wore on she recorded the many deaths of babies and little children. On 1 September five babies were buried. The terrible situation had become part of their children's play. Johnnie would rush to pick up a bullet while it was still warm and all the children would make balls out of earth to hurl at the wall in imitation of shells bursting. Johnnie often asked whether it was 'us' or the enemy firing and yet the children slept soundly during the heaviest bombardment and never appeared frightened.

Fanny wrote with remarkable frankness to her father about the reports that were reaching them from other centres of uprising: 'Poor Miss Jennings was dragged about the streets for hours in a state of nudity, tortured and finally killed. Mrs Chambers who was killed by a butcher was one of my most intimate friends, a lovely young woman and just expecting her confinement.' However, Julia and Fanny were fortunate to be with their husbands. Three officers were separated from their wives who were in Cawnpore and Julia wrote of the 'wretched face' of one. He barely spoke.

On 18 September there was a partial eclipse of the sun. A few days later the rain cleared the air, but the Residency building, which was close to collapse after months of bombardment, leaked badly. Julia was sitting in a small room when she heard the sound of distant guns. The noise filled her with hope and each boom seemed to say, 'We are coming to save you'. There were rumours, too, that bagpipes had been heard. On 25 September 'tremendous cheering' went up and they knew their relief had arrived. Julia shook hands with a short, quiet-looking, grey-haired man, whom she recognised at once as General Havelock and who said they must have suffered a great deal. She could hardly answer and longed to be alone with her husband. They snatched some time in private, but it was a fleeting moment of happiness. Havelock now merely became a new participant in the siege and Lucknow was not finally relieved until 16 November.

Fanny wrote her next letter home in December from the Fort at Allahabad and explained what had happened during the months between May and their eventual release, eighty-seven days later. She told her father how the Residency had been bombarded and that one of the first shots had struck a room she was in, where it took off Miss Valence's leg. The young woman died the next day. They retreated to the basement, but conditions were so foul that they braved the bullets to flee to a nearby house and then to the Brigade Mess – a site so close to the enemy lines that it had the advantage that the shells burst *over* them. On 13 July Georgie died from 'water on the brain', 'poor little angel I have grieved for him bitterly, but quite see now that he was taken in mercy for he must have been starved'. She had no milk or food for him. He was buried at night in the graveyard and she read the service over him.

Her husband, Walter, was worn down by the arduous work of burying horses, filling boxes with earth for barricades and taking sentry duty – all in the extreme heat. He was injured in the face and chest and also broke several ribs and hurt his knee when he fell through a hole in the hospital floor. When they were finally rescued they had to run under fire from the Residency and double march to Cawnpore. Fanny had grown so thin that it was painful to sit down and the guard on her diamond and emerald engagement ring became loose and the ring dropped off. It was never found. Like Harriet, it was only one of many losses she suffered. Everything in the world had been taken from them: carriages, horses, buggy, tents, piano, furniture and their clothes. Walter suffered from the cold because he had no drawers. In a letter to his father-in-law, he estimated their losses from the siege at 8–9,000 Rupees, which, including the destruction of the bungalow, amounted to around 10,000 Rupees or £1,000 in contemporary money (equivalent to over £100,000 today).

Fanny wrote to her father from Calcutta in February 1858 to say that they hoped to be on a steamer home on 9 March. It was so hot that she almost fainted in church. She wondered how much those in England knew of the mutiny and speculated that they probably had a clearer idea of events than those who had been in the thick of it. When they arrived back in April 1858 the *Bristol Times* wrote of the excitement that greeted 'the heroic band who bore the perils and awful anxieties of the long Siege of Lucknow'. Bells rang out and neighbours raised a 'triumphal arch'. 'Those who remember the fair young girl that a few years ago left their village a soldier's bride, could trace in the same countenance the wearing effects of painful anxiety, long watching and ceaseless danger, sustained within the "fire lapped wall" of the Residency . . .'

*

The Tytlers' escape from the Flag Staff Tower in Delhi was followed by a journey in which they did their best to stay ahead of the mutineers. Mrs Gardner had already become separated from her husband, but Robert insisted on returning to the city and found him stumbling about with his revolver. The two families drove 'at a terrific pace' north of Delhi, once glancing back at the cantonment to see that every bungalow was on fire. Harriet thought of all she had lost. Many items were irreplaceable: a lock of her dead child's hair, manuscripts and paintings from a book Robert was working on, her own artwork. She later calculated that the more mundane possessions – clothes, furniture, a large carriage, horses, buggy, her husband's uniform – were worth £20,000, a huge amount today.

After about 20 miles the wheels on the Tytlers' carriage collapsed under them and they were forced to abandon it; each husband and Marie carried a child and the two wives walked silently by their side. They commandeered a *dak gharree*, but the rear wheels rolled off. Passengers in a mail cart helped them to repair it, but the springs under Harriet's seat gave way and sent her and Marie up to the ceiling, 'from where we had with difficulty to be extricated'. There was nothing for it but to continue their journey in the heat of the night, unsure if they might, at any moment, bump into mutineers. They managed to commandeer a bullock cart from two Indians; it was unsprung and they were unsure how to drive the animals, but it was better than walking. The Indians, seeing their ineptitude, took pity on them and returned to help them drive it. There was no water except for the green mire by the roadside pools which Harriet drank, holding her nose and closing her eyes, from her husband's cupped hands.

Eventually, they reached a bungalow where they had breakfast before continuing to Kurnaul (now Karnal) and then Umballa (Ambala), where they stayed with friends, Colonel and Mrs Ewart. The Colonel was an old and nervous man who was not keen on children. Marie kept them out of his way by looking after them all day in the large bathroom, where they played with the water in the earthen pot and ate their meals. Mrs Gardner had no servant and her son, whom Harriet described as badly behaved, had to eat meals with the adults.

Everyone at the barracks at Umballa was nervous: there had been fire attacks a few months earlier and the cantonment was awash with rumours about plots. As a result, there were several false alarms when, Harriet, exhausted from the recent days' exertions, was forced out of bed in the bungalow to the greater protection of the barracks. Here she and Mrs Gardner were bombarded with questions from worried soldiers and their wives about their experiences in Delhi.

After a few days Mrs Gardner approached Harriet and said there were too many people staying at the bungalow and that because there were more of the Tytlers they should leave. There were no hotels in Umballa and they had no other friends to call upon. Robert bought a 'van', about 12 feet long and four feet wide, from a shopkeeper, who had used it to transport crockery. He had the railings around it removed and a thick thatch added; the sides were enclosed with matting – except for two places left for windows. The van was parked in the grounds of the 9th Lancers and each night they slept on straw under two traditional Indian quilts and were driven back to the Ewarts' in the morning. Their ordeal did not last long because Captain Maisey offered them his house while his wife and children were away in the hills. He also gave Robert his horse and asked him whether he would like to return with him to Delhi as paymaster to the troops, with responsibility for the military treasure chest out of which the soldiers were paid. As the Tytlers had lost so much in Delhi, even Robert's last month's salary, and had to find boarding fees for three boys in England, the offer was appealing. Probably because Harriet was so heavily pregnant, he made the unusual decision of taking his wife and two young children with him – with the aim of sending them on from Delhi to their cottage in Mussoorie. They offered to take Mrs Gardner with them, but she scoffed at the idea and, instead, set off by palanquin to Kussowlie. She gave birth on the way. Her husband had already volunteered to return to Delhi, where he was attacked and died later from his wounds.

The journey back to Delhi held several horrors. The day before they reached Alipore, Harriet saw a Muslim baker in clean white clothes hanging from the branch of an acacia tree. 'Tommie Atkins' had hanged him for being late with the breakfast bread several mornings in a row. Harriet thought the soldiers should have been hanged for their cruelty, but supposed every soldier was needed to fight the rebels. Soon after she saw the naked bodies of soldiers, 'swollen by the heat . . .', one had a hole in his forehead 'as large as a billiard ball'.

At Delhi Robert bought a tent to use as an office. It was pitched in front of the carts, or 'tumbrels', that carried the money and which were guarded by sixty soldiers. The tumbrels, open wagons which tilted backwards to tip out their load, resembled the carts used to move prisoners about to be guillotined in the French Revolution – a comparison which, had it occurred to her, cannot have reassured Marie. The Tytler family lived in another cart, where they took their meals, only leaving it in the evening for an 'airing' when they went for a stroll and their friends told them the latest gossip. By now there were other women and children refugees in the camp, who were to go by 'pad elephant' – that is, sitting on straw mattresses on the animal's back – rather than in the more comfortable and secure *howdahs*, to the comparative safety of Meerut. Harriet, who expected to give birth any day, begged to be allowed to stay. Much to the consternation of high-ranking officers like Lord Roberts and Major Hodson, her wish was granted. The baby arrived two days later, on 21 June, at two in the morning.

The child was born with dysentery and not expected to live. He lay near the opening in the cart with only a small flannel over him, 'with the setting moon shining brightly on him, with nothing but the sound of the alarm call and shot and shell for music to his ears for the rest of the siege'. Harriet was alarmed when Marie lifted him up by his leg to give him his first bath and instead washed him herself in a brass washbasin, or *chillumchee*. A week later the monsoon broke, flooding through the thatched roof of their cart and drenching them. Robert found an empty 'bell of arms' – a little tower usually made of stone where rifles were stored – and the family moved in. Harriet walked to it barefoot, her new baby wrapped in a wet sheet. They slept on straw and quilts. It was to be their home for the next four months, until the siege of Delhi finally ended.

Harriet thought she and her baby would both die, but she found she was able to feed him without 'the usual aid of a bottle of milk' (presumably, modesty did not allow her to say she breastfed him), which was a relief, as no milk or bottles were available. Clothing was a problem: her two other children had only what they had escaped in, but she managed to make the baby a few coarse petticoats. She spent most of her days in the bell of arms, darning their meagre garments and growing used to the sound of shells. When Captain Willock was startled by one, she replied casually: 'Oh! It is only a shell', an expression that became a catchphrase around the camp. The baby slept well throughout and became a mascot for the troops.

Despite the extreme circumstances, the family quickly established a routine. Every morning, before the sun rose, Marie took the two children for a walk and then they had breakfast and washed. It was impossible to keep Frank inside and, despite the lack of a hat, he scampered about, playing with the soldiers. On one occasion, Marie allowed him to go for a ride with a soldier, which led to an agonising period when Harriet thought he had been kidnapped. Edith, who was still fragile after her abscess, had to stay in the cart, where she would frequently faint. In her desperation to keep the girl inside, Harriet scratched her feet and told her to play doctor and dress her mother's wounds; the game was endlessly repeated.

They lived like cattle, bedding down in the straw. Harriet

sandwiched the baby between the wall and her body to protect him from a sleepy kick from the older children until one day when she was bathing him she noticed that his head, which was still the malleable skull of a newborn, had grown to one side. A reordering of the bodies helped to rectify the situation. She never got used to the flies, which multiplied because of the number of carcasses and appeared to be coming in via the *punka* strings that ran through the screens covering the two holes that acted as windows. Harriet covered the strings with cloth while bored officers took to laying a sugar trail for the flies before blowing them up with gunpowder. She was unable to find a nine-inch centipede she had glimpsed on the floor; she knew its bite was not fatal but worried any wound might become infected.

One day a group of rebels got into camp disguised in the uniform of Indians who had stayed loyal to the British. They killed some of the local people who would not join them and freed the horses so that they ran wild through the camp. The alarm was raised and the battle continued in the cantonment cemetery, opposite the bell of arms. As a precaution, Harriet put the children and Marie between the two apertures, where the walls were thickest, but was so anxious about Robert that she hung out of the 'window' to look for him in the battle, oblivious to the bullets ricocheting off the bell of arms. It was the only battle she ever saw and wrote later that she would never forget 'the glistening of the bayonets even through the smoke as both sides fired. Almost in the twinkling of an eye, all was over.'

Both sides in the rebellion were guilty of terrible atrocities. The British revived the barbaric Mughal custom of tying mutineers over the mouths of cannon before blowing them apart. At Jhansi, on 8 June, sixty-six British men, women and children who had held out for five days were killed after surrendering. At Cawnpore (now Kanpur, in Uttar Pradesh) the local prince, Nana Sahib, encouraged mutineers to besiege some 200 European, civilians and women and children, under the command of Sir Hugh Wheeler. The garrison surrendered after three weeks, but the men were killed as they boarded boats on the Ganges and about 80 women and 100 children murdered in a house known as Bibigarh; their bodies were thrown into a well that later became a much-visited shrine. Accounts of what was happening at other cantonments added to the tension within Harriet's camp and she asked her husband to get hold of a bottle of laudanum. 'In case of a hopeless reverse' she intended to give each of her children a good dose from it and then drain the bottle herself.

Reinforcements arrived in India from China, but it took until December 1857 for Sir Colin Campbell's army to restore strategic points along the Ganges valley. Small pockets of armed resistance continued to cause alarm until spring 1859 and the bloodshed left a legacy of mistrust: it was harder for soldiers and their families to feel safe. Places associated with the uprising became points of pilgrimage and constant reminders of the terrors earlier army wives had experienced. Some cantonment homes carried plaques commemorating those who had died and the red-brick, pock-marked ruins of the Residency in Lucknow became part of the tourist route, alongside traditional landmarks such as the Taj Mahal. The Tytlers took one of the first photos of the Residency when they visited in 1858; in the space of a few months the once elegant building had been reduced to what looked like ancient ruins.

For the next twenty years, visitors asked to see the bell of arms where Harriet and her family had lived. The dwelling lost its aura only in 1877, when Lord Lytton pitched his camp there and converted it to a house with glass windows and had the bullet marks erased. The baby who had been born in a bullock cart also became an attraction and there was much debate about his name. The soldiers wanted to call him 'Battlefield Tytler', but Harriet refused. Instead, he was given the only marginally less cumbersome name of 'Stanley Delhi-Force' after the last line, 'On, Stanley, on', from Sir Walter Scott's poem, 'Marmion', which her husband had read to her before the siege. A shell that had landed near the cart, and which Harriet had kept, intending to give it to the baby when he was older, was stolen.

In Britain, the mutiny presented a challenge for artists. No longer were they required to depict battle scenes; rather, the most dramatic moments were sieges which had as their epicentre civilian suffering, mostly by women. In 'An Alarm in India', exhibited in 1858, Edward Hopley, well-known for his paintings of fairies, shows an officer peering out of the window as his wife holds a second revolver for him to defend them from the mutineers. Frederick Goodall's painting, which has several titles, including 'The Campbells Are Coming' and 'Highland Jessie' (and 'Incident During the Siege of Lucknow, 26 September 1857'), but which was most commonly known as 'Jessie's Dream', relied on the legend of Jessie Brown. She was the young wife of a Scottish soldier whose optimism provided succour for the captives. According to the story, even she loses heart and falls into a feverish sleep until she wakes suddenly and claims to have heard the sound of bagpipes – proof that a Scottish regiment was on its way. She was not believed until, sure enough, others started to pick up the rousing strains and the 78th Highlanders arrived. In the painting she leans over the barricade to point to the approaching soldiers while an officer stands next to her, his arms folded in disbelief; another wife kneels exhausted, as a child clings to her skirt. The story inspired ballads, poems (including Tennyson's 'The Defence of Lucknow'), figurines, penny novels, plays and dioramas. Paintings such as 'The Relief of Lucknow' by Thomas Jones Barker, exhibited in 1859, were more detailed and more accurate. Newspapers, including the *Illustrated London News* and *Harper's Weekly*, carried 'before and after' illustrations of the Residency. The siege has also caught the imagination of more recent writers, including M.M. Kaye in *Shadow of the Moon* and Philip Pullman in *The Ruby in the Smoke* (the 'ruby' of the title refers to a jewel that went missing during the siege).

Joseph Noel Paton produced the most shocking image from the

uprising. His 'In Memoriam' (1858) shows women and young children cowering in a room at Cawnpore. Behind the group the viewer can glimpse Indian soldiers entering through the door – the implication being that they are poised to murder, and perhaps even rape, the innocents. As Hichberger has said, the taboo of white women in the hands of non-white men also represented another great fear: of the slipping of British control from imperial grasp. The painting caused a sensation when it was exhibited at the Royal Academy; for some critics it was quasi-religious, but audiences were shocked and *Punch* reported that a woman had fainted in front of one of the 'horrible Cawnpore pictures'. When it was shown at the Royal Scottish Academy in 1859, Paton agreed to replace the *sepoys* with kilted Scottish soldiers who had come to the women's defence; he also switched the setting from the massacre of Cawnpore to the relief of Lucknow. The second version became the popular engraving and was titled 'In Memoriam: Henry Havelock' and bore the legend, 'Designed to Commemorate The Christian Heroism of the British Ladies in India during the Mutiny of 1857'. Edward Armitage's imposing (nearly 9.5 feet) allegorical oil painting 'Retribution' showed the brawny figure of Britannia, clad in a vibrant pinky-red gown, straddling the bloodless bodies of a young woman and child, and about to plunge a sword into the chest of an Indian tiger. The message was clear: India would pay for the massacre of innocents.

The dramatic scenes, in which women played a key part, helped those at home to imagine what the soldiers and their wives had gone through. Dioramas of the sieges and theatrical re-enactments of episodes from both India and Crimea became popular. There was a demand for maps of Delhi so that readers could follow every twist and turn of the drama. But, while so many images associated with the Indian uprising focused on the suffering of women and children, the artist 'who was to do for the soldier in art what Rudyard Kipling was to do for him in literature' was female – and herself an army wife.

7

The 'Career Wife': Lady Elizabeth Butler

When Charles Dickens visited his friend Thomas Thompson in a crumbling palace in Italy, in October 1853, he was shocked by the state of his two daughters. He found Thomas's wife painting, while he tried to teach the girls their times tables in a 'disorderly old billiard room, with all manner of messes in it.' Elizabeth, the eldest, and her sister, Alice, were 'very pale and faint from the climate'; one had bare feet and both had short, cropped hair, with a bright bow perched on top of their heads.

Elizabeth was not obvious army wife material, but her future husband, William Butler, did not come from traditional army stock. He was born in Tipperary, Ireland, a Catholic who attended Jesuit college before joining the 69th Regiment. Although William was from a long line of medium-sized landowners, he grew up during the Potato Famine of 1845–49 and always harboured sympathy for those who worked the land. He was trying to climb the army ladder at a time when commissions were purchased and, since he came from a comparatively modest family – and a Catholic one at that – his ascent was slow. He spent twelve years as a subaltern and he might have stalled altogether had it not been for a distant relative who had done well in the Peninsular War. The British Empire turned William into a *Boy's Own* adventurer, who negotiated rapids and rugged terrain in the Red River Expedition (1869) sent to suppress rebellion in what is now Manitoba, Canada, and who charged into battle on a panting steed, while always remembering to treat the natives he conquered with a victor's magnanimity. He served in India and Burma, but his most significant posting was when he joined Sir Garnet Wolseley's West Coast of Africa expedition of 1873–74. The climate reduced his (6 feet 2 inches) frame to a 'ruckle of bones' weighing just eight stone, but his daring deeds got him noticed. Queen Victoria was said to have visited several times during his convalescence at the vast military hospital at Netley on Southampton Sound.

It was while lying on his sick bed that he first came across Elizabeth Thompson. He was recovering from 'Ashanti Fever' in England's biggest building, an echoing, quarter-mile-long behemoth built in response to the Crimea War and which would later treat men suffering from shell shock in the First World War. Elizabeth's name featured heavily in the newspapers William's sister Frances read to him to break up the tedium of recovery. Jokingly, he wondered aloud whether she would marry him. It was to be three years before he could put his musings to the test.

Elizabeth, who was twenty-nine when they met, had turned into a delicate-featured beauty at the centre of artistic London. John Ruskin, who was intrigued by her preference for painting soldiers, came to tea to praise her work and the Queen asked to borrow her most famous painting. The picture, which made her one of the most talked-about women in Victorian Britain, was 'Calling the Roll after an Engagement, Crimea' and depicted the pitiable sight of a ragtag of English soldiers struggling to assemble in the bleak aftermath of battle. It has been suggested that the scene shows the Battle of Inkerman; however, this was fought in rain and fog and Elizabeth was careful not to identify exactly which event she was portraying. As a result, 'The Roll Call', as it was more commonly known, became a generic Crimean painting – and ambiguity gave it added cachet.

'The Roll Call' broke many rules. As Germaine Greer, one of Elizabeth's most fervent modern supporters, has pointed out, the image of the thirty or so guardsmen ignores the traditional artist's triangle in favour of one plane of action. The painting is not especially large – 37 × 72 inches – and its palette is subdued; the occasional red tunic, blood and crimson flag provide rare splashes of colour. 'The Roll Call' is a cold painting: the birds wheel across a grey winter's sky, the officer's horse crunches across a road rutted with snow and the soldiers themselves wear long winter coats and bearskin hats. The subject matter, too, is sombre: the viewer faces a straggling line of exhausted soldiers. The fact of showing the fate of the ordinary man, and in the most sympathetic way, is unusual. In the foreground, a guardsman, his face deathly grey, has collapsed, while his comrade stretches out an arm towards him. The painting, exhibited twenty years after the Crimea War – the most recent war fought on European soil – fed an interest in that conflict and, in particular, in the lives of the lower ranks. Exhausted, the men lean on each other or on their rifles. The retreating enemy, dimly glimpsed on the hill behind; the discarded Russian helmet out of which spills bloody snow; and the erect standards point to a British victory – but the fact that the men can barely stand for the roll call and that several are bandaged raises the question of the cost of that victory.

Elizabeth could not have anticipated the response her painting would spark. She watched the men manoeuvre it down the narrow staircase outside her studio, feeling disappointed by the way it had turned out and convinced that it would be back with her after a swift rejection from the Royal Academy's selecting committee. But before she had received official notification, a committee member wrote to tell her of its warm reception and that he had urged the committee to raise their hats and give a round of huzzahs to the painting and its creator. He added that he would do his best to ensure that it was hung in the most suitable spot.

When she arrived at the Academy with brushes and paint box on 'Varnishing Day', traditionally the day when artists have the chance to varnish and 'retouch' their work, Elizabeth was overwhelmed by the interest and congratulations from artists such as John Everett Millais. One member even suggested she had a chance of election to the Royal Academy. At lunchtime she returned to her boarding house to retrieve a superior sketch of a Russian helmet to replace the Prussian version she had been forced to use, but found she could hardly make the alterations due to the crush of admirers gathered round her work. The following day the Royal Family attended a private view and the Prince of Wales declared he wanted the painting, although it was not Elizabeth's to give. James Galloway, a Manchester industrialist, had commissioned it and paid £126 without having himself seen the completed image.

'The Roll Call' was an instant success. The Duchess of Beaufort demanded to know the personal story of every man in the scene and The Honourable Harriet Sarah Jones Loyd, whose husband, Colonel Robert Loyd-Lindsay, had won the Victoria Cross for his bravery at Inkerman and Alma, burst into tears when she saw the painting. Florence Nightingale's sister, Frances Parthenope Nightingale (1819–90), introduced herself and asked whether the painting could be taken to the famous nurse, who was now bedridden. The Letters page of *The Times* buzzed with debate over the accuracy of the gait of the horse in the painting. Elizabeth countered that she had spent hours watching horses at various army manoeuvres and urged doubters to go down on all fours to try the sequence for themselves. The elderly Lady Lothian told her she had done just that. In fact, Elizabeth was one of the first artists ever to capture the movement, an achievement photographer Eadweard Muybridge's work confirmed later that decade.

On 4 May she wrote in her diary: '. . . I awoke this morning and found myself famous.' She was invited to balls and dinner parties and everyone wanted to own the painting. Queen Victoria, who had sent Elizabeth a congratulatory diamond bracelet, borrowed it for the night so that she could study it at Buckingham Palace and, eventually, Galloway succumbed to pressure to sell it to her.

The curate and diarist, Robert Francis Kilvert, recorded on 25 June 1874: '. . . went straight to the Academy exhibition at Burlington House which I reached shortly before 4 o'clock. There was a great press of people, 100 or more, round Miss Thompson's famous picture "Calling the Roll after the battle of Inkerman" [sic]. A policeman stands on duty all day by this picture from 10 o'clock till 6 in the evening saying, "Move on, ladies. Ladies, please move on".' 'The Roll Call' went on tour to Newcastle (where a sandwich board announced, 'The Roll Call is coming!'), Leeds, Birmingham, Liverpool (where 20,000 people saw it in three weeks), Oxford and Leeds.

The painting's popularity was, in part, due to the novelty of its creator's gender. There was much speculation about her background and it was even suggested that she might have been a nurse in the Crimea – perhaps due to her habit of including a red cross, the symbol of a small club she had belonged to at art school, above her signature. Her father wrote to the papers to confirm that she had never been a hospital nurse and that she was not married; in short, her life had been 'uneventful'. Meanwhile the press referred to her as 'Roll Call Thompson'.

Photographers started to 'bother' her. J. Dickinson & Co. (later, The Fine Art Society) sold a quarter of a million calling cards with her image on them. She thought she looked rather harassed in the photo, but a more objective observer would see a young woman dressed in fine clothes with sensuous eyes and lips, her luxurious hair piled high on her head. 'Nowadays one is snapshotted whether one likes it or not, but it wasn't so bad in those days,' she wrote later, 'one's own consent was asked, at any rate.' However, her aunt was shocked to see her niece's face on a costermonger's barrow full of bananas in Chelsea.

Although Elizabeth was still in her twenties when fame hit her, she had painted all her life and soldiers always held a particular fascination. When she was about fifteen, she produced a pen-and-ink study of 'military types': the caricature shows a line of British, Italian, Austrian, French, Russian, Egyptian and American soldiers distinguished by their different uniforms and exotic hats, each lunging forward, rifles over their left shoulders. Her early life had a roaming, Grand Tour quality to it, and offered many opportunities to paint different landscapes and different soldiers. It would also prepare her for her later role as an army wife. Her father, Thomas, had inherited money from his grandfather's sugar plantations in the West Indies, but had failed three times to fulfil his dream of becoming a Liberal Member of Parliament. Dickens lent him money and introduced him to his future wife, Christiana Weller, at a piano recital at which she was performing. The family spent much of their time abroad because it was cheaper than living in England and Elizabeth was born in Lausanne, Switzerland, in 1846. Her younger sister would become the poet and essayist Alice Meynell.

They often visited the Ligurian Riviera, where Thomas's daughter, by a previous marriage, had settled after marrying, aged seventeen, an Italian officer who was killed at the Battle of Volturno. The romantic notion of the ordinary man who was prepared to take up arms in defence of his country inspired Elizabeth from an early age. She 'stuffed' her sketchbooks with British volunteers in every conceivable uniform and entered a competition in the *Illustrated London News* to design a uniform for a short-lived corps called the Six-foot Guards. Her submission was returned with thanks.

Like Turner and other artists before her, she was fascinated by Waterloo and visited the battlefield with her family in 1865, when she was nineteen. The Thompsons enlisted the services of a veteran, a white-bearded sergeant-major who had fought with the 7th Hussars when he was twenty-seven and who now relived the experience with vivid detail for eager tourists. His stories transformed a field of turnips into a refuge for British soldiers and took them, as Elizabeth recorded, on a walk through 'ghosts with agonised faces and distorted bodies, crying noiselessly'. The encounter made a profound impression on her and was one of the first times she used an eyewitness account to help her to imagine an historic event. On the way back to England she started to draw the soldiers working on the new fort at Dover. The images convinced the headmaster of South Kensington School of Art that she had talent and she enrolled on a course that included Kate Greenaway, the future children's illustrator, among its students.

Her first success came when the Dudley Gallery accepted her watercolour 'Bavarian Artillery going into Action' (1867). Ruskin had told her to avoid sensational subjects and to study nature, but she found his advice impossible to follow once her father took her, in 1872, to watch the army autumn manoeuvres in the New Forest. The army, in turn, realised that it, too, had found a strong advocate who could, as the general refereeing the training exercise expressed it, 'give the British soldiers a turn'.

Elizabeth met William Butler at a lunch hosted by Lady Jeune (later, Lady St Hellier) after a private view of her second Crimea painting, 'Balaclava', in April 1876. She does not mention William by name in her diary; he is simply one of two 'distinguished' officers. But a photo of the time shows him as a confident, extravagantly bewhiskered man, dapper in civilian clothes and leaning on a prop covered with an exotic animal skin; he holds a cane in one hand and a top hat in the other. He gazes unflinchingly out of the photo.

According to her daughter, Eileen, Elizabeth was in 'abject slavery to good looks' and had a habit of assessing someone's face with an artist's eye. William was exactly the sort of hero Elizabeth enjoyed painting and they married just over a year later, on 11 June 1877. She and her sister, Alice (née Thompson), later Meynell, had followed their mother's example by converting to Catholicism and so the wedding was performed by Cardinal Manning. In some ways it was a typical army wedding and marked her departure from civilian life. The guests included men like Sir Garnet Wolseley and Redvers Bullers, who were important to William's career. He gave his bride the choice of Ireland or Crimea for their honeymoon and she chose to visit his home country. Ruskin wrote to Butler to congratulate him, saying, 'What may you not do for England, the two of you.'

As a couple, William and Elizabeth crossed the paths of the most eminent men and women of their age: on her sick bed Florence Nightingale had asked to see 'The Roll Call'; Queen Victoria, who viewed her army as an extension of her family, *demanded* to own it; Cardinal Manning officiated at their wedding; and William tried his best to save General Gordon. Of the Victorians carefully selected by the iconoclastic biographer and essayist Lytton Strachey, to satirise in the early twentieth century, only Thomas Arnold, headmaster of Rugby School, who died before Elizabeth was born, had nothing to do with the esteemed couple. But, while the Butlers were at the heart of the Victorian Establishment, they were also slightly apart from it. Not only was Butler an Irish Catholic, he also held views that did not sit easily with the tenets of British imperialism. He once described colonial campaigns as 'sutlers' wars', believed in Home Rule for Ireland and had a surprising degree of sympathy for the indigenous people of Africa and Afghanistan, who found themselves looking down the barrel of a British gun. He was also a successful writer and used his experience of army life to produce *The Great Lone Land* and *The Wild North Land* about Canada, an account of the Ashanti war and a history of his regiment. Later, he added biographies of generals, including Napoleon and Gordon, a boy's adventure story, novels and autobiography to his literary accomplishments.

Try as she might, Elizabeth never quite managed to settle down and devote herself solely to the role of army wife. Indeed being married to a famous soldier both helped and hindered her artistic career. Authenticity had always been important to her; now she had her very own soldier at home. As an unmarried artist she had relied on civilian models – many of whom were veteran soldiers. When she was working on 'The Roll Call' they posed for at least five hours a day in her studio at No. 76 Fulham Road. The sergeant with the full red beard and open book who 'calls the roll' had served in Crimea and offered her specific advice about details. Other veterans were not so reliable: another Crimean pensioner was unable to answer her query about the letters that would have been stamped on the soldiers' haversack. At first he was convinced they would be 'B.O.' for 'Board of Ordinance', then he changed his mind to 'W.D.' for 'War Department' before reaching a compromise of 'W.O'. The Thompson family doctor helped her to trace uniforms, helmets and haversacks, and together they rummaged through a 'dingy little pawnshop in a hideous Chelsea Slum', a visit she said she enjoyed more than a trip to a West End milliner's.

Now she had only to look out of her window to see a uniform or horse at first hand. When William was made adjutant-general in 1880 they moved to Plymouth with their daughter, Elizabeth Frances (their first daughter had died in infancy), and she made use of the clear light of Plymouth Hoe to work on 'Scotland for Ever!'. She had 'any amount of grey army horses as models'. She studied the tone and colour of horses in Wicklow for 'Halt on a Forced March: Retreat to Corunna' and finished the painting in Alexandria in 1892, where Egypt's half-starved animals provided realistic models. Her stay also allowed her to build up a good stock of watercolours of camels and members of the Camel Corps. After a picnic to the west of Alexandria she rode one side saddle and said she 'revelled' in the animal: 'Usually that interesting beast is made utterly uninteresting in pictures, whereas if you know him personally he is full of surprises and one never gets to the end of him.'

She was able to know him at very close quarters when she asked the general at Cairo if she could drive out to the desert to watch manoeuvres. In order to be able to see the beasts face-on, she left her carriage to stand in front of the advancing squadrons of 300 camels, their drivers urging them forward with whips. She stood aside at the last moment and then rushed off to her room in Shepheard's Hotel to record the scene, the different skin tones, the red morocco leather of the saddles, their fringes flying in the wind.

Every two or so years Elizabeth's life of painting was interrupted by a major upheaval in their household. William was regularly away on campaign: in 1879 he went to Durban, supplying Lord Chelmsford's forces in Zululand, and in the 1880s he served in Wolseley's Egyptian campaign and the abortive bid to rescue General Gordon. Often she went abroad to live near, or with him, sometimes taking some of their five children with her. As well as her trip to Cairo, she visited him several times in Alexandria, where he was in command of the garrison, and joined him in Cape Town in 1899. The couple also moved house frequently in Britain, depending on William's promotions. They lived in Devonport, Dover Castle and Aldershot and had a family home in Ireland. When William was invalided back from Wadi Halfa in 1886, the family moved to an old farmhouse in Brittany for eighteen months and were there when he was knighted.

Her wandering upbringing meant she was used to making a home in a foreign country and these trips gave her the chance to explore artistic subjects other than Crimea, which was beginning to pall. Shepheard's Hotel, where she stayed with their eldest boy and girl, proved a particular attraction. The former palace had been Napoleon's headquarters during the Egyptian campaign, and now catered for tourists to the Nile and travellers en route to India. It had a long association with the British Army and when officers of the 10th Hussars were moved at short notice to Crimea, leaving many unpaid bills, the hotel's founder, Samuel Shepheard, was said to have pursued them as far as Sevastopol, where he claimed to have 'settled all within fifteen shillings'. Elizabeth enjoyed watching the comings and goings of Ibrahim Pasha Street below from the comfort of the terrace's wicker chairs, or walking in the cool of the nearby garden. The family went on to Luxor, from where they continued their journey by houseboat to the ancient and dusty town of Wadi Halfa in north Sudan. They stayed until the intense heat of over 40°C (104°F) degrees centigrade drove her and the children back to Plymouth.

Elizabeth's careful research into battle scenes and their aftermath gave her an insight into the hardships and dangers of a soldier's life. It was a unique perspective for an officer's wife and may have made the separations, when she knew her husband faced danger, harder to bear. She found William's departure to fight against the Egyptian nationalists in August 1882, 'most trying to me of all the many partings, because of its dramatic setting. One bears up well on a crowded railway platform, but when it comes to watching a ship putting off to sea, as I did that time at Liverpool, to the sound of farewell cheering and "Auld Lang Syne", one would sooner read of its pathos than suffer it in person. Soldiers' wives in war time have to feel the sickening sensation on waking some morning when news of a fight is expected of saying to themselves, "I may be a widow".'

Although the travel and organisation involved in her frequent moves were disruptive to her art, she usually ended up somewhere that allowed her enough room to create a studio of her own. Art provided a uniquely portable pastime. She worked on two versions of 'Halt on a Forced March: Retreat to Corunna' on her trips to Egypt, describing the painting in her diary in a way that made it sound as if it were a piece of embroidery she could tuck in her bag for an idle moment. Her daughter, Eileen, wrote later: 'Whenever I get a whiff of lavender oil, the picture of my mother – rather small and slight, with delicate face but strong hands, standing at her easel in a long gabardine, a mahl-stick in one hand and palette and brushes in the other – is conjured up.'

Elizabeth also liked to use her children and servants as models. One son, who was thought to be particularly good-looking, took the part of a drummer boy and a visiting nephew was made to lie in one position for so long that he fell asleep and woke with a cold that lasted his whole visit. Their Breton cook left because she was made to pose for 'To The Front', only to discover that her rear view alone appeared in the final painting.

At Aldershot, where William commanded the 2nd Infantry Brigade (1 November 1893), she took to the old court martial hut, where four extra skylights made it easier for her to work. She was once in her painting dress with her sleeves rolled up when Princess Louise visited. Later in his career, William was offered the choice of Colchester or Dover Castle and left the decision up to her; her painter's eye dictated the choice. She preferred Dover with its views of the sea and the French coast. Here she worked on her canvases, holding them in place with an industrial monster of an easel that could be lowered and raised to suit her eyeline. Soldiers at Dover provided models for her Crimean painting, 'The Colours: Advance of the Scots Guards at Alma' (1899), in which she depicted the Scots Guards climbing the hill at Alma in full parade dress and Lieutenant Lloyd Lindsay carrying the Queen's colour. Lindsay, who by now had become Lord Wantage, heard of her latest artistic project and took her to the Guards' chapel, where the battered colours were lifted from the wall so that he could hold them once more for her to sketch and describe the original colours to her.

However, there were several ways in which marriage hindered Elizabeth's work as an artist. For one, she lost her famous name and the public and reviewers were slow to take to 'EB'. It is true that her career had probably started to wane by the time she married, but she also found that her choice of subjects and emphasis were sometimes at odds with her husband's view of military events and led to tension between them. At the peak of her earning power, she could bring in much more than his officer's salary. In 1877, for example, The Fine Art Society paid her £3,000 (worth over £312,000 today) for the copyright to the 'Return from Inkerman'. This compares to William's annual salary of £600 in 1881 (equivalent to about £65,000) when he was a lieutenant-colonel and senior staff officer at Devonport.

It was unusual for her to contravene her husband's wishes. A rare example of this came with her depiction of the aftermath of the battle of Tel-el-Kebir on 13 September 1882. The battle, in which Wolseley suppressed the Egyptian nationalist forces led by Arabi Pasha – or 'poor old Arabi and his "rebels"', as Elizabeth referred to them – was hugely popular in Britain because it followed a series of ignominious defeats in Southern Africa and Afghanistan. But Elizabeth's painting, which includes her husband in his red tunic astride a horse hurtling forward, focuses on the moment immediately *after* the battle. Elizabeth describes in her autobiography how Wolseley gave a 'fidgety' sitting at his home in London and that his wife tried to keep him quiet on her knee 'like a good boy'.

Although the painting appeared in the Royal Academy in 1885, William did not approve of it and had hoped his wife would abandon the project. He thought the subject matter unworthy and likened capturing Arabi's earthworks to 'going through brown paper'. He felt such sympathy for the nationalist leader that he did his best to have his death sentence reversed. Pasha was ultimately exiled to Ceylon, a change of heart that is unlikely to have been due to William's intervention, which nonetheless provided another example of his determination not to follow the most politic course. The painting's reception did not justify the tension it produced between the couple. By the time it was exhibited the campaign's moment had passed: the excitement that had brought hundreds of thousands of spectators to St James's Park in London to watch the review of the returning soldiers in 1882 had dissipated and other artists had depicted Tel-el-Kebir in popular newspapers like the *Illustrated London News* and the *Graphic*. Elizabeth's version had none of this early power and relevance. The original canvas no longer exists and she is thought to have chopped it to pieces when William died, or even before. It was also rumoured that he did not like her 'The Defence of Rorke's Drift' (1881), which allows the viewer a clear view of the anguish of the individual soldiers, and that he commented: 'One more painting like this and you will drive me mad!'

Their daughter, Eileen, witnessed this temper at first hand and later wrote:

> What is surprising is that one who, in public life, invariably championed the under-dog should, in his own home, have been a complete autocrat. No one there ever dared dispute my father's will – least of all my mother, in whom loyalty was an outstanding quality, who detested rows, and who, fortunately for herself, had her studio into which to retreat and there find tranquillity.

William could be domineering and refused to call the doctor if any of the children were ill (almost certainly because he thought his own judgement was better than the doctor's). His experience of the Potato Famine, if from a distance, gave him an abhorrence of wasted food and he would regularly reduce Elizabeth to tears by asking to see the household books. 'To me,' Eileen added, 'as a child, he was an idol; but an idol to be worshipped from afar.'

As the wife of a high-ranking officer, Elizabeth was expected to entertain dignitaries and their families, wherever they happened to be living in the world. She enjoyed certain aspects of this – but found small talk difficult; art was a useful starting point. Her daughter later revealed that her mother had been partially deaf since childhood and this may have contributed to her unease in social situations, although Elizabeth herself freely admitted that she had a knack for blurting out an inappropriate comment, forgetting people's names or failing to spot a famous person. At a dinner in Farnborough she spent the whole meal talking to her neighbour in French, assuming he was part of a group of French noblemen when he was, in fact, a journalist from *The Times*. On another occasion in Egypt she declared a dinner with heads of the departments and their wives, 'a difficult function' and, although she knew she should have been 'at her post all day' went out sketching in the morning. She found it impossible to know what to talk about to the Vice-Reine and resorted to illness, which, she said, she 'always found touches the proper note in a harem'. She was not the only one to struggle in a royal situation. At the Queen's Ball at Buckingham Palace she found the rush to the supper-room 'most unseemly', made worse by the fact that there seemed to be something wrong with the doors. 'Every one got jammed, and it was most unpleasant to have steel cartridge boxes and sword hilts sticking into one's bare arms in the pressure'.

Elizabeth was 'seldom up to schedule' in returning calls in the way that a general's wife should. She was loath to waste precious daylight on social niceties while wrestling with the conundrum of how best to foreshorten a rearing horse. Eileen remembered one school holiday when they were living at Government House, Devenport, and William's aide-de-camp arrived at her studio with a list of calls she should make – the most urgent, which had prompted complaints, was underlined in red. In one case, Elizabeth had delayed so long that the other wife had died before she could return the visit.

Part of her role also meant meekly accepting the occasional public criticism that was bound to accompany her husband's long military career. It was only later, in her autobiography, that she was able to blame the 'terrible tragedy' of the failure of the 'Great Gordon Relief Expedition' on 'maddening delays at home'. William was also heavily criticised in the months that would later prove to be the run-up to the Second Boer War (1899–1902). In 1898 he was made commander-in-chief in South Africa and acting governor of the Cape Colony and high commissioner in South Africa while Sir Alfred Milner was temporarily absent. Elizabeth went out with the children in March 1899 but returned in late August. William had been put in charge at a moment of high tension that coincided with an attempt by imperialist Cecil Rhodes and his followers to snatch the Transvaal and Orange Free State from the Boers. Directions from London were contradictory and William was convinced that war was avoidable. He had little option but to resign, and was accused in the press of being too pro-Boer and of leaving South Africa poorly defended. Later, he was vindicated, to some extent, when the army put him in charge of investigating the War Stores Scandal in which defence contractors were accused of profiteering.

There was no such reprieve when it came to a scandal that *The Times* referred to in a leader as a 'flood of filth' and which Elizabeth makes no mention of in her autobiography. The year 1886 should have been the highpoint of William's career: his adept handling of the Egyptian situation had earned him a knighthood (KCB) and promotion to the rank of brigadier-general. Instead, a 'revolting scandal' called into question his fitness to be called an 'officer'.

Gertrude Blood might have been remembered for several reasons. At 5 feet, 10 inches tall she was a talented sportswoman who swam, fenced and rode bikes and horses; her love of outdoor pursuits and years spent in the Mediterranean had given her an unfashionably deep tan and the nickname 'Arab'. She also wrote books: a short novel, *Top: A Tale about English Children in Italy,* appeared in 1878 and was illustrated by Kate Greenaway and *Etiquette of Society* (1893) sold 92,000 copies in her lifetime. Her roster of friends included George Bernard Shaw, James Whistler, Oscar Wilde and the Sullivan half of Gilbert and Sullivan. But, if she is remembered at all today, it is for Giovanni Boldini's oil painting of her in the National Portrait Gallery in London. Black dominates his sensuous depiction: Gertrude's smouldering black eyes, black hair and the long black dress that sheaths her body from a plunging neckline via a minute waist through broad thighs to tiny feet. As the National Portrait Gallery explains, Boldini 'imparted a special glamour to this alluring sitter by treating the rules of anatomy with magnificent contempt'. His representation is all the more daring because of the reasons why she was well-known to a Victorian audience.

Gertrude was the youngest daughter of Edmond Maghlin Blood,

of County Clare and it was later, convincingly, claimed in court that she was friends with Elizabeth and William Butler, and Elizabeth's sister, Alice. She met Lord Colin Campbell MP, younger son of the 8th Duke of Argyll, on a trip to Scotland and they became engaged within days. He had been an officer in the 1st Argyllshire Volunteers but his parliamentary career had only been distinguished by his decision, in 1879, to vote against a bill to abolish flogging in the army. He left the Commons early in the vote to avoid his action appearing on record.

Lord Colin, however, was reluctant to name a day and the marriage was twice postponed due to ill health. The wedding eventually took place on 21 July 1881 at the Royal Chapel of the Savoy, off The Strand. Guests included Queen Victoria's daughter, Princess Louise, who was also the groom's sister-in-law. But the honeymoon was not a success. Lord Colin persuaded his new bride that, due to medical problems, they should have separate bedrooms and a nurse even accompanied them to the Isle of Wight. They did not consummate the marriage until October when Lord Colin advised his bride that she should take precautions against infection. The truth was that Lord Colin was being treated for syphilis.

Campbell versus Campbell and the Mordaunt divorce case of 1870, in which the Prince of Wales was called to give evidence, have been described as 'Two of the most notorious scandals of the Victorian period [both of which] turned on marriages poisoned by venereal disease'. In the Mordaunt case, Sir Charles Mordaunt's wife, Harriet, confessed to her infidelity when she gave birth to a blind daughter – whose disability she blamed on venereal disease contracted from one of a handful of lovers. Syphilis was widespread among Victorian men and some doctors told their patients to delay marriage until all signs of the disease had passed, a futile gesture since the patient could remain infectious for five years after apparent recovery. Thus, despite Lord Colin's precautions, his wife soon became ill and her venereal disease formed the basis for cruelty charges when she sued for a judicial separation in 1884 and then divorce two years later. As a woman, she needed this additional cause (bigamy, incest or desertion would have served equally well) to divorce her husband, whereas a man was only required to prove adultery to divorce his wife.

Lady Campbell, then twenty-eight, claimed that her husband had committed adultery with a servant and had already been granted a decree of separation. He, in turn, filed for divorce, claiming his wife had been unfaithful with four men: the family doctor, Thomas Bird; a notorious philanderer, the Duke of Marlborough; the Chief of the Metropolitan Fire Brigade and an ex-army officer from Belfast, Captain Shaw; and General Butler. What followed was eighteen days of the sort of upstairs-downstairs titillation that kept the crowds who packed the courtroom and the nation's newspaper readers eager for each session's revelations. Cabmen and maids revealed a world in which ringing a doorbell, which could only be heard in the servants' quarter, rather than using a bold door-knocker, was a sign of complicity. The Campbells' domestic life was exposed to forensic inspection and the picture that emerged was often accompanied by a soundtrack of derisive laughter and even, at one point when a witness managed to reveal the lack of logic in a lawyer's questions, a Mexican wave of clapping started by junior barristers that spread to the public gallery until the judge was forced to appeal for silence. Throughout the ordeal, Lady Butler, like the good army wife she was, kept a dignified silence.

The evidence included details that newspapers deemed 'unfit for publication' – a label that allowed the reader's imagination to plunge into depths of uncharted debauchery. The court heard about servants peeking through keyholes – and a lengthy digression in which the court was asked to assess whether, in fact, that particular type of keyhole would have given a servant such a vantage point. When Gertrude's brother, Neptune Blood, claimed that the design of the keyhole at 79 Cadogan did not offer a clear view of the drawing room, the jury demanded to see for themselves and fought through the waiting crowds in Belgravia to assess whether the butler could have seen what he said he had seen. The foreman of the jury decided that the 'escutcheons' (heavy surrounds) of the keyhole were 'very stiff' and would have offered a clear view. One wonders what a music-hall turn would have made of his pronouncement.

William Butler escaped lightly when it came to the allegations he faced. There were no claims of figures on floors in states of déshabillé (as was said to have happened when Captain Shaw visited), or flushed faces (supposedly a result of the Duke of Marlborough's attentions). Instead, he was alleged to have spent several hours alone with Gertrude, during which time he made no effort to see her husband. She refuted this allegation and said that her sister who, inconveniently, had died before the case came to trial had chaperoned them throughout the visit. She told her husband she had known Butler since childhood, but she compounded the servant's suspicions by informing her that she was not 'at home' when a lady friend called and by later falling ill – due, it was claimed, to a miscarriage. (The eminent obstetrician John Braxton Hicks, who gave his name to the contractions that occur early in pregnancy, had been called in at the time and ascertained this was not the case.) A maid, whom Lady Campbell had refused to supply a reference for, said in court that she had found a photo of Butler in her mistress's bed; Lady Campbell counter-claimed that it must have fallen from the shelf above. The maid added to the farcical tone by telling the court that Butler left on tiptoes.

Despite the lack of lurid detail, William was, nevertheless, tainted by what he did *not* do. At the start of the trial he was introduced as 'a man who had distinguished himself by gallant services and had married Miss Thompson, a prominent artist, the painter of the "Roll Call"'. By Day Eighteen of the trial his reputation had sunk so low – due to his refusal to appear in the witness box – that the judge 'implored the jury not to let General Butler's conduct, however reprehensible they might think it, bring guilty consequences upon Lady Colin . . .'

The jury took two-and-a-half hours to reach a verdict and eventually decided that neither side had committed adultery. Butler bore the force of their opprobrium:

> The Foreman added that the jury desired to express the opinion that in not coming forward in the interests of justice General Butler's conduct was unworthy of a gentleman and an English officer, and was the cause of the difficulty which the jury had experienced in coming to a decision.

He was the only co-respondent to be singled out for criticism; his profession merely added to the weight of his crime of absenteeism. Elizabeth had made her name through 'The Roll Call'; William lost his by failing to fall in.

The Butler family spent that autumn in Brittany, partly sheltered from the battering William received in the press. The court case was reported in more than forty newspapers around the country. During a period when newspapers had none of today's bulk, *The Times* devoted 599 lines to the saga. A booklet, *The Colin Campbell Divorce Case*, proved a bestseller in England and a French version of the story also appeared. In marrying a high-ranking officer, Elizabeth would have expected to maintain a certain role in society, based on his adherence to the notion of honour. His involvement, no matter how innocent, with a woman who was married to a man so blatantly out of step with the modern soldier's code of ethics cast a shadow over his military career.

William retired in October 1905, aged sixty-seven, and the couple moved to Bansha Castle, County Tipperary, where Elizabeth continued to paint. In June 1906 he was made a Knight of the Grand Cross of the order of the Bath and three years later, member of the

Privy Council of Ireland. The Liberal Party courted him, but in the end his religion scuppered any chances of being an MP.

After his death, in 1910, Elizabeth continued to live alone at the castle. During the First World War, in which two of her sons served – one as a chaplain – she sketched soldiers, although her age (she was sixty-seven years old) and her gender meant she could not work as an Official War Artist. In the summer of 1922 she found herself, for the first time, in the middle of a battle as the Republicans fought the Free Staters. She grew used to the sound of mines exploding and gunshots ricocheting around, but was eventually forced to leave the castle. In her eighty-third year she died in her daughter Eileen's home, Gormanston Castle, in 1933. Eileen later lost two sons in the Second World War.

Part Two:

Loss and the Great War

8

The Army Widow: Clare Sheridan and Hazel Macnaghten

Clare Sheridan, Winston Churchill's cousin and the wife of a captain in the Rifle Brigade, rang the doorbell of an ordinary-looking, terraced house in Notting Hill, west London, in what she described as a 'suppressed state of excitement'. She felt sure that her husband, Wilfred, would know why she had come and would be prepared.

The room she was shown into reminded her of a Quaker meeting place. A small, middle-aged woman with grey hair pulled the violet curtains to darken the room and then took a seat opposite Clare. She placed a record by violinist Fritz Kreisler on the gramophone, explaining that the vibrations made it easier for her to work. The slow, mournful lovesong, 'Liebesleid', which he had composed himself, helped to create the perfect, wistful atmosphere. Then she covered her face with her hands and drifted into a trance. When the hissing record came to an end, she fumbled to turn the machine off from within her state of half-consciousness. Spirits of the dead were known to enjoy music, but Clare could only reflect on how much Wilfred hated gramophones and on what he must be making of this encounter. She did not comment on whether the room was infused with the smell of incense or dried flowers, as was usual on such occasions.

The woman rose and, in a voice that was suddenly not her own, prayed for help to put Clare in touch with those who had 'passed over'. When she sat down the spirits trickled through her like a line of customers waiting to use a public telephone box (an analogy Clare and others like her found helpful). When each came to the 'phone' her voice changed in keeping with the person calling. The medium's earthly assistant explained how the communication would work and who was waiting to speak to Clare. The medium would see faces, names or initials and hear voices and names called – all of which she would seek to identify – presumably much like speaking on a crackly telephone line. Clare's spirit guide – in effect, the operator who would connect the medium to various callers – turned out to be an Indian with a deep bass voice who spoke in broken English with no known accent.

It took a while for the line to be connected. This was not unusual. The millions of war dead had created congestion and the war itself had caused a thick fog to envelope the earthly plane. The mental condition of the grief-stricken families also interfered with reception.

Suddenly the medium fell silent and gave a convulsive shiver. It dawned on Clare that she was alone with an unconscious woman and she wondered whether she could creep out when the woman shivered again and began to speak in a 'queer new voice'. 'Oh, darling, my darling,' the woman cried and tried to embrace her client. Clare was torn: she did not wish to be kissed by the medium, but also did not want to quash her husband's joy at their reunion – 'But Wilfred should have known better, I felt. He should have realised the limitations of mediumship and not given rein to his impulse.'

Her husband went on to talk, in a voice that she did not recognise as his, about their two young children, Margaret and Dick. He told her that he was not lonely and had 'heaps' of friends on the other side and was working hard. Like other wives who attended séances, or read *Raymond, Or Life and Death* by Sir Oliver Lodge, she was given a detailed introduction to her husband's new world. Wilfred was helping the thousands of men who arrived daily from the trenches: many did not understand that they were dead; others needed guidance to return to their loved ones. He told her how, when she slept, her spirit joined him in caring for the newly dead on the battlefield while their little girl, Elizabeth, who had died as a baby, took her siblings to play on the children's plane. Clare already knew of these reunions because Margaret, who slept in her room, would tell her about the meetings and of seeing her father's shiny Rifle Brigade cap badge.

Raymond had given her a clear picture of what the dead got up to and she had selected the medium from a list printed in the book. The author, a former professor of Physics at Birmingham University and, significantly, given his interest in psychic matters, a pioneer of the development of wireless telegraphy, embraced spiritualism after the death of his soldier son in the same year, 1915, that Wilfred was killed. Although the Catholic Church and the Church of England were concerned by spiritualism, Sir Oliver, who was a committed Christian, saw nothing contradictory about his belief in both. He made contact with Raymond through a celebrated medium, Gladys Leonard, and gave lecture tours explaining what he had experienced. His book on the subject appeared in November 1916 and was reprinted four times before the end of the year and ran to a total of twelve reprints. Sir Arthur Conan Doyle, his friend and Sherlock Holmes creator, had lost a son, brother and son-in-law during the war, and was another keen supporter, although his conviction had started long before his son's death in 1918.

Spiritualism took wing in the Victorian period, swept along on a tide of scientific discoveries, but its popularity soared to new heights during the Great War as organised religion struggled to respond to the wall of grief. Although the Church of England brought back the tradition of prayers for the dead – a practice that had been banished during the Reformation – such gestures were not enough to deal with widespread mourning. According to one estimate there were some 4.5 million bereaved close relatives in Britain – roughly 10 per cent of the population. By 1919 around 250,000 people were attending séances in an attempt to make contact with their loved ones. In her memoir of the First World War, *Testament of Youth*, Vera Brittain wrote that friends had told her of the 'experimental compensations' of spiritualism. 'As always in wartime, the long casualty list had created throughout England a terrible interest in the idea of personal survival, and many wives and mothers had turned to séances and mediums in the hope of finding some indication, however elusive, of a future reunion "beyond the sun".' The number of societies affiliated to the Spiritualists' National Union jumped from 145 in 1914 to 309 in 1919 and continued to grow until the Second World War, which provided a renewed need. In 1932, a (admittedly partisan) reporter from *Psychic News* believed there were around 100,000 séance circles regularly gathering to hold hands in Britain.

Clare knew from reading *Raymond* that spirits often returned to their earthly predilections; for example, some continued to enjoy whisky and cigars and Raymond himself had girlfriends. Another author, Hereward Carrington, writing in 1918, explained how a woman he called Heather had learnt to become a clairvoyant and clairaudient in order to communicate better with her dead fiancé. The deceased soldier was doing his part by attending regular lectures and had graduated in methods of controlling earthly mediums. Carrington found the idea of this extramural study reassuring: 'Oh, how natural and sane is life beyond! This brave soldier-lover is not a white-winged angel in some far-off state, neither is he in the orthodox hell, he is just Heather's lover, working for her good, and learning the best means of communing with her and protecting her . . .'

William Frederick, known as 'Wilfred', and Clare were both socially well-connected in their different ways when they first met at a ball in 1903, when she was eighteen and he was twenty-four, but their families were short of money and tried to hold out for more lucrative unions. Clare was the only daughter of Moreton Frewen and Clara Jerome, who lived at Brede House in Sussex (when they were not 'economising' by staying in hotels). Her mother was a New Yorker and her aunt Lady Randolph Churchill. Wilfred's home was Frampton Place in Dorset and he was the great-great grandson of the dramatist Richard Brinsley Sheridan. The couple's friendship was based on books; Clare wanted to be a writer, and counted Henry James as a friend. She had already accepted a proposal when Wilfred, described by one biographer as 'the best-looking man of his time', appeared on the scene again and impetuously asked her to marry him. Although they had ambitions to live a bohemian lifestyle, lack of money forced Wilfred to work as a stockbroker for the first years of their marriage. They shunned London society and instead lived in the country, where Clare wore smocks, wide-brimmed sun hats and bulbous amber necklaces. She tried to cook peasant stews for 'Black Puss', as she called Wilfred, but did not realise she had to soak the beans first. At night they read poetry to one another and in spring 1914 Wilfred took her on holiday to Capri.

The marriage was blighted by tragedy when their second daughter, Elizabeth, died of tubercular meningitis in February 1914. It was while Clare was searching for a memorial for their daughter that she met the widow of Pre-Raphaelite artist George Frederic Watts. Mary Seton Fraser-Tytler was a Scottish designer and potter who had married when Watts was sixty-nine and she was nearly thirty-seven. She ran a pottery near Clare's house and encouraged her to make a kneeling child with the face of Elizabeth; this early expression of her grief was the first step towards a career as a sculptor.

Wilfred joined the City of London Territorials before it was really necessary – his age and marital status meant call-up was not imminent (conscription was not introduced until January 1916)

– and, due to a shortage of uniforms, drilled in his tweed suit. Although Clare hated militarism, she said a soldier made a 'happier and a pleasanter companion than a stockbroker'. Wilfred was promoted to lieutenant and transferred to the Rifle Brigade, just as Clare realised she was pregnant. He sailed for France in May 1915 and they wrote to each other daily; he managed to secure leave in August, hoping that the baby might arrive then. It did not, but they talked about what he would do after the war; his firm, into which he had poured his savings, was close to bankruptcy and he agreed that they could plan a new life in Canada after the war. He drew diagrams in the sand to explain to her the different fronts of what would be the Battle of Loos. She wrote later: 'Those war days were so tense one seemed too heroic to be human, it was like playing a set part in a great company of actors. Sometimes it was a big part, sometimes it was insignificant, but all the time it was the part that others had just played and were going to play.'

Their son, Richard Brinsley Sheridan, or 'Dick', was born on 9 September 1915 and Clare sent his father bulletins about his progress for the next nine days. Wilfred wrote back a 'hurried pencil scrawl' to say how glad he was and that he was under marching orders for the expected battle. Then silence. Her mother-in-law, whose first son had been killed in the Boer War, sat by Clare's side in her white dressing gown comforting her as she recovered from childbirth by reassuring her that they had heard nothing because the post was disorganised. Then a packet of Clare's letters was returned with 'killed in action' scrawled in red pencil across them. Wilfred died on 25 September, on the first day of the Battle of Loos when more than 8,000 men were killed in the opening hours, and is remembered with them at the Ploegsteert Memorial in Belgium. On hearing the news, Clementine wrote to her husband, Clare's cousin Winston, who himself was serving in the trenches: 'My Darling I don't know how one bears such things. I feel I could not weather such a blow – She has a beautiful little son 8 weeks old, but her poor "black puss" sleeps in Flanders . . .'

In Wilfred's writing desk, Clare and her mother found a letter addressed to his wife and written before his departure to France.

> You will only read this if I am dead, and remember that as you read it I shall be by your side: you will know that I shall be saying to you – "Now pull yourself together." There is nothing to cry about, only is there a great happiness in that he did not fail and that he has done the big thing; he has got into his eleven; he has won his colours; it is up to me to be proud of him and glad for him and not to weep. My head is up, my chin is out and I take my step forward into my new existence conscious that he is watching and approving.

On the same day that Wilfred was killed another young wife was getting ready for bed in Bournemouth. Her husband was in Flanders with the Devonshire Regiment; she had received several letters from him that summer – and even one that very morning – and was satisfied that he was well. It was about 10 p.m. and she was deep in conversation with the girlfriend with whom she shared the room. The light was on. Suddenly she stopped in mid-sentence and stared into space. Before her stood her husband in full uniform. She was struck by his look of intense sadness and he held her gaze for two or three minutes. Shortly after seeing the vision she received news of his death.

Her experience was not unusual. In a country focused on the dead, ghosts rubbed shoulders with the living in a way that came to be seen as normal. In Lincolnshire, until as late as the 1950s, it was common for a widow to have her photo taken standing behind her deceased husband's chair – which was kept vacant because it was believed that part of him was still present. In the absence of a body, or even a place to visit – although some widows and fiancées, like Vera Brittain, made the pilgrimage abroad and left cards on the grave – many families created shrines to their loved one in their home.

From 1915 the army's Grave Registration Committee offered families free photos of a relative's last resting place and details of its location. Often a box of soil from the cemetery or the battlefield was placed on the mantelpiece. Other 'secondary relics', which took the place of an actual body, arrived in the brown paper parcel, sometimes muddy and caked with blood, dispatched by the army and containing the man's effects: his watch, a last letter or poem found on the body, perhaps a cigarette case. As an officer bought his own kit, this had to be returned to him and his family might receive several packages. In one extreme case, a mother mounted her dead son's tattered uniform in a frame that she displayed in the hallway.

When the poet Edward Thomas died on the first day of the Battle of Arras his widow, Helen, received the contents of his pockets: a diary containing her photo, a slip of paper and a letter. The diary's pages had become rippled by the sudden lack of air sucked out of the atmosphere by the pneumatic concussion of the German shell. It killed him by stopping his heart as he stood in the doorway of his trench; outwardly, his body was unscathed. By comparison, the terrible package that arrived for Roland Leighton's family spared few details and allowed his mother and his fiancée, Vera Brittain, to imagine exactly how he had died. A tiny hole beside the right-hand bottom pocket of his tunic showed where the bullet – which they realised would have been an expanding one – had entered his body; his khaki vest, breeches and braces were soaked in blood and it was clear that the bullet had blown out his back. Brittain noticed how the breeches had been slit open at the top by someone 'obviously in a violent hurry' – she imagined a doctor or one of his men – and how the cap that she was used to seeing him wear 'rakishly' on the back of his head was bent and shapeless and caked in mud. He must have fallen on top of it, or the people who fetched his body may have trampled it. She supposed he had fallen on his back, as his clothes were more stained and muddy than in the front. She wondered why it was necessary to return these 'relics' and described how the 'charnel-house smell' pervaded the small sitting room to the extent that Edward's mother ordered their removal. They decided to keep the blood-stained vest, if it could be sterilised, and his Sam Browne belt. They threw the windows open wide, but it was a long time before the smell and even the taste of them dispersed.

On Armistice Day, a tradition started in 1919, Ada Deane uncovered concrete proof that the dead were still present and interested in the lives of the living. On developing photos of the solemn ceremony she discovered, as she bent over a kitchen table covered with a black cloth, that the faces of the mourners had been joined by the inquisitive faces of the dead. Ada, a charwoman from Islington, north London, joined forces with her brother, a chemist, to produce and sell these ghostly images. Spirit photos were not new – mediums had long produced scenes of ectoplasm in the shape of the dead hovering over their relatives at séances – but the mass ranks of the First World War dead created a new and eager market. Although to modern eyes the photos look like unsophisticated 'copy and paste' jobs and the *Daily Sketch* claimed the faces were really sports stars, there were many who wished to believe in these spirit 'extras'. Psychical phenomena flourished because of the sheer numbers of the dead. As Jay Winter says in *Sites of Memory, Sites of Mourning: The Great War in European Cultural History*: 'Among the major combatants, it is not an exaggeration to suggest that every family was in mourning; most for a relative – a father, a son, a brother, a husband – others for a friend, a colleague, a lover, a companion.'

The First World War's 1,500 days of industrialised killing produced tens of millions of mourners who needed a new 'language of loss'. Their inarticulateness was confounded by their physical remoteness from the grave, or, in many cases, the lack of a body. More than 300,000 British and dominion casualties had no known resting place. Around three million of the nine million who had died left widows, most with at least two children. During the war itself, and for the immediate years after, burial and commemoration of the dead was chaotic and could lead to unseemly disputes between parents and wives, each claiming ownership. Parents usually won these tussles by asserting their unbreakable familial ties; sweethearts or fiancées had even fewer rights and their name was last after parents and siblings on any card left on the grave; their presence was sometimes pushed to the background in memorial books.

Initially, it was, in theory, possible for a family to repatriate the body of their loved one – as happened with Lieutenant William Gladstone, the 29-year-old grandson of three-times Prime Minister William Ewart Gladstone. The politician's namesake, who had been killed by a sniper in April 1915, was – officially at least – one of the last to be brought back to England and was buried with full military honours in the family home in Flintshire. Five thousand people lined the funeral route and five hundred packed into the village church. The cost of repatriation meant that the custom was in practice open only to the very rich and went against the democracy of death. The United States, by comparison, allowed the repatriation of bodies and nearly half its dead went home; the last in the 1940s. Britain's decision not to allow repatriation led to a few secret exhumations.

Funerals like Gladstone's were exactly what Sir Fabian Ware, who started what was to be known as the Commonwealth War Graves Commission, aimed to stamp out. Ware, at forty-five, was too old to fight and instead became commander of the mobile unit of the British Red Cross. His experience prompted him to record and care for the graves his unit came across. In May 1917, a Royal Charter established the Imperial War Graves Commission, and land for graves and memorials was secured after the Armistice. By 1918, around 587,000 graves had been identified and a further 559,000 casualties were registered as having no known resting place. The task of commemoration was taken so seriously that a team of the very best practitioners of their time was assembled. This included the three most eminent architects – Sir Edwin Lutyens, Sir Herbert

Baker and Sir Reginald Blomfield – to design and build the cemeteries and memorials. Rudyard Kipling advised on inscriptions and Gertrude Jekyll had her say on horticultural aspects.

Despite the difficulties of travelling in a ravaged land a steady stream of relatives started to visit the place where loved ones had fallen. In June 1920 Thomas Cook offered tours of the Western Front and the South Eastern and Chatham Railway Company put together a two-night package. Thousands went in the years to 1925 and numbers picked up again every time a new monument was unveiled. In 1931, 140,000 widows and parents made the pilgrimage and 160,000 eight years later. The wives who went, particularly in the years immediately after the end of the war, cannot have known what to expect and many were advised not to go. The remnants of war – rusting rifles, human remains, scraps of clothing and boots – must have left a troubling memory.

Monuments to the dead started to spring up at home: outside churches (or inside as plaques or stained glass), on village greens, at factories and railway stations or on wealthy estates. The materials they were made from, marble or granite, meant they were expensive to build at a time when many veterans were jobless and starving. A statue near Cambridge railway station, for example, of a returning soldier called 'The Homecoming', unveiled in 1922, lost two feet in height due to lack of funds (at six foot, he still cuts an imposing figure). Nevertheless, these memorials formed a part of the 'community in mourning' and provided a physical presence by which to remember the dead – so physical, in fact, that the gesture of reaching out and touching the name of the fallen became in itself an act of remembrance.

The most strikingly imaginative monument was the Tomb of the Unknown Warrior. The dead soldier's appearance in the *Oxford Dictionary of National Biography* represents an innovative example of an entry for an anonymous person, and even his date of death cannot be pinned down precisely but is merely given as '*d.* 1914?'. The idea and ceremony behind his interment came about with such speed that there is still uncertainty about some of the key facts. Was, for example, the celebrated corpse chosen from four or six dead soldiers? They had been plucked from the mud of Arras, Ypres, Aisne and the Somme, but only one was chosen to return home to England, to lie next to poets, kings and exalted generals in Westminster Abbey. Each waited in flag-covered coffins in an impromptu chapel in Saint-Pol-sur-Ternoise for the senior officer, Brigadier-General Louis John Wyatt, to daub one of them with his touch of immortality.

David Railton, a military chaplain who had served in Flanders for most of the war, stumbled upon the idea of a monument to the unknown soldier in 1916 when he found an improvised grave in a back garden of a house near Armentières. A white wooden cross marked the plot and an inscription in pencil read, 'An Unknown Soldier'. He suggested the idea of a symbolic grave to General Haig but received no reply. In 1920 he broached the subject again, but this time he asked Herbert Edward Ryle, Dean of Westminster Abbey, to put the suggestion to George V. The King thought the ceremony would rip open wounds that were just starting to close and it took the intervention of the Prime Minister, David Lloyd George, to win him over. With the second anniversary of the Armistice fast approaching, the unknown soldier's journey home suddenly assumed a new urgency. The body was given a special guard and taken to Boulogne, where the coffin was transferred to a two-inch thick casket made from oak grown at Hampton Court Palace gardens and lined with zinc. Railton's flag, which he had used as an altar cloth during the war, was placed on top. From Dover the corpse travelled on a special train in the same luggage van that had carried the body of the British nurse Edith Cavell. Crowds gathered to mark the train's passing on its way to Victoria station.

On Armistice Day, 11 November 1920, it was placed on a gun carriage and made its stately way, attended by generals, admirals and field marshals through silent crowds to Lutyens' new Portland stone *Cenotaph* – the Greek word for 'empty tomb' – in Whitehall. The simple white monument replaced the hastily assembled wood and plaster original that had been erected for the victory parade of July 1919 and which, despite criticism, had proved popular among the public, who covered it in wreaths. The King, as chief mourner, placed a wreath on the coffin of the unknown warrior before it continued to Westminster Abbey, where a short funeral service was conducted. Afterwards, the grave was filled with soil from the main battlefields and the familiar, black Belgian marble from a quarry near Namur was added in 1921. Dean Ryle wrote the words that stand above it: 'Beneath this stone rests the body of a British warrior unknown by name or rank brought from France to lie among the most illustrious of the land'. In the days that followed, around a million people filed past the grave until it was finally sealed on the night of 17 November.

Although the idea of the Unknown Warrior was designed and implemented by men, it had a special resonance for women. A thousand widows and mothers whose sons had perished were invited to the service, 'titled ladies next to charwomen'; mothers were given precedence over wives. Lady Elizabeth Bowes Lyon (later, Her Majesty Queen Elizabeth The Queen Mother) was the first royal bride to ask for her wedding bouquet to be laid on the tomb when she married the Duke of York (later George VI) in 1923. She had lost a brother in the war and her gesture became a royal tradition. A more humble woman who visited the tomb left an account, anonymous and published privately, in which she described feeling as if the bones inside the casket belonged to her missing husband. A modern historian has described this account, *To My Unknown Warrior*, as 'almost hallucinatory'.

Wives and mothers cleaved to the Tomb of the Unknown Warrior, and to other memorials, because the alternative was too painful. A public focus for their grief took some of the sting away from the thought that their loved one was resting in a foreign field.

For relatives of around a third of the dead who had no marked grave, the reality was even more terrible: their beloved was lying in unconsecrated ground that they shared with strangers, a detail that carried the taint of a pauper's grave. Christian teaching also became problematic: how could the body be resurrected when it lay in pieces or had been atomised by the new technology of killing?

By the time of the First World War, Britons had lost the knack of mourning. The possibility of death in a far-off country was always a risk for the traditional soldier – many died serving the Empire abroad or left behind the grave of a child or wife in India or Crimea. But a distant grave was a new experience for families of conscripts. A dramatic fall in infant mortality rates meant that, unlike their Victorian grandparents, couples expected their children to outlive them. Better housing, diets, working conditions and medical care sidelined death. By 1910, life expectancy for a man was fifty-two, compared to forty in the mid-nineteenth century. In peacetime death now usually arrived at the end of life, not at its beginning or youthful flowering. The Edwardians turned their back on death and its rituals, whereas Victoria's reign had been dominated by her grief for Albert. Edward VII decreed a short period of mourning for his mother. As historian David Cannadine says, at the outbreak of the First World War: 'The English were less intimately acquainted with death than any generation since the Industrial Revolution.' Mourners of those who died in the First World War had few conventions to lean on. There were no funerals and mourning clothes were so commonplace that they failed to elicit special sympathy or acknowledgement. A black filter had descended on the entire country.

While local and national governments erected monuments to the fallen, families created more domestic shrines. In her cubicle in a nurses' home in London, Vera Brittain gathered together the books she had shared with her fiancé, Roland. And, although she had refused to wear an engagement ring because of connotations of possession, she resorted to tradition by buying a mourning engagement ring after his death and had it engraved with his name and date of passing. Not only did the ring help her grieve, it also gave her status among the grieving. Women found solace with each other and with friends of their husbands, who often paid a visit after a death. Wilfred's batman, David, visited Clare. Sometimes these visits provided extra details about how someone had died, although they may not always have been welcome. The letters an officer was obliged to write to a bereaved wife naturally focused on the fact that the man's death had been instantaneous and painless; occasionally a fellow soldier might contradict this.

But perhaps more painful than becoming a widow was the torture of knowing that the soldier was 'missing', a fate suggested by the cold words, 'Regret – No Trace' that appeared in letters and telegrams. Many families longed to believe that their loved one had been taken prisoner and that their name had yet to make its way through the official channels, or that they had suffered some injury that left them with amnesia: they were safe but had lost all sense of their true identity. Rebecca West was one of the first authors to tackle the theme of memory loss and the havoc a veteran's reappearance could wreak. *The Return of the Soldier*, published in the final year of the war, tells the story of a man's relationship with three women who love him in different ways: his aloof wife Kitty, who lives with their child in a beautiful home; his devoted cousin Jenny; and Margaret, a woman caught in stultifying suburbia. The soldier is trapped in a world of fifteen years earlier, before his marriage and when he was in love with Margaret, at that time the inn-keeper's daughter. The three women have a choice: whether to 'cure' him or to leave him in a blissful, prewar state.

Angus Macnaghten, an officer in the Black Watch, was officially reported missing on 29 October 1914 during the first battle of Ypres. He was thirty-one when he disappeared and had been married to Hazel for three years; his son and namesake was born in May 1914. A photo of Angus shows him as moustachioed and with tightly curled hair; he wears a kilt with an extravagant sporran. He was a quintessentially British mixture of aristocratic Highlander: while he was at Eton his trustees bought him 12,000 acres of 'hill and heather' in Perthshire and he became well known as a good shot, a piper and a scholar of Gaelic. He felt an instant bond with any Scotsman and on the troopship to France struck up a friendship with the chief engineer, 'one M'Donald', a Highlander who was 'Awful pleased' when Angus spoke to him in Gaelic. His elder and unmarried sister, Lettice, ran his house and spent part of the year at their father's other home near Southampton.

Hazel Irwin had known Angus for years before they married in 1911. She was the daughter of an officer who had served in the Indian Army and who died when she was six. More thoughtful and bookish than her husband, she was also pretty and flirtatious. As Angus had been in the Army Reserve for several years she was used to the idea of him in uniform. In his first two months abroad she received regular postcards and letters. He told her to tell Cousin Lesley (Sir Lesley Probyn, KCVO, 1834–1916) that he was known as 'the Zouave', due to his red waistcoat. He wrote, 'The Germans have been trying the "white flag" game with us, but it didn't pay them. I think it is a regular practice of theirs – they are awful brutes, no doubt about it.' He was rather ashamed of the interest he took in food 'among the most gruesome affairs', adding that nothing was nicer than the Quaker Oats porridge and condensed milk they sometimes had as a treat for breakfast. These comforts helped since he had not slept in a bed since leaving Aldershot; he usually bedded down outdoors or on straw in a billet. In early October his captain was wounded and he was put in charge of a company of more than 200 men. 'This life does bring home to one the Power of the High One,' he wrote to his wife, adding that he believed he would return home safe to her.

On 3 November the War Office sent Hazel a telegram saying that her husband had been reported missing on 29 October. It cautioned that this did not necessarily mean that he had been injured or taken prisoner and promised more information would follow. It seems likely that Hazel received a postcard from Angus after the first telegram. His sister also telegrammed to say that her husband, who was at the front, had learnt that Angus had been slightly wounded in the leg before being taken prisoner. So began years of speculation, rumour and counter-rumour.

Many of the rumours focused around fighting at a ridge north of Paris known as the *Chemin des Dames*. It was to be the scene of three major battles, each named Aisne after the river. Driving along the road at night today there is still something uncanny about the landscape – a certain quality in addition to the eeriness of the unending fields and deserted villages. In one account, Angus was the only officer to identify a group of men as Germans, rather than French. When they retreated to a wood he was chosen, because of his stalking skills, to find a way through the German lines in the midst of a storm. In another account, an officer spotted a bearded chieftain emerging in the mist and recognised Angus from his time at Eton.

The Black Watch suffered heavy casualties and Angus's fellow officers wrote to reassure Hazel that he had been taken prisoner. They warned her that he would be shown as 'missing' but was now safer than before. However, by November a note of caution had started to creep into the letters she received. Major James Murray of the Black Watch, who was convalescing in England, wrote to say he could not be certain she would hear soon. When Lettice met him she found his attitude to her brother's fate discouraging.

Towards the end of 1914 Hazel placed an advert in the personal columns asking for information about her husband. A Red Cross nurse in Dorset replied that she had cared for a private who remembered seeing Angus wounded in the leg, but that the injury was not serious. The same day a representative from Cox & Co., a bank and shipping agency the War Office used to return officers' effects, reported their representative in Paris had heard that Angus had been wounded in a trench. The Paris office of the Red Cross confirmed that they, too, had heard this story.

Hazel told Angus's personal bank, Coutts, to let her know if he withdrew any money. She started to collect newspaper cuttings about missing soldiers. An article in December 1914 gave her hope because it reported that many lists of POWs were delayed or incomplete. Relatives and friends used their contacts around Europe – from the Army and Navy Prayer Union to high-ranking generals and American Express, which the British Government employed to deliver parcels, letters and money to Prisoners of War in Germany – to pursue all sort of lines of inquiry.

After reading an article about him in the *Daily Graphic*, Hazel wrote to an American, Edward Page Gaston, who was acting as an unofficial go-between for POWs in Germany. In the article, he explained how he had set up a missing persons' bureau for Allied servicemen and that he believed hundreds, maybe thousands, of men were being held in German cottages, farms or hospitals, where they were not allowed to contact their loved ones. Gaston was one of several men who claimed, for a fee, to be able to trace missing servicemen. Hazel sent him the considerable sum of £50 (worth around £4,000 today) and a photo of Angus, which he promised to distribute throughout Germany. A few months later she wrote to Lettice saying that there were rumours that Gaston was a fraud but that she felt there was no cause for alarm. Although the War Office had already warned the press about Gaston and other fraudsters, Hazel was slow to see through him. Eventually, in June 1915, a letter from the American Ambassador in Berlin published in many British newspapers put paid to Gaston's scam. Hazel was lucky enough, with the help of a trustee of Angus's will, to recoup £35 of the £50 she had given him.

She and Lettice were understandably reluctant to countenance any suggestion – no matter how well meant – that Angus was dead.

Lettice instantly dismissed an account by a soldier she interviewed in hospital, who said he had seen Angus's grave. By contrast, Hazel and Lettice found solace in anything that kept Angus alive. He was 'gazetted' a captain in February 1915 and therefore could not be presumed dead. They read that commandants in German POW camps burned letters to save them the trouble of censoring them – although this was later refuted.

In June 1915 the War Office wrote to Hazel to say that they had two statements proving that Angus was no longer alive and would she allow his name to be added to the roll of honour. But still she clung on. By November the War Office said that, due to the length of time after he was reported missing, he must be assumed to be dead. In early 1916, moves were made to start winding up his estate but, nevertheless, Hazel issued a statement saying that, although his name would appear on the roll of honour, neither she nor his sisters had given up hope that he was still alive. Lettice told the *Southampton Times* that the announcement 'believed killed' was only included for business purposes and that, since no definite news of his death had appeared, it was still reasonable to hope. Hazel continued to visit hospitals, seeking out men who might tell her what she wanted to hear. At the end of 1916 she received official condolences from Buckingham Palace and the following year Angus's life insurance was paid out. But still she hoped. After the end of the war, in 1918, one of the trustees of Angus's will wrote to Hazel to say that he had interviewed three men from her husband's platoon who had given him a detailed account of his final hours. 'I am afraid this leaves practically no room for any hope, as the man was telling me exactly what he saw himself, and I have every reason to believe that his information is correct.' He added those words that had become almost a benediction: 'death was instantaneous'. But still she hoped.

Door-to-door inquires were made in Belgium. In 1921 his medals were sent to her. She continued to make inquiries. Occasionally reports emerged of men who, having been reported dead, were found to be alive and on their way home after being held in some far-flung camp. In other instances, obituaries had been written, memorial services given, estates wound up; sometimes widows had remarried. Every time a newspaper report surfaced of a soldier who, having lost his memory, suddenly returned home, Hazel's hopes were raised, only for her to sink back into mourning. As late as 1930 she wrote to a man who had only recently recovered from amnesia after serving in the First World War.

This gnawing sense of not knowing was not usual. The new form of warfare obliterated bodies and the volume of the dead meant officials could not keep up with statistics. One fiancée was given six different dates on which her sweetheart had died. The various memorials to the missing contain seemingly endless rows of names. The Menin Gate, where Angus's name eventually appeared – his surname misspelt but in time corrected – holds more than 50,000. Nor was Hazel unusual in refusing to give up hope: Kipling's son was reported missing in October 1915, but his father continued to believe he was alive for the next two years.

It would have been unusual if Hazel had not, at some stage, turned to the supernatural for help and she chose a clairvoyant who claimed to be able to see into a subject's past as well as his current and future state. Hazel sent the man one of Angus's letters and from this he told her that he was in a hospital, unable to walk and unaware that Hazel did not know where he was. The clairvoyant gave her the names of places where he had been held, which, of course, Hazel investigated.

Clare Sheridan spoke to her dead husband, Wilfred, for half an hour during her first visit to the medium in Notting Hill. She asked him if he had been to the memorial service at Winchester Cathedral and he told her, 'Of course, we were all there . . .' before berating her for losing control of her emotions. He reassured her about money and that there was no need to consult him about financial affairs. She asked him what death was like and wanted to know whether it was similar to childbirth. He compared it to going to sleep. He told her not to cry and said he was closer to her when she was happy. Then he was gone. He was replaced by a child's voice saying, 'Mummie, Mummie, I can't see you, it's all dark' and the smell of lilies of the valley. She recognised the voice of her daughter, who told her they were playing hide-and-seek. Elizabeth made a clutch at her mother's hair, saying: 'Mummie, I don't like this dark; I like being out in the light.' The medium's guide described a child who had continued to grow after her death and said Wilfred had wanted Elizabeth to talk to her mother, but the child had not been happy and had returned. The medium's assistant then announced that she was tired and that the session must end. She had been in a trance for forty minutes.

Clare was convinced that she had been in touch with the other side, although she found it deeply unsatisfactory. She returned several times to speak to her husband and also met other friends who had been killed in the war – as well as Henry James, who wrung her hand warmly. Her American grandparents spoke to her and a sister who had been stillborn. She chatted to Wilfred as if he were still alive and allowed herself to disagree with him. She continued to visit the medium for several years until the relationship came to an abrupt end. She had brought her son, Dick, along and they had been talking to his father for about an hour. Dick was thrilled to hear of the new discoveries being made on the other side when the conversation suddenly took a more earthly direction and Wilfred asked about their forthcoming trip abroad. When she said they were going to live in Turkey, he replied: 'Don't be a fool'. Clare was so affronted at this outburst that she never returned.

Hazel took much longer to come to terms with her husband's death and, ironically, it was her privileged position of well-connected friends and her moneyed background that perpetuated the pain. In 1931 a female friend, whom Hazel had known since childhood, casually mentioned that when travelling in the Balkans ten years earlier she thought she had caught a glimpse of 'dear old Angus', either in Serbia or 'one of those countries between Bulgaria and Trieste'. She was tired, dazed and ill, so she could not be quite sure, but she thought she had seen him on a train on the opposite track. The sighting, no matter how unreliable, was enough to reignite Hazel's hope. She contacted the British legation in Sofia and a search was started; the Red Cross in Geneva were also approached but held out little hope. A brother-in-law asked the authorities in Berlin if it was feasible that a POW could have been sent that far. No trace of Angus was found.

In August 1939, on the brink of what would be the Second World War, Hazel went with her son, Angus, to the Menin Gate to see her husband's name – albeit misspelt. They were accompanied by the two officers and her husband's closest regimental friends, who had written to Hazel to reassure her that her husband had been taken prisoner. After a quarter of a century of searching and grieving this was the closest she would ever come to a reunion with her husband. For many other women the intense sadness they felt at the loss of their husband or fiancé would never leave them, even if they were fortunate enough to find someone else to love.

9

The Letter: Lena Leland, Clementine Churchill and Ethel Cove

Coming up with a coded language was not difficult for John Ronald Reuel Tolkien. Even as a child he relished secret forms of communication. When he met his future wife, Edith Bratt, they were both orphaned teenagers, living in the same boarding house in Birmingham, and would whistle to one another as a sign to hang out of their windows for a clandestine chat. Ronald trained for the army while he was still studying English at Oxford University and deferred his call-up until he had completed his degree. He took a first in June 1915 and a commission as a 2nd lieutenant in the Lancashire Fusiliers, where he specialised in signalling. He learnt how to send messages by Morse code, heliograph and lamp, how to signal with flags and discs and how to use rockets, field telephones and carrier pigeons.

Ronald and Edith married in March 1916, when she was twenty-seven and he was twenty-four. Edith decided that she would not make a permanent home for herself but live in furnished rooms as near his camp as possible until he was sent to France. He wrote later, 'Parting from my wife then . . . it was like a death'. Edith found it hard not to worry about her husband's safety and the couple developed a code that allowed Ronald to give her extra information about his whereabouts, without troubling the censor. He incorporated a pattern of dots into their correspondence that told her where he was in France and she traced his movements on a map pinned to the wall of her lodgings in Great Haywood, Staffordshire. Many of Tolkien's friends were killed in the First World War and he was eventually sent home suffering from Pyrexia, or fever.

Although letters from the First World War always carry the shadow of the censor's pencil hovering over the page, the frankness with which soldiers wrote to their wives can still be surprising. The writer was not supposed to mention his location, military strategy, defence works, anything about the organisation or numbers of troops or armaments, morale or physical conditions of the soldiers, casualties or criticism. But, while most soldiers were punctilious about not giving away precise military details, many were less inhibited about discussing the mood of the troops, deaths and injuries. Professional soldier Captain Herbert John Collett Leland told his wife, Lena, in Edinburgh: 'I wish I could write to you as I want to and give you news, but it is impossible as you know they are most frightfully strict, and very rightly too.' Instead, he dropped hints in the hope that she would reach the right conclusion. The following comment, written on 7 October 1916, might, perhaps, refer to a hotel with a French name: 'You ask me where I am. You will have to guess. It is where we spent an afternoon in Newcastle, but we have moved and Armentieres will perhaps fix it. (If the Censor gets hold of this he will probably delete the last.)' In another letter that month he told her that 'dykes' should give her an idea of his whereabouts, before querying whether he had spelt the word correctly.

On 1 November 1916 he reassured her that every letter she sent had reached him, despite the difficulties faced by the Field Postal Authorities. He warned her that they might not arrive as regularly soon, adding, 'I must leave you to guess the reason.' Seventeen days later he confirmed that she had guessed where they were heading and that they were 'in for the big show'. On 7 December 1916 she had 'quite grasped the situation out here' and guessed the position of her 'worser half' – 'Try and read between the lines as you always seem to do.' The following summer he told her to buy the *Daily Mail* on 31 May 1917 because he was within a dozen yards of the noticeboard mentioned in the article; in early August he had to stop in a certain 'wood', 'renowned in history'. Other soldiers relied on literary references to hint at their location.

Herbert was forty-one at the outbreak of war and already had an impressive career in soldiering behind him. His father had been a doctor but died when Herbert was three. His mother remarried – a rector, twenty-nine years her senior – and by the age of eighteen Herbert was in the army. In his twenties he spent two stints of four and three years in West Africa. According to a grandson he would have preferred the cavalry but did not have the money to support the necessary lifestyle. During his first tour he was part of the Gold Coast Constabulary, 1896–1900, and on his return served as captain and adjutant, Gold Coast Regiment, West African Frontier Force, 1900–03. He was mentioned in Despatches during the Ashanti campaign and became a companion of the Distinguished Service Order (DSO). While in Africa he contracted dysentery, which laid him low for several months, but he had a more congenial time in Ireland, where he was adjutant, 5th Battalion, Royal Munster Fusiliers, 1904–09. He married Lena in 1902 and was promoted into the 1st South Staffordshire Regiment in 1909. Their postings together included a spell in Gibraltar.

But despite his experiences in Africa and other parts of the Empire, nothing could prepare Herbert for the trenches of the First World War. It was a horror he had no qualms about sharing with his wife. He sent his first letter to her on 16 September 1916 and the months that followed chronicled life at the front in unsparing detail. At the start his tone was almost jolly; by the end he had descended into deep despair. On 21 September 1916 he wrote:

> We are in the front line. Those who have been out for some time say this is quite a quiet spot, but, oh! What will the noisier place be like. One continuous roar. The only thing is to keep smiling and look as if you enjoyed it. I suppose I shall get used to it in time . . . [the shells] looked exactly as if some giant with a watering can was pouring water on the earth from the clouds. Some new devilment, but thank goodness it was some distance away from us.

He explained about the threat of gas and how they had to carry two helmets with them at all times. One night he was woken at three in the morning by the sound of buzzers, gongs and bells and cries of 'gas, gas'; sometimes the 'Huns' would launch little red balloons before an attack. He had also seen several 'horribly exciting' aerial dogfights. On another occasion he went for a long, night-time ride. His horse was 'very clever in dodging the shell holes' his rider could not see 'as you know what a fool I am in the dark'.

He painted a vivid picture for Lena back in Edinburgh, telling her how the writing paper he was holding had twice in the last ten minutes been blown from his hands by what was known as 'Back Fire'. The previous day a shell had dropped three feet from the orderly room but it was a 'Dud', which, he explained, was a shell that fails to burst. He also acknowledged how the war was changing his character: 'I could not believe that it was possible to feel so callous as one does out here.' In the same letter he told her that they were going into the trenches in four days' time, adding, 'Perfectly safe, so you need not worry.' On 26 September 1916 it was 'absolute hell' and he urged her to 'read between the lines'. A few days later he told her the Huns had been shelling them: one within 10 yards of him, and two others not 15 yards away. They had 'shaken him up' and left him with 'a nasty taste' in his mouth. He said that he would not have been able to imagine what it was like if he had not experienced it himself: 'The continual roar of the guns, the whirr of machine guns, the ground shakes as if by earthquake, and it never ceases day or night. At night the lights and star shells light up the whole sky and the effect is most extraordinary.'

He knew that, like other army wives, she would be visited by men who had served with him and would be able to fill in the gaps. He told her that Macgregor, an RAMC doctor, would be passing through Edinburgh and that she should give him the best lunch or dinner possible, although he warned her not to mention anything he had said in his letters. Macgregor would deliver a 'Boche shell' that had missed Leland by a few inches and which their son, Tony, would appreciate.

He described everyday life: the rats 'more like rabbits' that wake him in the night by pulling his hair out at the roots to use for their nests, the prostitutes (just like the ones they had seen when visiting Las Palmas – he reassures her that they have not touched him), and the food, 'great thick slices of salt bacon and tomatoes'. He makes sure she understands that 'over the top' means entering no man's land. He tells her of the different places he is staying: 'a small wood, sand bags piled up all around me, my Adjutant a young detail, lying beside me, and a field telephone at my ear . . . nuts and acorns drop round me, but it is quite warm and no rain, and really very comfy'. He is lucky to have a good servant, who never seems to sleep. He is on the top floor of a chateau, in a bed that would hold six, 'but there is only one wall standing and it is very rickety'. Next, he is billeted with a French family and the coffee is 'very good', although he is driven mad by the cuckoo clock. He pins two pictures of her to his billet wall, and later, a humorous poem she has written about their rum ration that even the padre found amusing.

Lena, for her part, sends him items he requests: a waistcoat that keeps him warm under his tunic but which makes his uniform so tight that he fears he will burst out of it, writing paper and cards, an electric lamp that is envied by his fellow soldiers, toffee and cigars. He nearly loses a four-leafed clover that floats out of a letter and which he almost overlooks in the poor light; as his watch will not open he cannot store it there; instead he places it with his daughter Jean's milk tooth in his breast pocket. He asks Lena to persuade other friends and family to send him a stick of shaving soap, two toothbrushes, a jar of toothpaste and some cough lozenges. He also needs the latest musketry regulations, parts one and two, which she should be able to buy from any bookseller. She is keeping the home fires burning, but not in the way he remembers. She talks of fitting a bar-less grate in the drawing room and he teases her by asking whether this means he will no longer be able to gaze at the coals (which burnt below eye-level in the new model). He worries about whether or not they have enough to eat in Edinburgh and thinks they will be better off if the price of meat is fixed – 'Give an idea in your next letter as to what you are able to get and how you fare.'

Herbert urged Lena to get his mother to send him cake and the well-off provided a mouth-watering supply of food and drink to officers in the trenches. Fortnum & Mason's sent ready-made parcels of goodies and wives clubbed together to buy Christmas puddings, oranges, nuts and cakes. When Winston Churchill was serving in France in November 1915 he bombarded his wife, Clementine, with regular requests. He was given command of a battalion of the 6th Royal Scots Fusiliers with the rank of lieutenant colonel and one of the first things he asked for was two new pairs of riding pants, without laces or buttons at the knee. A long list of other items followed and he declared the pillow she had sent a 'boon & a pet'. Later, he wanted a small box of food to supplement rations; it should contain sardines, chocolates and potted meat, and be sent weekly. He also asked for a new pen to replace the Onoto he had lost and then a small Corona typewriter. She could not find his trench wading boots and woke in the middle of the night, worrying about him being cold. On 25 November she told him that she loved him more than ever and felt as if 'more than half my life has vanished across the Channel'. She cut out a 'delightful snap-shot' from the *Daily*

Mirror of him in uniform leaving the house, 'There was a thick fog & the figure is misty & dim & so I feel you receding into the fog & mud of Flanders & not coming back for so long . . .'

Winston reassured her and then went on to request two bottles of his old brandy, plus a bottle of peach brandy. This consignment should be repeated every ten days. He later added that this was important because it was common practice for officers to share their treats from home and Clementine wrote in distress that the first consignment of food had gone to the wrong mess. His next list included:

> 2 more pairs of thick Jaeger draws [sic], vests & socks (soft)
> 2 more pairs brown leather gloves (warm)
> 1 more pair of field boots (like those I had from Fortnum & Mason) only from the fourth hole from the bottom instead of holes there shd be good strong tags for lacing quicker. One size larger than the last.
> Also one more pair of Fortnum & M's ankle boots only with tags right up from the bottom hole (the same size these as before)

He apologised for his extravagance but said that he needed spares because he was repeatedly drenched and had nowhere to dry his clothes. She wanted to know all about his life: does he have a nice servant, where and what does he eat? She said she would hate the rats more than the bullets and wonders whether he can shoot them, or would that be considered a waste of bullets?

On 4 December he asked for a big bathtowel as 'I now have to wipe myself all over with things that resemble pocket handkerchiefs.' By 12 December the food parcels had started to arrive regularly, plus 'the most divine & glorious sleeping bag . . . I get daily evidences of the Cat's [Clementine's] untiring zeal on my behalf. The periscope was the exact type I wanted. How clever of you to hit it off.'

As well as sending him comforts, Clementine also acted as his political adviser and cuttings service. She kept him up-to-date with the latest intrigue and sent him snippets from the newspapers and his cabinet papers that he asked for. He was pleased that she had entertained Lloyd George for lunch and urged her to keep in touch with him, as well as friends and 'pseudo' friends. He wanted a verbatim report of her meeting with the Prime Minister. She said she has been 'hobnobbing' with so many politicians on his behalf that she deserved the Distinguished Service Medal. When she bumped into Lord Esher in the Grill Room of the Berkeley Hotel, he said he had recently seen Churchill in France and that he looked well.

Clementine was also busy organising a canteen for a new government factory in Hackney Marshes that was to operate twenty-four hours a day and which was officially opened by Lloyd George. She admitted to Winston that she felt lonely and in January 1916 she wrote that they will be proud that he was a soldier, and not a politician, for the whole war, adding, 'soldiers and soldiers' wives seem to me now the only real people'. But, in a later letter, she also acknowledged her dread of coming home from 'canteening' to find 'a telegram with terrible news'. Now if the telephone rang it might be the War Office to say that he had been killed. She admitted she would spare one of his arms or legs if it meant his safe return.

In August 1917 Herbert had a few days' leave. By the time he had taken the train to Edinburgh he had barely a week with his family, and his journey home reminded him of what he was returning to: Charing Cross in London had been bombed and he shared a sleeper compartment with an officer who had lost an arm and who needed help dressing. Back in Flanders, he had time to reflect on the life he was missing: 'This leave has been nothing more than a dream. I cannot really realize yet that I have been at home. How I hate leave. The returning is just too damnable. You cannot come down to my present state of misery (no not misery – melancholy).'

*

Letter writing played an important part in maintaining morale among troops at the front and their families waiting at home. But the importance of the letter was a relatively recent development and possible only because of higher levels of literacy. The Education Act of 1870 arrived too late for some working-class parents of soldiers who served in the First World War and, of course, letter writing did not come naturally to everyone. But, as Michael Roper points out in *The Secret Battle*, 25 per cent of army recruits worked in central or local government, the professions, finance or commerce and, for this group, writing had been at the core of their peacetime job. War turned them into prolific writers. Officers were more used to writing letters, particularly if they had been at boarding school; their quarters, which were usually better lit and drier, made composing a letter slightly easier, although, as Herbert Leland told his wife, a blast was still capable of knocking a candle out of his hand.

Before 1795 the Postal Service drew no distinction between soldiers serving abroad and other customers living overseas. An Act of Parliament introduced a penny rate for soldiers receiving and sending letters. The innovation encouraged correspondence and also saved the soldier a potentially large bill when forwarded mail eventually caught up with him. During 1855 over three-quarters of a million letters were sent through France to the Army and Navy in Crimea and 1.2 million went in the other direction. The war marked the last time civilian postal workers were sent out with the British Army.

The sheer volume of post during the First World War presented a challenge. After 1914 letters home that weighed under 4oz were free of charge because they were seen as good for morale. By 1917 soldiers on the Western Front were dispatching 8.15 million letters a week. It was impractical to sort the mail in France and instead a massive sorting office, said to be the biggest wooden construction in the world, covered five acres of Regent's Park. As many postal workers had enlisted, it was staffed by men who were medically unfit to fight, and women too. They had to deal with a variety of packaging and addresses; in one bag, for example, 'expeditionary' was spelt forty-three different ways, including 'X.Perdition'. The Post Office also delivered £2 million per week in Separation Allowances to wives of men in the armed forces.

At the start of the war a letter from France took about ten days to arrive, but this eventually dropped to four as communication lines improved. Soldiers in Mesopotamia, Salonica or Gallipoli might have to wait months for news from home and when letters finally arrived, they were often out of sequence. Letters home, like a popular magazine, usually had a readership that was much wider than the original recipient. The letter might be read at the breakfast table, passed round friends and family and even printed in a local company's newsletter (as happened with Lever Brothers) or a local newspaper. Wives whose husbands were serving in Europe found it easier to imagine what their men might be up to because they shared a similar climate and time zone. When it was snowing hard in London, Clementine Churchill worried that Winston was wet and cold. It was harder to conjure up a loved one if they had been posted to a more exotic place, such as Mesopotamia.

In 1917 Herbert and Lena's letters were among those packed into the 19,000 mailbags that crossed the channel daily. As the British Army moved around less than in other conflicts, a reliable system of lorries and carts became established to convey the post to and from the front. At home, though, the lack of men, and the need to conserve fuel, led to cuts in deliveries that, nevertheless, by today's standard, reflect an enviable service. Before 1914, for example, a rural village received around 12 deliveries a day; the war reduced this to one or two; in inner London there were *only* five daily deliveries. The wartime drain on government coffers also brought the demise of the Penny Post in June 1918, when postage was raised by half a penny.

During the Boer War letters passing through the army postal system were censored, as well as some private mail and dispatches from war correspondents. The Boers in turn censored letters sent by British Prisoners of War. Censorship was haphazard in the First World War and there were ways round it, even without the need for codes. Men posted letters for their pals when they were home on leave and injured soldiers used the Red Cross to deliver letters. Field Service Post Cards and strictly rationed 'Green' envelopes, which contained letters covering sensitive family matters, included a declaration in which the sender promised that he had abided by the rules, and were not censured. It was the officer's job, or sometimes the padre's, to censor letters written by Other Ranks, but as he might have to read as many as 300 letters in an evening the officer was forced to limit his scrutiny to obvious breaches such as place names and details of troop numbers.

The very fact that letters were so treasured has meant that few from army wives have survived. They were read and re-read but often had to be jettisoned when the soldier moved on. Far fewer have survived from the wives of ordinary soldiers, but the exchanges between Wilfrid and Ethel Cove and their small daughter, Marjorie, give some idea of the impact letters could have on the whole family.

Ethel and Wilfrid had been together since they were sixteen. She was twenty-five and he was a year older when they married in north London in 1908. It is not known why they took so long, but their letters show a touching devotion. He was her 'darling boy'; she was his 'darling girl'. They had two young daughters: Marjorie, who was five when her father left for France in June 1916 and whose phonetic spelling (she tells him she 'orlwase' says goodnight to him and writes fairy as 'fear is') lightened their correspondence, and Betty, who was born in 1914. Wilfrid was a cashier in the Piccadilly/Regent's Street branch of London and Smith's Bank and, under the new Derby Scheme (named after the Director-General of Recruiting, Lord Derby), registered his willingness to serve in December 1915. Ethel was a schoolteacher from Southend, whose father had been a theatrical manager before turning to the more mundane career of insurance. She and Wilfrid had made a home for themselves in a respectable, villa-style, semi-detached house in Harrow, Middlesex. Gunner Cove, Royal Garrison Artillery, looks dashing in his uniform, with his neat moustache.

One of her first notes to him, in June 1916, contained news that Marjorie was to be a 'real live fairy' in a '*Dansante*' and she had been busy teaching her the steps. Ethel had received one letter from him that morning and hoped for another later that day. Seven months later, at the end of January 1917, she sounds weary. She has been writing from 7 p.m. to 9.30 p.m. and his is the fifth letter that evening. Her letter is full of the minutiae of domestic life: the clock has started striking an extra two hours; she is worried about the pipes in the bathroom; the broken window has yet to be fixed; she has lent Mrs Morgan a storm lamp; she popped in to see his 'folks' and found they were short of coal so invited them round for tea. Like many soldiers at the front, he becomes a helpless eavesdropper on family politics. He tells her not to worry about what her uncle, Oscar, said to her.

Money is a major preoccupation. She needs some new boots but cannot afford them; it sounds as though she has had to let a servant go – 'Yes dear I quite "got you" as regards money matters when you come back, & quite realise what we'll have to face then. But there'll be two of us to do it, so it will be easier. I will try to keep the right side of the ledger . . .' In February they had £18 in the bank: 'It seemed such wealth. But it's dwindled now to £3 off after paying rates etc'. The window has still not been mended and the house needs a good clean.

Marjorie and Betty are both 'pretty fit', although Betty, in particular, suffers from chilblains and they argue over who should 'love' his photograph. Betty is very attached to the boy doll her father gave her and it needs mending daily. One of the daughters, probably Marjorie, said to her one morning: '"Mummy!", "Yes? What is it?" "I do want my Daddy!"'

A few days later Ethel says how relieved she is that his injury has not caused permanent damage to his eye. She has seen a lot of discharged soldiers and some are 'pitiable'. She also prophesies misery from the 'hurried war weddings' and tells him about one girl who visited a man in hospital three times, took him for a walk and then married him. Coal and sugar are hard to come by, but she has found some 'awfully nice butter at 1/3 – a mixture of the real thing & margarine'. She thanks him for the souvenirs he has sent and appears daunted by his ardour: 'As for your feeling – I shall be rather nervous when you come home – can't live up to it.' When Wilfrid writes to her on 14 November 1916 he notes that it is the first time they have been apart for either of their birthdays since she was seventeen – 'Heaven send that by your next birthday – or mine come to that – this terrible war will be over & that we may both be spared & united on each of our birthdays and those of our dear little kiddies for many years to come.'

Her mother has written to tell him how brave and cheerful she was being and he promises that, if he is spared, he will do his best to be worthy of her: 'It causes me many regrets and much sorrow when I remember that my selfishness has more than once caused you unhappiness and I sincerely hope that my future conduct will make you realize I had notwithstanding my shortcomings I do love you with all my heart and I do realize that I have one of the best little wives in the world. I can now quite understand the Late Lord Kitchener's preference for bachelors as soldiers.' He tells her that he does not fear death itself, just not being reunited with her. He believes he is in a safe place.

His fifteen-page, handwritten letter goes on to describe the cakes and sausage rolls she has sent as 'A1', but 'the eggs! Oh! The eggs!!!' He had managed to put them in water and then carry them to a shell hole before they exploded. Like Churchill, but on a more modest scale, he makes sure she is aware of his preferences: condensed Nestlé rather than Ideal milk, because it is sweeter, goes further and is less likely to spill. When he gets home he is going to show her how to make a meal from bully beef, onions and biscuits. In a later letter, he asks for Boots toothpaste. She does not need to send cigarettes, as they have plenty (this remark may have prompted Marjorie to ask him if *he* will send them cigarettes for the 'poor' soldiers in Harrow hospital).

He has heard rumours of big zeppelin raids over England and is worried about her safety, particularly if he does not receive a letter. He is reading *The Pools of Silence* (1909) by the popular Irish author Henry de Vere Stacpoole. Their gramophone record has broken, so they make their own entertainment using mess tins as drums to accompany their whistling and singing. On 16 November 1916 he tells her that he has been made batman to the Second in Command, but says he would rather stay 'on the guns'. For Christmas 1916 he sends Ethel one of the popular embroidered cards that French and Belgian women make to earn extra money. His is green, white, brown and yellow, and urges her to 'Enjoy Joy This Xmas'.

Marjorie sends him letters in large childish handwriting with blocks of kisses and drawings of leaping fairies, people in a strange assortment of hats, stars, birds, fruit and a family portrait of a man with a moustache, his wife and two girls. He writes to tell her how proud he is of her and compares the picture of the bulldog she has sent to the German eagle – 'The eagle quite represents the Germans for it is a nasty bird which lives on dear little lambs.' As so often happens when a father writes home from the front, unaware of the burden such words can place on a child, he tells his daughter to be kind to her mother and to help her sister. He makes light of his experiences – 'Fancy sleeping every night in a cellar!' – and tells her about the German planes trying to find Daddy's big gun (a description that inspires one of her drawings). He tells her he cannot come home for Christmas because there are so many families who are more needy than he. She must tell Mamma that he will remember them at 2 p.m. on Christmas Day.

He praises her writing and drawing and has pinned her crayon pictures of tulips next to her photo in his dugout bedroom. He sketches the room with its stove and shows them making tea and Oxo; he compares it to her little pink room. On 15 January 1917 he writes:

> My dear Little Marjorie, This is the first time this year I have had a chance of writing to you, but I have never forgotten you and I am very pleased to see by your clever little letters that you have not forgotten your daddy.

He thanks her for the dominoes she has sent and looks forward to playing a game with her and reading her a bedtime story. He longs to give her a piggyback ride down the stairs. 'It must be funny to be big and little at the same time,' he tells her. She is now tall enough to reach the door latch without standing on tiptoes and her legs no longer dangle when she sits on a chair. He says he is sorry that she has so many disappointments about his leave and asks her to polish the brass in the front room for when he does come home. Her letters make him laugh. One of his most treasured notes from home reads:

> My Dear Dad, I hope you are . . . mum has had her hair wosht as well. I was very tierd when I kame home from dancing larst night mum has got some new boots blak boots thay are from your . . . I . . . a nice skooter a red handool and red weels it is not a very nice day to day I have had my ...

This was one of a handful of mementoes of his family that were recovered from his body after his death on 7 March 1917. The other items include a torn, black and white photo of Betty; a beautiful hanky that looks like silk, pale blue and embroidered round the edge with white flowers, mottled and beginning to tear along the folds; and a printed white card, about the size of a matchbox. On one side a branch with several flags bears the words: 'I'm ever thinking of you'. The reverse has the handwritten words: '"Somewhere in France" Nov. 1916 To my Darling Wife with fondest love and wishing you many many happy returns on your birthday, from your ever loving Hubby'. There is also a torn piece of writing, in a child's hand of big loops, in pencil on lined paper, decorated with printed blue forget-me-nots, and the words: 'The riches that we prize, May sometimes end, But not the riches of, A true friend' and a torn drawing of a tree with a green pear and a note 'Her first tree' and another scrap with 'Little "girl" skipping' written by adult hand.

Looking back on events, Ethel felt that there had been signs that her husband would not return to her. She remembered how the grandfather clock had started to behave in an odd way and frequently struck twenty-three. Some time before his death the mirror he used in the bathroom fell down and when she wrote to tell him he seemed unconcerned, telling her to 'hang the mirror up & carry on'. On a Friday, his favourite picture, a large one by Fred Morgan, who painted sentimental country scenes, 'crashed to the ground, splintered' – 'This I must own made me feel uncomfortable, & I told him nothing.' On 1 March 1917, he was slightly wounded in the head with shrapnel and taken to hospital. On Sunday, 4 March, he went to a church service in the hospital and enjoyed a sermon on the theme of 'Thy will be done'. On 7 March, she experienced an 'awful restlessness' and the next day, Marjorie told her: 'Mummy, I had such a funny dream last night. Daddy came to the bedroom window, and beckoned. He was dressed all in black, & the bandage on his wounded head was black too.'

Lieutenant Carroll wrote to Ethel to tell her how her husband, his batman, had died. He had become 'very attached' to him and knew all about Ethel and their two daughters. Wilfrid had been killed by a shell and death was 'instantaneous'. Carroll had seen him immediately after he had been killed but, due to heavy shelling, had not been able to remove the body until that evening. His body had been wrapped in the union flag and given all the honours worthy of his 'heroic death'. He was buried at the cemetery at Vlamertinghe. Carroll wrote to her again in June to say that the War Office would send notification of death, her pension and any money she was owed. He wrote again, a few days later, to say he was ill and that she should contact the War Office about the matters she mentioned. He said he would visit next time he was in London.

He may have been referring to Ethel's attempts to obtain a death certificate. Just three weeks after Wilfrid's death she had written – from Southend, where she must have moved to be with her family – to the Army Record Office in Dover to ask for 'certain certificates'. She needed the documents because she had applied to send Marjorie, who was barely six, to an orphanage.

Ethel was awarded a pension of 22/11 a week, with effect from 24 September 1917, and the cash returned with Wilfrid's effects amounted to about £9. As she told him in one of her letters, she found it difficult to keep on the 'right side of the ledger' and perhaps putting her oldest daughter in an orphanage seemed like a sensible solution. So many wives lost their husbands that she may have felt it wiser to apply for a place for Marjorie as soon as possible; she may even have discussed the possibility before her husband left for France.

Although Ethel referred to it as such, the boarding school Marjorie was sent to was not an orphanage in the traditional sense of the word. Children who attended the school, and others like it, were funded by the Bank Clerks' Orphanage, a fund set up in 1883 to give educational grants to families whose fathers had died or who could not work through illness or injury. It was funded through subscriptions from bank workers, donations from banks and fundraising activities such as staff sports days. The First World War placed a terrible strain on the fund: there were more children who needed its help at a time when fewer bank clerks were paying into it because they had joined the army. In the final two years of the war contributing banks agreed to double their donations. However, the increase in the cost of education put further pressure on the fund and demand for places remained high throughout the 1920s. Each year payments were made to around 80 pupils, and children whose fathers had died of illnesses related to the war were admitted as late as 1929. Students left the scheme when they started work or turned seventeen.

In the same year that Marjorie went off to Bray Court, Maidenhead, four-year-old Anthony Buckeridge's father Ernest, a private in the Honourable Artillery Company, was killed in France, half an hour after arriving at the front line. His mother, Gertrude Alice, took a job as a bank clerk and, at the age of seven, Anthony won a scholarship from the Bank Clerks' Orphanage to attend Seaford College boarding school in Sussex. When he left school he worked, as was the custom, for his father's bank and eventually found himself in the same department in which his father had been employed. However, he did not enjoy banking and ended up as a teacher and, finally, the author of the 'Jennings' books about life in a boarding school.

Ethel may have thought that sending Marjorie to boarding school offered an ideal opportunity and one that took some strain off a widow with two young children, but Marjorie's letters to her mother in that first term of September 1917 are painful to read. She tells her that she shares a room with five other girls and that one has hair just like hers. She has lent one of the girls a painting book and tells her mother that Dolly did not wake up once in the night. Her mother sends her a beautiful dinner set, and a pretty little coat and bonnet for her doll. The letters also reveal a touching solicitude for her mother:

> Have you had any visitors at home lately, if you have I hope not very many because you know how dear the things are. Have you had any trouble to get sugar? I hope not, you did not before I

> came here, did you love and kisses from your loving child, Marjorie.

Letters from absent fathers had helped families to maintain some semblance of normality, often featuring a surprising frankness from both sides about what husband and wife was going through. When the letters stopped, their absence contributed to the heaviness that descended on the home.

10

The Damaged Husband

The flickering black and white film cuts from a French suburban street to a bustling, well-lit room on an upper floor of a house in Paris's leafy Latin Quarter. Each of the three soldiers inside the room demands the full attention of the person looking after them. The room has the brisk, business-like air of a quartermaster's office, where men are fitted for their uniform, but these are obviously not raw recruits. The walls are adorned with the French, American and British flags and vases of fresh flowers are dotted around. These homely touches, however, fail to cancel out the ranks of human faces, deathly white, each with a different expression, mounted on the walls like rows of stags. In each mask the eyes are closed; some have moustaches. In the higher tiers the faces are terribly disfigured: whole jaws have been gouged out, noses erased and mouths reduced to caverns. On the next row down, the features have been restored and the faces are serene. Fragments of face, each with a perfect skin tone, lean against the wall on a table below: a nose with glasses perched on the bridge; a strong jaw with a bristling moustache; a nose, moustache and one eye gazing at another nose.

The camera zooms in on one of the soldiers so that it is possible to see his two medals and the fact that he is casually lighting a cigarette. The matronly woman in her heavy Red Cross uniform with large pockets and epaulettes starts to fuss round his nape, turning him gently by the shoulders, as if she is about to give his hair a trim. They both smile momentarily and conspiratorially as he unhooks something from his right, and then left, ear and hands it to her; suddenly the whole of his lower jaw disappears to reveal puckered scar tissue. He looks vulnerable and embarrassed, somehow younger. She turns to a person out of shot, smiling and perhaps seeking approval, then helps him to reapply the prosthesis, fusses with the hooks over his ears and holds him by both shoulders, studying him like a tailor fitting a new jacket.

The camera switches to another woman who is dressed in a white, high-necked blouse with a ribbon keeping her hair, which is swept up above her head where it sits in an untamed cloud, out of her eyes. She is painting an object she holds in her left hand; as she studies it, she turns it constantly until it is possible to make out the shape of the lower part of a face: the left cheek, half a mouth and part of a nose. She puts it down and picks up an entire face, its eyes closed, lips parted, in a death mask. Then she has a face in each hand: one smooth and perfect, the other an imprint of flesh ripped apart and dragged down, reminiscent of Charles Laughton's Quasimodo.

In the next scene a young woman in the same dark Red Cross uniform, nipped in at the waist, helps a bearded male artist in a white smock. This cheerful version of Van Gogh works away with a potter's smoothing tool at sections of more death masks that he hands to her to form into one face.

The female painter is studying a wire contraption with an ear suspended from it; carefully she lays several over a large *marmite* or earthenware pot, as if to dry. Then she starts to add colour to a man's face, applying it from a palette and smiling as she tickles the flesh between nose and moustache. 'Van Gogh' is fitting glasses to another young soldier who has one eye, no nose, only the suggestion of lips and a crumpled jaw. Every time the artist removes the man's spectacles his nose disappears – now you see it, now you don't.

It is hard to pin down the atmosphere of the room. It has the intense creativity of an artist's studio and yet the rows of masks provide a torture chamber backdrop. But, then again, both artist and subject smile and smoke. It is as if actors from a horror movie are waiting to have their prosthetic make-up applied – except that in this instance the process will work in reverse: all the artists' efforts are focused on making their subjects look as little like monsters as possible.

The smoking, the flowers and the patriotic posters were all designed to create an informal atmosphere. Anna Coleman Ladd (1878–1939), who looks rather matronly in the film but who, in reality was barely forty, liked to drink cocoa and tea while she chatted with the 'brave faceless ones', as she called the soldiers who came to the American Red Cross Studio of Portrait Masks she founded at the end of 1917 and which she ran with four assistants. Faces were important to Ladd, from a practical, aesthetic and spiritual perspective. She was a trained neo-classical sculptor, whose work before the war concentrated on dancing sprites and mischievous nymphs. Born in the genteel Bryn Mawr area of Pennsylvania, she was educated in Rome and Paris before settling in Boston with her paediatrician husband, Maynard. Ladd might have been content to concentrate on nymphs if Maynard had not been appointed to the Children's Bureau of the American Red Cross in Toul. At about the same time, she heard of the work of the British sculptor Francis Derwent Wood (1871–1926).

Wood was a well-established artist and sculptor, who had exhibited at the Royal Academy in London and in Paris. During the Great War he joined the Royal Army Medical Corps (RAMC) as an orderly, together with other members of the Chelsea Art Club, and worked at the 3rd General Hospital in Wandsworth, London. He was soon given the task of helping disfigured patients in a part of the hospital the soldiers referred to as the 'Tin Noses Shop'. In an article he wrote for the *Lancet*, 23 June 1917, he explained how his work began after the surgeon had done as much as possible to heal the wounds, support the fleshy tissue and cover other areas through skin-grafting: 'I endeavour by means of the skill I happen to possess as a sculptor to make a man's face as near as possible to what it looked like before he was wounded.' He dealt with 'extreme' cases that the plastic surgeon had had to abandon but the results were the same: 'The patient acquires his old self-respect, self-assurance, self-reliance, and, discarding his induced despondency, takes once more a pride in his personal appearance. His presence is no longer a source of melancholy to himself nor of sadness to his relatives and friends.'

Wood believed there were cases that only the hands of a sculpture could help because such hands were 'trained to serve both plastic and sculptural manipulations, or a process combined of both'. He employed three other sculptors, a casting specialist and a plaster mould-maker. The team began by making a cast of the patient's face out of plaster of Paris – an ordeal that was suffocating and may have taken a few patients back to the trenches they had survived. Any wound cavities were filled with dressing or cotton wool. Further casts followed and a photo taken before the injury, or simply observation of the sitter, helped to create a true likeness. For Ladd, who followed most of Wood's techniques, 'psychological insight' was just as important as a photo in recreating the pre-battle face. A final plate was made from thin copper one thirty-second of an inch thick – or, as a lady visitor to Ladd's studio described it, 'the thinness of a visiting card'. It weighed between four and nine ounces and was attached via spectacles, spirit gum or ribbons. Oil paint chipped, but a thin coating of cream-coloured spirit enamel came close to flesh colour and could be blended with the skin's tone and contours. The colour had to be renewed over time as scar tissue changed the contours of the face. Wood painted the eyebrows to match and made lashes from thin metallic foil, soldered to the plate and tinted. Ladd often used real hair for eyebrows, eyelashes and moustaches. Glass eyes could be incorporated, but occasionally Wood painted the eye on by hand.

It took about a month of careful work to produce one mask and by the end of 1919 Ladd's studio had made 185 for mainly French and American veterans. Wood's team probably created a larger number before the department closed in 1919; Ladd's studio lasted a year longer. Correspondence from grateful patients shows how the mask gave their wearers a chance to re-enter the world and to start to rebuild marriages; they may never have looked 'normal', but they 'passed'. One disfigured man had not been home for two-and-a-half years because he did not want his mother to see his dreadful injuries. Ladd wrote that the letters she received from soldiers and their families were so full of gratitude that they 'hurt' – 'Thanks to you I will have a home . . . The woman I love no longer finds me repulsive, as she had a right to do . . . She will be my wife.' Another sent good wishes from his wife and two children: 'Please accept from a poor disabled Frenchman and from his little family our best and most sincere regards and warmest greetings.' In his memoir of Paris in the 1920s, *A Moveable Feast*, Ernest Hemingway describes seeing the disfigured victims of the Great War in the café, the Closerie des Lilas. He admired the skill with which their faces had been repaired, 'There was always an almost iridescent shiny cast about the considerably reconstructed faces, rather like that of a well packed ski run . . .'

Although the skill of both Ladd and Wood is remarkable, particularly in the days before 3D computer modelling and versatile materials such as silicone and acrylic, there is no record of the long-term effects of the mask on its wearer and his family. While it is true that they hid some of the most gruesome wounds, they were still unnerving to the uninitiated and suggestive of something sinister lurking below the surface. This effect must have worsened with time as the paint began to fade and the mask itself became damaged or rusty. The ex-soldier was trapped with an unchanging, immovable expression and, because it was not part of his anatomy, failed to address disabilities such as the inability to swallow or chew; it might also distort his voice.

Ladd and Wood used their skill as sculptors to try to ease the path of injured soldiers back into society and into a marriage that had been fundamentally changed; the work of two other artists – Henry Tonks and his student at Slade School of Art, Kathleen Scott – also acted as a bridge between the worlds of art and science. These four artists and many of the pioneering surgeons they worked with came from unusual or mixed backgrounds and did not fit neatly into the social norms of the time. They were foreign, of mixed race, Jewish, or female. Like the men, and by implication their wives, whom they tried to help, 'the problem of "passing" was and remained a central figure in their psychic lives.' Scott, whose husband, Robert, had died just two years before the outbreak of war on the ill-fated expedition to the South Pole, was a widow but one who was still only in her early thirties and still hungry for fresh experiences. She had thrown herself into war work, helping to raise money and to organise the transportation of cars and ambulances to France and setting up a hospital in a French chateau. At first, she gave up her sculpture and found a position making coils in the Vickers factory. Here the young women she worked with fell under her exotic spell and she took forty of them in a charabanc to see a production of *Peter Pan* written by her friend, J.M. Barrie. She was also friends with the Prime Minister, Herbert Asquith, who came to her for advice and sympathy and whose son was killed in 1916. Kathleen did not believe in female suffrage – she felt more influence lay in persuading husbands of the right course of action.

She was pursued by various officers who had survived the trenches – often with terrible injuries. Her biographer, and granddaughter, the novelist Louisa Young, said she always had a 'weakness for wounded heroes' such as Clifford Erskine Bolst, a captain in the Black Watch, whom Kathleen described as 'rather a bounder but so full of life in spite of having been burned alive, wounded and gassed'. He wanted an affair, but she took him instead to the zoo with her small son, Peter. The dashing, New Zealand champion swimmer Bernard 'Tiny' Freyburg also pursued her. Freyburg arrived in England to enlist after hearing about the war when he was in Mexico, reportedly fighting in its civil war. He quickly notched up a string of honours. Early in the Gallipoli campaign he won a Distinguished Service Order (DSO) for swimming ashore and lighting flares to distract attention from the main landing. By the end of the war he had added two bars to his DSO, won the Victoria Cross through 'splendid personal gallantry', and become a Companion to the Most Distinguished Order of Saint Michael and Saint George (CMG). He was mentioned in dispatches on several occasions and wounded nine times. When he took Kathleen out in 1917, she remarked: 'five wound bars: a great gash on his neck, one arm stiff, another both bones broken, a gashed tummy and a bullet through both legs – what about that for sentimental blackmail!' He made some 'delicious suggestions', with which she 'longed to comply', but did not.

But by 1918 she was feeling drained and despondent, and suffering from headaches and fatigue. She found her salvation at the Sir John Ellerman Hospital for Disabled Officers at St John's Lodge, Regent's Park. The cream wedding cake building, which was built in 1818, stands to the North of the Inner Circle and was surrounded by tranquil gardens. The Treasury and Office of Woods and Forests lent the site to the British Red Cross Society to use as a hospital for fifty or so officers and the shipping magnate, Sir John Ellerman, agreed to fund it for an initial period of one year.

Kathleen's role was to create casts of men's faces, which the surgeons could then use, together with photos of the patient before his injury, to rebuild the visage without the need to experiment on the actual man himself. Tonks, her professor at the Slade, who had practised as a surgeon before becoming an artist, led the way in keeping records of these cases using diagrams and pastel portraits of men treated by Harold Delf Gillies and other surgeons at the Cambridge Military Hospital in Aldershot and later, Queen Mary's Hospital, Sidcup, in Kent. An amateur artist himself, Gillies needed someone to record the progress of a wound and its treatment. Kathleen's new role meant she had to model the patients whose faces were much more disfigured than any other ex-servicemen she had encountered. In October she wrote in her diary: 'At the hospital I worked on the man with no mouth – rather bad. They asked me if I could stand it, and I replied confidently that I could, and I did, but I was very unwell when the tension was over. That is what happens to me in emotion. I am very sick, I never cry. Why am I not made like other people in this? It's most annoying . . .' A fortnight later, she had to model a chin and wrote in her diary: 'I feel terribly like God, the creator. The surgeon said with a smile, "Don't make it too long, or we shan't have enough to cover it." Sad! It's a fantastic world.'

Often she could allow her artistic sensibilities to take over from the natural horror of what she saw. 'These men without noses are very beautiful, like antique marbles,' she wrote in November 1918, and described how she became so engrossed in a 'magnificent head' of Captain Budd that she forgot about lunch. She found it harder, however, to distract herself during an operation to remove scar tissue – 'The anaesthetic and heat were rather overpowering but I stuck it out and it was very beautiful to watch.'

Harold Delf Gillies, often referred to as the 'father of plastic surgery', went some way towards providing an alternative to hiding behind an artificial mask. Such is his fame in the medical world that there was a point, not so long ago, when nurses of a certain age would ask if I were related to him (I am not). Gillies was born in New Zealand in 1882, the great-nephew of Edward Lear, author of *The Book of Nonsense*. This familial connection may explain Gillies's love of practical jokes – he had a toilet roll holder fitted in the gents at St Andrew's golf club which surprised users by playing a tune every time a customer extracted a sheet; he also made a golf ball out of plaster of Paris that covered the player with a white cloud when it was hit. Or it may be that he simply shared the sense of humour so often associated with doctors, and surgeons in particular. He studied at Cambridge University, where he played golf and rowed for the university. On graduation he moved to St Bartholomew's Hospital and eventually specialised in otorhinolaryngology, more commonly known as Ear, Nose and Throat.

In 1915, he joined the RAMC and served in France, where he was impressed by the reconstructive surgery achieved by French and German surgeons. He took what he had learnt back to England, where he set up a facial ward at the Cambridge Military Hospital in Aldershot. To ensure suitable soldiers were sent to him, he bought £10 worth of labels from a local bookshop and had 'Faciomaxillary injury – Cambridge Hospital, Aldershot' printed on them. The labels were dispatched to field hospitals in France to be pinned to the chests of those suffering from jaw or facial wounds. The first naval casualties arrived in January 1916. After the Battle of the Somme staff expected to receive 200 casualties – 2,000 arrived. In 1918 the unit moved to Queen Mary's Hospital, Sidcup, where the team treated 5,000 soldiers and was eventually administered by the Ministry of Pensions, to which Gillies became honorary consultant.

Terrible, life-changing facial injuries were one of the 'innovations' of the First World War. They were the result of the method of fighting, mainly in trenches that protected the body more than the head; the technological advances of machine guns, hand grenades and high-calibre artillery, which elevated killing to an industrial level; and improvements in medical care which meant that, although millions died, thousands still had a chance of survival – albeit with deep physical and psychological scars. Soldiers did not always appreciate the dangers of popping their heads above the trenches. Perhaps this was because so many were volunteers, or because they

Left: Rebecca Gillies was the first of three generations of army wives. She met her husband Donald when he was serving in the 1st Dunbartonshire Rifle Volunteer Corps.
Author's private collection

Above: 'The Girl I Left Behind Me' by Eastman Johnson (*c.*1872). A young bride looks longingly after her departing soldier. Her cloak's red lining hints at their passion and her wedding ring suggests fidelity. © Archives of American Art, Smithsonian Institution

Above: Elizabeth Evans with Chelsea Pensioners of the King's Own Royal Regiment (*c.*1912). She accompanied her husband to the Crimean War and was later allowed to wear his medals.

Right: Fanny Duberly with her beloved horse, 'Bob' in Crimea. The photo was taken by Roger Fenton in 1855 and became popular among the soldiers.

Above: 'News from Home' by John Millais (1856–7). Art critic John Ruskin questioned the likelihood of a soldier wearing such elaborate dress while reading a letter at the front during the Crimean War. PD-UK

Above: In 'Home' (*c.* 1855–6), the artist, John Noel Paton places the courageous soldier at the very centre of his adoring family. PD-UK

Above: Robert and Harriet Tytler endured what she described as the 'Great Sepoy Mutiny'. Harriet gave birth to a son in a bullock cart during the siege of Delhi. PD-UK

Above: Lieutenant Simon Fraser Hannay of the 50th Regiment Native Infantry spent his entire career in India supported by his wife, Margaret. Courtesy of the 6th Gurkha Rifles Regimental Trustees

Above: Colonel John Inglis, Julia Inglis and two of their three children after the siege of Lucknow. PD-UK

Above: The Residency, Lucknow, pictured before the siege in 1857. © Dinodia Photos / Alamy Stock Photo

Above: The Residency was reduced to ruins after the siege of Lucknow.
© The British Library Board

Above: In 'Highland Jessie', attributed to Frederick Goodall (*c.*1858), a Scottish corporal's wife tries to convince those around her that she can hear the sound of bagpipes, indicating that they are about to be rescued. © National Army Museum

Below: 'Calling the Roll after an Engagement (The Roll Call), Crimea' showed the ordinary soldier in a desperate state and – most unusually – was painted by a woman.

Royal Collection Trust / © Her Majesty Queen Elizabeth II 2016

Right: The artist Elizabeth Thompson (later Butler) became a celebrity after her painting, 'The Roll Call' toured England.
© Mary Evans Picture Library/Alamy Stock Photo

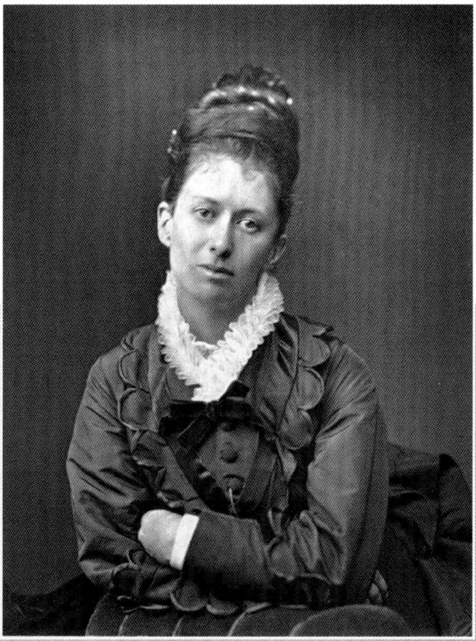

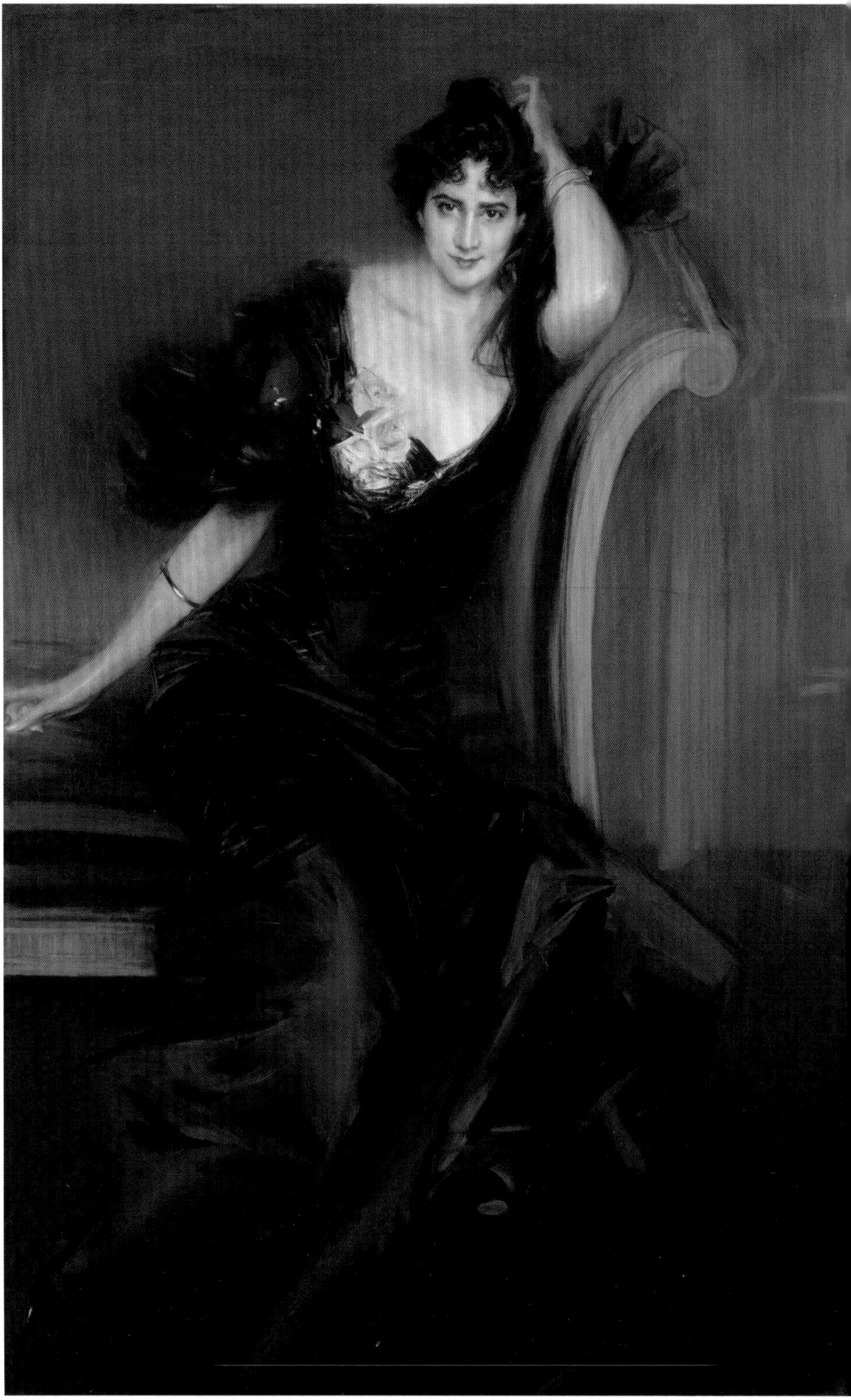

Opposite: Boldini's portrait of Gertrude, Lady Colin Campbell (née Blood), treated the rules of anatomy with 'magnificent contempt'. *The Times* devoted 599 lines to her divorce case. © National Portrait Gallery, London

Right: The faces of fallen soldiers appear to have joined the ranks of mourners on Armistice Day, 1922, in this photo developed by cleaning lady and medium Ada Deane. PD-UK

Above: Clare Sheridan communed with her dead husband through a medium but broke contact with him after a falling out over the family's plans to move abroad. © *National Portrait Gallery, London*

Above: Gunner Wilfrid Cove wrote regularly from the trenches to his wife, Ethel and their two daughters Marjorie (left) and Betty. PD-UK

Above: William Michael Spreckley (standing, right) behind wife Eileen with Michael Gillies Spreckley on her knee, 1922. The family photo was taken just five years after his surgery. Courtesy of the Estate of William Michael Spreckley

Above: William Michael Spreckley underwent revolutionary surgery to replace the nose a sniper removed in 1917. In later life his face showed few signs of the gruelling treatment. Courtesy of the Estate of William Michael Spreckley

Above: In Anna Coleman Ladd's studio in Paris artists created life-like masks to hide the terrible facial injuries of trench warfare.

© Archives of American Art, Smithsonian Institution

O DRY THOSE TEARS (2).
O lift thine eyes to the blue skies,
See how the clouds do borrow
Brightness, each one, straight from the sun;
So is it ever with sorrow.
'Twill come, alas! but soon 'twill pass,
Clouds will be sunshine to-morrow.
Then lift thine eyes to the blue skies,
Clouds will be sunshine to-morrow.
O dry those tears, life is not made for sorrow.
BAMFORTH (COPYRIGHT).
WORDS BY PERMISSION OF CHAPPELL & CO., LTD., LONDON.

O DRY THOSE TEARS (1).
O dry those tears, and calm those fears,
Life is not made for sorrow
'Twill come, alas! but soon 'twill pass,
Clouds will be sunshine to-morrow.
'Twill come, alas! but soon 'twill pass,
Clouds will be sunshine to-morrow.
BAMFORTH (COPYRIGHT).
WORDS BY PERMISSION OF CHAPPELL & CO., LTD., LONDON.

Right above and below: Wives and girlfriends kept in touch with their loved ones through letters and postcards which were often passed around family and friends.

Author's private collection

Above left: Higher levels of education among all classes increased communication between husband and wife during the Great War. Author's private collection

Above right: Diana Carnegie's photo in the society magazine, the *Tatler*, just before her marriage to James in 1939, hints at her mischievous nature. © Illustrated London News Ltd/Mary Evans

Right: James Carnegie faced long months of separation from his wife Diana and their daughter Susan, born in 1943. © Carnegie Estate

Opposite: Diana's letters to her husband, James, throughout the Second World War, are both flirtatious and full of domestic detail. © Carnegie Estate

like this —!

The enclosed I leave for you to deal with. Lady W.'s letter would you like to answer & <u>then return to me</u> & I will answer later!

Letters from Nancy— mentioning of course that her husband had been away for 3 wks with the Sec. of State & the Monarch! Producing in Nov.

Was it in *your* camp that the Ats were overheard— I hope not?

Don't think a certain amount of travel could poss. hurt Susan as, the water wld really be the only thing

Left: Mass Observation diarist, Rachel Dhonau, hoarded luxuries to help her look her best when her husband returned on leave. PD-UK

Above: Renee was so proud of Tom Boardman's promotion that she persuaded him to wear his uniform when they married on 19 August 1940. Courtesy of the Boardman family

Above: While a Prisoner of War in the Far East, Tom Boardman made a ukulele out of wire and Red Cross packing. He was photographed playing it on the ship home. © Handout/Getty Images

Above: British Army wives rifle through articles of clothing for sale in the NAAFI Families' Shop during the Soviet blockade of Berlin, 1949. © IWM (BER 49-118-004)

Left: US Major Terri Gurrola embraces her daughter Gaby on her return from a tour of Iraq, 2007. Army wives are no longer always the partner waiting at home. © Louie Favorite/AP/Press Association Images

were slow to realise that they faced a much more sophisticated killing and maiming machine. At the same time, doctors were becoming better at treating injured men at the front and their skill ensured that more survived.

The Royal Army Medical College at Millbank, which was founded in 1903, helped to improve the training of army doctors. The Boer War, too, had offered valuable lessons – albeit in dry, warm, sandy conditions that provided no preparation for the cold, wet mud of the trenches. Advances in medicine and hygiene meant that illness killed far fewer soldiers at the front than in other conflicts, such as the American Civil War. The relentless fighting also gave doctors and orderlies the chance to practise innovations. Saline drips reduced the effects of shock; blood transfusions – which were revolutionary at the start of the war – appeared in clearing stations in 1917 and then advanced dressing stations in 1918; and doctors became much more adept at treating and avoiding gas-gangrene caused by injury in the manure-rich killing fields where tetanus was rife. Surgeons became better at saving men with awful stomach wounds and the simple innovation of the now commonplace Thomas splint brought death by fracture of the femur down from 60 to 30 per cent.

For some soldiers, the fear of facial injury was as great as the fear of death. The face represented so much more than simply a physical wound. Major Francis Gull of the 13th Rifle Brigade wrote, 'Only one thing do I dread, that is disfigurement – real disfigurement, it would be too awful for my girl.' He was killed a month later. There was a clear distinction between different types of maiming. More than 41,000 British soldiers lost a leg in the First World War; of these, 69 per cent had one leg, 28 per cent lost one arm and nearly 3 per cent lost both legs or arms. But amputation was easier to hide, earlier photos of veterans from the Crimean War show that this was not viewed as necessary and such a disability was not regarded as repugnant. During and after the First World War, it became common throughout England to see men with an amputated limb. Disfigurement of the face was viewed as much more emasculating for the victim and horrific for the viewer. Gillies reported that the children of one veteran fled from their father's robotic face and the Government recognised the stigma of disfigurement in a more practical way – by awarding a full pension to a soldier with 'very severe facial disfigurement'. In terms of a pension, disfigurement was deemed equal to the loss of two or more limbs, total loss of sight or lunacy. But in other, subtler ways, disfigurement was seen as *greater* than the loss of sight. Gillies made this clear when he commented that a soldier who was given a prosthetic nose and dark glasses to conceal his terrible disfigurement had become 'presentable enough to be a blind man'. Those who had lost their sight were generally seen as more cheerful; the 'merriest banter' in a war hospital was to be found in the ward for the blind, according to one orderly. When Kathleen Scott was introduced to blind officers at a dance club she described the visit as, 'a most extraordinary experience. All pity vanishes in a wonderment of admiration. They were amazing dancers.'

Likewise, press reports of men recovering from amputation portray the vigour with which they engage in pastimes on the road to recovery. They run on their new limbs, ride bikes, play cricket and football, chop wood and play one-armed golf. They are so in tune with their new identity that they are even employed making new prosthetic legs for injured soldiers. As Suzannah Biernoff comments: 'Physical agility and manliness are re-inscribed into the prosthetically remade body'. And, although they still suffered prejudice such as the widely held belief that disabled ex-servicemen would produce similarly deformed children, their masculinity was less bound up with their injuries.

The 'Surplus Women' problem of the post-war years, when the war siphoned off much of the pool of eligible bachelors, offered some hope for injured servicemen. The *Matrimonial Times*, a magazine founded in 1904, provided help for single men and women looking for lasting partnerships. Many of the females who placed adverts were not shy about their openness to form a relationship with an injured soldier, if all other criteria were suitable. Among the adverts the term 'war widow' became as distinct a category as 'spinster' or 'young lady' and usually appeared at least once on every page. There was also demand for officers. Although the adverts from women frequently specified the willingness to accept a disabled soldier, usually an officer, the male counterparts did not mention any disability.

> INDEPENDENT SPINSTER, 5ft 7 ins, 24 years of age, very good looking, good figure and fair hair, would like to marry an officer who has been wounded in the war.

By comparison, adverts from men often went into great detail about what they expected from a prospective mate.

> I AM A LONELY SERGEANT (waiting for my commission), but still serving with the E.E.F., 26, good-looking, well educated, dark hazel eyes, 5ft. 6 ins., steady, little money, would like to correspond with affectionate and lovable Young Lady (spinster or widow), dark preferred, Church of England, but do not want to marry for money, feels very lonely.

> LIEUTENANT, 25, (bachelor), considered good-looking, fresh complexion, good teeth, med. fair, blue-grey eyes, med. height and weight; of Scottish birth and education; smoker, temperate habits; can ride, shoot, swim, cycle, play tennis, cricket, billiards; loves horses and dogs; fond of outdoor life (Scoutmaster) and sea; dances (anything) and loves music; broadminded; Presbyterian – has the 'play cricket' outlook on life; loves and knows children very well; amiable disposition; eldest of family, brother killed in action, parents simply 'gems,' though almost pennyless [sic], have

> lots of faults, I suppose, but believe give and take spirit is the essence of happiness; ambitious – has office position to return to in Canada (in glorious, dry, bracing climate); Army income £260 – no other means (never had capital nor incentive – never dreamed of marriage and was rather unlucky, and too home-sick, though loved Canada, to save); wants to meet a good-looking and good-natured, sensible, well-educated Girl, with a good, clear eye and good carriage – one who could take any position in society, not older than self.

Gillies and his team performed more than 11,000 operations on around 5,000 servicemen at the hospital at Sidcup between 1917 and 1925. As antibiotics had yet to be invented, it was difficult to graft skin from one part of the body to another without infection taking hold. Gillies built on earlier Russian research to perfect the concept of the 'tubed pedicle' that could be used to transfer healthy skin from one part of the body to the site of an injury – usually in the face. A flap of skin from the chest or forehead remained attached to the original blood supply, while the other end was swung into position where needed. This 'bridge' offered two big advantages. The original blood supply was preserved, and the connecting flap was stitched into a tube shape, the skin facing out, so that the inner exposed flesh was protected from infection. Eventually, once the graft had 'taken', the flap could be detached from the 'donor' site and remodelled. The tubed pedicle, which has been compared to a suitcase handle, could remain in place for weeks without the risk of infection.

William Michael Spreckley, a 23-year-old second lieutenant in the Sherwood Forresters, was one of Gillies's most successful cases. Michael, as he was known to his wife and friends, was on a year-long visit to Germany, when war broke out. He was staying near Dresden as part of an apprenticeship in the lace-making industry because Germany was more technically advanced than Britain and he wanted to bring home expertise for his family business in Nottingham. His return was hampered by the fact that he spoke such good German that the authorities believed he was fleeing recruitment.

He was admitted to hospital in January 1917 after his nose was shot off by a sniper; he also had a foot injury that meant he walked with a stick. Gillies took a section of rib cartilage and implanted it in his forehead, where it stayed for the next six months until it was teased down into the centre of his face to become his nose. This was not instantly seen as a success. Gillies wrote later: 'When the huge, oedematous forehead flap was slowly lowered over the pyriform opening, the new bloated columella stuck ahead like an anteater's snout and all my colleagues roared with laughter.' The surgeon removed excess tissue at the top and, gradually, a new nose emerged. The process took three years and Michael was finally discharged in October 1920.

A photo of Michael in his sixties shows a face that is certainly rugged but, to an outsider, offers no clue that his nose had started life in a different part of his body. He was still wearing bandages when he met his future wife, Eileen Nora Donoghue (sometimes written O'Donoghue), a draughtsman's assistant in the Nottingham lace trade, and they married a few months after his discharge, in January 1921. The first of eight children was born that August and named Michael Gillies Spreckley. His father was open about his experience in the war and his family still has a photo album of his time at Sidcup, part of the pictorial record he was given of his operations and the progressive transformation of his face. Michael returned to help run the family lace-making business, but it went into liquidation in 1931, partly due to a fall in the popularity of lace. Like many ex-servicemen who struggled during the post-war Depression, he took to the road and became a travelling salesman. A young brother who had also fought suffered from shell shock. Michael's financial situation was not helped by a propensity for gambling, a habit he picked up in hospital – perhaps as a way of whiling away the hours of boredom. He enlisted at the start of the

Second World War, although he was assigned to barracks after his arrival in the Middle East because the strong sun and sand affected his wound. The plastic surgery also meant that the inside of his nose did not offer a natural filtering mechanism and he suffered severe rhinitis. Later on, he was put in charge of a group of German Prisoners of War in England and then spent four years as part of the post-war peace-keeping force at the British Army headquarters in the Hotel Sacher, Vienna, a rare point of grandeur in a devastated city and the background for Graham Greene's *The Third Man*, which was being filmed at the time. Michael's granddaughter, Ally White, believes the injury distorted the way he felt about himself and even in Vienna he said that women hid from the sight of him. He retired from the army aged fifty-seven in 1950 and died from cancer of the oesophagus when he was eighty. Eileen lived on until 1968, and benefited from one of the first plastic aortas.

Gillies and his patients had a close relationship, perhaps to the detriment of their family life, which was often fragmented due to the need to spend months in a hospital and, often, from a reluctance to show their face in the outside world. And yet the surgeon credited the patients with some comic banter. In one story he recounts how a private who had lost much of his face was caught peering into a mirror (an object normally banned in the wards) with obvious amusement at his inability to grow a beard. When asked what he found so funny he told the medical officer, 'phwat an aisy toime the barber would have in future.' This, Gillies added, was 'characteristic of the cheerful resignation of faces cases in general.'

Another soldier who had his jaw blown away found it incredible that privates and officers received the same care and that Gillies dressed the wounds himself. He told Gillies's biographer, Reginald Pound: 'Today, instead of being hideously deformed, my features are almost normal and I am happily married. I owe much of my happiness to him.' Patients kept in touch with their surgeon for years, often for the rest of their lives. One even became Gillies's tailor.

Gillies noticed that:

> if we made a poor repair for a wretched fellow the man's character was inclined to change for the worse. He would be morose, break rules and give trouble generally. Conversely, if we made a good repair, the patient usually became a happy convalescent and soon regained his old character and habits. This seems but to emphasise again the powerful influence that our physical appearance wields over our character. For instance, if my bald head suddenly flourished with a crop of curly red locks and my receding chin became thick and square, imagine how pleasant my personality would become. This might be offered here as an excuse to all those nice people to whom I have been so rude.

Nurse Catherine Black, who worked with Gillies at Aldershot, had, perhaps, a more realistic appreciation of the effect of their injuries. She described how the ward was largely silent as only one in ten patients could mumble a few words: 'Hardest of all was the task of trying to rekindle the desire to live in men condemned to lie week after week smothered in bandages, unable to talk, unable to taste, unable even to sleep, and all the while knowing themselves to be appallingly disfigured.'

She remembered the case of a corporal who arrived with the mud of the trenches still sticking to his clothes. The photo of him as a young man that he showed her revealed a handsome figure. Soon Black heard of Molly, who wrote to him nearly every post; the letters were full of plans for when she would be able to come and see him. He kept putting her off and did not want her to visit until some of the 'beastly bandages' had been removed for they would 'scare her to death to see me lying here looking like a mummy.' On the day they were taken off, his mother visited and turned ashen. Nurse Black was worried she might faint 'but not the slightest expression of face or voice betrayed her . . .' Later, she found the Corporal using the shaving glass in his locker. She pretended not to see it when he called her over to put the screens round his bed. 'Every nurse learns that there are moments when it is better to leave a patient alone, because sympathy would only make matters worse. I think he must have fought out his battle in the night, for early next morning he asked for pen and paper and wrote a letter to Molly.' When Black suggested he was well enough to see her, he replied: '"She will never come now," . . . and there was the finality of despair in his voice.'

11

The Changed Husband

Some of the symptoms of what became known in the First World War as 'shell shock' had been recognised hundreds of years earlier. When Swiss mercenaries in the seventeenth century complained of extreme physical tiredness, found it difficult to concentrate and lost their appetite, doctors diagnosed them as suffering from 'nostalgia' – a longing for home. In the First World War that longing, usually of an idealised home, provided an emotional crutch for soldiers at the front. The reality rarely matched the imaginings – either because the man had changed too much, or his wife and country failed to meet his expectations.

In his memoir *Goodbye to All That*, the poet Robert Graves remembers moving to Harlech with his wife and young daughter. He discarded the army uniform he had worn for the past four-and-a-half years and rifled through his trunk to see if he had any suitable civilian clothes. His one suit – other than a school uniform – no longer fitted and he realised that, having gone straight from school to the army, he was 'still mentally and nervously organized for war'.

> Shells used to come bursting on my bed at midnight, even though Nancy shared it with me; strangers in daytime would assume the faces of friends who had been killed. When strong enough to climb the hill behind Harlech and revisit my favourite country,

> I could not help seeing it as a prospective battlefield. I would find myself working out tactical problems, planning how best to hold the Upper Artro valley against an attack from the sea, or where to place a Lewis-gun if I were trying to rush Dolwreiddiog Farm from the brow of the hill, and what would be the best cover for my rifle-grenade section.

Graves still had the army habit of commandeering anything that did not seem to be obviously owned by someone else and of lying his way out of a corner. He approached problems as if he were assessing billets or trenches and progressed through a mental checklist: food, water supply, possible hazards, communications, sanitation, weather, fuel, light. Still a soldier at heart, he had a soldier's habits: he stopped cars for lifts, chatted without embarrassment to fellow train passengers and felt no qualms about relieving himself by the roadside – no matter who else was about.

Returning soldiers faced the twin difficulties of adjusting to domestic life and of finding a job, a task that grew more difficult as the Depression dug its heels in. Pilots who had survived the aerial dogfights of the First World War took to the skies again to offer 'five-bob flips' at fairs and flying circuses around the country. They joined the army of tramps who trudged Britain looking for work. Poet and novelist Laurie Lee encountered this band of vagrants in 1934 on his way from his home in the Cotswolds via Sussex to London – 'They were like a broken army walking away from a war, cheeks sunken, eyes dead with fatigue'. In *Down and Out in Paris and London* (1933), George Orwell recorded having problems sleeping in a Salvation Army shelter because he shared a room with a man who had 'some nervous trouble, shell-shock perhaps' and would cry out 'Pip!' at regular intervals. As Robert Macfarlane says, more recently, in *The Old Ways* (2013): 'Some of the returning soldiers, wounded in body and mind, retreated to the English countryside, hoping that by recovering a sense of belonging rooted in nature and place they might dignify their damaged lives (the wish that it had all been *worth* something).'

My grandfather, Alex Gillies, who had survived the war and the equally deadly flu pandemic, left his young wife in 1923, and their three children, to look for work as a carpenter in America. He took a third-class berth at Greenock, on the west coast of Scotland, knowing that their fourth child was due in December, and sailed for Boston. There is no record of how much money he managed to send home or how long he spent abroad. It must have been a painful separation so soon after the anxious waiting of the war years, but the decision may even have been a form of self-sacrifice – with jobs hard to come by in Dumbarton he was another hungry mouth to feed; by absenting himself, he was at least leaving more for the children.

Robert Thomas Wright, my maternal grandfather, who had married Ada, when he was twenty-three and she was twenty-four, in 1916, first joined the 23rd battalion, County of London (later, just London) Regiment, a prewar territorial battalion based in Camberwell, in 1909. At the time he was a 17-year-old out-of-work tram bus assistant and served as a territorial for seven years until he re-enlisted on the outbreak of war. When he returned to the regiment in 1914 it was as a lance corporal, and he was quickly sent to France. He was wounded in the shoulder in May 1915 and injured severely enough in 1916 that he spent six months convalescing in the Royal Hospital, Chelsea before being discharged, now a corporal, in February 1917, with a weekly pension of 14/6. In a questionnaire he filled in just before his release, he gave his qualifications for employment in civil life as '5 years experience in a warehouse, 9 mts motor driving and 2 mts electric tramway driver'. He hoped to find a job as a warehouse man or munitions worker. His daughter, my mother, remembered him as a distant parent, who suffered from backache and sudden outbursts of temper. She was told that he had been gassed during the war.

Gas was a particularly frightening form of attack that could leave men with life-long respiratory, heart and eye problems. It was a form of attack that the British were ill-prepared for; early protective action included breathing through urine-drenched socks, a pad made from cotton wool stuffed into a sachet of muslin or flannelette, or even sanitary towels supplied by French and Belgian chemists (the loops at either end of the pad which, in normal circumstances, were attached to a sanitary belt could be conveniently hooked over a soldier's ears). After the first use of gas at the Second Battle of Ypres in April 1915, the War Office and the *Daily Mail* mounted a campaign for women to make the pads and the very next day thousands flocked to the Army Clothing Depot in Pimlico with mountains of the sachets. The 'Black Veil Respirator', which made the troops look like female mourners, was more sinister and the smoke helmets that followed slightly more effective. The fear of gas, and watching it attack other soldiers through 'froth-corrupted lungs' as Wilfred Owen expressed it in 'Dulce et Decorum Est', could be as mentally damaging as a physical assault.

Although my grandfather eventually found a job as a private chauffeur, his wandering took the form of infidelity. Their first child, Bob, was born on 23 August 1918 and two daughters followed in quick succession, but the marriage was not a happy one. By the time my parents' wedding photo was taken in 1946, he was estranged from Ada and had at least one child by another woman. In the wedding group his smile appears strained and he is standing slightly in front of his wife, as if he had left her behind. He died a few months later at the age of fifty-four.

The writer Doris Lessing believed that the First World War robbed her parents of their happiness. Her father lost a leg and met his future wife in the Royal Free Hospital, which was then based in London's East End, where she nursed him back to health. Although Emily was a talented and ambitious nurse, the encounter locked them together in what would prove to be a joyless union. The couple moved to Southern Rhodesia, where both continued to be haunted by their memories of the war. Alfred talked about the trenches obsessively, as a way of ridding himself of his memories, whereas his wife suffered in silence from her own hospital nightmares. 'So there was this load of suffering deep inside my mother, as there was inside my father, and please don't tell me that this kind of pain, borne for years, doesn't take its dreadful toll,' Lessing wrote later.

Reunited couples found themselves with a range of experiences that needed sorting and reconciling. Husbands had acquired a new bank of memories, a new set of intimate friendships, perhaps even a new nickname. Wives, in turn, had tasted independence and many, like my Scottish grandmother, who worked in a munitions factory, had discovered different, more masculine jobs; others, from more privileged backgrounds, had felt the satisfaction of voluntary work and the exposure it gave them to women from a variety of homes.

While husbands like Alfred Lessing felt the need to share their experience, just as many men – if not more – found it impossible to impart what they had seen and heard. How could they possibly convey the horrors, the noise and smell of the trenches and how could they explain futuristic weapons like the tank, the hand grenade or the machine gun? Some of these experiences seeped into their vocabulary. As in any large organisation, jargon helped to bind together members of the British Army. But, in addition to army slang, returning soldiers acquired the specific language of the First World War. The very term 'Trench Talk' suggested a new way of living that would be unfathomable to a wife. Terms such as 'barbed wire' (invented in the previous century but rarely seen in Britain); 'duck-boards' (sometimes known as a 'bathmat') to transport the soldier across mud; and 'No Man's Land', all conjured up a mythical landscape. Places were Anglicised and sanitised: Ypres became Wipers; Monchy Breton, Monkey Britain; and Ploegsteert, Plug Street. Other words concealed the true purpose of an object: a 'pip-squeak' for a high-explosive, high-velocity shell fired from a field gun;

a 'toffee apple' for a British mortar that looked like an apple on a stick and a 'flying pig' for a large, unpredictable mortar bomb. Soldiers also brought home a particular form of Franglais: I grew up baffled by my father's frequent reference to Sand Fairy Ann, which he, in turn, must have picked up from his father's version of *Ça ne fait rien*.

One new word which emerged in late 1915, and eventually replaced the Victorian term of 'neurasthenia' – for the public, at least, was 'shell shock'. (It has now been superseded by the modern label of Post-Traumatic Stress Disorder [PSD]). The term 'shell shock' first appeared in print in an article in the *Lancet* by Sir Charles Myers (1873–1946), a Cambridge academic and consultant psychologist to the British Expeditionary Force who worked at Le Touquet. By then, it had already started to appear among soldiers. While other countries recognised shell shock in the First World War, only Britain used a term that was alliterative in a way that suggested the early, and soon dismissed, theory behind it: that tiny particles from the shell had damaged the brain. A 1922 War Office committee acknowledged that mental breakdown associated with war was far more complex than this simple explanation. In France the same malady was referred to as *hystérie de guerre* or *commotion par obus*; Germans used a term that was much closer to neurasthenia: *Kriegneurosen*. The change in terminology was part of a reassessment of mental illness. The *Spectator* had pointed out as early as 1894 that the meaning of the word 'nerve' had undergone a complete about-turn: while once it was used in the singular to denote a steely resolve, it now appeared in the plural and carried the opposite meaning.

The list of physical complaints attributed to shell shock varied widely – from the bulging eyeballs of a private whose look of horror suggested he was condemned to relive forever the original scene that had sparked his illness, to the stumbling gait and convulsions that overtook the whole body. One patient's way of moving was compared to the French tightrope walker Charles Blondin. In the 1930s, the writer Roald Dahl observed the phenomenon in one of his most feared prep school masters, Captain Hardcastle: 'Rumour had it that the constant twitching and jerking and snorting was caused by something called shell-shock, but we were not quite sure what that was. We took it to mean that an explosive object had gone off very close to him with such an enormous bang that it had made him jump high in the air and he hadn't stopped jumping since.'

Other symptoms were only noticeable to the victim's close family members. A soldier who lost his memory after the Battle of Ypres in 1914 was treated in Manchester, where he spoke with a Lancashire accent. After a course of hypnosis his original Wiltshire burr returned. Others were struck dumb, lost their sense of taste or smell or went blind – despite showing no signs of physical injury. The hair on one patient's head stood permanently on end and no amount of water or oil would tame it. In some patients shell shock took the form of a change in personality: a quiet man would become excitable, an honest type turned to crime or a rowdy soldier plunged into shyness. A wife reported that her husband would burst into tears and had started to paint the house in odd colours.

While this behaviour was obviously distressing, there were also instances in which the husband's changed personality put his wife and children in physical danger. One patient was so worried that he would kill his wife and six children that he wandered around the Midlands for a week before giving himself up. The wife of a cotton twirler, who had been invalided out of the army suffering from shell shock, reported that he often burst into tears and had tried to strangle her. Another wife petitioned for her husband to be returned to hospital only weeks after his release because he had threatened to 'thrash' her, kill his doctor and drown himself.

Rebecca West's novel, *The Return of the Soldier* (1918) and Virginia Woolf's *Mrs Dalloway* (1925) both focus on men who are traumatised by war in a way that has devastating effects for their family. In Woolf's novel the soldier is driven to suicide and the newspapers of the time show that this was not an outlandish plot twist. It was generally believed that the civilian, or 'home man', rather than the professional soldier, was ill equipped to cope with war and was more liable to suffer mental distress. This weakness was often given as the reason for the many tragic cases that followed in the war's wake, as, for example, when an ex-soldier jumped from a bridge, killing himself and leaving a wife and four children. In another sad case, in October 1920, a man threw his five-week-old-baby off Blackpool Pier. The inquest stated that he was suffering from shell shock and had come to the seaside resort to try to improve his health.

Private Harry Barrow, who had lost one brother in the war and had three others in hospital, hoped that he would be allowed to follow his trade and become a regimental tailor. But when he was ordered on parade he feared this meant he was about to be sent to the front and hanged himself in the toilets. He had been in the army for only six days. His widow was at first not granted a pension until she testified that he had always been a good father and husband and had worked as a tailor for sixteen years. By June 1917, 1,216 men had been discharged from the army for insanity and given pensions, but many were not granted this financial support and it often took an MP or doctor, or in rarer cases, a wife, to stand up for a man's right to a pension. Some soldiers did not even make it home and were shot for desertion when, in fact, the unbalance of their mind had caused them to wander into No Man's Land or to fail to respond to an order. The numbers of those who were executed in this way remains disputed, but what is for sure is that each death carried reverberations for those who attended it and for the dead man's family.

The first men suffering from psychological injuries were sent to ordinary military hospitals such as the Royal Victoria Hospital in Netley, Southampton, which served as a clearing station. But it quickly became apparent that a more specialist approach was needed. In December 1914 the Red Cross Military Hospital at Maghull, Liverpool, became available for patients who needed greater supervision than an ordinary hospital could offer. By the war's close,

80,000 cases of war neuroses had passed through army hospitals.

At the same time, charities started to raise money for the special care of shell-shocked men. Viscount Knutsford raised £7,700 (about £707,000 today) for a 'Special Hospital' at 10 Palace Green in Kensington which, although not originally designated as such, became, at the War Office's stipulation, a refuge exclusively for officers. Nearly all of the thirty patients had their own room in the detached private house, lent by the estate of Lord Rendal. They were looked after by a resident doctor, a matron, three trained nurses and three 'probationers'. *The Times* commented: 'It would not be easy to find a more sequestered and restful spot in the midst of a great city. Within sight are lofty trees, green spaces and the time-mellowed brick of Kensington Palace – as much tranquil old-world charm, perhaps, as survives anywhere in London.'

Knutsford stressed the gallant and masculine qualities of the afflicted and a visit from Queen Alexandra on 16 January 1915 went some way to reduce the stigma attached to mental illness, as did an article in *The Times* on the effects of shelling. In it, *The Times* Medical Correspondent described the 'wounds of consciousness' and how they are 'the result of the wear and tear of a war of high explosives'. He went on to say that, 'Quiet, rest, the "home feeling" of sympathy and kindness, and specialized treatment are the means by which good results can most speedily be achieved.' Number 10 Palace Green was 'home-like' and 'cheerful' and patients could meet other men in the communal rooms or large garden or go for a drive with visitors. Treatment included 'electricity, massage, and dieting' – 'In a few instances psycho-therapy is resorted to. Always the larger psycho-therapy of cheerfulness and encouragement is practised.' By May, more than 100 officers had passed through 10 Palace Green, and, according to Knutsford, with 'but very few exceptions all have recovered'.

Captain Herbert John Collett Leland, who had written such frank and vivid letters to his wife, Lena, in Edinburgh, arrived by motor car at 10 Palace Green at the end of 1917, accompanied by a nurse. In October he had written of being so 'horribly War worn'. His tone becomes ranting as he writes that 'about the only friend' he had has just died – 'You tell me that your letters are thrilling and make your heart standstill! I have told you nothing, nor can I describe what it is like. Multiply a dozen times what I have told you, and even then, it is nothing. I never want to go through another ten days like the last.' It must have been terrifying for Lena to receive such letters. The next day he wrote: 'I want to come home. It is cowardly to talk like this, but I do feel so rotten. I have not fed for two days'; he was glad that she was working at the 'bandage rolling business'. He urged her to take as much work as she could because it would help her to forget. A few days later: 'I have never got over that dose of shell shock. My head is just bursting. The shell fell within a few yards of me and everything was blank for several minutes. I do not mind saying openly that I have had quite enough of this. I will, and have, volunteered to go over the top time and time again, but this back area shelling is about as much as human limits can stand.'

At the end of October he was hit by tear gas and cried for three hours. He told her to write letters of condolence to the parents of at least two men – although he was not entirely sure whether they even had parents. In answer to her question, 'Parkes' was 'sniped' and died instantly. Sitting writing to her in an attic, presumably at the top of a requisitioned house, was his one comfort – a conversation with no answers. He had discovered the reason that Hilton, most likely his batman, had been acting strangely was that his wife had 'gone off the rails' and wanted nothing more to do with him. Herbert wrote to Hilton's wife encouraging her to contact Hilton, although he held little hope that it would help.

By 22 November he had been moved to an officers' hospital, where he complained of heart and head pains and insomnia. He believed he was suffering from 'delayed action shock' and a chill caught from travelling in an open-top car. He was told he needed rest but was full of self-loathing: 'I feel so disgusted with myself and such a damned rotter. . . .' (26 November 1918).

A few days later he was taken by hospital ship to England and on to 10 Palace Green, which he described as a 'luxurious establishment' that served 'exceptional food'. He was visited by a specialist in civilian clothes, who looked 'very learned'. The routine could not have been further from life at the front. He was woken every day at 7 a.m. and given a cup of tea. He had a bath and was shaved by a 'very superior looking valet' before going back to bed. But he felt a sense of shame: 'I am so sorry that this has happened, for your sake. But I stuck it as long as I could, and I don't think I deserve all this fuss.'

A major from the RAMC wrote to tell Lena that her husband had had a breakdown in France, owing to overwork. For a few days there was 'slight mental confusion and profound exhaustion'. He reassured her that her husband was doing well and asked if she could make the journey from Edinburgh to London to visit him. Fortunately for Lena, her parents could look after their three children. Over the next few years he wandered in and out of convalescent homes and joined the Reserves. He helped to keep order in Edinburgh during the miners' strike of 1921 and then moved several times in England, living off a meagre army pension.

His daughter, Jean, later remembered the tension when her father finally returned to Scotland. Her mother was 'very Scottish and shut in' while he was 'irascible': 'They had an excellent relationship, except for when he was in his cups then he'd fight like Kilkenny cats.' He knew to avoid alcohol but occasionally someone would pour him a drink and his anger would flare up. Once he told his daughter to fetch his bike, saying that he was returning to France. He got as far as the port of Harwich – this was probably when they were living in Colchester, Essex – but the family doctor managed to ring ahead so that officials told him that his papers were not in order and he was sent home.

The number of officers who were suffering from mental illness is likely to be far higher than official figures would suggest – partly because many were treated privately. Treatment varied from hospital to hospital and might range from an emphasis on physical exercise, such as working in a garden, kitchen, workshop or farm, to isolation and rest, hypnosis, psychoanalysis (particularly in the case of officers, as favoured by Dr W.H. Rivers at Craiglockhart in Scotland), massage and a milk diet.

As cases grew, more military hospitals became available and eventually neurological sections were opened in many general hospitals around the country. During the period between April 1915 and April 1916, 1,300 officers and 10,000 Other Ranks were admitted to special hospitals in Britain, while some were treated in wards in France. The years after the war saw a jump in the number of ex-servicemen in public asylums – by October 1921 the figure was 6,435, according to a public meeting in the House of Commons. A parliamentary debate in February 1922 revealed that nearly 12,000 servicemen whose disorders were said to have been caused or aggravated by the war had been certified in the asylum system. According to Peter Barham in his book *Forgotten Lunatics of the Great War*, the death rate for war veterans in English mental institutions in 1918 was more than 20 per cent, compared to a prewar average of 10–11 per cent. Barham speculates that many of these deaths may have been due to malnutrition as asylums tried to save money by cutting diets. In other instances a husband might be held in an asylum that was an expensive train ride away from his home; one man, for example, was kept in Scotland while his family lived in south London. In another case a wife used her husband's pension to buy a bike so that she could cycle the 40-mile round trip to visit him, a journey that meant leaving the children alone at night.

Many patients were sent home before they had properly recovered. They often arrived under military escort – a shaming experience for the family. In addition, the man's wife and children might be unable to cope – particularly if he made violent threats to them or himself. In other instances a man might stay at home – although this could mean decades of misery when the wife acted as her husband's principal carer, sometimes at great personal risk to herself. Occasionally, the wife divorced her husband after years of such care.

The increased number of sufferers led, in some quarters, to a more sympathetic approach to mental illness, questions in Parliament and debates about a man's eligibility for a pension – if a Medical Board had declared him fit for active service in the first place, surely his wartime experience was at the root of his illness?

Since shell shock encompassed so many different symptoms and was treated in such a variety of ways – as well as not at all – it is difficult to give an accurate figure for the number who suffered. In 1918, the Government awarded 18,596 pensions for shell shock, neurasthenia and other similar complaints; the figure peaked at 65,000 in 1921. According to official figures, in 1937 the Government was still paying out around 35,000 war disability pensions for ex-servicemen with mental disabilities. The 1930 Mental Treatment Act officially, at least, banned words such as 'asylum', 'pauper' and 'lunatic', but the stigma lingered.

Men also returned home with profound experiences of friendship – sometimes forged with a man from a different class. This was perhaps most likely in the case of the officer and his 'batman'. The term dates back to the eighteenth-century word 'pat horse', or 'pack horse', an animal used to transport the officer's baggage; the batman was the soldier in charge of the horse. By the First World War the batman had become the officer's personal servant or valet; he woke his master in the morning, provided hot water for his wash and shave, kept his uniform clean, polished his boots, buttons and belt, cooked and cleaned for him and arranged for items to be sent home; he was also expected to stay by him in battle.

In the trenches this close relationship became even more intimate. Each saw the other at his most vulnerable; if the batman were older and more experienced, the relationship might have shades of a father/son bond. It was common among the lower ranks for soldiers to make a pact among each other that one would write to the other's wife or sweetheart if he were killed, but if an officer died the batman might also write to his widow. He would visit her and return objects such as his master's watch. The batman was often asked to contribute to the memorial book created after an officer's death. If both survived they might stay in touch for the rest of their lives, a pattern that was common among the non-officer class. An example of this enduring bond appears in the relationship between Dorothy L. Sayers' fictional detective, Lord Peter Wimsey, whose former sergeant, Bunter, saves him from shell shock and becomes his valet after the war.

Although historian Joanna Bourke has argued that relationships between servicemen during the war 'failed to result in any true reconstruction of masculine intimacy', fighting, nevertheless, gave men the *opportunity* to experience that intimacy and could enhance male friendships. As Bourke explains, the army has several techniques, such as the wearing of uniform and parading naked, for uniting men into a disciplined fighting machine. These strategies also breed intimacy, especially in the absence of women. As the British subaltern Sidney Rogerson says in his brutally honest memoir, *Twelve Days on the Somme* (1933): 'We were privileged to see in each other that inner, ennobled self which in the grim struggle of peace-time is too frequently atrophied for lack of opportunity or expression. We could note the intense affection of soldiers for certain officers, their absolute trust in them. We saw the love passing the love of women of one "pal" for his "half" section . . .'

For some soldiers, friendship formed the impetus for enlistment in the first place. It also defined which part of the service they joined. Occasionally volunteers wanted to stay in the ranks to be with their friends, even though they might be officer material. In the early years of the war particularly, many joined a certain battalion to serve side-by-side with workmates or men they had known from boys' clubs or sports teams, as in the many 'pals battalions' such as the Accrington, Hull, Liverpool, Leeds, Swansea, Oldham and Manchester Pals. In a more affluent version, the 10th Royal Fusiliers were known as the Stockbrokers' Battalion. According to one estimate, nearly 40 per cent of the service and reserve battalions formed between August 1914 and June 1916 emerged from organisations other than the War Office. Local connections provided an added safety net and a wife knew she could write to an officer to ask for help and he would be able to use his influence at home. A wife of a man in the Northumberland Fusiliers, for example, contacted a temporary captain in her husband's regiment, begging him to send her husband home because their daughter was suffering from a mental illness. The captain refused but arranged for his mother to approach a local relief fund. On another occasion, the captain asked his mother to find work for family members of men in his platoon. Those who had served with men from their local community often found returning to civilian life easier because there was less to explain.

The strength of these friendships and new roles was partly based on an enforced domesticity in the trenches and other places of war. Ordinary soldiers who had served at the front became used to darning their socks, washing their clothes and boiling up a meal together. When there was time, particularly in prisoner-of-war camps, men danced together and put on drag to take women's parts in plays and sketches. For some, this was the first time they had tried out a feminine identity. Occasionally, soldiers would refer to a close friend in a joking way as their 'wife'.

Men returned with an attitude to their body and its functions that was subtly changed. My maternal grandfather, Robert Wright, knew that, aged seventeen when he first joined the territorial service, he was 5ft 5 in tall, weighed 112 pounds (nearly 10½ stone) and that his chest measured 34½ inches and had a 2½-inch range of expansion. Alexander Gillies (at 21 years and 8 months) was an inch taller and was slightly heavier; his chest was 37½ inches and had a range of 2 inches. As well as a greater awareness of their own body, they had seen men at their most vulnerable, sometimes literally inside out. They had endured physical extremes of cold and wet and, as Robert Graves noted, lived in the same set of clothes for several years. Their senses had become attuned to a limited spectrum of muted colours, violent noises, harsh textures, bland food and the smell of gas and the grave. Even something as basic as underwear required adjustment: in the poorest of households vests and undergarments were unaffordable or worn for several days at a time; in this context, army issue clothes seemed a luxury, although in the worst of the fighting socks and other items could be worn for weeks. Officers were obliged to sport moustaches; the decision about whether or not to shave them off after the war could be a significant rite of passage and one that some men preferred to leave to their wives – perhaps because a wife was best-placed to judge which was more attractive and also because they were guardians of their home.

As in other conflicts, some soldiers also brought home venereal disease. Around 417,000 men were admitted to hospital suffering from VD during the Great War. Treatment for syphilis meant a hospital stay of fifty days – which was easier to hide from a wife than the accompanying cessation of pay and her separation allowance. Officers had a slightly easier time for they might be able to persuade a doctor to treat them privately. Although the army gave advice about how to avoid contracting VD, some soldiers welcomed it as a respite from the trenches. As historian Clare Makepeace has pointed out, this form of 'self-inflicted wound' meant that some prostitutes suffering from syphilis or gonorrhoea could command higher prices.

While more timid soldiers were frightened to enter a brothel, there was also a belief that denying a man an outlet for his natural urges might actually be harmful to his health. Parts of northern

France housed legalised brothels, or *maisons tolérées*, where professional prostitutes faced regular medical inspections. Makepeace estimates that, by 1917, there were at least 137 brothels in some thirty-five towns. (In parts of India in the late nineteenth century the army ran regimental bazaars – in effect, brothels.) Some displayed a blue lamp for officers and a red version for the ordinary soldier. One young corporal who surveyed a queue of soldiers outside such a house was told: 'these places were not for young lads like me, but for married men who were missing their wives'. There was a sense among some soldiers that they should squeeze as much life out of what could be their final hours.

The birth rate fell during the war years due to the absence of so many men and the effects of Spanish flu, but the returning soldiers led to an 'extraordinary baby bubble' in 1920, with 957,000 births in England and Wales – the highest number in a single year until the present day. This sudden fecundity gave many women the new experience of motherhood, and took others back into a role – as primary carer for a young child – that had been superseded and supplemented by other tasks during the war years. Although it remains debatable whether women's status in society was permanently altered as a result of the war, what is indisputable is that many had experienced new freedom and powers during the conflict. The female workforce rose by 50 per cent during this time and by the end of the war 700,000 women had filled jobs previously held by men. While my Scottish grandmother worked in an ammunitions factory on the Clyde, many of her female friends and relatives had joined the previously all-male shipyards. The *Daily Mail* of 5 June 1918 maintained that this could only damage women's health. Necessity meant that during the war there was more chance to go out unaccompanied and after the war the loose, flapper styles of dress gave a physical manifestation of a perceived freedom.

Officers' wives, then as now, were expected to offer support to families at home, while also dealing with their own worries. This was especially true in territorial or Pals' battalions, where those left behind were concentrated in one geographical area. Eleanore Stephens, wife of Lieutenant-Colonel Reginald Stephens of the 2nd Battn of Rifle Brigade, set up a support network of the wives of ordinary soldiers which was both practical and humane. Her husband, Reginald, also shared his worst moments with her in the frank letters he sent home. As his battalion was involved in heavy fighting at the village of Neuve Chapelle in March 1915, there were many moments of anguish. After losing twelve officers and 300 men, he wrote to Eleanore that he refused to give a further order to advance – a decision that he confided to his wife might have put him on a charge of cowardice. Reginald was forty-five and an experienced career soldier who had fought against the Sudanese Dervishes and the Boers. During the first year of the war he was stationed in northern France. They had been married for ten years and had three children.

Eleanore ran the brigade's 'comforts fund' and, with help from other wives and mothers and donations from Vickers, the local employer and armaments manufacturer, arranged for warm clothing, cigarettes, regular tins of milk and food to be sent to the soldiers serving at the front. As she wrote to the quartermaster every few days, she was able to tailor the packages to the soldiers' immediate needs. In March, he told her not to send mittens or comforters because the weather had improved but added that socks, milk, sugar, cocoa, hankies, black buttons, small towels and pocket books were in demand. In November, by contrast, the soldiers needed safety pins with which to fasten their greatcoats. Surprisingly, the soldiers craved curry powder – perhaps because their previous posting had been India or because they used it to disguise the taste of the food. As someone who was used to writing letters, she also helped wives to claim their Separation Allowance.

As the war dragged on, her support extended to the families of those who were killed or missing. The quartermaster supplied her with families' names and addresses and she wrote to them to say she was willing to help. Some asked if she could track down any possessions belonging to their dead husband so that they had a memento by which to remember him. Another wife, while hoping that Colonel Stephens would return home safely, asked whether Mrs Stephens had any black clothes she could pass on, as she was struggling financially. Others were desperate to hear news of the battalion. These pitiful letters reveal a genuine bond between women of different classes. They also show how a wife bore some of the anguish of war that was hidden from her husband.

Eleanore and Reginald seemed to have been brought closer by their shared experience, but for some couples the war served to accentuate differences. Many couples had rushed to the altar in the excitement of the first months of fighting; others felt obliged to commit to a relationship that might otherwise have petered out. Some found that the years apart had brought about too fundamental a change. Whichever the reason, there were three times as many divorces in 1919 as 1913. This figure might have been higher, had incurable insanity been grounds for divorce – as it would be after 1937. There was also a startling jump in the number of bigamy cases. In 1912, 2.75 per cent (34 out of 1,232) cases brought to the Central Criminal Court concerned bigamy; by 1918, this had jumped to around 20 per cent or seven times the prewar level. Many of the accused women worked in ammunitions factories or other industries linked to war work. This is not to say that these women were morally lax; it may simply have been easier to cite them in proceedings.

Just occasionally, official documents shine a light on a domestic situation in which the wife longed for the separation offered by war. The Middlesex military service appeal tribunal heard more than 11,000 appeals against men being forced to join the army. Several are accompanied by heart-rending letters saying why a man should be spared: a young carpenter, for example, was allowed to stay at home because his four brothers had all died in the war. The wife of Percival Brown, by contrast, wrote to urge the tribunal to ignore her husband's claims of a back injury. The mother of two added: 'he leads me such a life, I was looking forward to him joining up as I have had nearly 11 years of unhappiness through him . . . [his behaviour] as [sic] caused me to go short of money, food . . . besides selling part of my house.' Her husband, she said, had threatened to make sure 'she did not get a penny' if he were sent to the front. Mrs Brown's appeal was successful and her husband's application for a reprieve was rejected.

The rate of legal marriages jumped immediately after the war and was 30 per cent higher in 1919 and 1920 than before. Marriages among widows, aged twenty to forty-five, increased by 50 per cent and their husbands had to contend with the ghostly presence of a first husband who had died fighting for his country, often at a young age. Harry Patch, the last survivor of the trenches, married Ada, who had been engaged to a young soldier who died at the front. She was not able to countenance a new relationship until she was convinced her first love was not coming back and, even then, their engagement ring had a place on her dressing table for years to come. Ada was one of the lucky women who managed to find a man when so many women were searching for a soulmate.

Part Three:
World War Two

12

Life on the Home Front: Diana Carnegie, 1940

Did you listen to the 9'o'clock news last night & did you hear the bomb (it must have been one) I thought Bruce Belfrage was very brave – I should have thrown myself flat on the floor!

Diana Carnegie, who included the comment in a letter to her husband, James, a second lieutenant in the 352 Search Light Battery, Royal Artillery, was right: the crackle and crump that she, and millions of other listeners heard, *was* a bomb.

Just after 8 p.m. on Tuesday, 15 October 1940 a delayed-action 500lb explosive smashed through a seventh-floor window of Broadcasting House in central London, before settling in the music library, two floors below. In the basement of the monolithic building just moments before; Belfrage had waited for Big Ben to strike the hour before launching into his script. As was normal at a time when the population was braced for a German invasion, he identified himself and continued in his measured tones to pass on good news to the nation:

This is the BBC Home and Forces' Programme. Here is the news and this is Bruce Belfrage reading it. There is an Admiralty communiqué giving the full story of recent naval successes in the Mediterranean. Besides the latest details of RAF successes

> against Berlin, and other vital objectives, there is more news of the good results of our air raids in Africa. More daylight air attacks by enemy fighters have been broken up. There is comment, both from Moscow and London, on the news from Rumania. Tonight's talk after this bulletin will be by Lord Lloyd, the Colonial Secretary, . . . [explosion]

Belfrage paused momentarily before continuing with his script. The bomb, which exploded when staff tried to move it, rocked the building and left a light dusting of plaster and soot on Belfrage's suit which, under the more relaxed regulations of the time, was probably not a dinner jacket. Three men and four women were killed.

For those listeners, like Diana, who recognised the interruption for what it was, the thought that an institution that specialised in conveying encouraging news about 'naval successes' and 'good results about air raids' could itself come under attack was shocking. But 1940 was a time of great upheaval – especially for families. Rationing was introduced at the start of the year: butter, bacon and sugar first, followed in March by meat; in the summer tea, margarine and other fats were added to the list, although free, or at least cheaper, milk was made available to mothers.

Diana and James had married a few months before the start of the war, on 25 April 1939 at St Mark's Church, North Audley Street in Mayfair, London. The guest list was grand: although James's father, the late Hon. Sir Lancelot Carnegie was not related to the American industrialist and millionaire of the same surname, he had, nevertheless, been ambassador to Portugal and both mothers-in-law were Ladies. The small church, built in 1828 in a classical revivalist style, lent the occasion an intimate air. The reception was held at the bridegroom's London home in Cadogan Square. The wedding was announced in *The Times* and the *Tatler* and the latter carried a photo of Diana looking mischievous, wearing a plain black top, her hair pinned up in ringlets and a faint smile playing on her mouth. James, in peacetime a stockbroker, was thirty when they married and his new bride five years younger.

Like many couples in the Second World War, Diana and James endured long periods of separation even while he remained in the United Kingdom. Although Diana was usually living in a house that had a phone, she preferred to pour out her heart to 'My darling', 'Darlingest', 'Angel' in the hundreds of letters she sent to him over the next few years. Her day was punctuated by the rattle of the letterbox and the absence of a few lines from James could plunge her into despair. Her letters reveal a young woman who has had independence thrust upon her and most of the time simply gets on with it but who occasionally is worn down by the responsibility of running a household by herself. When dealing with their financial affairs, she asks him what it means if a company has 'passed a dividend' and tells him she wished he had seen her driving the 'old Hillman', 'very upright' from Crewe and back: 'I nearly killed the District Nurse, who looked daggers at me and I had to crash some red lights – both owing to my inability to stop the car! Everybody laughed as they passed me!'

She tells him about the minutiae of life: that the mice have eaten his cricket trousers and how she is 'suffering from the Test again', when talking to her beloved brother, Horace: 'Hokey's dotty about it & when we're not hearing it on the wireless indoors – his man shouts the score etc out of the window! . . However, I feel it has greater possibilities since I learnt that there were such things as "silly-mid-ons" and "silly mid-offs"!! Lovely—' (He was probably referring to the 'victory tests' that took place after the end of the war.)

The couple were devoted to Bengie, a small white Sealyham terrier, who divided his time between wherever Diana was living and James's army camp. Bengie was often in trouble for mounting his 'girlfriends' in the garden – Diana put it more bluntly – or for having to sit on her mink coat in the train to keep him away from another dog. The breed was popular because many Hollywood celebrities like Alfred Hitchcock and Gary Cooper owned one. Bengie provided companionship, and a degree of security, for Diana and travelled with her in the car and on long journeys on overcrowded trains. She worried about how she would feed him at a time when many people had their pets put down because they could not spare food. Later in the war she was reduced to giving him potato skins.

Diana's letters to James reveal a deep concern for his health and the conditions in which he was living. 'Oh darling – it makes me weep to think of you alone in your dripping tent . . .' She wondered whether a previous heart problem might be enough to allow him to be moved from the Regular Army to the newly formed Local Defence Volunteers, or Home Guard, a body recruited specifically to see off the German parachutists who were expected to descend from the skies and snatch away a British way of life.

She gossips about their friends and is rude about both their mothers – she is relieved that her mother, whom, like everyone else, she refers to as 'her Ladyship', has not lost Diana's white knickers. But she is annoyed when her mother writes 'reams' in which she warns her about '"staying quiet & not being unreasonable" about the situation – & not "making a laughing stock" of you', which Diana assumes refers to an incident in which a colonel friend allowed her into a Defence Area when he should not have done.

They discuss books – particularly *Gaudy Nights* by Dorothy L. Sayers – and she is excited that the famous writer, Noel Streatfeild, author of *Ballet Shoes*, is coming to tea but the following day declares her 'a frightful woman'. Her letters are playful – her cousin, Vivien, has sent him a packet of Players cigarettes for Christmas which she intends to smoke, but she reminds James to write and thank Vivien, even though he will not enjoy the gift. She longs for him both physically and emotionally; at times her letters represent a sort of epistolary version of 'phone sex'. In the following extract, she highlights the supposed antics of a member of the Auxiliary Territorial Service (ATS). Members of the ATS were frequently the butt of ribald humour and in some quarters were known, unfairly, as 'Officers' Groundsheets' or, after the arrival of US troops, the 'American Tail Supply'. They may have attracted such criticism because of British suspicion of women in uniform. Such was the concern about the supposed loose morals of these women that the Government set up a parliamentary committee in November 1941 to investigate claims about the high rate of pregnancy among ATS women. In fact, the committee found that, at 15.4 per 1,000 per annum, the ATS rate was lower than among civilians of a similar age, which was 21.8 per 1,000 a year. The figures were also distorted by the fact that many of the ATS were already pregnant when they joined up.

> Well – I don't know what to think of your goings on! Falling into a ditch with an ATS sounds very peculiar to me – & I expect the next thing you'll know she'll be accusing you of the paternity of her coming child (probably quite rightly!) and she is probably the only person who knows what did happen – or have you had a flash of guilty memory?! You must have gone pretty far to have got anywhere near a ditch – still I don't really mind as long as you didn't go the whole hog – but don't suppose we'll ever know whether you did or not!?

She could be even more explicit: 'Incidentally – I'm all for your having an affair with Mrs Fisher – or even a jolly good fuck if you feel like it – but do not behave unseemly again in front of Mrs Russell.' As their leave together was so precious she speaks freely about 'the Curse' and whether it will mean she has her period when they meet.

By spring 1940 she knew that she was pregnant with their first child. At that time she was living near Henley-on-Thames and James was stationed in Lincolnshire.

> I wonder how you got on in the air raids last night? I had awful visions of bombs having being dropped onto you – when they

said Lincs – but pulled myself together, as if I imagine you're dead every time they say that I shall be in the looney bin in no time! But do tell me all about it & whether you picked any up, & where the nearest bombs were etc. I wonder whether all my friends at Woodhall are running away – I hope not? Have a v. nice letter from Frs F enclosing to [2] photos of her child which I shall speedily consign to the dustbin – I do hope ours will have some form of eyebrows & eyelashes. By the way they did the 'pencil' test over one the other day – & it was firmly 'boy' – suppose it would please the family more than a girl – any way as long as it isn't a freak or a minor [?] (which I sometimes feel it's bound to be! (quite seriously!) I don't give a damn. . .

I suppose we're in for really big attacks now so do take care of yourself darling, & keep well away from the searchlight & don't hesitate to be the 1st to leap into the nearest ditch, for my sake.

I do love you angel. D.

She visited the maternity hospital and said it had nice views but that the walls were 'café au lait'. Like other mothers-to-be she was conscious that she was about to give birth at a precarious moment in Britain's history; some women even worried that their children would grow up speaking German. The Phoney War, when the expected onslaught had turned out to be nothing more than an anticlimactic 'Sitzkrieg', had ended and the German Army had swept down through the Lowlands with indecent haste. By the summer an invasion was expected daily and the Government published leaflets warning families to 'stay put' rather than clog the roads as refugees had done in mainland Europe. Diana alluded to the invasion in many of her letters; she usually referred to it in a jokey way, but it was obviously preying on her mind – 'Well, I suppose everyone's as gloomy as they could be – there's no reason to be anything else – but I do feel for you alone on that bloody site – I only hope you'll remain alone on it & won't be joined by cohorts of Germans!'

Their daughter was born on 25 June 1940 in Wareing Cottage Hospital, Oxfordshire, and weighed a tiny 4¾ pounds; the doctor said he had never seen such a small baby who was not premature or a twin. Friends called her 'The Snippet' or 'The Very Little Girl', while another preferred 'Cyrène Bombina' because of the bomb attacks that Diana was so worried about and perhaps the siren suits that were popular at the time. But Diana herself had another suggestion: 'it was really the parachutists who brought her on – so I think "Paraldehyde" which includes them & is the name of the filthy drug I was given – per rectum – which did as much good as a whiff of eau de cologne & smelt vile!'

The baby arrived on the day that France capitulated to the Nazis, prompting Diana to write to James: 'How bloody the French are, though I still can't believe that the whole bag of tricks will surrender – anyway one gets deadened to bad news – it's quite powerless to make me feel anything after a bit.' The dire situation abroad meant that it was impossible for James to obtain leave and Diana refused to send him a photo of their daughter until he had met her in person. They continued to struggle to find a name and referred to her as 'BN' for reasons that remain a mystery, although the 'B' probably stood for 'Baby'. Diana found it a particularly painful period to be separated from her husband who, like the majority of the army, was still stationed in Britain. By 1 July 1940, over half the male population between the age of twenty and twenty-five was in the armed services – representing 20 per cent of British males. Diana wrote to James: 'it wouldn't matter if we were all killed together – but I'm not maternal enough to want to go on living even with BN without you (& Bengie!).'

Eventually, they settled on 'Carolyn' as a name, chose godparents and arranged for a christening, although they decided not to squander his '48 hours' [leave] on it. The celebration did not go quite to plan, 'Rather sad C's christening cake has had all the icing decorations round the sides knocked off & instead of writing Carolyn on the top they've put silver decoration & what's more they've charged 15/6 . . . & what are we to do about it – let me know by return as I must write.'

Over the next months Diana led a peripatetic lifestyle. Although she was never part of the mass evacuation of women and children to parts of the country that were deemed safer, she, nevertheless, spent much of the war moving from one house owned by a friend or relative to another so that she could be nearer her husband. She stayed with her mother in Eye, Suffolk; Stone Hall, Balcombe in Sussex (which was probably where she strayed into the Defence Zone); Dorfold Hall, Nantwich, Cheshire and Crofthead, Longtown in Cumberland, close to the Scottish border. Her mother was not sympathetic and in one phone conversation 'went on for a long time about how we "presumed on our rights" & the Army didn't allow wives to flow round etc.!!!' Diana said it was a waste of a phone call but at least her mother had promised to send warm pyjamas.

For Diana, the priority was to be near James. She missed him more than ever – especially since Carolyn was struggling to put on weight and had to return to three hourly feeds. She chastised him for eating the baby's glucose, partly because it was so expensive: 'I'm all for your taking Halibut oil as you know, or even Bease – but feel the other is unnecessary taking your girth etc into consideration?!'

As the autumn approached, the intensity of bombing increased. On 7 September the Luftwaffe sent 1,000 German aircraft – more than 300 bombers escorted by 600 fighters – across the Channel in what proved to be the start of the Blitz. Apart from one night, when the weather saved Britain, the bombers attacked London and other major cities every night – and sometimes during the day – for seventy-six consecutive nights. When Diana put Carolyn's gas mask on her for the first time she described it as 'a horrible thing & she looked awfully pathetic, but was very good – I do hope we won't have to use it'.

James was promoted and moved to Chester, but she was told it was rather 'bomby' and full of troops. So they stayed with friends nearby. Another friend had left for America and she wondered whether they should send Carolyn to Scotland for safety. She wrote to James: 'I hate being bombed (or the thought of it) when I'm all alone! Even here it is rather unpleasant – it's a horrid feeling hearing the Germans overhead all the time & knowing that you're more or less the objective & that they're not just passing over you – the R's Royce works is under 4 miles & one hears the noise of it all day, & it's covered with Blimps [barrage balloons]! I gather the reason I'm so frightened nowadays is that Carolyn used up all the calcium & stuff that supplies the nerves – so p'raps I shan't always be such a coward?!!!' Her anxiety was justified: the house was bombed and took out a window, which left them shivering until it was mended.

As a precaution, James's mother took her wedding veil from its safe deposit in the bank, but Diana continued to worry about their own possessions, which were in storage with Harrods, being hit. She also told him to make sure that one of the other officers had her telephone number and address so that she would know if a bomb dropped on him. Carolyn put on weight – but slowly. James's sister-in-law urged them to send her to a specialist in Edinburgh, but Diana did not think it was worth it because she was making progress and it would involve a long train journey. She was furious that her mother had written to James with her concerns about Carolyn and her insistence that she should be drinking cow's milk. Diana maintained this was impossible because they moved around so much and blamed her ill health on the change in climate – from Suffolk to the northwest. At times Carolyn's hair looked almost pink and someone referred to her as the 'teeny-weeny girl'. But Diana tried to be positive: 'I think C.'s colour was a bit better – & she was talking away to herself when I went in – but she still looks a pathetic little thing, all the nurses are fond of her now, & pay her a lot of attention.' In another letter she writes: 'Carolyn looks & is, I think, much better, in fact she's in very good form – but she's very rude as, when I sang "Pop goes the Weasel" to her when I was giving her bottle to make her eat, a broad grin spread across her face & she let go of the teat altogether, so I shan't sing to her again till she can appreciate it!'

Diana visited James as often as she could; usually they stayed in hotels. Once she treated herself to a perm in Penrith – '[my hair's] been falling out like mad which is very sad & I expect I shall soon be nearly bald!'

As 1940 neared its end their luck appeared to be changing. She was 'completely overcome' by news of his promotion and Her ladyship had 'presented' her with £12 (about £700 in today's money). These two facts made their worst experience of bombing easier to bear:

> Friday
> Sweet one,
> What a night we've had – bombed incessantly from 7–4 – we all went to bed in Lydia's [her cousin's] room. L & me in the bed, C. on the chaise longue – Bengie & Otto – we lay with bombs crashing around us, listening to the glass falling out of the windows – then about 1 o.c we decided it was madness to stay up there & got up & then saw the most frightful glare from Celia's window & thought the house was on fire – we looked out & there were 4 parachute flares over the house lighting up the entire place (you've just rung up!) then we fairly fled downstairs expecting the house to be obliterated at any moment – we were promptly blown back by blast – & all the windows that weren't blown open were broken. We spent the rest of the night huddled in the servants [sic] sitting room with the icy wind whistling in through the open window that had burst their locks. Poor Bengie was scared out of his wits & nearly burst his bladder by (very sensibly) refusing to go out!

However, Diana was wrong about their luck changing. On 28 December 1940 Carolyn Mary Carnegie, aged six months, died in St Mary's Hospital, Manchester. The causes of death were given as: gastroenteritis and anaemia neonatorum (Erythroblastosis fetalis). Today, the second illness is more commonly known as 'haemolytic disease of the newborn' and can occur when a mother whose blood group is negative has a baby who inherits the Rhesus positive group from the father. The baby may be born anaemic and after birth becomes yellow. In severe cases the newborn can die; others, like Carolyn, never thrive and an additional setback such as gastroenteritis might be enough to end their life. Treatment is difficult and involves blood transfusions; in Carolyn's case the doctors may not even have been aware of the root of the problem. Diana and James were extremely unlucky.

The anxiety of Carolyn's brief life was even harder to bear because Diana was, in effect and like many other army wives of the time, a single mother. James could not be with her all the time, although from Diana's side of the correspondence, it seems evident that he did his best to console and reassure her. There is no record of how exactly they coped with the enormity of such suddenness. For some couples the tragedy of losing a baby – perversely – can make it more painful for them to stay together, but Diana and James's marriage remained strong – perhaps helped by the fact that they were able to be so frank with one another in letters.

13

Life on the Home Front: Rachel Dhonau, Summer 1941 to December 1942

> The thought that Jakob may be coming on Saturday makes me feel quite ill with excitement. It does awful things to my tummy, making it feel in just about the same turmoil as when a bomb falls near [me].

Rachel Dhonau's longing for her husband was as intense as Diana Carnegie's and assumed a physical form that escalated as the date of his expected arrival grew near. Like Diana, she was frequently disappointed: 'I was just going to bed when there were heavy steps to the door and my bell rang. I thought it must be my husband, my heart started beating violently and my tummy turned completely over, but it was only a special constable come to ask if it was a car of mine left without a light outside, which it wasn't.'

However, Rachel did not have Diana's resources and contacts and could not wander the country, hoping to make the most of her husband's leave. Norfolk, where she lived in the seaside resort of Sheringham, was viewed as a first line of defence – particularly in 1940 and early 1941 – and everywhere she went, she was reminded of this, from the anti-tank ditches on the cliff edge to the pill boxes and scaffolding on the shingle beach. A few miles east, Cromer, once a slightly more elegant holiday destination, had become 'a depressing place'. The windows in the big hotels and guest houses were all boarded up and the town had a 'general air of dilapidation'.

Rachel's world shrank. Barbed wire unfurled along the beach and pushed her back towards the sturdy, semi-detached house, studded with traditional Norfolk flint, which she rented with her mother and young son, Timothy. Army lorries rumbled down the road outside and when she walked to the post office to post her daily letter to Jakob, she listened to soldiers moaning that they had not had a smoke for a month. When the bombing started in earnest it fitted a tight lid on her landscape: 'It is a funny feeling just now living on the edge of England, particularly when it is cloudy and anything may drop out of the clouds.'

Jakob, a private in the Intelligence Corps was still in Britain – but only just. He was stationed in the Shetland Islands, an important military base in the North Sea, 534 miles and a long sea crossing away from Sheringham. In one letter he pointed out to Rachel that the Orkneys, a mere staging point on the way to the Shetlands, were sometimes referred to as *Ultima Thule*, or the end of the world. His new base put him beyond the end of the world. What he failed to mention was that he was much closer – a mere 204 nautical miles – to Nazi-occupied Norway.

Rachel envied her husband his chance to visit Scotland and the Shetlands. As she told the diary she kept for the Mass Observation organisation – founded in 1937 to foster an 'anthropology of ourselves' by recruiting thousands of citizens to record their thoughts – she would have loved to have gone too. She felt, however, that their son, Timothy, who was five in 1941, needed at least one parent by his side. Sheringham was both cut-off from world affairs – by its poor road and rail links to London – and at the very centre; from April 1942 its nearest city, Norwich, became a focus of heavy bombardment as part of the Luftwaffe's Baedeker raids on historic sites. When the Germans' progress began to stall, East Anglia assumed the role of holding pen for American soldiers and airmen poised for the assault on Europe.

Although Rachel was born in Norfolk, and turned thirty just after the start of the war, her view of the world stretched far beyond the flat Norfolk landscape. Her maiden name was Piechowicz and her father was born in Aachen, Germany, one of seven children. He emigrated to England, where he worked as a chauffeur and became a British citizen, just after Rachel's birth in 1909. His death in 1915 meant she remained an only child and she and her mother moved into Avondale, a respectable, late-Victorian house on the Cromer Road in Sheringham, with her maternal grandparents. Before his retirement, Rachel's grandfather had worked as a stationmaster at a small rural railway station; it was a position of benevolent responsibility that seemed to sum up everything the Nazis threatened to overthrow, just like the avuncular figure in E. Nesbit's *The Railway Children*, portrayed so perfectly by Bernard Cribbins in the 1970 film adaptation.

Ernest Dhonau, or Jakob as he was more commonly known, was not the obvious husband for Rachel to find in Sheringham. But the couple, who probably met in their teens when the Dhonau family spent their annual holiday boarding at Avondale, were well-matched. They were originally from southwest Germany but during the 1930s ran a bakery in southeast London. Jakob was active in the local Labour Party.

Rachel won a scholarship to a nearby girls' school before continuing her studies at Bedford College, University of London, where she read English and German. She graduated in 1931 with an Upper Second Class Degree before training to be a teacher in Oxford. At about the same time, Jakob was reading Modern Languages at Exeter College. They were engaged at least once before they married, in secret, in Norfolk in early 1935. The couple spent their first two years of married life in London before Jakob took a job as a translator in Paris. They had planned to holiday in Brittany in the summer of 1939, but this idea melted into history when Rachel opened a copy of *Paris-Soir* as she sat outside the Luxembourg Gardens. News of the German–Russian pact turned them into refugees and robbed them of their last chance of a family vacation. They returned to live with Jakob's family in south London a few weeks before Prime Minister Neville Chamberlain declared war and then, in 1940, they moved back to Sheringham, which, at the time, seemed safer than London.

By then Jakob had joined the Intelligence service and was scrupulous about not giving much away. Rachel speculated that this would encourage him to fill his letters with details of the history, customs and language of the Shetlands. In another person this comment might sound snide, but they were equally bookish and photos of them reveal a stolid couple with heavy features and thick round glasses. Rachel relaxed by reading Proust and knitting, or picking up a book on the Shetlands to help her imagine her husband experiencing the landscape.

In July 1941 they had been apart for five months. When Jakob rang from Aberdeen he said he expected to be given leave within a few days but Rachel became despondent as the telegram confirming his leave failed to appear. 'It seems almost like a dream that we once lived together,' she wrote in her diary. Her mood was further knocked by news that a friend's husband, a pilot, had been killed. Ironically, it was about this time that the 'V for Victory' campaign took hold. It appeared on walls and envelopes and, Rachel surmised, must even have been chalked on chairs, as she noticed several people with white 'V's on their backsides.

The next few weeks turned into an agony of waiting, a pattern that would become all too familiar: 'No letter from my husband, but I hope. I live very much in a state of hope. Hope for a letter – hope for his leave – hope for the end of the war.' A few days later, she was relieved that her periods had started and that they would not disrupt her husband's leave, as they had last time. He had told her how some men had been 'deprived of marital rights for the whole seven days' for this reason. She mused about how it would be interesting to collect the euphemisms used for the menstrual cycle; she noted how the men in her husband's battery referred to it as 'having the Admiral on board' because when an admiral visits a ship the crew is obliged to fly the Red Ensign.

When Jakob's leave was just a week away she dared not think about the prospect of seeing him again: 'It will be like being newly married all over again – at least almost.' She went to bed later and later, as there seemed no point when there was no one to share it with. She wished that the clocks would go back during his leave so that they could steal an extra hour together. She darned her stockings frantically, relieved that she no longer had to repair his socks since he had learnt how to do this in the army. 'I feel quite nervous at the thought of seeing my husband again after six months' separation – but I don't suppose I shall feel shy for very long. I watch the sea anxiously in case it should be rough so that he can't come.'

Avondale was just across the road from the railway station and it was no hardship to meet the train she thought he might be on, but she was disappointed. She received a telegram saying that he would arrive the next day, a Sunday, but she was unable to believe it. Her mother held back the best food so that Jakob could enjoy it. '. . . it is only by exercising great self-control that I am able to concentrate sufficiently to write this diary,' Rachel wrote.

Sunday morning dragged on until 11 a.m., when he finally appeared: 'I didn't listen to the news, I didn't read the paper, I didn't do anything except be pleased that we were together again and think what a shame it was that we were parted.' In a practical, but perhaps not overly romantic, gesture, he brought her eggs from Scotland. The next week was a mixture of courtship and a return to family life – both within the confines of a wartime setting. They went to the cinema in Norwich, but the film was interrupted by a siren (in the event, it proved to be a false alarm). They shared a cup of tea and bread with just the hint of butter scraped over it; there were no rolls or cakes on the menu. On his last day they treated themselves to a chicken for lunch, followed by a walk in the woods; later, he chopped some logs. After tea, Jakob spent an hour polishing each of his army boots. Rachel cut a mountain of sandwiches and they went to bed together for the last time in 'who knows how long?'.

She got up at 5.30 a.m. to see him off at a station humming with soldiers and members of the ATS and WAAF (Women's Auxiliary Air Force). 'I feel so desolate without Jakob – and I don't even know when he will come again. When he has been away for a long time, I feel somehow resigned, but not at all when he has just gone away.' Their son, by contrast, was 'not altogether sorry that Jakob is going. He likes his independence and monopoly of my attentions.'

She went to the cinema to try to counter her desolation but afterwards felt upset that she could not find a particular letter he had sent her. She started to worry about the perils of the long sea journey he faced. It was five days before she knew that he had arrived safely at his army base. They quickly fell back into the usual routine: 'I had a letter from my husband, in which he told me little beyond the fact that he couldn't tell me anything of what he had been doing lately.' A few days later she discovered that she was not pregnant, 'which though a good thing in one way, in another is always something of a disappointment.'

Like many people during the war, Rachel was susceptible to anything that appeared to hint at what the future might hold. In September 1941 Kiev fell to the Germans and shortly afterwards she saw the *aurora borealis*. She felt sure this was a bad omen: the last time she had seen the Northern Lights was just before the outbreak of war. A year later, when she happened to glimpse the moon through glass, she was worried that this might foretell a disaster. Most Monday mornings in the Food Office where she worked, they discussed the prophesies of Edward Lyndoe, the balding, moustachioed astrologer who wrote for the *People*, and who forecast in July 1941 that the war was in its final stages, although Rachel was sceptical. She also bought

Psychic Review – just out of curiosity, she said. She found the idea of reincarnation reassuring because it meant that time spent apart could be made up for in the after-life.

Her work in the Food Office placed her at the very centre of her community and she had a broad range of responsibilities. She issued allowances for farmhands who were bringing in the harvest, dealt with requests from young women who wanted the name on their ration book changed but did not have proof that they were married, handed out permits to shopkeepers and the Home Guard and licences for slaughtering pigs. She worked every day, except Sunday, 9 a.m. to 6 p.m., and grew to know her colleagues well. Her job gave her a unique insight into the world of people she would not normally mix with; they talked about the most intimate aspects of life – from sex to constipation. After a visit to the library she confided to her diary: 'I thought how desolate life would be without books and music. I heard someone boast the other day that she hadn't read a book for over a year . . . I didn't even know that people like that existed until I worked in the Food Office.'

She was also well placed to pick up all the town gossip. 'I didn't ever really believe in the "lowering of moral standards by war" but I am beginning to, now,' she wrote after hearing of two more cases of bigamy that she was adamant were not hearsay. Anxiety about being duped by soldiers was confirmed when a young woman she started chatting to in a shop told her of a fool-proof way of finding out if a man in uniform was married. She would work the conversation round to money and tell him she had never seen an army pay book. If he were single, he would unfailingly agree to show her his book; if he were married, he would quickly change the subject.

Rachel was honest about her own needs. 'I miss my husband much more physically while I am at home than when I am at work. I suppose while I work I indulge in a little Freudian sublimation of sex. I hadn't had a holiday for so long that I didn't realize this.' But she could be censorious about other women. She partly blamed the 'sordid' calendar of crimes at the County Assizes, with its emphasis on rape, on women – 'I have seen them in Sheringham thrusting their attentions on soldiers and Rona and Peggy in my office dress in a most provocative manner, but are almost prudish in their behaviour. But the stimulus is there.'

She felt films encouraged women to dress in this way and claimed she could tell which female film star was appearing at the local cinema by the way Rona behaved. Rachel knew of several ATS girls who were forced to leave the service because of their 'condition' and of five who, when asked to identify the father, had named the same man. In another case, reported in the newspaper, a woman from the 'slums' of Sheringham and an airman had been fined for performing an indecent act in an air-raid shelter, although she did not believe the 'embroidered' additional details in which the woman was said to have been married for six months and that when they were found, he was naked and she was just wearing her vest. Rachel had heard it was possible to buy a powder in Sheringham that would induce an abortion and commented that the typist who narrowly avoided committing bigamy changed her fiancé as easily as she might her job.

With touching naiveté, she pointed out in her diary that Japan's invasion of Malaya had cut off the region's rubber exports, which meant that hot water bottles were no longer freely available. Soldiers and army officials, however, were more concerned by the effect this dearth of latex had on birth control and the rate of VD. The shortage of condoms not only made unplanned pregnancy more likely but also drove up the instances of sexually transmitted disease. Cases of venereal disease escalated after GIs started to arrive in Britain in spring 1942. It is hardly surprising, though, that an influx of young men had this result; the same pattern would crop up when the GIs arrived in Paris and Brussels. A public education campaign in October 1942, which included a talk on the BBC – naturally after 9 p.m. – and continued the following year in newspapers and on posters, went some way to educate the public about the disease. A Defence Regulation allowed VD patients to cite their contacts, who could then be forced to seek treatment, and the introduction of penicillin towards the end of the war made the disease easier to treat.

Rates of illegitimacy rose sharply during the war – particularly among married women. Morals had been put under such strain that one bishop even suggested that married people who had committed adultery should be forgiven by the Church and allowed to renew their marriage vows. Nearly a third of all illegitimate children born in the last two years of the war were the product of extra-marital affairs. If the husband had been away for more than nine months, the infidelity was hard to conceal. If, however, the timing of his leave made paternity less easy to ascertain, there was a sense of neighbours and family silently counting the months off on their fingers. Some men, even if they knew, or guessed, they were not the father would still accept the child as their own; others could not forgive. The divorce rate, which had plunged during the economic Depression of the 1930s, soared in the war years. The annual number of adultery petitions filed after 1942 rose by 100 per cent above the 1939–42 average. By the final year of the war, the number of husbands suing for divorce on the grounds of adultery jumped eightfold – two out of every three petitions were brought by men. This contrasted with 1940 when men filed most of the petitions.

Rachel was sceptical about the rush to the altar – particularly among young women. An eighteen-year-old typist who worked in the Food Office was among those desperate to find a husband in uniform. She seized her chance at the end of September when the 18th Division descended on Sheringham determined to make the most of their embarkation leave. The typist's fiancé was due and she managed 'almost no work' that day. By the time the division left many weddings had taken place and the typist announced that she would marry her fiancé on Saturday afternoon when he returned on 48 hours' leave. He was expected on the morning of the wedding and would be back with his regiment on the Monday. 'She is very young and knows nothing about the man she is marrying,' Rachel pointed out, adding that she would not be surprised if he did not appear. Even before the wedding the planned honeymoon was cut short so that he could return to his regiment on the Sunday before being sent abroad. Rachel concluded it was a 'silly business': 'If they want to sleep together, they ought to do it without all this fuss and bother and the finality of a wedding ceremony. She is only eighteen and doesn't know anything about him or his family. But I suspect that the separation allowance has something to do with it.'

However, when the typist discovered just in time that her fiancé was already married, Rachel was sympathetic: 'She is very miserable and was dripping tears all over the typewriter. Poor child!' For those women who did go through with their wedding to a soldier in the 18th Division the next four years and – in some cases – the rest of their lives – would be marred by the tragedy of their death or the scars left by the terrible conditions of captivity their husband would endure in the Far East.

Many women left it too late to marry their soldier lover and instead faced the social stigma and financial hardship of bringing up a child alone. Their fate was raised several times in Parliament, particularly in the years after 1942 when more men were posted abroad. A handful of MPs campaigned for women to be allowed to marry 'by proxy' – a system by which the bride could post her consent to a soldier serving overseas and he could return his vows in the same way, thus saving a future child from the shame of illegitimacy. Two women Labour MPs, Janet Adamson (MP for Dartford) and Ellen Wilkinson (MP for Fulham, West), were at the forefront of the appeal, but the Government refused to countenance an innovation that might have ramifications in peacetime. Adamson argued that many soldiers, who were now in the thick of fighting and unsure whether they would return, had been given no embarkation leave and had therefore missed the opportunity to fulfil their promise to marry their girlfriend. Hundreds of other soldiers had written to the MP, complaining that they were serving their country but did not have the chance to do the right thing by their pregnant girlfriends. She added that this sorry state of affairs gave the mother no rights to a pension, or even the same rights as a couple who had been living 'in sin' before the soldier was sent abroad. Wilkinson added that, as a doctor, she had seen several cases of very young 'stupid' teenage girls, rather than the 'designing' women feared by opponents of marriage by proxy, who had fallen pregnant to servicemen who were then sent abroad.

Opposition to the principle seemed all the more unjust because many other countries allowed it. In October 1943, *The Times* reported the case of a German private held as a prisoner of war in Canada, who was allowed to marry his fiancée in Germany. A British POW, Andrew Hawarden, wrote home to his wife to tell her about a wedding that had taken place between a French prisoner and his fiancée at home. However, not all marriages by proxy went to plan. An injured GI who had promised to marry his English sweetheart but had been invalided back to the US posted her an engagement ring and, to speed up her visa application, arranged for a marriage by proxy. The service was held in the Catholic church where his family worshipped; it was broadcast on the American radio network and reported in local papers. The bride listened in to her own wedding over a transatlantic telephone link and could even make out the organ and the vows being read. Despite all the hoopla, the state of North Carolina did not recognise the union and the bride never, in fact, made it to the US.

When husbands returned on leave, it could feel like a second honeymoon. Rachel hoarded luxuries – like the last bath salts – that would make her more alluring when her husband returned, a time when she often felt nervous about seeing him again after such a long gap. She decided to let her hair grow out of its bob because it was hard to obtain a perm and then she avoided the hairdresser's altogether because she feared servicewomen had head lice. It soon became difficult to buy a comb, as there was said to be only one factory in England that still made them and before the war the country had relied on imports from France and Japan. The dentist said there was even a shortage of false teeth. Occasionally, she regretted not buying clothes and shoes in peacetime. In the office the women discussed how they were running short of nighties and underwear and were forced to 'economise' (presumably going without or not washing their clothes as often). Rachel noted that this was not such a problem while her husband was away.

In November 1941 she reflected that Jakob had joined the army a year ago and in that period they had spent only fourteen days together. The blackouts and lengthy days in the office made her long for natural light. She remembered the prewar dazzle of London but reminded herself that the last time she had seen the city was in the Blitz. The gloom was compounded by the domestic crises she faced without the help of her husband. The house was overrun with mice that fed off the scraps left for the pigs and chickens that so many people now kept. There were fewer cats to keep their numbers down because many owners had had their pets destroyed to save food, although she would later relent and allow her son Timothy to keep a kitten. She was also worried about his cough, which sounded dangerously like whooping cough.

Letters from Shetland were taking longer to reach her and the couple were experiencing the familiar will he/won't he tension about his next leave. Eventually she heard that he should be home at the beginning of December: 'which is nice but a most unfortunate time. I think the army should consult the men, so that their leaves can be dated properly – at all events married men.' She would not allow herself to be too excited, in case the break was cancelled, but she received a telegram when she was washing her hair to say that he would be on the late train that day. The hours before his arrival passed in such a state of excitement that she was unable to record in her diary anything else that happened that day. His trip home followed a familiar pattern. Before he arrived she wondered how they would get on: she had filled her life with so many superficial things to blunt the pain of separation that she feared there was no room for him. Inevitably, their short time together was bliss. When he left, she felt physically ill and could not even find consolation in books.

Although Christmas 1941 was miserable without Jakob, a few cracks of light started to appear in her blacked-out world. When he visited in the New Year, she accompanied him to London to see him off – she had longed to visit the city for months and noticed how untidy it was and how the women were wearing less make-up than last time. She also decided to take up a new job as a teacher at a boys' school in Norwich. It was a big decision because it meant leaving Timothy with her mother for several days a week while she lived in a hostel.

The year 1942 was when she became aware of the full horror of aerial bombardment. On 19 January she was eating a quiet tea at home when there was a load bang that drove Timothy and his kitten to hide in the cupboard under the stairs. She and her mother went out to see if they could discover what had happened. They saw a wisp of smoke and a neighbour told them four houses had been destroyed a few streets away. Rachel immediately thought about her friend, Peggy Smith, who had worked with her in the Food Office since the start of the war. The next morning her worst fears were realised: Peggy and her parents had been killed by a lone, low-flying bomber that had dropped two 500-kilo bombs. Rachel was deeply affected by Peggy's death and the loss of someone close to her made her more fearful for Jakob: she felt that because one person she knew had been killed, it somehow increased the risk of others dying.

A few weeks later Sheringham was rocked by news of the

desperate battle to save Singapore from the Japanese. Many local men, who were part of the 18th Division and had so recently spent their demarcation leave in the town, were now fighting for their lives several thousands of miles from home on a tropical island. Local people felt 'dismay and certainly disgust' at the way they had been abandoned. Although Rachel continued to worry that she had not heard from her husband, she was hugely grateful that he was not one of the soldiers sent out to the Far East. She was delighted when he was posted to Winchester, which meant she could see him more often and they could speak on the phone, but worried that the move was a prelude to her worst fear – an overseas posting.

On the night of 27/28 April 1942, it was Jakob who had the greatest cause for concern when Rachel witnessed the start of a massive aerial bombardment of Norwich. Before that evening, the city had enjoyed a period of eight months without any attack. This had led to some complacency and there were even stories that the council had locked up some public shelters to avoid them being vandalised. It was a moonlit night and the sirens started wailing at about thirty minutes past midnight. Rachel had already had a bath, knitted a few rows and then retired early. Even before the sirens had sent up their warning two pathfinder planes dropped parachute flares that lit up the streets. They then swooped down to machine-gun the centre; incendiary bombs started a blaze at the Midland and Great Northern Joint Railway Station. The fire spread to coaches waiting at the platform and then became an inferno that attacked a nearby grain store. A few minutes later, twenty-six aircraft dropped nearly 200 high-explosive bombs; the air vibrated with the throb of their engines. By then Rachel was sheltering in a reinforced scullery with other women who were 'jittery' at first, but gradually settled down. Having experienced the Blitz in London, she felt it sounded worse because the planes were flying lower and later commented that the people of Norwich lacked the grit and humour of Londoners. It was all over by about 3 a.m.

The next day everyone looked pale; only half the children came to school and many staff were absent. The city was transformed: the bombs had blown the roof off the Regal Cinema and pubs, churches and terraced houses looked jagged and shocked – Norwich had suddenly taken on the mantle of the East End of London. Rachel knew that there were heavy casualties – although she could not have realised that as many as 162 people had died and 600 were injured. To put her mother's mind at rest, she went home to Sheringham that night. A few days later, Jakob sent a telegram and then telephoned in a 'state of dreadful agitation'.

On 4 May 1942 another two bombs dropped on Norwich without any warning sirens; but there were no casualties. The weather suddenly turned very hot and the heat, together with the bomb damage, made the city dusty. Everyone seemed to be coughing. Firemen spent their time damping down blazes and some people slept in haystacks outside the city. Later, it was reported that one of the pupils from her school had been killed, but when the head boy attended the funeral there was no burial because they could not identify the body.

There was good news that month, though, when she learnt that Jakob was being posted to Maidstone in Kent. She would have liked somewhere nearer, but at least he was staying in Britain. A colleague of hers was devastated when her husband was sent abroad: 'She says she feels quite empty inside and can't settle to anything at all. She can manage a day at school, but at home she wanders restlessly from room to room and feels lost. She feels so dreadful because she wouldn't know if he were ill or needed her. But she has been married only a month – it is worse when you have lived with your husband for years before your whole life is torn apart.' Another colleague, a 'Mrs L', said the shock of being bombed had completely upset her, particularly her 'feminine function': 'She wants a baby desperately and doesn't have one. It annoys her when people think she does things to prevent it because it is one thing she really wants. It is funny how half the world wants babies and can't have them and the other [half] can have them and doesn't want them.'

But the threat of a bombing had its advantage for housewives. Rachel's mother had abandoned spring-cleaning, as it did not seem worth the bother since they might be bombed. She was 'half-shocked' at her own daring but admitted that the house was just as clean. Rachel observed that their landlady used the same reason as an excuse not to repair or paint the house, which Rachel said was falling down.

The arrival of the Morrison shelter produced a stir in Sheringham. The shelter, really just a large bed in a cage, was popular because, unlike the Anderson shelter, it was kept inside and was therefore warmer and less damp. Timothy grew to like it and would use it as a den in which to read. It took a while for others in Sheringham to adapt to it and Rachel reported one case where the owners slept *on top* of it, rather than inside. News of the mass bombing of Cologne led to jubilation among many of Rachel's acquaintances. Even her mother said she wished 50,000 German had died and 'that everyone with any German blood in them should be exterminated – quite overlooking the fact that this would include me.'

Rationing and shortages provided a constant refrain throughout her diary; she became a forager – not just in the hedgerows of Norfolk, but in the shops of nearby Norwich. She was glad that she lived by the sea, where fish was plentiful and there was no shortage of nutritious crabs. Their garden yielded gooseberries, peas and blackcurrants. The appearance of lemons in Sheringham led to great excitement, but the lack of soap – which she used as a form of contraception – caused anxiety. 'I shall soon have to have a baby because we can't do anything else. Not that we have quite reached the end of our resources yet.'

Rachel began to feel more conscious about those men who were not in the army, such as aerodrome workers, and who appeared to throw their money around. She was also acutely aware of the difference between army ranks: 'My aunt always makes me think that my husband is the only man in the ranks in the army. Her acquaintances and relatives are all married to officers.' The news that both teachers and soldiers were to receive an increase in pay highlighted for her the inequity of the system, even though, by now Jakob had been made a lance bombardier and would eventually earn promotion to corporal: 'And I can't see why a soldier's child should have 1s per week increase but an officer's 1s per day. A child is a child, whatever his father, but I suppose without a revolution this sort of thing will always go on. But I don't think it's right.'

As the summer drew to a close, Rachel confessed that something fundamental in her outlook on life had changed. She had spent her husband's forty-eight hours' leave with him in Norwich and then they went to the golf links. She lay on the beach reading while Timothy played in the sand. 'Every time he goes it seems much worse to me. I feel as though I just can't bear it, though I know I must & can. And then I discovered that despite everything I wasn't going to have a baby, which disappointed me very much indeed, because I want another baby. . . . I shall go to bed. I feel lonely and miserable. I wish the war were over.'

At the end of September she noticed American soldiers on the streets of Norwich. They looked unhappy, but she speculated that this might be because they were largely ignored and because of the cold weather. By the following summer, Rachel had less sympathy for the Americans and their tendency to spend money freely and to encourage their adoring women to drink heavily. She blamed the GIs for Norwich's 'scruffiness'. A restaurant that had been 'all right' before the war was now 'nauseating' – 'It was dirty and the food was appalling and the prices were exorbitant. There were several Americans with girls and they were all drunk to the point of vomit.'

A friend had encountered a group of females who were drunk at 2 p.m. and could not stand without help. The head of a girls' secondary school had been forced to warn the pupils about the way they were behaving with the Americans. In the Midlands, Diana Carnegie had also had an unpleasant encounter with Americans: 'Disgusting – Leicester platform was covered with USA soldiers passing out & being sick when I arrived – really revolting.'

Certainly, some women found the GIs irresistible. Their polite manners and greater ease with females and children made them seem like Hollywood stars stepped down from the silver screen. They knew how to smooth-talk a girl and they were less uptight than most British men – a trait that was most evident in the way they danced: not a courtly ballroom glide but a frantic jitterbug or smoochy shuffle. A GI earned about five times more than a British private and, as well as being 'over-paid', had ready access to luxuries such as chocolate, Nylons and talcum powder. Rachel noted how it had become commonplace to see children in Norwich chewing gum they had been given by Americans. And, on top of all these many advantages, the GIs were *here* – not in the Far East, or Europe or some distant British Ack-Ack gun emplacement.

Many of the romances between GIs and British women – some of whom were married – emerged from sheer loneliness. Even if letters arrived regularly, not every husband or boyfriend in the British Army was a gifted writer capable of courting his wife or sweetheart by post. The officers' handbook, *The Soldier's Welfare*, recognised this problem and encouraged officers to give their men advice on letter writing. Rachel also did her bit by helping a young soldier called Fred, who was living next door. He could read but not write and, as a result, found it difficult to hold onto a girlfriend. When Fred, who was from Bolton, finally proposed to an Irish girl, Rachel, who knew the importance of letters as a way of sustaining a relationship, wrote to her to help fill the gap left by his stuttering correspondence. Soldiers could also request compassionate leave but, as Diana Carnegie discovered, this was not easily granted. Applications soared as the war progressed and had risen to 419,000 in its final year, compared to 16,000 in 1941. The Soldiers', Sailors' and Airmen's Families Association and local police could be drafted in to help establish whether leave was really necessary. In extreme cases, worries about who was keeping their wife's bed warm could lead to mental breakdown or a soldier going absent without leave.

Although many romances faltered once the soldier left for Europe, about 80,000 women became GI brides after the war. One estimate suggests that the American soldiers also fathered around 70,000 illegitimate children. It was easy for a GI to apply for a transfer if he wanted to dodge his responsibility, while it could take months to secure the necessary paperwork to allow a British woman to marry a GI. The procedure involved lengthy checks on the man's situation in America to see whether he could afford to support a wife.

The influx of bored young men, who might also be missing home and keyed up at the thought of going into battle, could lead to violence – often triggered by jealousy over a woman. In Norfolk a British soldier who returned home unexpectedly to find his wife in bed with a GI threw him to his death from a second-storey window. There were at least two cases of Canadian soldiers killing their lovers in acts of jealousy. In March 1943, a Canadian was hanged for murdering his lover, a Brighton woman whose husband was a POW, after he discovered she was having an affair with another Canadian serviceman. Such stories filtered back to British soldiers and helped fuel their insecurities.

The arrival of black GIs on British soil added another level of tension. Few Britons had any experience of soldiers from a different ethnic background and in many instances the black soldiers received a warmer reception than in their racially segregated home states. British women were oblivious to the idea of a 'colour bar' and were keen to dance and drink with the black GIs. This relaxed attitude angered many white American troops and, at its worst, led to outbreaks of violence. American troops fought one another in the Cornish town of Launceston in September 1943 and the following year, riots erupted after a black sailor was spotted kissing a white girl at a railway station in Manchester. There were other cases of white troops ejecting black soldiers from pubs and bars. Rachel reported an instance in September 1942 when some white American soldiers had refused to eat in the same restaurant in Norwich as black GIs. A local woman stood up and said that if the men were good enough to fight, they were good enough to mix with, but the lone protest failed and the black soldiers had to leave. The most serious case arose in May 1944, when a US Army court martial sentenced a black soldier to death after allegedly raping a woman in a village near Bath. The *Daily Mirror* found several holes in the woman's testimony and a petition signed by 30,000 readers prompted General Eisenhower to overturn the conviction.

Rachel's friend on the other side of the country, in Barrow-in-Furness, had a theory about why passions were running so high and why this led to a sudden surge in fecundity: she believed that love making was more passionate after a long spell apart and that this increased the chances of conception. Her friend was herself expecting – although they had been taking precautions. She added that she knew someone who had been married for five years without falling pregnant and then managed to conceive on only her husband's third leave. By September 1942, Rachel too had become part of the 'epidemic' of pregnant women. Although the pregnancy had been planned, she suffered occasional bleak moments: 'I can't imagine why I ever decided to have another baby. . . . It was a very silly idea, but alas! I fear there is very little I can do about it. I can't imagine what makes me feel like this suddenly. I have been so happy about it until now. I sometimes feel that I should be really grateful to a bomb which scored a direct hit on me.'

She bought a cradle sooner than she might have to avoid not being able to find one later; knitting a matinee jacket made her feel a little more optimistic. Her mood lifted further when Jakob visited in November and declared how pleased he was about her pregnancy and that he hoped it would be twins. 'No one reading this diary could believe how happy we are – yet the only thing that could make us happier would be for us to be together always.' She even began to hope that the baby would be born into peace.

During her last few days at school she felt distanced from the other teachers, although she appeared to find humour in the tragic and the absurd. When, in November, her uncle tried to take his own life, two teachers commented on his lack of patriotism at wasting gas when there was a shortage of fuel. She also heard how a couple were using their Morrison shelter as a cage to lock their children in so that they could go out for the night.

The Allied attacks on German towns intensified in 1943 and provoked mixed feelings for her. She had lived in Düsseldorf and knew people there and was distressed by the bombing of her father's birthplace, Aachen. When her second son, Nicholas, was born in June 1943, his arrival made her reflect on the tragedy of war: 'I look at Nicki and think of the other mothers and babies in Germany. It might so easily have been me.'

14

The Prisoner of War's Wife: Renee Boardman, 1942–44

As a girl of thirteen, Irene ('Renee') Isherwood was known in the mining community where she lived as the 'Gracie Fields of tomorrow'. In 1932 the British & Continental Film Company offered her a screen test, but her parents, who ran the local butcher's in Leigh, a few miles southeast of Wigan, viewed both the movie business and London with deep suspicion and so she stayed in Lancashire. Instead, she sang and danced at church events, colliery performances and the occasional bigger venue such as The Theatre Royal, Leigh, and a 'go as you please', a sort of *X Factor* of its day, at the much-grander Manchester Hippodrome & Ardwick Empire. She became known for her rendition of the music hall number 'Burlington Bertie', and cut a diminutive figure in her shiny black suit, a top hat over her girlish bob, a cane tucked under one arm.

Tom Boardman met her when they were both young teenagers performing in the pantomime *Dick Whittington*. He was immediately star-struck. Tom came from a nearby mining family in Howe Bridge, a suburb of Atherton, near Manchester. As well as amateur dramatics, he enjoyed sport and playing the ukulele, inspired by Wigan-born George Formby, who would soon be bringing his special brand of winking innuendo to the troops.

Tom and Renee appeared to be the perfect match. They were

both miniatures: small in stature, but with an outgoing, optimistic personality; they loved dancing – particularly the quickstep and cha-cha-cha. One Sunday afternoon, when they were strolling in the park, Tom, who spoke with a strong Lancashire accent, proposed. At the time he was working in an office job at Lancashire United Transport, a bus company that dominated the routes around Liverpool and Manchester. Both families were delighted and Tom's father fried up some steak in butter to celebrate. When they were at the jeweller's to pick out an engagement ring, Renee suggested that Tom should have something to wear too and chose an unusual gold ring with a two-headed serpent with ruby eyes. A few days later, just before the outbreak of war, Tom joined the Royal Army Ordnance Corps (RAOC), which was responsible for the repair of military vehicles and equipment, among other tasks.

They married on 19 August 1940. Tom had hoped to wear his civilian clothes, but Renee was proud of the fact that he had been made a sergeant and persuaded him to come in uniform. Despite wartime shortages, they had four bridesmaids and Renee's dress was made of white silk and taffeta inlaid with lace. He looks solid in his uniform and she is petite, her head barely reaching his shoulder. About eighty guests came to their reception in the Co-op Hall Restaurant. They honeymooned in Blackpool before she returned to her job as a weaver in charge of eight looms at Courtaulds, a cotton mill in Leigh, and he went back to barracks.

In 1941 he was posted to Nottingham and she joined him there for his week's embarkation leave in February. They managed to combine both their interests by ice-skating at the Palais de Dans and watching the Scottish fly-weight boxing champion, Jackie Paterson, retain his Commonwealth and British titles. They pussyfooted around what Renee should do if Tom failed to return and did not get as far as discussing whether she should remarry. He had no idea where he was being posted. They said their goodbyes during the week's leave and Renee decided not to wave him off from Liverpool.

Once Tom and his mates realised their ship was heading away from Europe and towards distant and peaceful Singapore he thought, 'We're quids in here!' He sent Renee a cable when he arrived in May 1941; it was followed by months of silence.

On the night of 7 December 1941 Japanese troops invaded Thailand and started to fight their way down the Malayan Peninsula towards Singapore with a speed and efficiency that shocked their enemies. On 15 February 1942 Lieutenant General Percival surrendered the island and 14,000 Australian, 16,000 British and 32,000 Indian troops became POWs. Tom was among them. In the sweltering heat of the tropical island, he knew that once he became a prisoner the guards would rob him of his valuables. For most soldiers this meant a watch, fountain pen or jewellery; Tom's most precious possession was the snake ring. He scooped out a bar of soap he had been carrying in his haversack; then pushed the ring into the centre and smoothed it over. Once it had been used a few times the ring became firmly embedded in its hard, soapy case. Although soap was a prized possession in the extreme heat and amid the physical exertion of the slave labour the POWs were to endure, Tom never once used the bar over the next three-and-a-half years of captivity.

It took months – sometimes years – for families of men captured in the Far East to discover whether their loved-one was alive. Renee listened to the wireless and pored over newspapers for snippets of news. Wives also faced financial hardship. Once a man had been classified as 'missing', he was assumed after a reasonable amount of time to have been killed and the wife lost her allowances and received a meagre pension of around £1 per week plus about 6 shillings per child. It was not until August 1942 that Renee knew that Tom had not died. By then her days were filled with her own arduous war work. As so many men had been called up there was a greater need for women to play their part, and from March 1941 all women aged from around eighteen to forty-five had to register at an employment exchange and were asked to opt for the type of work they felt they could do and to give details of their domestic situation. At the same time, the Ministry of Labour, which was keen not to wreak further disruption on families, asked for female *volunteers* to help with the shortage of workers.

In December that year, the National Service Act (No. 2) conscripted childless widows and single women aged twenty to thirty; this was later extended to include women, single or widowed, of between twenty and thirty years. Mothers with children under the age of fourteen could ask to be exempt and women who were teachers, nurses or who had specific domestic responsibilities and pregnant women could usually remain as civilians. By mid-1943, almost 90 per cent of single women and 80 per cent of married women were employed in essential war work.

The government further divided the workforce into 'mobile' and 'immobile' workers. Mobile workers could leave their home to work in another part of the country where the shortage of manpower was particularly acute. Married women, regardless of their age and whether they had children or not, were 'immobile'. As the war progressed the rules were relaxed and some married women ventured further afield. Parts of Wales, where women had traditionally stayed firmly at home, were exposed to bus and train loads of females wearing slacks, turbans and lipstick, who descended on the valleys in search of extra money. Although government posters and films such as *Millions Like Us* (1943) stressed the excitement of leaving home to live in hostels and work in factories, the reality was more complicated. Many women, who had barely been outside their town, suffered from homesickness and found it difficult to adjust to communal living. Several of the jobs, too, were extremely dangerous.

At first, Renee continued to work at Courtaulds, but then she was moved to the Royal Ordnance Factory at Risley, near Warrington. She travelled there daily by bus and was lucky that her sister, Joyce, and a good friend, Elsie Gittins, also worked at

Risley. The setting seemed perfect for her extrovert character. Factories could be vibrant, cheerful places where young women consoled one another about the absence of men or plotted the acquisition of a boyfriend or husband. Loudspeakers broadcast programmes from the wireless. *Music While You Work* brought popular singers into the workplace, while *Workers' Playtime* transported audiences to a works canteen 'somewhere in Britain', where a variety of performers entertained a live audience. Factories also organised their own choirs or am-dram groups to perform at lunchtime and Renee enjoyed entertaining her workmates.

Some women relished the physical expression of making anonymous mechanical parts, while others felt the hard work was only really worth it if they knew what the final product would be. Although they had no official uniform and were forbidden from talking about what they did, they were, in a more direct way than any other British women, helping to kill the enemy. In her hugely popular comic song 'The Thing-Ummy-Bob (That's Gonna Win The War)', Gracie Fields compares munitions workers to Florence Nightingale and Grace Darling. Workers had a definite pride in what they were doing. Some factories kept a running total of how many shells they had produced or pasted posters on the wall of the ships they had sunk. There were stories of notes of encouragement that workers had tucked into shellcases and how, occasionally, the woman who had signed the note received a message, or even a visit, from the soldier who had fired the shell. One Ack-Ack emplacement in Southern England even named a gun after 'Mary', the female worker who had slipped a note to them.

Working at a munitions factory also paid well – which was an important consideration to the wife of an ordinary soldier like Tom. Wives usually received about a third of their husband's pay, but this calculation was worked out based on a very low rate. A woman such as Renee, with no dependants, received about 10 shillings a week – less than a sixth of the average wartime factory wage for a female.

However, a munitions worker could earn between £2 and £4 a week, which could rise to £8 if she did overtime or earned a bonus for meeting targets. The days were long and usually organised around a shift system of, for example, 2–10 p.m., 10 p.m.–6 a.m. or 6 a.m.–2 p.m. The work required intense concentration and could involve a long and complicated journey by public transport.

As well as the camaraderie suggested by Gracie Fields' song, munitions workers also had to put up with the usual petty squabbles, rivalries and bullying by fellow workers and the occasional sadistic boss who enjoyed the power he held over his female workforce. Some women, with limited experience of the workplace, found these trials difficult to bear. Renee's talent as a performer gave her a special place in the ammunitions factory but, like many young women, she found the inherent danger attached to producing deadly weapons difficult to cope with. Factories, although camouflaged, were among the Luftwaffe's most sought-after targets. And if the enemy did succeed in hitting one, it was a case of bomb colliding with more explosives in a devastating cocktail. Tom did not know exactly what kind of work his wife was doing, but he heard from the radios, hidden at great risk by the POWs, that the industrial areas of northwest Britain were being bombed regularly and he worried about his family's safety.

Even without the help of the Luftwaffe, the munitions factories were highly volatile places. As they were working with ingredients such as tetryl, cordite and trinitrotoluene (TNT), staff were searched on entering and leaving the building – not just for reasons of national security but to check that they were not wearing anything that could spark an explosion. They were forced to hand over objects like jewellery, hair clips and combs, which all reflected their personality and history but which could be dangerous in such an explosive environment. Wives had to remove their wedding band, or if this was impossible, have it taped over. Even a boiled sweet was seen as deadly since it might put the worker at risk of transferring some of the toxic material she was handling straight to her mouth.

Thousands of miles away in the tropical jungle of Thailand, Tom still carried a studio photo of Renee in her Saturday-best clothes and coiffure; he had no way of knowing that her hair was now hidden under a scarf or turban. Just as he was shedding clothes in response to the heat and slave labour and was reduced to a 'Jap Happy' or loincloth, she was covering up to comply with strict rules. Munitions workers like Renee wore regulation overalls or dungarees and donned sturdy, flat shoes. Their work was closely supervised – for obvious reasons: if a parachute had not been packed properly it could mean a man's death. But the scrutiny added another level of tension to a shift of eight hours – or longer – when women were already under pressure to maintain high levels of production. Smoking was allowed in the canteen only.

Risley was a desolate place: it was flat and frequently wrapped in mist – which at least gave it the advantage of being hidden from the German bombers. Sheep often wandered into the bunkers where the women sat out air raids and could provide a woolly perch. The site was said to be haunted, but Risley's real horrors were man-made and explained why people who worked in its most dangerous parts, and workers in other shell-filling factories, were described as being 'on the suicide squad'. Nearly 22,000 staff worked at Risley – mainly women but a few ex-miners – who were bussed in from local towns or hostels. They were divided between 'clean' and 'dirty' areas. The 'clean' areas were the most dangerous because, if an accident happened here, it could kill or maim. Women like Renee had the fiddly job of filling shells, protected by a glass screen or goggles and cumbersome gauntlets. But the gloves made the job harder and many women were tempted to remove them. This was a perilous strategy because the heat from their fingers could trigger an explosion and lead to the loss of fingers and hands; at least one woman was blinded. New workers were sometimes shown round by these mutilated women, but the reason for their deformities was not usually explained – making their disfigurement all the more sinister.

Renee found the powder they handled particularly troublesome. Despite the scarves and turbans, it turned hair, face and hands yellow and refused to wash out; some women made the affliction even worse by scouring their skin with bleach, peroxide and detergents. Blowing your nose produced a hanky full of yellow mucus, an all-too-vivid reminder that the deadly substance had invaded the body. After a humid night's sleep a woman might wake to find herself wrapped in jaundice-coloured sheets. The problem was not new: in the First World War women who worked with TNT were known as 'canaries' because of their colour. Occasionally, a woman might view the change in hair colour as a perk of the job, although hair did not always turn the desired shade: if you were naturally blonde or red-headed, then your hair might turn green; black hair could become red. Even more disturbing, the whites of your eyes might become yellow.

TNT and other toxic materials, such as mercury powder, caused awful rashes in many women, including Renee. Some endured weeping boils on their faces and, as a result, had to wear bibs covering their upper bodies. A few factories issued 'barrier' creams and thick Max Factor 'cake' make-up, but most women preferred to plaster on their own foundation – which may go some way to explaining why factory workers look so glamorous in publicity photos. Many workers were also exposed to high levels of lead and given milk to drink in an attempt to counteract its effects. We will probably never know the long-term health implications of exposure to so many toxins.

Renee found the emotional stress of working at Risley harder to bear than even the physical discomfort. There were many accidents at the site – partly because it was used for testing new explosives – but also because financial incentives and targets drove workers to turn out as many shells as possible. Renee helped to assemble detonators, which were among the most dangerous commodities because they contained the most powerful powder. The merest judder or spark could trigger an explosion. The worst accidents, in which women were maimed or even killed, usually involved detonators – for example, if the person carrying them tripped or stumbled. The workers were fully aware of the risks they faced. They were given a detailed safety booklet to read and were constantly reminded of the precautions they should take. A woman carrying a tray of detonators was often accompanied by two other workers – one in front and the other at the back, both carrying red flags to clear a route for the hazardous load. For the workers who saw accidents, the sights were as searing as anything a soldier witnessed on the battlefield.

Eventually, the strain of working in such a dangerous, driven place, plus a severe skin complaint that had to be treated in Manchester, led Renee to suffer a breakdown and she was transferred to a factory, Burgess Ledward, at Walkden, Greater Manchester, which made parachutes. Though now relieved of the stress of working under such volatile conditions, she lived with the constant uncertainty about Tom. Japan had signed, but not ratified, the 1929 Geneva Convention concerning POWs and far fewer Red Cross parcels reached prisoners. Just as significantly, Japanese guards viewed the act of being taken prisoner as a great dishonour and, since the Allies captured very few Japanese soldiers alive, there was no sense of mutual respect for prisoners and their families waiting at home. As a result, families of Far East POWs did not benefit from the much more frequent exchange of letters that was normal between POWs held in Europe and their loved ones. Renee and Tom, however, were – comparatively – fortunate in that she knew he had been taken as a POW.

But anxious relatives waiting at home had no inkling of the conditions in Thailand – where Tom was taken from Singapore. In

1942 the British Red Cross began to publish a free magazine for relatives of POWs held in Europe, called *Prisoner of War*, but families of men in the Far East remained in the dark until the first edition of *Far East* appeared in 1944. Although the information could not be as detailed as in the magazine aimed at families of European POWs, it did, at least, make relatives feel less isolated. The British Red Cross also set up centres around the country to support worried family members of Far East POWs. Relatives were encouraged to drop in or to telephone or write for advice.

Many families received some communication, even if it was just the most basic of facts, about their loved ones in 1943. But the place names and red Japanese characters on the pre-printed card Renee received conveyed little more than an exotic foreignness. It was only later that place names like Changi, the military cantonment on Singapore, and then Thai names such as Ban Pong, Chungkai, Wampo, Tarsao and Takanum started to form a picture in her mind. Like other families of Far East POWs, she could not imagine the jungle, the humidity and the tropical illness. Nor could she know that Tom was one of thousands of POWs who were being used as slave labourers to build the Thailand-Burma Railway, later known as the Death Railway. Around 22 per cent of British labourers died working on the line. It was not until Sir Anthony Eden's speech to Parliament on 28 January 1944 that anyone in Britain had any clue of the privations suffered on the railway: the disease, starvation and violence.

While Eden was attempting to describe an unimaginable world, Tom still had his bar of soap with the ring Renee had given him hidden inside and was still entertaining his fellow POWs. He was still cheering himself up – and those around him – by making music. While he was a patient at Chungkai hospital camp, close to the crossing that became famous in the 1957 film *Bridge on the River Kwai*, he made a ukulele from packing cases and telegraph wires. At home, Renee found some release for her anxiety by going to church and praying. She wrote to Tom two or three times a day, but only a handful of letters reached him. On one never-to-be-forgotten day, when he was 'up country', deep in the Thai jungle, 'several inches' of letters arrived at once and in one Renee had enclosed a photo of herself.

Until the war, Renee had had no reason to write letters because all her family lived close by, but, like many couples, the war meant separation and letters became the main way to communicate. Writing to a POW in the Far East was an act of faith. It could take a year or more for post to arrive in England and, even then, the communication might be little more than a series of pre-printed statements such as 'I am interned in [space to fill in camp name]'; 'My health is excellent . . .' The rules about how to write to POWs in the Far East also changed constantly. Adverts in the British press warned that the Japanese had stipulated that communication must be in typed letters, then limited to twenty-five words, then restricted to pre-stamped airmail postcards.

As in the First World War, women became adept at using networks to support one another when they faced months, sometimes years, of silence. And, also as in that earlier war, it was often the officer's wife who was at the centre of a web of information that stretched out across the country to disseminate meagre facts about a captured soldier and his regiment. Phyllis Baker fulfilled this role for the wives, mothers and sweethearts of men who were held with her husband, Captain Barton (known as 'Barry') Custance Baker, of the Royal Corps of Signals, 27 Line Section. Phyllis and Barry met after a May ball at Cambridge University, where they were both undergraduates, and married two summers later in July 1939, by which time Barry was a commissioned officer in the Royal Signals. Their son, Robin, was born in December 1940. The seventy men in the signals section under his command came from a diverse background and included workers from Glasgow's Post Office Reserve Unit, as well as men from the West Country. Many had already survived the evacuation of Dunkirk of 1940; eighteen months later, they were at the fall of Singapore.

From that point on, Phyllis, Renee and other wives wrote into a void. The Royal Signals Record Office had no idea what had happened to the men and could only give them the official tag of 'missing'. In mid-February Phyllis circulated a letter to all the families in Barry's unit for whom she had addresses and received several letters in reply saying how grateful they were to feel that someone else was in a similar position. Over the years that followed she kept in touch with families, who in turn sent her any news that they received. At regular intervals during the war she wrote a letter that she circulated to the families and friends she had addresses for. It was a laborious task that meant retyping the same letter over and over and presenting a positive front in the face of silence and rumours. She also wrote letters of condolence to those who had heard that their husband had died – usually from a tropical illness. Families wrote back to her: more than 80 letters in 1944 and 100 in 1945. Phyllis's stoicism is even more impressive because she did not hear from her own husband until January 1944.

Later that year the Allies torpedoed or bombed several Japanese transport ships, unaware that they were carrying POWs. The survivors, who included members of the Royal Corps of Signals, were debriefed in an attempt to find out more about the fate of the other POWs. Phyllis, with the help of another wife, compiled a dossier of information and photographs about the missing men from the Signals Unit and sent it to the War Office. She also relayed the information she received from the War Office back to the families and reassured her readers that conditions after the completion of the railway must have improved and that the men who had been chosen for the transport ships were among the healthiest. It would not be long before they all realised how wildly optimistic her well-meant words had been.

*

In Norfolk, another wife, Daisy Duffield, was listening out for POWs – this time those in Europe. In autumn 1944 she wrote to a Mrs Dolly Booty with news of her husband, Ernest Francis Booty, a farm worker who had joined up in 1942, when he was twenty-two. Daisy was enjoying a foreign radio station when she heard that E. Booty Number 11407484, a private in the Durham Light Infantry, had been taken prisoner. He was well and Dolly was not to worry about him. (Although Daisy did not know this at the time, he was being held in Stalag XI-B, Fallingbostel in Lower Saxony.) Daisy finished by saying: 'I hope he will be able to write to you soon and that this war will soon be over so that you will have him back with you again, I also hope you will not mind me writing to you, but I thought perhaps you would like to know, if you have not already heard.'

Mrs Booty, who lived in Norwich, was delighted:

> Just a letter thanking you very much indeed for letting me know about my husband. I haven't heard from the war office yet and I'm ever so glad that I got your letter first as it is not such a worry knowing that he is a prisoner as to get the usual war office letter to say that he is missing. I had a letter from him last Thursday and he was in Holland so they were quick putting the news through weren't they. I never listen to the foreign stations and I'm glad I don't as it was much better to hear it from you. Do you ever come into Norwich in the mornings as I should like to meet you and thank you personally. I work at Buntings on the Haberdashery from 9 till 1.30 every day. So goodbye for now.

A week later, Daisy wrote to say that she had heard his name on the wireless again. His message was, 'Dear Dolly I am quite well, hope you are, I will always love you'. She said she was pleased to receive Dolly's letter but did not need thanking, 'if my husband was abroad, I should like some news, I think that word missing is awful'. She told her not to be surprised if she called in to the haberdasher's where

Dolly worked, 'I should love to know if you get letters from him, which you will as soon as he gets to a permanent camp'. A friendship quickly grew up between the two women and Daisy visited the shop where Dolly worked. Dolly gave her some ribbon and a hair grip for Hazel – presumably her daughter.

Daisy spent long evenings scribbling down names, addresses, numbers and messages snatched from the wireless via the crackly ether: 'Hello my darling don't worry I'm well You and ? are always in my thought (Vivian, Grimsby, 4804333)'. She wrote to Mrs Thompson in Sheffield about her two boys and the grateful mother replied: 'If you have anyone dear to you serving with the forces please accept our best wishes for their well being.' Nellie Kersham from near Oldham wrote: 'I am glad there are women like yourself that try to help people in this way. Its heartbreaking news but it could be worse, glad he is alive.' Mary Chambers, near Newcastle, said: 'it is so nice to have such kind friends' and that she would keep the letters to show her husband when he returned.

Nor was Daisy the only one to write. Many of the mothers and wives she contacted told her that other strangers had been in touch to pass on messages they might have missed. In such cases, the fact that a stranger wanted to comfort them seemed to provide nearly as much solace as the knowledge that their son or husband was alive.

15

The End of the War: Surviving the Peace, 1943–45

Whether Diana Carnegie wrote any letters after the death at just six months of their baby, Carolyn, from a form of childhood anaemia, is not known. If she did, none have survived. Her correspondence resumes again in 1943 – when she has good cause to celebrate.

She thought 'it' was more likely to arrive on 28 June 1943 and, since she knew James, who was stationed at Holsworthy in Devon, could not be there for the birth, she suggested he should come a day or two after the event, 'as one always feels wonderful the next day, with relief & then the reaction sets in & one feels very low & weak & so it would cheer me up more then.' She had scrubbed the cot, but 'it's a terrific business trying to get all the clothes aired' and had sprained her wrist with all the 'washing and wringing'. The unborn baby, whom she referred to as 'Whirling Willie', kept her awake at night: 'I've never known anything like it – he seemed to be trying to burst his way out of my tummy – most wearying!'

Diana went into labour at a nursing home near Windsor on Sunday, 26 June 1943. Through the agonies of birth she heard the guards' bands marching to church and reflected that if she gave birth to a boy it would probably be 'frightfully martial'. When Susan

Diana was born on Monday, 27 June, Diana revised her assessment, 'I suppose she'll always run after the soldiers'.

Friends visited mother and baby in the nursing home and declared her 'lovely because she is so miniature' (she weighed just over 6½ pounds). The nurse could not stop kissing the back of the baby's head – as if she, not Diana, had given birth – and sat with her on her knee. Not surprisingly, after the tragedy of their first baby, Diana's letters to James were full of Susan's progress and milestones on her way to a healthy childhood. Susan eats 'like a Roman Emperor (or her father!)'. 'WE WEIGH 7LBS. TODAY – AREN'T WE CLEVER?!'; Diana 'enclosed' a hiccough from Susan.

Rationing and shortages played a much greater part in her second pregnancy. She asked James to hurry to obtain Susan's ration book because there was a chance they might avoid the new regulations – 'It's the limit increasing pregnant women's rations [they were allowed more meat] just when I've stopped being one – & cutting down babies['] as soon as I've got one!' She asked him to send her jam and eggs, and to bring soap, marmalade, biscuits 'on her points', and orange juice, which was a luxury allowed to babies, pregnant women and the sick. Hospital visitors brought food: cakes, sandwiches and buns or raspberries, peaches and tomatoes from the garden, rather than the traditional wilting flowers and tired grapes. James used up all his ration vouchers sending her a packet of chocolate. Rites of passage, like taking a photo of the new baby, were harder to achieve in wartime and she was delighted when James managed to find film: 'You've made my day for me! I'm longing to have some photos of the little poppet.' Later, though, when she sent him some photos she thought that she looked like 'a v experienced but ugly French tart – and I suppose you realise that in the other which you've been gaily showing around . . . I've got a completely bare & rather repulsive bosom –which luckily they haven't touched up in the painting?!'

Soon after giving birth, Diana was starting to think about her figure: 'I have a top like Mae West & legs like Marlene Dietrich – neither of which will last for ever I feel – but I'm rather pleased, as I was measured for the awful battleship [probably a type of corset] yesterday – & taken fairly tightly was 26" round the waist & 32" hips – which is pretty good for a week after giving birth I feel.' Underwear was a major concern for wives in the Second World War – especially once Japan's entry into the conflict made materials such as silk and rubber almost impossible to come by. These shortages may explain why Diana became so obsessed with a missing pair of knickers. She had a 'rather unsuccessful battle on the tel.' with the laundry she was convinced had lost them and made James write to demand compensation. She found their reply 'really rather nice & very shaming "your wife's knickers"!!!' and hummed and hawed about how much compensation she should ask for: the knickers probably cost about 5/6 and would last another year but it would be impossible to find the same material now. She was relieved when the undergarments turned up at her ladyship's house.

Magazines and newspapers encouraged women to take their appearance seriously and to see a trim figure and well-fitting outfit as part of the war effort. Clothes rationing started in June 1941 and in May the following year, the Government introduced Utility Wear to ensure well-designed, good-quality affordable clothing. Even the celebrated *haute couturier* Norman Hartnell was called upon to create 'utility dresses and skirts'. By standardising production, the Government hoped to make factories more productive. But there was only so much suffering Diana would take in the name of fashion: 'I wore my new battleship till tea time today, when I couldn't bear it any longer – it is agony – sitting in it is a nightmare & my hipbones are raw! And I had to pay £5.5.0. for it & 3 coupons!' She was more optimistic about a prewar suspender belt that a friend had never worn and had promised to give her as a Christmas present; it was much nicer than anything she could buy now.

Over the next two years Diana sent James updates on Susan's

progress. She told him about her first tooth and her first steps, how she had learnt to say 'good-bye' and, if she found something difficult, 'aw dear [oh dear!]'. But she did not spare him graphic details of exploding nappies and unusual items found in potties. Their dog, Bengie, spent time with James in Devon but returned to be with Susan and Diana as the war progressed James was sent to different parts of the country and attended courses and helped command searchlight batteries in Blackheath, Eastbourne, Carlisle, Lincolnshire and London. After the birth, Diana, Susan and Bengie moved from Bletchley to a cottage near Haywards Heath in Sussex but also visited relatives in Suffolk, Scotland, Carlisle and Cumberland.

Diana found herself left to run a household alone and to deal with domestic chores that would not have concerned her in peacetime. It was her responsibility to catch mice and rats, to take the car to have its plugs cleaned and to mend the windscreen wiper. Finding and retaining a nanny was a major problem. One woman needed constant reassurance during the air raids; another was so slovenly that Diana's friends started to comment on how dirty the house looked. There were times when she felt like a drudge – 'Nanny is still a wreck, & I'm feeling more & more ghastly – have now got a boil in my arse, which is acute agony, & a sprained wrist from wringing nappies . . .' She added that she had ordered a new Dutch cap and hoped he would have 'the pleasure of meeting it next week!' but warned him that she had not washed her hair for a fortnight – this abstinence later stretched to three weeks.

The cottage's garden proved an unexpected solace, as well as an important additional source of food. She even asked for a hoe for her birthday. The sweet briar was 'heavenly' and she enjoyed the abundance of melons, onions, carrots, parsnips and sprouting broccoli. She tried to roll the lawn with Susan 'cackling with laughter' as she 'slithered & slipped'. A ride on a donkey caused further merriment.

Like families all over the country, Diana had to spend more time alone with her in-laws. Her letters to James are dotted with the irritations of family life – 'The m.in.law has taken to doing the most shattering & revolting pharts [sic] very loud – frightfully embarrassing!' His visits home offered a break from the drudgery, when he would bring her breakfast in bed, but his departure plunged her into despair: 'all the joy goes out of life when you go & it becomes just a dreary existence. I miss your help with the house, the coke, the wood, the mouse traps – pretty well everything.'

She was cheered by the war news but always worried that the Allies' advance might mean he would be sent abroad; she was alarmed when he joked about going to Burma – 'Don't like all those people being whisked away for the 2nd front, it's not likely to happen to you is it?' The start of what became known as the 'Baby Blitz' in summer 1944 brought her renewed worries about his safety – although he was still on British soil. In June the Germans dropped some 2,452 V1 pilotless 'flying bombs', or 'doodlebugs', on England. Whenever she heard the slow, throaty buzz of the V1, she was gripped with fear for him, especially when he was in London, and asked him to ring her after a raid. She was convinced that the barrage balloons tethered near their cottage in Sussex made them more of a target and, in truth, they did experience several raids: 'We had a horrible doodle last night, sounds as though it was coming straight towards us, then it's engine stopped – & it was 3 mins before the explosion – I was in my bath, & spent 3 v. unpleasant mins crouched up at one end of it, wondering if I dared get out & put a towel round me.' Another night a shell's tracer path flashed past the window and she could hear the anti-aircraft Bofors guns responding in the distance. On another occasion she was caught in a raid when stepping down from a bus and was forced to dive into a doorway, fearing she would be struck by shrapnel at any moment.

The V2 rockets, the long-range terror weapons which the Nazis started launching at England in September, gave her 'the creeps' and she was 'terrified' that he might be hit. The V2s killed more than 2,500 Londoners in the following six months, in addition to the V1 fatalities. James was part of the anti-aircraft force that managed to bring down a large proportion of both weapons before they reached their targets and his role and frequent visits to London made Diana particularly anxious. Susan started to imitate the sound of the V2s and one landed in a street close to her ladyship's house in London. She was shaken by the near-miss and a burglary in which her furs were taken. During the worst of the V2 attacks Diana and Susan went to Scotland, where she was grateful to sleep without fear of attack – 'The war really is going marvellously – why can't the Germans admit they're done & end it all,' she wrote to James.

By the start of 1945, she was allowing herself to think the unthinkable. 'Isn't the news wonderful only how much would I give to be with you the day Peace is declared – I wonder if it would be possible? I suppose it's pretty certain you'll all get a bit of leave to celebrate? If not I suppose I could get to you for 1 night . . .' She was cheered, not just by the prospect of peace, but by the fact that they had finally managed to buy their own home near Godstone in Surrey. It had taken her months of futile trips by pushbike, bus and train to see properties that turned out be 'n.b.g.' ('no bloody good'). Significantly, houses were now being advertised 'with possession *after the war*' and buying the cottage was another acknowledgement that they would soon be together permanently.

'I must say, I love the cottage more & more – it really is divine, even with nothing in it, & the garden's looking heavenly even though the grass is hay – & apparently it's the chickens that have been eating the veg. not the rabbits, which is a relief.' There were still annoyances: it was hardly worth painting the windows because wartime paint simply washed out during rain and she asked James to look out for light bulbs, which were in short supply. But she was cheered to find her bike nestling against his. 'Rather touching, they must have missed each other!' Susan, too, was growing stronger daily and could push the table away when she sat on her mother's lap. 'I have awful visions of a vast woman striding about in tweeds & brogues!' Diana wrote to James.

When the war in Europe officially ended and Tuesday, 8 May 1945 was declared a public holiday, Diana was determined to enjoy the celebrations, although she was forced to do so without her husband. James, who had so far been fortunate enough to avoid an overseas posting, was sent with the Royal Artillery to Germany and then Scandinavia. Diana travelled to London with friends to experience the biggest party the capital had ever seen. Afterwards she wrote, rather shamefacedly, that for the first time she had been 'naughty' and not written to him for two days. She wished she had, but it had been impossible with the 'V' celebrations going on. They started by cooking an enormous lunch for nine people at her cousin Lydia's before going to Westminster Abbey at 3 p.m. The service itself was 'disappointing', although there was standing room only. Afterwards they drove round 'rather aimlessly with nothing much happening' before heading home to Lydia's for tea. They drank whisky until they were 'fairly tiddly' and then went to the Athenaeum Club in Pall Mall, where James was a member. Diana had a 'set to' with the barmaid, who refused to serve them because James was not there. When Diana pointed out the reason why he was not there, the barmaid conceded and served them a rum and orange. They had a good dinner before stumbling out into the night.

Pathé and other news services recorded scenes of innocent jubilation that night – young women and servicemen entwined in paper streamers or dancing an unsteady, coiling conga; bemused children on their parents' shoulders waving union flags; thousands of fingers raised in a definite 'V' for victory sign; young couples wading in the fountains at Trafalgar Square, their trousers hoicked high to reveal pale flesh and exuberant youngsters hanging off trucks and lampposts. But Diana saw the bigger, uncensored picture. As they left the Athenaeum, heading for Buckingham

Palace, they tripped over 'fucking couples (in the dark)'. When they reached the Mall, they discovered they had just missed the King and Queen's appearance on the balcony and decided to head for Whitehall in the hope of seeing Churchill. Their pace slowed as the jostling crowds pressed in on them, but they managed to make their way behind a 'string of sailors with their girl friends rather like follow my leader – when they skipped & danced we had to keep up & we sang whatever songs they were singing'. Parliament Square was a 'seething mass' – 'We actually all got on to a jeep – but thank heaven it got so bad that it couldn't move as otherwise I know I should have been killed as I was only able to get one toe onto something that was sticking out and balance myself by a hand on the American's helmet! At that moment [Clement] Attlee [Deputy Prime Minister and leader of the Labour Party] & co appeared on the balcony – so we made a dash & got right in front of the crowd & immediately underneath him, we cheered suitably at all points of his ridiculous & boring speech at the same time mentioning that we'd like to see Churchill . . . & when Attlee had finished [Ernest] Bevin [Minister for Labour and National Service] (looking like a revolting gargoyle) came to the mike to speak – so we just yelled "we want Churchill" . . . & quite a lot of the crowd took it up, & he never got a word out & had to retire! We were terribly pleased with ourselves, as it was entirely our doing & he'd probably have said packets if it hadn't been for us. – wonder if you were listening to the wireless – if so you heard us?!'

From there they made their way back to the Palace, where their bones were 'nearly broken in the swelling mob'. They could hardly move or breathe, but eventually the royal family emerged and Diana and her friends 'cheered ourselves hoarse'. They left, disappointed not to have seen Churchill, but 'delighted at our efforts re Bevin!' When they got home the buildings were floodlit and 'looked lovely' – 'oh darling, you can imagine how I ached for you to be there, it would have been marvellous – & we'd have gone wild together &

never stopped. . . . I did enjoy it, & it's cheered me up mentally, I must have let off steam – but I just couldn't really get the proper spirit without you – it seemed so terribly wrong not to have you there. . . It's rather wonderful to feel there's no more war – oh – for the day when you're home again.'

The end of the war provided a painful reminder of their loss to thousands of widows. For wives like Renee Boardman, whose husband Tom was still a prisoner in the Far East, the celebrations only heightened their frustration. She celebrated both VE and VJ Days in Leigh, but felt 'lonely not knowing'.

On 6 August 1945 the Americans dropped the first atomic bomb on Hiroshima; Nagasaki was bombed three days later. Diana wrote to James, who was still in Germany, 'What news! What with the "atom" & Japan – wish they'd hurry up & surrender – needless to say, all I can think of is whether it'll mean that you'll be home any sooner – you jolly well ought to be – oh – I do hope so.'

For families waiting to hear what would happen to their loved ones in the Far East the news of the bombs, plus the Soviet invasion of Manchukuo, made the end seem tantalisingly close. Finally, on 15 August 1945, Japan surrendered and a slightly more muted version of VE Day was repeated on VJ (Victory over Japan) Day. But wives like Renee still had a long wait to see their husbands and during that time they began to suffer from acute worries about how they would adapt to life with a man they had not seen for four years. As they waited, stories of the appalling treatment suffered at the hands of the Japanese started to emerge.

Tom Boardman was flown in a Dakota plane to Rangoon and then boarded the SS *Corfu*. It took him twenty-eight days to reach Southampton, compared to the eight-week journey out to Singapore. In wartime the troops had been forced to travel via South Africa; his return trip was much more direct, via Sri Lanka and Suez. The *Corfu* was the first ship carrying former Far East

POWs to arrive back in Britain and reached Southampton on 7 October. Other soldiers had much longer journeys home. POWs and internees in Hong Kong who had been held for the longest time in captivity – since Christmas Day 1941 – were among those who travelled via the west coast of America. At ports such as San Francisco, they were transferred to hospital trains that took them north to Canada and then the five-day train journey to the east coast of America and the final Atlantic crossing.

Both routes were achingly long for anyone desperate to be reunited with their family, but, in retrospect, the tortuous route played an important part in the ex-POW's re-entry into normal life. Today, a wounded soldier can be flown home from a conflict zone in a matter of hours; even a planned departure, including a few days of Rest and Recuperation, can mean transporting a man from a battlefield to Britain within a week. The lengthy voyage for survivors of the war in the East gave them time to readjust and to do so surrounded by men who had gone through the same experience. They were 'weaned' off their meagre rice diets and reintroduced to European food. They started to wear 'proper' clothes again, and at each port of call they received their mail and sent cables home. The British Red Cross's *News from Britain* magazine helped them to fill in the gaps in their knowledge of the progress of the war and changes at home. Lectures suggested new careers and training opportunities. For many, a nurse or WREN provided their first encounter with a woman for several years. Some were shocked by the sound of a female voice and a tinkling laugh, and by their own shyness in speaking to a woman again after so long. There were flags and presents along the way but, for a few, the welcome only drove home a sense of guilt and shame that they had been forced to sit out the war – albeit in the most terrible of conditions. These feelings, together with an order not to talk about their experiences, only made it harder for returning POWs to share what they had been through with their families who, in turn, had been advised not to question their returned soldier about his experience. At the time, it was felt that dwelling on the past was not healthy and that details of the conditions in the camps would only upset the bereaved and the public in general. The emphasis led some men to believe that the country did not want to acknowledge what they had gone through.

Tom's parents had planned to welcome him home at Southampton but had decided not to because of the crowds that were expected. Indeed, the September edition of *Far East* advised families not to meet their men off the ships as the congestion might delay their disembarkation. Instead, Tom made his way to London and then on to Manchester. On 9 October he came 'plodding' down the street to Renee's parents' home, 12 Smithy Street, a three-bedroom, terraced house in Leigh. He arrived at about 11 p.m. Her father was still awake and there was a light on, although she had gone to bed. Mr Isherwood shouted up the stairs and Renee emerged in her dressing gown and burst into tears.

Despite strict instructions not to speak about his time in captivity, Renee wanted to know what he had gone through. He had suffered from malaria and dysentery and was still troubled by the effects of strongyloidiasis, a worm infection. As the years passed, he started to give talks about his imprisonment and he also made two trips to Singapore – both times with Renee. They travelled as far north as Wampo and Tom even described the holiday as 'quite romantic'. Although he had kept all his letters from Renee, they decided to burn them because they felt they were just too personal for anyone else to read. At first they lived with Renee's parents, but soon moved to 19 Clarence Street in Leigh, which had been owned by Tom's uncle. Their son, Ron, was born in 1949.

Returning to normal life after the war was difficult for most couples. There was little awareness of how the trauma of war might have affected servicemen and women and, unlike today, couples did not have the benefit of counselling. Many wives were frustrated at the length of time it took for their husbands to come home and then to leave the army. Diana Carnegie wrote to James of how envious she felt when she saw other people's husbands – James was now in Oslo and likely to stay there until at least November. Although he, too, was desperate for normal life to resume he had plenty of distractions. Diana had heard that it was possible to find lemons and champagne in Norway and wrote: 'I envy you your parties & the drink my goodness – if you don't bring me some back I'll divorce you for cruelty – Jean says you're allowed to bring 1 bot.scot free but most people bring stacks – but it is probably best to declare some of it? Thrilling about the stockings – please get me 4 pairs as fine as poss. Size 9 (English?!) & a sort of beigey-tan not brown & not whitish – I'm sure you know any way! I don't really know between a white or silver fox cape (or rather little coat with short sleeves if poss.!) I've no idea what the fashions will be – what do you think?' She also wondered if there was 'any chance of a rubber h.w.bottle?'

James, though, had obviously not been paying attention and was unsure exactly what colour stockings he should bring home. Diana wrote in exasperation: 'Darling, I can't cut up one of my few remaining stockings for the colour! I'm sure you know? A sort of sunburn colour not fawn or grey, I shall never forgive you if you don't bring me some.'

Their old flirtatious banter had also returned. She warned him to be prepared for 'the wreck of the woman you knew' and added that it was 'a bit fishy your having to go to Oslo for specs so soon after meeting the lovely blonde! . . . Glad to hear that your still being faithful to me! But sorry you're feeling so randy – expect I would be too – were I not so bowed down with care, (not that a little intercourse wouldn't be v. soothing to the nerves) think I'll have to do a course of "pink pills" before you return!'

She hoped that the Government would speed up the demobbing process and complained that the date when he was due to leave the army kept changing. If his letters continued to arrive only once a week she would scream. But she was also thinking of the new, postwar world. She was shocked by the election result in which the country rejected Churchill, its wartime leader, and returned a massive Labour majority: 'Pretty staggering isn't it? I wonder what'd happen to us all – I'm all for them settling their beastly labour difficulties – & there's quite a theory that whatever govt. got in now, couldn't cope with the situation successfully, & will be thrown out – but will we survive while they last?' Despite her fears, she paid a 'terrifying amount' for his membership of the London Stock Exchange so that he could return to his work as a stockbroker.

Although the immediate threat of bombing had disappeared, the exuberance of VE Day quickly faded into a bleak realisation that the next few years would be austere. Diana said she did not blame nannies for wanting to go abroad – 'England is completely grim at the moment.' She still faced petty domestic troubles alone. Ten of the local farmer's cows had broken through the hedge and run riot in the garden, eating all the turnips and beetroot and trampling the dwarf beans, onions, lettuce, winter greens and spinach. The invasion was all the more painful because rationing of many foods continued after VE Day. 'It's heart-breaking . . . Oh how I wish you were here to cope.' Later, she wrote, 'how utterly grim the winter looks – with no fuel, no food, & no petrol! Really if we go below our present rations, I don't know how we will manage – things have reached rock bottom . . . & it really is a problem, what to produce for each meal.' If it were not for him, she wrote with great melodrama, she would kill herself, adding, 'for God's sake bring as much drink as you can I'll need it anyway! . . .' And, in another letter, 'Oh darling – I ache & ache for you to be here – to back me up in my battles (not that you're ever v. good at that!) & advise me with all my worries but I suppose one day it will be so – though I fear I may be an old grey haired, pinched, harridan by then!'

But, as their reunion drew nearer, she began to feel nervous about seeing him again after their longest period apart as a couple: 'You'll be so sated with parties that you'll only want to sit at home, while, I who've done nothing else for a year will only want to go to parties!' In reality, she longed simply to go to the nearest pub with him and, like so many army wives through the ages, started to prepare for his return by planning to look her best. She booked herself in for a haircut and ordered a new dress and suit from a tailor in East Grinstead. The thought cheered her, although the purchases would swallow up thirty clothing coupons between them and in the end the tailor was unable to obtain the tweed she wanted for the suit. Instead, her dressmaker in London managed to find material for a new outfit. She wondered whether they could spend a night in the Savoy, although she had heard that most London hotels were fully booked. As their reunion drew nearer, she wrote to say that, as her period had arrived, they would not have the curse to 'thwart them'.

Suddenly, she realised that everything was about to change. 'Horrid to think I shall have to stop writing soon, I like being able to tell you everything (mostly my worries!) but still, for such a reason it really won't matter. I still can't quite believe it, can you? I feel it'll probably be put off – or you'll be held up or something?! Oh, I do hope not.'

Her father's arrival home also marked a turning point for Susan, who was now two-and-a-half years old and far too young to understand the momentous change that was about to happen. She was at an age when she was up to all sorts of mischief: unravelling the precious spool of film her father sent from Norway, trying to clean her shoes but daubing the polish on her face and eating from Bengie's dog bowl. Both her parents worked hard to make sure that she knew that her father had a special place in her life. James sent her a telegram, presents and pictures from Norway – one of a pig – and Diana bought a wooden telephone and a car from him for Susan's birthday. She asked him to bring her back a doll from Sweden. Susan kissed his photo so often, and so vigorously, that it was in danger of disintegrating. She said 'Dad-dad' to it, but Diana admitted that she had said the same thing to an ATS girl at the railway station.

Thousands of children around Britain were also adapting to the tangible presence of a male figure ever-present in a photo and in conversation, but fundamentally absent, for the past few years. The returning husband and father had to fit into a complex web of relationships that had developed over the past few years. In her memoir *Bad Blood*, Lorna Sage describes how her grandparents turned her mother, whose husband was in the army, into a 'domestic drudge' who did most of the housework in their home, a vicarage on the Welsh borders. When her father returned, elevated from private to captain, they found it difficult to shake off the prejudices that had existed about a marriage between a vicar's daughter and a haulier's son: 'Like many who'd married in the war, my parents were finding it hard to survive the peace.'

The war had picked up traditional relationships and flung them down in a surprising pattern: family friends became 'aunts' and an older woman might be 'Nan', even though she was not related. Neighbours, friends, brothers, brother-in-laws and a whole array of relationships took on a greater significance. The title 'Uncle' could be applied to any ambiguous relationship, as in the case of John le Mesurier's character, Uncle Arthur, in the BBC sitcom *Dad's Army*. The returning father was yet one more off-centre relationship that needed accommodating.

The absent father had usually been represented by a head and shoulders photo occupying a sacred place in the home, which had quickly became out-of-date. As a result, children were confused and distressed when a different man walked through the door. The father who came home was older and often thinner (although, sometimes, as in James's case, he had put on weight) and gaunter than the image they had been gazing at for years. He might be tanned, have little or no hair or be sporting a beard or moustache. Some small children were shocked to discover that he was bigger than the photo and had legs. Even a detail such as whether or not he returned wearing the same cap as in the image played a part in the ease with which children received him back. One child persisted in kissing the photo on the wall goodnight, even when she had the real thing by her side. Older children felt awkward calling a stranger 'Dad' or 'Daddy' and could manage only 'Uncle' or 'Mister'. And some boys, as still happens sometimes today, had been told by well-meaning fathers and other relatives that, no matter how young, they were 'the man in the house' while their dad was away. This could place a huge burden on the child and sometimes led to any uneasy relationship between mother and son. In France there were instances of boys writing reports about their mother's behaviour to their POW fathers.

How the child was introduced to their new father was important. Many fathers were understandably keen to hug the child they had not seen for years, but for a small child being embraced by a stranger in a rough army tunic could be traumatic. Lorna Sage's early memory of her father was of being picked up by a man in uniform and being sick down his back. Asking a young boy to guess which of the commandoes in his front room was his father, as happened to my brother-in-law Bob at the end of the war, seems to modern sensibilities a particularly cruel way of dealing with a reunion. Perhaps shifting the emphasis to the child helped the adults in the room to cope with the awkwardness of the situation.

The arrival of a husband also upset the dynamics of the family. Even in the most loving households, the child could be left feeling displaced. Throughout the war years many children had shared a bed with their mother or grandmother due to shortage of space – if they were living with relatives – or because the child was afraid of the air raids. Now there was no room for them and many felt aggrieved. There might be added tension because, although couples were desperate to start their married life in their own home, the housing shortage forced several families to stay with in-laws.

Feelings of jealousy towards the father were often exacerbated by the arrival of a sibling. Long periods of separation meant that many children spent the war years as only children and it was a shock to have to share their mother – not only with a man – but also with a new baby. Not all of these additions led to anything other than the usual sibling rivalry, but the arrival of a new sister or brother was yet another major upheaval. In some cases, the husband obviously favoured the younger child who represented a new life started, significantly, in the period 'after the war' and one in which he could play an active part.

Many men who returned were physically injured or had mental scars to contend with. This was especially true of soldiers who had served in the Far East. As well as bouts of tropical illness, such as malaria, families had to learn to cope with unpredictable, and sometimes violent, mood swings. Some POWs refused to sleep on a bed, hoarded food or abhorred waste, noisy eating or eating outside; a traditional family picnic became a tense occasion. For others the time of year or change in weather could trigger painful memories. Many soldiers, whether POWs or not, suffered from nightmares and there were times when children were simply told to be quiet or to keep out of their father's way.

It was not only the soldier who had been changed by the war. Wives, too, had gone through life-altering experiences. One hundred and thirty thousand civilians died in the Blitz; of those 63,000 were women. As well as the loss of loved ones, women had been injured and seen their homes destroyed. It could take months, even years, for a family to settle into a new rhythm. Women like Diana and Rachel had been forced to become heads of their household while their husbands were away, often with help from other women, such as a sister or mother. They had become used to taking on responsibilities and to doing things their way. Adapting to a new authority figure was often difficult – and sometimes impossible. Many women had been forced to work and had enjoyed the independence and confidence that came with having a job outside the house. By contrast, the economic situation after the war meant jobs were hard to come by and the unemployment figures dealt men a further emasculating blow. Parents found they had developed quite distinct parenting skills – the husband influenced by the strict discipline of service life or from talking to other men about their attitudes to parenting. These differences in approach often became most evident at mealtimes when manners were put to the test. Officially, too, it was believed that the missing parent had led to wayward children. Research that appeared in the 1950s and earlier police reports suggested that boys born during the war years were more likely to lose their way. A rise in juvenile crime after the war was blamed in Britain, as well as France and the United States, on the lack of a father figure during the war years.

It is this period of adjustment – when expectations are so high after the longed-for return of a husband – that modern army wives still find tricky. Twenty-first century spouses have the army network to support them and, over the years, they work out a routine that eases the resumption of family life. Army wives in the Second World War had only one chance to get it right.

Part Four:

The Modern Army Wife

16

The Cold War Wife

The USA's unexpected success in the 2014 FIFA World Cup in Brazil was a direct result of the Cold War and the romances it made possible. Six of the thirty players on the USA's squad were the offspring of a German mother and a US serviceman. As an American commentator put it: 'One could say with only the wryest of smiles that the Soviet blockade of Berlin was the most important event in US soccer history.'

Like the kedgeree, curry and shampoo that British army wives brought back from their imperialist adventures in India, international soccer players proved a surprise by-product of a foreign military presence on German soil. When Jermaine Jones, one of the US World Cup squad, scored his first ever goal for the national side his instinct, before even embracing his team-mates, was to dash to the sideline, puff out his chest with pride and deliver his crispest military salute. The gesture was a tribute to his soldier father who met his future – German – wife in Frankfurt.

Romances between German women and British servicemen started to flutter into life once the Germans stopped being the enemy. In terms of football, the unions have offered not so much a 'soccer pipeline' for Britain as a spout through which unexpected heroes sometimes dribble. To date, the most successful athletic offspring of the Cold War has been international goalkeeper Maik

Taylor, whose father, a staff sergeant in the Royal Electrical and Mechanical Engineers, met his future wife in Germany.

For the British soldier and his family, Germany has assumed many shapes since the Second World War. Immediately after the end of hostilities, it was seen as a drab and dangerous posting – a country that was in a worse state even than war-ravaged Britain. Once the Cold War set in, though, relationships with local Germans thawed and the Soviet Union became the new bogeyman. Soldiers and families in Germany were suddenly on the front line, with a nuclear warhead trained on them. When Germany became an ally, British soldiers, wives and children started to mix more freely and, by the 1950s, Germany was an attractive posting, compared to Britain, which had yet to throw off its austerity shackles.

Until recently, a professional soldier could expect to spend large chunks of his career in Germany. Its wide open spaces became a military play area for training exercises that could not be accommodated in Britain's next best thing, Salisbury Plain. During the 1970s and 1980s it was the home to which the soldier returned after tense tours of duty in Northern Ireland at the height of the Troubles. In the twenty-first century many soldiers set off for Iraq and Afghanistan from the Rhineland. The wives left behind in Germany did their best to keep their spirits up through a round of intense social activity and by creating a bubble of Britishness.

When army wives first went out to Germany, in the late 1940s, they encountered a country in ruins. The nation was grey and battered, hardly able to feed itself and full of disease and danger. It was swollen with refugees and displaced people. More than 400,000 Germans had been killed and 800,000 injured by Allied bombing, which had also wiped out 1.8 million homes and badly damaged other buildings. Around 5.3 million German servicemen had died in the war and there were still bodies – civilian and military – waiting to be buried. The British Army of the Rhine (BAOR) stepped in because, in the words of a newsreel of the time, 'We cannot live next to a disease-ridden neighbour'. The British Army was there to help rebuild the infrastructure, to prevent starvation and epidemics, but also to guard against a reinfection of diseases of the mind, especially new strains of Fascism. When the Allies sliced Germany up at the end of the war, Britain's section was found to hold many dark Nazi secrets, most horribly the Bergen-Belsen concentration camp. Such discoveries intensified the wariness with which the army regarded the local inhabitants. It was to take many years for that unease to subside.

As a booklet entitled *A Guide for Families in BAOR*, written in 1949, explained, there were 12,000 British wives and more than 12,000 children in Germany. This was comparable, the book went on to say in reassuring tones, to a town the size of Windsor. The choice of a place – and one as well-behaved as the Queen's nearest town – of that size gave the impression of safety in numbers, not of a mob tempted to overstep the rules. And there were plenty of rules when it came to living in a country that had so recently been the enemy and one that had laid waste to large sections of Britain, just as British bombers had flattened parts of Germany.

A pamphlet, *Your Journey to Germany* (October 1946), attempted to make the relocation into a jolly adventure. Cartoons showed a woman in high heels and a fur coat next to two children and a caption, 'Goodbye England!' But the comic drawings and nursery colours could not disguise the fact that families were moving to a country that was recovering from war, and once they set foot on foreign soil their journey became a nightmarish intelligence test. Luggage had to be colour-coded – depending on which part of Germany they were travelling to – and a different train had to be taken – again depending on their route through the divided country. A bewildering map tried to explain the colour coding. Despite the many challenges of the journey, the pamphlet ended with a cartoon, 'Journey's End', showing a soldier, his wife, two children and a dog outside a Hansel and Gretel style German house. In reality, there was not normally such a fairy-tale start to life in the new country.

While soldiers found they were using the same 1930s buildings that had once housed their enemy, and which still carried traces of Nazi insignia, families moved into houses and flats recently occupied by German civilians. Although these were foreign homes, they were still governed by Byzantine army regulations. Rent paid by officers' families was linked to a husband's rank, while the rent paid by Other Ranks was decided by the size of their quarters. There was a charge for fuel and lighting and, in the case of officers, one servant. All quarters were furnished – right down to the provision of dishcloths – and families were allowed to bring only small items of furniture. As with all army quarters, the wife had to be aware of the battalion of rules to be followed – especially when it came to 'marching in' (moving into a new home) and 'marching out' (vacating a place). Only the Royal Engineers were permitted to carry out repairs – rather than local tradesmen. The Barrack Stores, on application through the quartermaster, would re-cover, upholster and polish furniture. Up to 30 per cent of a wife's entitlement of crockery and glassware was exchanged each year. Fifteen per cent of this was free and each piece of crockery or glass was graded on a complicated points system. If you found yourself in a house with a piano, you were responsible for the tuning of it. If the previous German owner had left behind any 'chattels', they became part of your entitlement – except if they were valuable, in which case you were expected to hand them in. On no account should you give them to your neighbour. The conquering army was entitled to the spoils of war – so long as their receipt was acknowledged in triplicate.

Families who had left behind rationing in Britain had to get used to a different system in Germany. The defeated country was not self-sufficient and many foods and services were imported. In addition *A Guide for Families in BAOR* was frank about army rationing '[b]eing fixed and inflexible, it is not the ideal basis for family catering.'

It reassured the housewife that it was acceptable to buy goods from German shops – so long as they were not rationed locally – but warned that the list of rationed foods changed frequently. Bread, cereals, meat (excluding fish, game, poultry), fat, cheese, milk and sugar were most likely to be rationed. There was no fresh milk and housewives should buy tinned milk – which was nutritious and hygienic.

Some of the questions in the booklet must have dismayed, rather than reassured, wives new to postwar Germany. For example:

> Q. Why do vegetables, fruit and fish often lose some of their freshness when received by families?

The answer conjured up limp lettuces, mouldy apples and rank fish: produce often looked and tasted tired because German shops were not allowed to buy food in bulk and all vegetables, fruit and fish had to be imported from The Netherlands and Denmark. Fast trains delivered the goods to Royal Army Service Corps Supply depots, but occasionally the trains were late and many deliveries had to cover very long distances. However, there was good news about some foods: the sugar ration was twice that in Britain and the meat ration far greater. But, again, the booklet's question added a caveat:

> Q. Why do families get a proportion of bad joints of meat?

All meat was imported from Argentina and the housewife shopping for the small requirements of her family was not in a position to demand the best cuts. The booklet urged her: 'Remember, that the population in the UK where the ration is at present 8d. worth per week, could not possibly buy meat three times a week; in most cases, they get it only once'. The implication was clear: the meat might be bad, but you could buy it three times a week!

Although Germany was just a few hundred miles away from Britain, the distance was multiplied by poor communications and prejudice against a country that had caused such suffering and fear. For the past six years, Britain's propaganda machine had done its best to turn the whole country against Germany. In the 1940s and 1950s the Government began to execute an about-turn. It was a tricky manoeuvre, which, in the end, it could manage only with the help of a common enemy.

Before the Soviet Union took up its role as Big Bad Wolf, however, Germany was still seen as a dangerous posting and soldiers and families rarely strayed far from their home bases. The army strongly recommended that wives and children should be vaccinated against smallpox, typhoid and diphtheria. *A Guide for Families in BAOR* included the following list of 'Don't's:

> DON'T Let your children eat ice cream manufactured from German sources. It is not subject to British medical supervision and is forbidden by GRO.
>
> DON'T Drink any milk in this country unless it has first been boiled.
>
> DON'T Let your children play with stray dogs – they may carry disease.
>
> DON'T Bathe in rivers or other places not authorised by the medical authorities – it is unsafe. Authorised bathing places are hygienically treated to protect the health of you and your family.

By the 1950s a wider selection of better food was readily available in Germany. A 1953 version of the previous booklet, *A Guide for Families in Germany*, explained that it was now possible to obtain all food in German shops or the army stores, the NAAFI, and that it was safe to eat in German restaurants. As before, there were still caveats. The pamphlet admitted that frozen fish lacked the taste of its British equivalent and that pork and pork products such as sausages should be cooked thoroughly to avoid the many worm diseases that were still prevalent in Germany. All milk should be boiled and cream cakes and ice cream avoided.

Sue and Richard Middleton were only twenty-two when Richard was posted to Germany in 1967. They had met on a blind date when Richard was at Sandhurst and Sue was living with her family nearby. Sue did not come from an army background and her father, who was a chemist, had not fought in the Second World War, although he was a stretcher-bearer during the Blitz. She always suspected that he might have felt rather guilty about his reserved occupation. Looking back, she says that everyone from her circle of friends wanted to go out with an officer cadet from Sandhurst because they were so dashing, and Richard was the first boyfriend her parents had liked.

They were too young to be eligible for army quarters and instead lived in a second-floor flat owned by a German couple in Iserlohn, southeast of Dortmund. Although some local people were still hostile to the British, Sue and Richard's landlords were kind. They watched over Sue when Richard was away on manoeuvres and the landlord lugged coal up from the cellar for her boiler.

Their youth meant the Second World War seemed like a very long time ago – although it had finished little more than 20 years earlier and some of the older army wives told her about their experiences. One, as a young wife, had been transported with her husband, children and all their possessions from north of Hanover to the Ruhr in an armoured 'half track' – a hybrid personnel carrier that looked like a conventional Jeep from the front, but which had tank-style caterpillar tracks at the back for roaming over rugged terrain. When the family arrived at their new unit, the quartermaster told them to find a German house and tell the family to move out. They did this, but allowed the previous occupants to live in the cellar. Sue remembers the army wives from an earlier age as 'very stalwart ladies – that's when it seemed near to me because I was a baby when the war started, so I knew nothing about it and was told all about it by these lovely old ladies.'

Sue had worked as a window dresser for the John Lewis department store before she married, but there were no job opportunities in Germany. To stave off loneliness she 'girded her loins' and went to the wives' club, which met every fortnight or so. She played bingo and went to beetle drives and drank coffee. When the other wives realised she lived 'out in the sticks', they asked her over to the base. As was her duty, the battery commander's wife also paid her a visit. Life became easier when Sue's first child, James, was born after eighteen months and they moved into a barrack block. From then on there was always company: other young wives and children. What was missing, though, were grandparents. James was several months old before Sue's parents were able to visit him. Phone calls were rare because they could not afford their own phone and had to book a line in the officers' mess. She wrote a letter to her father every week for the twenty-nine years she was an army wife.

One innovation that helped relatives in Britain feel closer to Germany and other overseas postings was a radio programme called *Forces Favourites*, which later became known as *Two-Way Family Favourites* and then *Three-Way Family Favourites*. From London, Jean Metcalfe, a typist with a girl-next-door way of talking who became the first presenter of *Woman's Hour*, and her co-presenter in Hamburg, RAF Squadron Leader Cliff Michelmore, read dedications and played record requests for members of the armed services and their families. The two broadcasters did not meet in person for six months, although Michelmore said it was 'love at first hearing' and they married in 1950 – an act which seemed only to confirm the show's emotional potency. The programme aired on Sunday lunchtimes and its combination of heart-warming vignettes and a rare chance to listen to popular records won it an audience far beyond the armed services. For many people, myself included, it takes only a few bars of the show's theme tune 'With a Song in My Heart' to be transported back to the steamed-up windows of a dining room, braced for a Sunday lunch of boiled cabbage and rubbery beef. At its peak, 26 million listeners tuned in.

Sue Middleton had arrived at the height of the Cold War. Six years earlier, the Soviets had erected the Berlin Wall – an ugly grey scar that carved up the city into East and West. The wall represented a concrete manifestation of the growing antagonism and mistrust between the two power groups. Churchill had made his Iron Curtain speech on 5 March 1946 and the curtain descended on 24 June 1948 when Stalin cut off all rail and road links to West Berlin, a city stranded deep in the section of Germany controlled by the Soviet Union after the end of the Second World War. The airlift, in which American and British planes flew supplies in to the beleaguered city round-the-clock for the next eleven months, preserved part of Berlin as a Western enclave, an anomaly both on, and behind, the front line.

The tension between America and her allies and the Communist countries reached boiling point in October 1962, when an American spy plane spotted nuclear missile sites being built on Cuba. Suddenly, Soviet-backed weapons put every American town within reach of an attack and President Kennedy's address to the nation confirmed the seriousness of the situation. Negotiation defused the immediate threat, but the realisation of what might have happened led to a nuclear arms race and gave the Rhineland a strategic position. Those who lived there were haunted by the spectre of a new kind of war. The men commanding the armed forces knew that, should the Soviets decide to strike, they could only ever delay them for a matter of hours. One troop leader later calculated his life expectancy at eight hours.

Wives and families were also aware of their perilous position. Sue Middleton remembers being given a sheet of paper advising her what to do in the event of an evacuation – although, unlike the

Second World War, it was difficult to imagine where might offer any shelter against a nuclear attack. The paper told wives to leave their animals behind and asked what skills the wife possessed (Sue put down driving). She also witnessed several exercises in which the men 'bailed out'. The siren went off and her husband leapt out of bed to scramble into his camouflage or biological warfare kit before disappearing for several days. At first she was terrified by the alarms: 'I was quite nervous when I first went to Germany because I felt a long way from home. Living in a German flat I did feel that I didn't know quite what would happen to me if they did come.' But it was much more alarming for the local Germans, who would sometimes pile into their cars, convinced this was the real thing.

One of Sue's closest friends, Barbara Wilton, who arrived in West Germany ten years later, realised that anything the British Army could do to halt the Soviets would only ever be a delaying tactic. When they were at Minden, west of Hanover, her husband Chris was a Flight Commander in the Army Air Corps (AAC) and flew frequent air patrols along the Inner German Border (IGB), which divided West and East Germany. Later, in the 1980s, when they had returned to Britain, he was ordered to man a nuclear bunker. The Cold War threat was less acute than in Germany, but Barbara still told him: 'You'll be lucky to get to the front door alive if you're going to leave me and two small children.'

Life in Berlin was a world apart from the other army units. Sue remembers living in the city as 'party, party, party'; she had a daily maid, as well as an evening maid. It could be difficult for the second maid to clock up enough hours, so they would use her as a babysitter while they went to the cinema and the maid would stay the night to add more hours to her tally. By then, relationships between local Germans and the military were much warmer, particularly after the Berlin Airlift. 'They adored us. We could do no wrong,' Sue remembers.

The novelist Elizabeth Speller has less happy memories of Berlin. She arrived there in 1972 when she was nineteen and heavily pregnant; her son was born eight weeks later. The family lived in a 'solid' semi-detached house in the Berlin suburb of Spandau, an area dominated by a prison that housed just one, infamous occupant. Fürstenweg was a 'middling kind of street, with plane trees and cobbles and an air of quiet respectability'. Anyone who lived there had to abide by the rules governing car-washing, bush-planting, tree-pruning, radio playing, snow-clearing and the days on which washing could be hung out.

Elizabeth was acutely aware of the Soviet threat. During her first year in Berlin, three people died trying to cross the wall from East to West and one child drowned when he fell in the river and neither side was prepared to rescue him. She noticed how Soviet spy cars with darkened windows roamed West Berlin, just as the British equivalent, no less identifiable, went through an identical routine in the East. Fighter planes buzzed the suburbs and every day a junior British officer took a train to the West. The purpose of his journey was always the same – to reinforce the right to travel across eastern Germany. On Fridays, crates of rations were handed out to every military family. The food represented supplies which were nearing their 'use-by' date and which had been stockpiled in case the Soviets attempted another blockade. But the most frightening experience was being woken in the middle of the night to hear sirens blaring and a loud speaker announcing that 'Operation Rocking Horse' had been called and all men should report to barracks immediately. Elizabeth and her two babies were often woken in this way as her husband jumped out of bed and armoured cars laboured down the cobbled streets in the unnatural brightness of Arc lights. 'Operation Rocking Horse' was yet another dry run for the Soviet invasion and the men were expected to reach the barracks in two hours. For years later Elizabeth's children had nightmares about marching monsters called 'Left Rights'.

The Cold War tension existed side by side with a determined hedonism of curry lunches, tennis matches and seedy nightclubs.

Elizabeth remembers the British sector as being more British than Britain itself and how other sectors assumed their national stereotypes: the French area was well-known for a particular restaurant, fine cheese and perfume; the American zone was remarkable for the gas-guzzling cars and the lavish white goods on sale in their PX (the American version of the NAAFI store).

She also had to contend with the Army Wives' club and its pecking order. The commanding officer's wife was top, followed by the adjutant's spouse and then, in theory, at least, Elizabeth. The sergeant major's wife came next but, in reality, ran the club. She was from an army family and was trained to drive a tank, should the Soviets invade. Elizabeth, as she freely admits, was barely out of adolescence and the club provided 'undreamed of opportunities for rebellion': in the Mess she flicked idly through the pages of the *Guardian*; wore a miniskirt and bare legs or mused that her disapproval of apartheid would make it impossible for her to follow her husband on a posting to South Africa or the southern states of America.

Carol Armstrong, another army wife in Germany in the 1970s, did her best to avoid the Army Wives' clubs. She was born and brought up in Belfast and as a teenager was keen to escape the religiously divided community. Even before the Troubles and the arrival of troops in Northern Ireland, she knew that there was 'something not right' in the society she had grown up in. She had wanted to train as a teacher in England, but her family felt this would give her little security. The army, which provided bed and board, offered the perfect safety net and her parents, who were English and who had moved to Northern Ireland for work, had no objections to her joining. When she first started her training in the Women's Royal Army Corps (WRAC) in 1965, she shared a room with three other 'girls' and it took her a whole week to discover that one was Catholic: a revelation that would have been obvious within minutes in Northern Ireland.

Although Carol was unsuccessful the first time she applied to become an officer, she was promoted to sergeant within two-and-a-half years, at the age of twenty-one. She says she rose so quickly partly because when other female soldiers married, they usually chose to leave the army, and others who became pregnant *had* to leave. Most of the other sergeants in the Sergeants' Mess were older men – and married. This was not usually a problem at a function restricted to serving members, but a 'ladies' night' was awkward. When Carol had a boyfriend who was a corporal, he was not allowed to accompany her because of his rank. And because she had little option but to talk to the other sergeants, their wives thought Carol was 'after their husbands'. There seemed no end to this speculation and she was driven to reapply for a commission. She was successful and started her officer-training course. This included marching, map reading – and flower arranging because female officers were expected to help with this duty at dinners. It was a skill that Carol refused to become anything other than competent at. This was not what she had joined the army for. 'You see women on television now, carrying weapons, wearing combats . . . [but] it was like being a civil servant in uniform because I didn't go on exercise, I didn't carry weapons, I was never issued with anything but a skirt.'

Carol met her future husband, Richard, when she was posted to Germany with the 16th Signal Regiment at Krefeld, northwest of Düsseldorf. Although she retired from the armed services in 2005, she still struggles to refer to his title without its army acronym, '2IC' (second-in-command). By the time they met she was a lieutenant (she was promoted to captain just after they married) and he was a widowed major, twenty-three years her senior. She felt more comfortable in the Officers' Mess because at least four other women shared her rank and there were more single men, so she was seen as less of a threat to the wives. Carol's WRAC officer commanding (a major) disapproved of a courting couple working so closely together and transferred her to Bielefeld, in North Rhine-Westphalia.

The separation failed to dampen the romance and they were married in the garrison church at Krefeld in 1970 and held the reception in the Officers' Mess. Eventually, they lived in married quarters in the sprawling, 1,161-acre BAOR (British Army of the Rhine) site at Rheindahlen, 50 miles from Bonn. Unusually for an army wife, this was to be Carol's married home for the next seventeen years, albeit it in three different houses. She had to leave the army when she became pregnant with their first child in 1973.

When it opened in 1954, the Rheindahlen Garrison felt like an upmarket, extremely well-kept holiday camp. Most of the buildings were cream-coloured, two- or three-storeyed blocks, and included barracks, offices and quarters for more than 1,100 married couples. Soldiers and their families had a choice of two cinemas and three churches. Wives could shop at a giant NAAFI store or smaller stores, including one that was German. Commerzbank had a branch and there were two post offices, a bookshop, library and cafés, as well as club houses and the usual messes for different ranks. Around 10,000 people lived or worked on the 'township'.

Carol's home was a major's quarters when their first son was born in 1973. It was a solid, four-bedroom house filled entirely with G Plan style, army-issue furniture. Like other army wives, she made it her own by filling it with lamps and ornaments. Later, when they bought their own house, she discovered the truth of the army saying that they had 'all the extras, but none of the basics'. Becoming a mother meant she was forced to give up her job. This coincided with her husband's retirement, although he continued as an RO (retired officer) – in effect, a civil servant with army experience. This strange halfway existence meant she lost many of her friends, who followed the normal army pattern of moving on to a new posting every two or three years, although one particular friend was a great support during her first child's early years. The friend, who came from a teaching background, was also struggling to fit into army life. Carol remembers, 'I used to say to her: "You kept me sane" because it was somebody else to talk to. And in later years she said, "You know, *you* kept *me* sane." At the time we didn't realise the mutuality of our support.'

Once her children were older, Rheindahlen came into its own. She was surrounded by other mothers with young children and there were lots of activities for them, as well as a range of very good facilities, such as a 50-metre, outdoor swimming pool, six primary schools and two secondary schools and the chance to go on ski-ing holidays. Although Carol's husband would have qualified for an allowance to send her two sons to boarding school in Britain, they decided that the boys should be educated in the schools at Rheindahlen. She was partly swayed by the fact that they would still be in school when her husband retired and the couple would not have been able to pay for them to continue in private education. Her sons were unusual in enjoying an unbroken spell of education in one place. Most army children – 'BRATS' as those who live abroad with their parents are often affectionately called, after the acronym British Regiments Attached Travellers – change schools frequently. Making friends quickly, and being able to cope when their pals move on, become useful skills. This ability to strike up a rapport with an audience, albeit in a classroom, may go some way towards explaining why children of parents in the armed forces like Juliet Stevenson, Jenny Agutter, Joanna Lumley, Jennifer Saunders, Ade Edmondson and Dawn French become actors and others, including James Blunt, Engelbert Humperdinck, Tanita Tikaram and Pete Doherty, go on to careers as musicians.

Schools in Rheindahlen were run by the British Families Education Service, which drafted in civilian teachers, who became used to detecting the rhythm of army life reflected in the classroom. Children could become unsettled when their father was about to leave and excited when he was due to return. They had completely different reference points – as one teacher discovered when she asked her class to draw a fish in a tank. Several children showed the fish inside an armoured car.

Both Barbara and Sue decided to send their children to the same boarding school in Suffolk from the age of nine and chose a school that was close to their grandparents so that they could visit often. Sue promised her son, James, that she would visit him every *exeat* (a short break) and every half term. In the days before cheap air travel, this meant a long car journey across Europe followed by a ferry crossing, three times a term, often in bad weather, for the nine years they were in Germany. Barbara and Chris did not spend as long in Germany before moving back to Britain. At the time, boarding schools were less flexible about allowing students to change their status to 'day children'. They sent their son, Luke, and daughter, Lucy Jane, to the same boarding school to make it easier to co-ordinate school holidays. Luke found it hard to cope with the paradox of seeing his mother more often than when she had been in Germany, but not to be allowed to go home. The flipside of boarding school was that children always had an interesting place to spend the holidays. Barbara and Chris decided to buy a house near their children's boarding school so that the children could say they *came from somewhere*, even when their parents were abroad.

Instead of joining the wives' club, Carol threw herself into the Girl Guide Movement. Each of the primary schools on Rheindahlen had a Brownie pack and there were several Guide companies. She became county secretary and her remit covered the whole of West Germany and Berlin. Girl Guiding is not so far removed from the discipline and outdoors activities of the British Army, but the aspect that Carol enjoyed most was that the women 'didn't wear their husband's rank' – 'So the County Commissioner was often a brigadier's wife but then we'd have guiders who were lance-corporals' or privates' wives, but we'd go on training together and everybody would be on first name terms and that was really lovely because the army – and the Royal Air Force – are so hierarchical and everybody knows everybody else by their rank so Guiding was a lovely escape for me.'

Sue and Barbara agree that some wives were 'more officer than their husband' and a few, in the saying of the time, had 'pips on their handbag'. Maintaining their own identity, in Germany or wherever else they were based, was difficult. All too often they were 'Wife of . . .' or simply known by the last three digits of their husband's army number. Even as recently as 1980, when Barbara tried to join an army library, she was told she needed her husband's approval and that if she lost a book, the library could fine her husband, not her. By then she had both an undergraduate and postgraduate degree in social work. Over a decade earlier, Sue remembers pushing the pram through the army base to be greeted by one of the soldiers with the words, 'Mornin', Ma'am' and then, after he had peered into the pram, 'Mornin', General.' On other occasions, the ordinary soldiers might become so nervous about the right way to address the officers' wives that they sometimes panicked and called them 'Sir'. Barbara says that the infantry and artillery regiments were more formal than the Army Air Corps, where she was always called by her first name, or 'Ma'am' if a soldier did not know her.

Officers' wives were also expected to be adept at socialising. In Berlin, Sue went to several dinners with local dignitaries, mayors, business leaders, members of the German armed forces and representatives from different consulates. Each wife was given a square of floor to stand in and had to make sure she chatted to each guest as they were guided around the room in a seemingly spontaneous round of 'mingling'. Once you were married, you knew that the minute you arrived at a party you and your husband had to separate and talk to anyone *except* your other half for the whole evening. The same strategy applied at a 'ladies' mess night': in the British Army, at least, a wife would never be seated next to her husband. At first, Barbara found it hard to throw off her natural shyness, but encouraged by her husband, she grew to enjoy the opportunity to meet other people. She concedes this was not the case for every young wife and that when she worked as a social worker for SSAFA (Soldiers, Sailors, Airmen and Families Association) in Germany there was concern about many young women – particularly if they had never lived away from home, let alone abroad before and could not drive. Friendships with other wives helped many to survive what could be a lonely existence; the other army wives became the family they had left behind.

When Barbara was expecting their first child, Chris was serving as a pilot in Northern Ireland for the last six months of the pregnancy. She was ordered to take six weeks bed rest in hospital and Sue looked after her; she and other friends assumed the role that parents and in-laws would normally have taken by visiting regularly and making sure she had everything she needed. When she went into labour, Chris flew to Gütersloh and rang the BAOR hospital in Rinteln, between Hanover and Osnabrück, from the arrivals hall to be told by the nursing staff that he had a son. Chris rushed to their home in Detmold only to find that their car would not start, but Sue lent him hers so that he could drive through the snow to be with Barbara and Luke.

Although Sue and Barbara remained good friends, there was no sense of obligation to return favours. Sue says, 'I remember someone took my child across London once and I said I'd do it for her and she said, "No, you won't, but you'll do it for somebody else."' Barbara adds: 'No one ever asked anything of you again. You just knew there was someone else somewhere who would return the favour. There was never "Oh, you did that for me so you owe me".' Support networks became even more important when husbands were absent. The army would fix anything that broke in the house, but there were still several times when a wife relied on her network of friends. Sue remembers one occasion 'when the men had just started to dribble off to Ireland' when she was walking home one day and saw a woman standing outside the house holding the chain of her little boy's bicycle and saying tearfully, '"You'll have to wait until someone's daddy comes home." There was a lot of that, "You'll have to wait until Uncle So and So gets home".'

There are several stories about affairs when husbands were away. The most infamous is the tale of wives placing packets of OMO washing powder in their windows to indicate they were 'On My Own'. But it seems likely that these rumours have been inflated: the cheek-by-jowl existence lived by wives would have made such trysts difficult to conceal. Carol certainly cannot remember any and believes that they would have been difficult in such a close-knit community.

From the 1970s, many soldiers who were based in Germany were sent on tours to Northern Ireland and the armed forces became a target for terrorist attacks, both there and in mainland Europe. The military and their families were warned to be on the alert after a bomb was defused at Rheindahlen in 1978 and over the next twenty years the military suffered a series of attacks on individuals and bases in Germany and other countries where the armed forces were stationed, or where they went for a break. In bars over the border in The Netherlands, their car number plates made them easily identifiable as British.

At 10.30 p.m., on 23 March 1987, a 300-pound bomb, placed by the IRA, exploded outside the Officers' Mess at Rheindahlen, injuring thirty-one people – most visiting Germans. Two years later, a corporal from the RAF and his six-month-old baby daughter were murdered by the IRA at a filling station near the Dutch border.

Barbara was more aware than most of the dangers associated with the conflict because she came from Northern Ireland. None of her immediate family had been in the army, but she joined the Officer Training Corps at Queen's University, Belfast, as a way of supplementing her grant. She met Chris when he was posted to Northern Ireland as a lieutenant in the Royal Corps of Transport (now the Logistics Corps) and a mutual friend, who was also in the army, introduced them. This was 1970 – just after the start of the Troubles. As she shared a flat with a girl who had republican friends, she made sure Chris and the girl's friends visited at different times.

To anyone other than her closest friends (who knew the truth), Chris's work was always described vaguely as 'in the bank', an occupation that suited his army haircut.

Looking back, she realises how dangerous Belfast was then. But she became inured to the bomb scares and often could not even be bothered to leave the university library after a warning – 'It was just part of life. You were just careful, you just carried on.' She remembers the car she was in with Chris breaking down on the Falls Road (the Republican area of Belfast) and recognises now the danger they were in. Chris was given 'one or two "extras" [punishments such as extra guard duty]' for being in a Republican area or for taking Barbara, as a Protestant, on a shortcut through a Catholic street. She looks back in horror at the time she carried her husband's gun for him in her handbag so that they could go to a disco where they knew he would be searched but she probably would not. Sometimes the risk of an attack was so great that Chris could not come out and she would meet him at Thiepval Barracks. They were married in Barbara's hometown in 1973 but were 'sensible enough' not to have a military wedding. Nevertheless, there were several members of the congregation who were discreetly carrying guns – partly because Barbara's brother was in the Ulster Defence Regiment.

Fear is part of the job description of being married to a soldier. Although it may not be ever-present, there are usually moments when an army wife feels anxious for her husband in a way that a civilian never would. Sue remembers once being phoned when she was in Germany and asked whether her husband was at home because he had disappeared from the exercise he was on. 'It frightened the life out of me,' she confessed. When he was serving in Africa he came home several days later than she had expected. He had been delayed and had not been able to contact her. But for many army wives, the most stressful time is the period *just before* their husband is about to leave. It is then that rituals and routines come into their own.

17

The Modern Army Wife[1]

It was the moment every army wife dreads. Annabel opened the door of her thatched cottage, which sits opposite a village green in a traditional English village, to find her husband's commanding officer in full uniform. At the time, her husband David was serving as an army helicopter pilot in Afghanistan and they had two young children. The officer's presence, in uniform, could mean only one thing. As she stared at him in disbelief, she realised that something in this horribly familiar tableau was not right: it was his expression. He lacked the sombre countenance of someone about to break bad news – and he was alone. There was no padre by his side, no welfare officer. As she waited for him to frame the dreadful words, his relaxed, Sunday-morning face evaporated to be replaced by dawning realisation and then horror. Finally, he said, 'I'm so sorry, Annabel.' But his words were a direct apology, not a condolence, when he saw the misunderstanding his sudden appearance in uniform had caused to an anxious wife waiting at home. He was not the harbinger of bad news but had merely been sent by his own wife to invite Annabel to dinner while her husband was away.

Although communication has changed beyond imagination since the First World War, and the army is much better and more sensitive about delivering bad news, army wives still dread the unexpected

1 All names of serving soldiers and their wives have been changed.

knock at the door, or the stranger standing on their threshold. When a soldier is away from home, the cheerful trill of a doorbell at the wrong time of day or night can be as ominous as the squeak of the telegram boy's bike was during the First World War.

In so many other ways, though, the contemporary army wife is a different creature from her historical counterpart – even compared to the end of the twentieth century. Army wives are more likely to want a career of their own and less likely to come from an army background. Annabel, for example, first met David at university, where she was studying Modern Languages and he was reading History. He was sponsored by the army and came from a military family (his father and grandfather had both been solders). They met again in their thirties, by which time he had served in Bosnia, Iraq and Northern Ireland, and had been married and divorced. Annabel was a qualified accountant and had been living and working in London for ten years.

The courtship worked in the same way as any other in which one, or both partners, is working away from home. He was based in East Anglia and they would take turns to visit each other, until he got posted to the Ministry of Defence in London. Getting married forced her to confront the reality of life in the army. As part of the preparations for the wedding the vicar gave them a general book of advice, but they took it more seriously, probably than most couples, because of the particular demands of the army and because the pressures of being apart had contributed to the breakdown of David's first marriage.

Owning their own house has helped to bring a sense of normality to a relationship in which David is away about half the time. It was an important stipulation for Annabel and, although it means she is not as involved in as many activities as army wives living on base, she values the chance to 'switch off' from army life and to build friendships in her village. More and more army couples are buying their own home with a view to life after the army; it is an option that the army itself encourages as good housing stock becomes increasingly rare. As one wife says, the solid 1950s house with a serving hatch is 'ideal for a brood' but not for a couple without children. Another, older wife looks back on the eighteen times she has moved during her career and points out that this has meant getting used to the vagaries of eighteen different ovens. While David is likely to move several times in his career, he should be able to commute daily – if he is given a desk job in London – or weekly, if he ends up in Yorkshire, Northern Ireland or Wiltshire, for example. If he is posted to Germany, they might consider moving because living abroad would be 'an adventure' for the family.

Annabel's life outside the army keeps her busy when he is away and offers an alternative social network. She has friends in the village whose husbands travel a lot because they work for international companies and in the past they have entered quizzes under the ironic name 'The Deserted Wives' Club'. She has used her qualification as an accountant to undertake voluntary work for the church and her daughter's school's parent-teacher association; she works one day a week as a school bursar and has set up her own accountancy firm. On the face of it, accountancy would seem as transportable a skill as teaching, hairdressing or social work, but, as with all jobs, frequent moves erode continuity of service and the benefits that can bring in terms of pensions, maternity pay and other perks.

Two weeks after they returned from honeymoon, David was posted to Afghanistan. Because he is an officer in the Army Air Corps his tours are slightly longer than for other soldiers and there are no trips home for 'R and R' ('relaxation and recuperation'). On his next tour of Afghanistan their daughter was just two and Annabel was eleven weeks pregnant so that by the time he was back in England she was physically very different. When he went abroad again they had two children and she was working full-time.

Like many army wives she finds special occasions such as Christmas, birthdays and Valentine's Day the hardest to bear. Weekends and bank holidays can also be difficult and most wives try to pack them with activities, especially if they have children. Many army welfare officers organise special outings to the seaside or indoor play areas to help families. When David was in Afghanistan for Christmas 2011, his daughters drew a big 'Happy Christmas, Daddy' banner that they coloured in, photographed and emailed to him. They spent the day at Annabel's parents, where they raised a glass to him but were careful not to be too sentimental in case it cast a shadow over festivities. Many wives keep a calendar on their kitchen wall, phone or computer to count down the days until their husband's return. For others, this seems like tempting fate and will mean he will be delayed or fail to come home at all. Some families mark the passing weeks in terms of coffee mornings or swimming lessons, 'Only four more coffee mornings to go'.

Louise, a teacher, met her future husband at a nightclub in Worcestershire. She did not come from an army background and, before they got to know Nigel her friends and family were worried that he was using his claim to be a pilot as a chat-up line. For a while she would avoid these sideways looks of pity by introducing him as a 'pylon fitter', or some other outlandish occupation. When they were first married he would tell her when he was due to fly over the house so that she could stand in the garden and wave, but after a while the novelty wore off and she told him, 'Nigel, if you were a taxi driver I wouldn't expect you to drive past the house and beep the horn every time you took someone out on a taxi ride.' She says he values the way she keeps him 'grounded'. Unlike her husband, she enjoys moving house. She likes the chance to have a clear-out and to make new friends. They have stayed for about four years in each of their postings, which have included Northern Ireland, Middle Wallop in Hampshire and a 'hiring' (a rented private property) in East Anglia.

The frequent moves have also marked her husband's progress up the ranks. When they met he was a corporal, now he is an acting major. The change in status was brought home to her when they were living in army housing at Middle Wallop and the officers' and Other Ranks' accommodation was separated by a road. When Nigel was promoted they had to move across the road to a house that had one more bedroom than the one they had left and whenever she went to the mess she was called 'Ma'am'. Although Louise says rank is immaterial to her, she admits that she did lose some friends when Nigel became an officer. Being a member of an army wives' choir has been very good for breaking down barriers between ranks.

The period just before a husband leaves can be hard to bear. He is engrossed in training and preparations and, mentally, he may already be absent. As Kitty, a management consultant who met her future husband Patrick at university, says: 'You're thinking, "Please just go. This is killing me, just get on with it because the sooner you go, the sooner you can start to be coming back."' If they are sensible, as Annabel is, they face the unthinkable – what sort of funeral he wants – and the more prosaic – how to access joint accounts and policies held in both names. Other wives know these details are kept somewhere safe, together with a letter to them, in case they do not return.

The role of the welfare officer varies slightly from base to base, but they usually organise informal family days as part of the 'pre-deployment' briefing. Couples can bring members of their wider family such as parents, siblings, nieces and nephews. It is a day for children to clamber over camouflage netting and army vehicles, but also for wives and girlfriends to make sure they have all the contact numbers they need and can ask any questions about the tour. They are reminded of practicalities: are there jobs that normally fall to their husband – such as checking the oil in the car or cleaning the gutters – and which they might find difficult while he is away? Is there anything he normally deals with and which they might need to find? The person giving the briefing usually refers to 'your soldier' to avoid any emphasis on rank and reminds the wife that she must know his army number in case of an emergency. After all the preparations and tension, it can seem almost a relief once the husband has left so that the wife can steer the family towards a routine. As Annabel says, 'It's a chance to eat and drink what you want, when you want, and to watch what you like on TV.'

There are now plenty of networks to support families while the soldier is away and to supplement the usual coffee morning rota. 'Welfare' often organise trips to London or the theatre and other outings. Facebook, Twitter and other forms of social media provide platforms for WAGS (Wives and Girlfriends of Soldiers) to let off steam and to comfort and console. 'Mrs P.', for example, tweeted: 'Deployment bonuses: wearing clothes boys "don't get" without having to explain yourself. Example A: pinafore dress' next to a photo of herself in the outfit. Someone in a similar position is often the only person who can understand the particular pressures; chatting to another army wife means there is no need to explain the jargon and idiosyncrasies of the armed forces. As Kitty says, 'If there's a housing issue they [army wives] just know what you're talking about. Even talking to my own family, I might mention Modern Housing Solutions [the partnership that at the time carried out maintenance on an army house] and someone will say, "So is that the MOD?" and you end up explaining who this organisation is before you even get on to the issue. And they might say, "Well, can't they just call another plumber?" and you're like, "No, forget it, it doesn't matter."'

Army choirs have become popular in the wake of choirmaster Gareth Malone's TV series and offer another way in which the increasing number of wives who live off-base can support one another. They are also an important network for women without children to connect. Charlotte, whose husband Scott is in the RAF Regiment but attached to an army unit, found that teaming up with her neighbour, a supply teacher, allowed them to support each other when their husbands were absent. She describes creating a 'third marriage' in which they asked each other how their day had been, cooked for one another and took turns walking the dog. They would also buy 'a load of old junk' and convert the garage into a 'sweatshop' in which they could restore battered furniture. They kept busy while their 'boys' were away.

Some women find it helps to have certain rituals or superstitions to follow when their husband is not there. During the Falklands War in 1982, one army wife played mind games with herself and fate: her husband 'couldn't' die on particular days – their daughter's birthday, for example. More recently, a woman refuses to sleep in their marital bed until he returns. Kitty always says goodnight to Patrick before she falls asleep; if she forgets, then she has to get out of bed and switch the light on to do it. She also finds comfort in the knowledge that they are looking at the same moon – no matter where in the world he is. In America some army wives have 'his' and 'her' clocks on their wall: one shows the time in the family home and a second, 'deployment' clock gives the hour for the country where their husband is serving. You can buy clocks with slogans such as 'Afghanistan Time', 'My Marine is worth the wait' and 'Half my heart is deployed'. This focus on a different time zone can help to keep an absent father at the centre of a family and make communication easier.

The waiting wife's awareness of what her husband is going through has changed greatly in the last few decades – partly because the armed forces have learnt from mistakes made in the Falklands War. While it may be argued that the Crimean War was the first time war arrived at the breakfast table, the conflict between Britain and Argentina brought the camouflage-blackened faces, plumes of smoke and stretchered victims into sitting rooms around the country – albeit in a heavily censored and time-delayed way. ITV showed the fleet departing from a sunny Portsmouth in April 1982 and Ministry of Defence spokesman Ian McDonald, once described as 'a man with the delivery and charisma of a speak-your-weight machine', rationed out the carefully controlled gobbets of news. There were no 'real-time' TV reports and no photographs for the first fifty-four days of the conflict. The manner in which news was released led to rumours among families who were uncertain who to believe. The conflict itself was difficult to understand: it was a war fought with computers and modern technology (what did an Exocet look like and what injuries could it inflict?) and yet the hand-to-hand fighting for Goose Green was closer to the trenches of the First World War.

One wife had heard that the island was devoid of trees and buildings and worried that her husband would have nowhere to take cover. But the war was different from others in so many respects. The treatment of wives varied depending on which armed service their husband served in, his regiment and where the wife lived. When nineteen men from the Special Air Service (SAS) drowned in a freak helicopter crash in which an albatross caused engine failure, local people in Hereford, where the SAS is based, raised £63,000 for widows. The response may have had much to do with the fact that many members of the SAS marry locally and the wives remain in the area, no matter where their husband is posted. In other parts of the country, women huddled together round radio and TV sets to hear the news reports that punctuated the day and reassure one another. The House of Commons Defence Committee later investigated the handling of press and public information during the war.

Media coverage changed again after the Iraq War of 2003. At the time it was thought that releasing vague details about the numbers killed and where would cause less worry for families; instead the opposite happened. Since then the army has enforced a strict protocol about letting next-of-kin know before anything is released. If a serviceman is killed or injured in Afghanistan, all communications with friends and relatives are shut down until the immediate family has been informed. This has proved an effective way of throwing a spanner in the rumour mill, although, in recent years, the army has had to contend with the instantaneous and uncensored nature of social media. Video footage of one of Fusilier Lee Rigby's killers, standing blooded in the street, was broadcast the evening of the attack, after images had already appeared on Twitter and Facebook. Ofcom, the broadcasting watchdog, received some 700 complaints about the item.

Wives differ in their approach to news. At first Annabel avoided any item on the army; now she is much more interested and will google 'Afghanistan helicopters Britain' in the hope of filling in the gaps in what David can tell her. His job has made her more aware of world politics and the implications for the British Army. Other wives avoid hearing or watching the news altogether when their husband is away. However, civilians often do not realise that the next-of-kin is always informed before a death or injury is announced. This can mean that an unsuspecting army wife can cause an embarrassed silence simply by walking into a room where people suspect she may not know she is a widow.

Facebook, Facetime, email and telephone calls all make it easier to keep in touch. Skype works well for North America and other parts of the developed world, but is unpredictable in places like Afghanistan, where the internet connection can break down if too many people are using it. Chatting on the phone can also be difficult, especially for children. Annabel does not always know what time David will call and it could easily coincide with bath-time or another important part of the daily routine. If he is using a satellite phone, there is often a delay and it can be difficult to match moods: he may be gearing up for the day ahead while his family at home is winding down for the night.

As Iraq is three hours ahead of the UK, it was not usually feasible for soldiers serving there in 2004 to call home at the beginning of the day. Instead, queues would form in the evening in the Portakabins at bases such as Abu Naji, where banks of telephones would allow soldiers to indulge in intense dialogue. Every soldier had a phone card that allowed him twenty minutes of free calls a week; extra minutes could be bought. For security reasons, soldiers had to be careful about what they said. This was often particularly tricky when trying to reassure relatives that they were safe – despite what they might have seen on the TV news. Occasionally the line was so clear that relatives could hear mortar rounds exploding and the soldier had to pretend that these noises were doors being slammed. One private commented, 'They must have thought it was the windiest place on earth.' When mortar fire hit the satellite dish at Abu Naji, troops' families went from regular communication to silence. Wives and girlfriends of American troops serving in a remote part of Afghanistan in 2007 and 2008 became used to military language seeping into their phone calls home. Intimate conversations would be punctuated by 'break' and 'over'.

When David was on his six-month tour of Afghanistan, Annabel sent him a photo of their two young children every day. The pictures arrived via an 'e-bluey' – a letter that is composed and sent as an email but printed out at the other end as an aerogramme (hence 'bluey') and delivered by British Forces Post Office (BFPO). About a million people a year now use the service, which accounts for 80 per cent of letters sent between British forces and home. The e-bluey is faster than a normal letter and gives the recipient the thrill of holding something tangible that was composed by their loved one. During the first three months after the invasion of Iraq, more than 250,000 e-blueys were sent each month, a record that still stands. You can also send a handwritten letter via a fax-bluey and, inevitably, the BFPO now has an app which can help find addresses, calculate the cost of sending packages, tell you which retailers will post directly to servicemen and women overseas, and reminds you of posting dates for Christmas and other important events.

The e-bluey is the child of the Forces Free Air Letters (FFAL) – the original 'bluey' – which is free to families of those serving in the armed services and can be dropped into a civilian postbox free of charge. Despite technological advances, the arrival of a big sack of mail still causes a flurry of excitement in postings such as Afghanistan and soldiers still slink off to savour the written word in quiet corners of the base.

The ritual of collecting treats to send in a parcel has been going on for generations. Annabel sends her husband several copies of *Motorcycle News* in one go; a stash his children call 'his pile'. They tried posting him flapjack, but it arrived as a mound of oats. Anything with chocolate rarely survives the journey, but sweets go down well. As Kitty says, 'There's probably more Haribo in Afghanistan than there is in the whole of the UK.' Wives send items that might be in short supply or just impossible to get: shampoo, deodorant, after-sun cream, dried fruit, beef jerky or the South African dried, cured meat, *biltong*. They try to think of items that will help disperse the boredom: books, a boomerang, a pack of cards, a kite, or a bouncy ball.

Birthdays are a particular challenge. Post can take anything from seven days to a month to arrive in Afghanistan. It is slower towards Christmas when the volume increases or if the planes are grounded or are taken up with medical emergencies. When Annabel ordered her husband an iPad on Amazon for his fortieth, she wondered how close to his birthday it might arrive in Afghanistan. She imagined his delight at receiving something so unexpected and sophisticated in his comfortless quarters. The surprise did not unfold quite as she had planned because the postal service proved so efficient that the package arrived three weeks early, emblazoned with labels announcing its contents.

The connectivity of the modern world is not always a force for good. In the past, writing a letter to a soldier at the front required consideration. The writer and the recipient knew what they were saying might be shared with friends, family and the censor; they were more circumspect. Today, soldiers are spray-gunned with news from home – not all of it welcome and some of it containing domestic trials they are powerless to do anything about. However, many husbands argue it is the trivia of life that they miss most and, besides, there is so much that they are not allowed to talk about. Charlotte says when her husband was in Afghanistan he enjoyed hearing about the banal side of life – that she had bought a new tool with which to trim the hedge and which sections she had attacked first. She also believes that telling him what is happening while he is away makes it easier for him to adjust when he returns. She tries to send him images that will make him laugh, like the dog with a bucket on its head.

Some members of the army, though, worry that this instant and regular communication with home makes men less able as soldiers because they are straddling two worlds. They hear about the quarrel at work, the fact that their son is struggling with his Maths homework or the dishwasher has broken, but are helpless to do anything about any of these problems. A director of the US Army's suicide prevention task force has suggested that hearing 'near real time' about conflict at home can be dangerous – 'It forces you to literally keep your head in two games at one time when your head should be in just one game, in Iraq or Afghanistan.' The bored soldier in a distant camp can become obsessed with tracking his wife or girlfriend's movements on Facebook and other sites. Jokey photos of a wife with her arm round a stranger as part of a harmless night out with girlfriends can easily be misconstrued by an absent husband.

The speed with which soldiers return home can also lead to unexpected difficulties. A long journey back from the Falklands in 1982, or from the Far East at the end of the Second World War, might have been frustrating for the soldier and his family but gave both time to adjust to what had happened, and in the soldier's case he was doing so among people who had shared the same experience. Today, when soldiers return from somewhere like Afghanistan, they usually stop at Cyprus to let off steam by playing sport and relaxing with other soldiers. Welfare officers inform families of when to expect their husband home and if he has been delayed, which he often is. Communication tends to be via brief texts, 'Husbands are fine. You'll hear from them in a few days' or 'Flights changed'.

Wives and families can meet them at somewhere like RAF Brize Norton, which feels like a commercial airport with its bank of arrival and departure screens, or at their base, when soldiers spill off coaches like children returning from a school trip – many reluctant to reveal their excitement at being home. Different wives follow different rituals in the run-up to their return. For some it's a matter of shaving their legs and making sure the fridge is stocked with their husband's favourite drinks. Louise and her two young children usually make a 'welcome home' banner to decorate the house with. At the base she says: 'When they come out, it's weird: you don't cry because there are just so many people there. It's just so overwhelming. It's so rushed, you get this whole build-up, and then I think it's a day or two later you let your barrier down. You just let it all out.'

Fathers often ease the transition by making sure they have a present to pluck out of their rucksack – even if it happens to be bought by their wife. After the initial euphoria of the homecoming has subsided, it can be difficult for a husband to fit back into a routine in which the wife has been in command. One wife remembers her two children resenting not having their mother's undivided attention and her son saying, 'Isn't it time Daddy went away?'. If a soldier has returned from active service he may be 'hyper vigilant' for weeks on end. Lingering worries about land mines will mean he finds it difficult to walk on grass or becomes cross when a family member parks the car on grass. He might be sensitive to loud or sudden noises. When Annabel's husband returns, he is usually back at his desk the very next day and he is expected to attend several official dinners too. Usually he stays the night in the officers' mess afterwards because they tend to be long and boozy affairs. Once the dinners are over and he has resumed his office life, he is allowed several weeks' leave and he and Annabel will make sure they have a break alone together, as well as family time with the children.

Being a soldier is a strange career. The army forms the staple narrative of many computer games, appears regularly on the news and in the cinema, and carries a political dimension. I remember, as a very young child, asking my father, as part of the bedtime storytelling routine, to tell me about the people he had killed in the Second World War and being bemused that it was the one question he would not answer. Today's army parents have to face the same question, but in the present tense. They also have to explain to children what Daddy does when he goes away. When one army wife's husband was posted to Afghanistan, the couple decided simply to tell their young son that 'Daddy had gone to the desert'. The primary school he attended tried to be supportive by discussing the war in Afghanistan in the Personal and Social Development (PSD) classes that are part of the primary school curriculum in the UK. However, it transpired that the school's approach was more direct than his parents would have liked – partly because the parents of another, older, army child at the school took a less opaque tack. The five-year-old boy suffered nightmares and was sick after the classes. He explained to his parents, 'I had this imagination and you were dragging me, Dad, and I was screaming, "I haven't done anything wrong" and you said to me, "It's alright, I'm just trying to hide as the Afghans are trying to kill us".' After talking to the army welfare officer, they responded by telling him that Daddy was just trying to make peace by ordering the baddies: 'Go home, stop fighting' and by making sure the 'baddies' knew that they were being watched. They also tried to make his job sound more everyday by talking about the meetings he goes to and by play-acting this part of his work. As a family, they held a meeting and Daddy gave a PowerPoint presentation during which tea and biscuits were served. After that, the child had a more benign impression of what her father did for a living.

Some wives detect a subtle pressure to take part in the many social events organised by their husband's regiment. Mess functions remain an important part of army life and can be as formal as long dresses and gloves. A wife can expect to be invited to at least three or four dinners a year and maybe a summer and Christmas ball. If someone is leaving a unit there might be a 'dining out'; when new people join there is often a 'dining in'. There might also be a dinner at the end of a tour to celebrate everyone's safe arrival home. This usually includes a toast to the 'ladies' and a speech in which the wives and families are thanked for their support. Some wives can find this level of formality daunting, especially if she has not been an army child. Louise takes a more pragmatic view and acknowledges the common saying: 'A wife will not make your career; she can break it, but she won't make it.' And not everyone wants to join in everything that is on offer. Some regiments also organise 'wives' exercises' in which the women wear their husband's kit and spend the night camping and drinking out of mess tins. This is designed to show wives how their husbands train, but it does not appeal to everyone. One wife refused to go because this would not happen in any other job – 'In no other industry would you say, "Right, all you doctors, your wives are coming into the hospital next week" and you wouldn't do it with vets.'

The other aspect of life in the army that is beginning to pall for some wives is the culture of competitive drinking. Eating and drinking have long been used as a way of fostering camaraderie and of helping soldiers to release tension. Some wives, however, resent the pressure put on them to join that culture – either by drinking a lot themselves or by putting up with heavy consumption from their husbands. At its worst, social events can turn into drinking games or 'drunken Olympics'. One wife was disgusted to hear that the fund for the Christmas ball had been diverted from harmless pleasures like dodgems and entertainers and poured into alcohol – 'Women passed out in the ladies' loos and were vomiting in the potpourri.' Another wife believes a lifetime in the army turned her husband into an alcoholic, a disease that eventually killed him. He was of a generation that was less aware of the dangers of alcohol abuse and she believes his addiction was made worse by the fact that alcohol was duty-free when they were living abroad. While the stories of wild drinking binges are rare, a drinking culture remains engrained in some parts of the army.

The secret language of the armed forces, studded with acronyms and jargon, can also take a little getting used to. Annabel remembers her husband trying to direct her to a meeting place at his base. 'He said: "Just turn up at this time at the RHQ", and I said: "What, where is the RHQ?", and he said: "Well, that's opposite the Old Guard Room", and I said: "What's the Old Guard Room?".'

Louise found the jargon difficult to follow at first but now realises that she is using it herself. She will say the weather is 'doggers' (there is poor visibility), or use some other term that Nigel will tell her is '*so* Army'. Kitty is also conscious of the army slang that has infiltrated their life:

> 'take a knee' – listen – a term used in basic training when a trainer calls a soldier over to tell him something. The soldier has to reduce his visibility but cannot lie down because the weight of his kit would mean he could not react quickly. Instead, he 'takes a knee';
> 'squared away' – beyond reproach;
> 'screw the nut' – finish something, usually to return the favour for someone who has helped you out;
> 'scoff', *n.* – food;
> 'crunchie', *adj.*– difficult;
> 'patch brat', *n.* – army children who live in army housing (the patch).

Someone might work in 'loggies' (logistics) or 'tankies' (tanks) and the well-established slang for civilian life, 'civvy street', is still widely used.

It can take a while to be able to spot someone's rank and position by the uniform, but harder still is reading a map for a professionally trained navigator. One tip army spouses learn early on in family outings is that using your finger to trace your journey on a map is never an adequate 'pointer' and that every trip needs to be treated as a complex navigational operation. In other ways, though, making army slang part of family life can be just another 'in joke' enjoyed by parents and children. Kitty remembers telling her husband to 'take a knee' by the frozen goods cabinet in their local supermarket while they worked out what to buy for a dinner party.

Epilogue:

Life After the Army

A job as head of security on a container ship skulking through the Indian Ocean seemed like a sensible way of putting the skills Ian (not his real name) had learnt in the army to good use. It was also a chance to earn a lot of money in a short time. His girlfriend, Jenny, had got used to the long months away from home, but neither he nor his family realised how much they would miss the routine and dependability of army life. When Tom Hanks' film *Captain Phillips* (2013), which tells the story of a real-life merchant seaman whose ship is hijacked by Somali pirates, became the film everyone was talking about, Ian's job no longer seemed like an easy way to make money. Fortunately, he survived the experience and used part of his savings to retrain as a central heating engineer. His army background has given him the right credentials for this job too: he is polite, punctual, carries out the task without any fuss and cleans up afterwards. For Jenny, it means he comes home every night.

From Kandahar to container ship to central heating van is not an obvious career progression. But the army is such an all-or-nothing, one-off lifestyle that the next step is bound to seem like an about-turn. While for most of us retirement represents a speck on an increasingly distant horizon, the army offers many financial incentives to stop work sooner. But leaving the army can be a shock to a relationship and, after years of being followed, the husband can suddenly find himself trailing after his wife or, like the bumbling major in the BBC comedy *Fawlty Towers*, forever out of synch with the modern world.

Picking the moment to leave a job that has become a way of life for both partners is a momentous decision. Every soldier reaches an age when they must decide to continue with the army or break the ties while they are still young enough to hop onto another career ladder. That decision will be influenced by many factors: their chances of promotion, whether they have learnt a trade – such as engineering – that will help them gain a foothold in a different world and whether their children are still at boarding school.

One army wife described retirement as 'like falling off a cliff. You lose your identify and status and become "another retiree" without your communication network. Few understand the life you have led. Nor are they interested generally.' She and her husband, who left the army at fifty-six, found it particularly difficult because their last tour was abroad, from where he was unable to build contacts that might have helped him to find a well-paid job or consultancy work in Britain. Instead, he spent his first year of retirement carrying out DIY tasks on the house they had bought in a rural part of England while she went out to work. Several years later, they still value the many friends they made around the world who understand their army background but, equally, they have 'moved on' and their new social network is not interested in their previous life. Their daily routine is quieter, but they find adventure in travel – the only difference is that now they have to pay for it themselves.

Sue and Richard Middleton, who had spent much of their army life in Cold War West Germany, started to think about a new life in the early 1990s when he was forty-nine. For them, the timing seemed right: the army was shrinking and offered attractive redundancy packages. As they had had their children early in their marriage, there were no longer school fees to pay; their youngest son, Charlie, was in his final year at university and James, their eldest, was at Sandhurst. Sue remembers sitting on the banks of the River Thames at Richmond working out exactly how much money they needed to live on. They were not looking for a big salary, just enough to cover the shortfall from Richard's pension.

The army offered him a useful resettlement course – although Sue comments that there was nothing similar for wives. She had found it impossible to work while they had been in Germany and had wanted to be home for her children during the school holidays. As a consequence, she entered the final decade of the twentieth century with no computer skills and doubts about whether she would ever be able to find paid work. A Women Returning to Work course, funded by the European Union, gave her the skills and confidence she needed and she found a job for the last few months of Richard's time as a soldier. The business was run by three 'chaotic but brilliant guys' who needed someone to keep them in order. Sue's experience as an army wife allowed her to organise them and she even, on occasion, ended up looking after a baby in the office. The woman who replaced her was an ex-army captain.

Life outside the army required some adjustment. At first Sue enjoyed not being alone for long periods, but she also found that she missed having time to herself. Like most army wives, she had learnt how to be self-sufficient, and sacrificing some of that freedom caused 'friction'. When she found a full-time job, as PA to the Eastern Region Shops' manager of the Sue Ryder Foundation Charity, Richard became a house-husband for five years. He was ready to leave the army and loved being at home. They had two dogs to look after and he filled his time with DIY, cooking and household chores. She would return at night, soak in the bath and ask, 'What's for supper?'.

Neither was Sue prepared for how their social life would change. When she tried to join the usual networks, such as the Women's Institute, she found it hard to adjust to a less regimented way of getting things done. She admits she was easily irritated by the slowness with which events were organised, and the absence of a 'sense of duty' from volunteers who often failed to carry out what they had promised. 'This of course was *my* problem, not theirs,' she concedes now, adding that she finds it harder to relate to people who have stayed in the same place all their lives. Most of her non-army friends have lived wandering lives too and her closest friends are ex-military. The fact that the husbands are also likely to be close makes it easier to form lasting bonds.

She was also surprised by how much she missed the peripatetic life of the army. For many wives the regular upheaval of packing and unpacking is one of the worst aspects of the job – but Sue loved it: 'If something didn't suit, you always knew it wasn't forever! New places, new friends, life was rarely humdrum and boring.' She also missed the sports facilities and 'on tap' medical cover – in Germany, in particular, hospitals were 'over-staffed'. It took her about ten years to feel content to live in one place – 'I couldn't get used to living in the same village, same house, same neighbours. Now I actually don't hanker for moving. But having said that, if there was ever a reason to move, even as far as New Zealand [where her son lives], or for other reasons it wouldn't be a drama.' This *wanderlust* seems to have extended to her children and her friends' children: nearly all are in the armed services or living or working abroad. Her son, James, thinks this may in part be due to their private education, which was inevitably quite old-fashioned and focused on the idea of Empire.

In recent years, the army has become more aware of its obligation to the 20,000 people who leave the Forces each year. Its Career Transition Partnership offers careers advice, tips on interview preparation and guidance about financial planning. In 2013/14, it helped 84 per cent of those leaving the service to find 'sustainable employment' within six months. The Government Forces' Help to Buy Scheme, launched in April 2014, offered financial assistance to more than 5,000 personnel to allow them to buy a first home or move up the property ladder. If all of this sounds like the sort of advice a school leaver might receive – albeit at a more sophisticated level – that is because the transition from army life to 'Civvy Street' can feel as momentous as leaving home for the first time.

Retirement was an alien concept for wives of soldiers in the nineteenth century, many of whom continued to travel and to endure gruelling lives, albeit in exotic settings. Until 1847 the ordinary soldier enlisted for life or until released on medical grounds. After this date enlistment was reduced to twenty-one years for the infantry and twenty-four in other corps. The Cardwell reforms (1870–1) cut this further to six years in the regular army, followed by the same period in the reserve. The scope of Britain's empire meant that between 1861 and 1885 over half the army was stationed abroad – predominantly in India – and a regular soldier could expect to spend two-thirds of his time in the army overseas. For much of the Victorian period officers were not obliged to retire.

Wives of professional soldiers in the Victorian period might spend years in distant parts of the empire, or accompany their husbands from one seat of unrest to another. Henry Duberly's regiment, the 8th Royal Irish Hussars, left Crimea for seventeen months in Ireland before being sent to Bombay in October 1857 to help mop up the dangerous vestiges of the Indian mutiny. Fanny again disobeyed orders to become one of the few officers' wives to accompany her husband to a country that, in Britain, was famous for the massacre of women and children. She marched 2,028 miles with the regiment – 1,800 miles of it on horseback, often at the front to avoid the dust kicked up by the horses and soldiers – to the far northwest of India, then called Rajutana. Here she visited the private quarters of the six wives of a local prince in a walled city before continuing on the punishing march.

Fanny was struck down with dysentery and blood poisoning from an abscess so painful that she had to be transported by palanquin, only leaving the vehicle to watch the battle in which the Rani of Thansi was killed. In 1859 she published a journal about her experiences but, unlike her Crimean book, it was not a bestseller. She and Henry spent the next five years in India, resuming the peripatetic lifestyle of an army wife as the 8th Hussars flitted between barracks in England, Edinburgh and Dublin. Henry eventually became staff paymaster to the 44th Brigade Depot in Essex and retired in 1881 with the rank of lieutenant-colonel. Like many other 'army people', they put their exotic travels to one side to settle in a cosy villa, in Cheltenham, Gloucestershire. Henry died in 1891 and Fanny lived on for another twelve years until her death, aged seventy-one, in 1903.

Harriet Tytler, who gave birth to her son in a bullock cart during the siege of Delhi, continued to live an energetic and dramatic life and to travel widely. In 1862 her husband, Robert, was appointed superintendent to the Andaman Islands, an archipelago in the Bay of Bengal between India and Burma, which the British had annexed in 1858. Today, the islands are represented by scenes of idyllic beaches and azure seas. When the Tytlers were posted there the region held convicts – many whose lives had been spared after the Mutiny – and Harriet had been told that the locals were cannibals. Over the next two years she helped supervise the prisoners' road-building projects, ran the governor's house and laid the foundation stone for the first church. Under her husband's aegis land was cleared on the South Island and a hill named 'Mount Harriet', now a national park. However, their stay was blighted by two incidents. The government in Calcutta criticised Robert for over-reacting when local people killed a naval man – supposedly in an unprovoked attack but which, it later transpired, had been sparked by his attempt to rape a local woman. Robert had been too quick to believe the naval party's version of events and, as a result, demanded two companies of *sepoys* be sent from the mainland to help restore order. During his term in office, too, 2,908 of the 8,035 prisoners died and 612 escaped.

The couple returned to India and from there she went back to Britain with her children to raise money for an orphanage she hoped to open in Simla. Her visit included speaking at a public meeting in Glasgow, an ordeal she found terrifying. While she was away, Robert, whose health was fading, opened a museum. At the age of forty-two, Harriet gave birth to a tenth child, a daughter, but the child lived only a few months. Robert died the following year, aged fifty-four. Harriet, who married when she was nineteen, quickly adapted to the role of widow. Although, as the wife of a colonel, she received a pension, the orphanage had used up funds and she economised by dismissing the servants and giving painting lessons for extra income. When she heard that two of her children in Britain were ill, she booked a second-class berth for herself and three other offspring. She was upgraded when an archdeacon on board heard about her plight.

Harriet returned to India in 1876 and in the 1880s held a successful exhibition of her own paintings and furniture in Hyderabad. In 1884 she visited her daughter 7,000 miles away in British Columbia, Canada. On her return to Simla she began to write her memoirs and completed them before her death, aged seventy-nine, in 1906. They were passed on to her daughter, Mabel, who married Captain Benbow of the 1st Dragoon Guards. Many of the 300 photographs taken by the couple have been preserved in the British Library; Robert also left behind at least one learned article on natural history based on their travels.

Lady Julia Inglis, who had survived the siege of Lucknow, had even less time with her husband. Promoted to major-general on 26 September 1857, he was made KCB 'for his enduring fortitude and persevering gallantry in the defence of the residency'. He became colonel of the 32nd light infantry on 5 May 1860 and was sent soon after to Crete, where he commanded troops in the Ionian Islands. In 1862 he died on leave in Hamburg, aged forty-seven. The couple had been married for eleven years and had three sons, all of whom had been at the siege. Julia died in Beckenham, south London, forty-two years later, on 3 February 1904, aged seventy.

Unlike Lady Inglis, and Fanny Duberly, few wives of ordinary soldiers could expect a lengthy old age in cosy suburbia. Elizabeth Evans, who went with her husband to Crimea before being sent home suffering from fever, was an elderly lady when she was buried with full military honours in Richmond, southwest London. She wrote later of her journey back to Britain as a sort of paradise after the horrors she had seen; she was given port and stout to help her recovery. 'But the greatest joy of all' was her reunion with her husband. However, they had barely settled to 'our home happiness' when he was ordered to India. Although he arrived after the Mutiny, he and Elizabeth both witnessed its legacy. She made a long journey without him to stay with a missionary's wife who had not seen another European woman for nine years. Elizabeth wrote that, 'The terror of the Mutiny had turned her hair quite white'.

While in India she observed how quickly husbands can be replaced. When a drum major died, a young soldier was promoted to his role and went to pick up his predecessor's staff and tunic. The replacement had sworn never to marry but decided that he might as well take on the man's widow, as well as his uniform. They were married within days. This was not an isolated example of a speedy remarriage. In other accounts widows were proposed to on the church steps after they had buried their husband; there were even tales of wives securing a promise from their future mate as their spouse lay dying. The shortage of European women and the high mortality rate meant that a bereaved wife usually had several new suitors to choose from.

Elizabeth's husband, William, joined the army when he was twenty and served for twenty-two years; she spent about fourteen years as a widow, during which time she took in laundry – just as she had as a soldier's wife. When an officer read an account of her time in Crimea, he got in touch with the Royal Patriotic Fund and secured a pension for her. Rebecca Box, another wife who was present at Crimea, died a few months before Elizabeth but saw out her final days in the Royal Cambridge Asylum for Soldiers' Widows in Surrey. The home, founded in 1851 by the Duke of Cambridge, was not as grim as the word 'asylum' suggests to modern sensibilities and still exists (renamed), although it has broadened its remit to help widows from different parts of the armed services.

Nell Butler, another veteran of the Crimean War, struggled to survive on 'out-relief' and battled for nearly forty years to secure the pension she felt she was owed. She was one of a handful of ordinary women who fought for financial help. Widows and orphans of officers had been receiving some kind of pension since the early eighteenth century, but it took nearly 200 years before similar rights were extended to the families of the lower ranks. The Crimean War did much to highlight the plight of the ordinary soldier and the press was eager to defend their role as part of the deserving poor. Several charities emerged to help them. The Patriotic Fund came to the rescue of wives both 'on and off the strength' – that is, those who were both officially part of the regiment and others who were, in theory, outside its protection, but who could prove that their husbands had died as a result of their wounds, which was not always an easy task. The Fund also helped with childcare but withdrew financial aid if the widow's morals were felt to be dubious or if she remarried. In the 1860s and 1870s the Fund provided allowances to around 3,000 widows a year. In 1881 the Government agreed to give widows of men and NCOs who were killed in action or who died as a result of a wound one year's pay.

The Boer War (1899–1902) provided the impetus for further reform. At the start of the conflict, the *Daily Mail* launched a fund to help the soldiers, many reservists, and their families, who suddenly had to leave their jobs for lower-paid soldiering and the prospect that they might not have a job to return to. Rudyard Kipling's poem 'The Absent-Minded Beggar', which was later put to music, highlighted their plight and became hugely popular, earning thousands for the fund. His words drew attention to the women left behind: the 'girl' married in secret because the soldier knew parents would not have approved; the wife struggling to pay for food, fuel and rent – and probably with a child to feed too; the lass he had stepped out with in a casual way, who was now missing her soldier. These families, Kipling urged, were too proud to beg but needed help – whether their husband was 'gardener, baronet, groom'; 'his mates (that's you and me)' have to look after '*her*'. Such patriotism highlighted the plight of families and added to pressure for official aid for widows – of whom there were 2,359 by the end of 1900.

In 1901 widows and orphans of ordinary soldiers were able to claim a state pension of five shillings a week, and 1s 6d for each child if their loved one had died while on active service. However, the state pension for soldiers' families came with many strings attached and it took courage to challenge the existing order. Only widows who were on the strength could apply, and dependents of black soldiers were excluded from the scheme, although discretionary payments might be made. A widow who remarried or was considered to have behaved in an immoral fashion also lost her pension. The National Archives in Kew includes the records of a woman who was given a pension of five shillings in 1901 but then had the payment taken away when she gave birth to an illegitimate child – presumably by her dead husband – the following year. The pension was finally restored twenty-two years later.

As in the past, widows whose husband had died while in the army, but not as a direct and obvious result of fighting, were frequently excluded. Josephine Downey had a pair of daughters under the age of two when her husband, Private James Downey of the 2nd Battalion of the Royal Lancaster Regiment, was killed in August 1900 in Paardekop, northwest of Cape Town. He died never having seen his youngest child. The following year, Josephine, who was thirty-one and originally from Ireland, wrote to the War Office to ask whether the new rules meant she was eligible for a pension. By this time, she and her two daughters were living with her widowed mother and two younger brothers, both single, in Gorton, Manchester. In her letter she pointed out that her husband had served in the army for sixteen years and that the only money she received was a few shillings a week from a local charity that was 'entirely insufficient to do anything like keeping us respectable'. Her application was turned down because James had not died in action or as a result of wounds, but had been killed in a tram accident. The rules were subsequently changed to include cases like James's and the introduction of a pension for soldiers' dependents proved an important milestone on the way to old-age pensions for the general population in 1909.

During the First World War pensions were extended to volunteers and women off the strength. But the sheer number of casualties meant that payments were slow and inflation was such that few families could live on it alone; most had to resort to help from charities and other sources. The subject of pensions for army widows continued to be a source of rancour well into the twentieth century. In the Second World War widows were taxed on their pension. The allowances for children were also lower for families who had lost a father, compared to the help for offspring of serving men. The debate continued to rage until strong lobbying from the War Widows' Association helped to remove taxation in the late 1970s.

For women whose husbands or fiancés have been killed on active service, the anniversary of their death – or of the moment when they first heard the news – can become a painful punctuation mark throughout their lives. After the First World War some widows chose to spend Armistice Day with similarly bereaved women so that they could cry together; others preferred to hide away from the world and do their grieving in private. One young woman would always write to her fiancé's parents on the anniversary of his death.

Clare Sheridan, who had kept in touch with her husband via a medium until he criticised her decision to live in Turkey, managed to find self-fulfilment as a widow. Having discovered a talent as a sculptor after modelling a statue for her first child's grave, she made a career as an artist. Following her husband's death she exhibited her sculptures, including one of Churchill, and visited the Soviet Union in 1920 in order to experience communism at first hand and to sculpt Lenin and Trotsky. She travelled to Mexico before settling for a while in America, where she became friends with Charlie Chaplin and turned to journalism. When a second trip to Russia, in 1923, left her disillusioned, she took her children to live in Turkey and then Algeria. She continued to sculpt and write, and died in 1970.

Modern army wives who become widows can often seem as if they have lost more than just their husbands. Although the army tries to be as sensitive as possible, there will come a time when a wife and her family must leave the 'patch'. If their child has an army-sponsored boarding school place this, too, may disappear. As well as the sudden change in their financial situation, the widow may lose the social life that was such a key part of life in the 'army family'. As a naval widow said after the Falklands War, 'gradually it all stopped and I felt as if I was no longer a member of the family. You never find the same camaraderie outside the Forces.'

In recent years efforts have been made to recognise the role of the widow and the suffering she continues to endure long after the end of a war. From the 1980s organisations representing widows have been invited to take part in many official remembrance services and parades. While many widows from the First World War could not afford to visit their husband's final resting place, efforts have been made to give modern wives the opportunity. Falklands widows were allowed free travel to visit the island and more than 200 widows of Far East POWs have been funded to visit their husband's resting place – usually in one of the beautifully kept Commonwealth War

Graves Commission's sites such as Kanchanaburi in Thailand. In 2000 former Far East POWs and their widows were given a tax-free £10,000 payment as a debt of honour to mark the particular suffering they had endured. Some 4,500 widows were among the 16,700 people who received the payment. Since 1967, the next-of-kin of a serviceman buried abroad would be invited to attend the funeral or to visit the grave within two years of the death with a companion and at the state's expense. Modern warfare means that sometimes the body is 'unviewable' and, particularly in America, a widow or mother may be given the flag that covered the coffin. In wars such as Vietnam the grieving process and the role of the widow has also been affected by the extent to which the war was generally seen as just or even heroic. Accepting the death became even harder when families had to wait weeks for the body's return from the other side of the world.

The issue of next-of-kin becomes contentious if the soldier's girlfriend is pregnant at the time of his death and, in a few high-profile cases, has set grieving mother against grieving mother-to-be. While in the First World War, the dead soldier's mother clearly held a position of prominence in the rank of mourners, the girlfriend now plays a significant part. In at least two cases, following the tragic death of young soldiers in Afghanistan, disputes over who should benefit from the financial compensation awarded by the Government and life insurance policies ended up in court. The arguments revolved around the wording of eve-of-battle wills and the UK's inheritance laws that allow dependents to make claims on an estate.

The army is still grappling with the role of the girlfriend and single-sex and long-term partner. At present, unmarried couples are not eligible for married quarters, but times have moved on since the days when single mothers would be asked to produce family photos or letters as proof of the relationship with a soldier who had been killed. Pension rights remain complicated and depend on the scheme to which the soldier belongs. However, the army defines an 'eligible person', in terms of pension benefits, as 'someone (same sex or otherwise) with whom an individual has an established and exclusive relationship of dependence or interdependence'.

It is a sobering thought that prisoners of war are unlikely to figure in future conflicts. Men captured by the enemy today are more accurately 'held hostage', taken to ground and moved from one hiding place to another, or subjected to mental or physical torture and, at worst, public execution. They are no longer confined to the large camps that started in the Boer War and continued in the major conflicts of the twentieth century. It was in these camps that intense friendships flourished. Being a POW delivered, for many, a more profound camaraderie even than simple soldiering. That camaraderie often lived on in regular reunions and social events to which wives were frequently invited. In the case of Far East POWs, it was sometimes true that veterans would share their memories only with others who had gone through the same experience or would talk about their trauma only to their grandchildren. Others found returning to the site of their imprisonment, often accompanied by their wife, the only way to stop the nightmares.

Although the two world wars represented a comparatively short stint in the army – at the very most, six years in uniform in one war – the period could assume a significance beyond the length of time. The war years, and the memory of that time, might represent to the wife a period to which she could never fully be privy. Or it might mark the high tide of their relationship, when a pattern of absence followed by reunion and spiced with danger lent their marriage a never-to-be-repeated intensity. She, too, might have experienced freedom, friendship and fear that could not be equalled in peacetime.

James and Diana Carnegie were eventually able to resume their normal life. James returned to the City, where he worked as a stockbroker. But history repeated itself in 1948 when another daughter, Sarah, survived for only a few months. Susan, their wartime baby, was fifty-seven when she died, but, happily, twins Sophie and Charlotte were born in 1954 and continue to thrive. There are five grandchildren: one, James Carnegie, has become his grandfather's namesake. Diana never talked about the baby who died in 1940 and Sophie and Charlotte had no idea that their mother had kept up a correspondence with their father during the war years. The daughters learnt about their mother's years of dedicated letter-writing only when the letters, which had been stored in a trunk that was stolen in a burglary, turned up at auction. For them it was a joy to hear again their mother's irreverent voice as she wrote to James about Bengie, barrage balloons and property that was 'n.b.g.' ('no bloody good').

Other veterans of the Second World War slipped back into their former lives. Jakob Dhonau ended the war as a sergeant in the Intelligence Corps, but Rachel had to wait until March 1946 for him to be demobbed. It was a relief for both to return to family life and books. They eventually bought the house in Sheringham they had rented during the war and both turned to teaching, Jakob training for a profession he would follow until retirement. Rachel gave birth to a third son, Max, in 1948, and then climbed up the teaching career ladder to become a deputy head. She died in 1987, aged seventy-seven, and Jakob eleven years later.

When my father-in-law, Brian Kelly, was demobbed, he rejoined an organisation that was very similar to the one he had just left: the Metropolitan Police and then Scotland Yard. His wife, Peggy, went from being an army wife to a police wife. There were many similarities: a close-knit, male world that kept her husband away from home for long periods of time. Their first son, Bob, who was asked to pick out his father from a line-up of newly returned commandoes, emigrated to Canada after graduation and found out only on his mother's death in 1995 that he had spent many months as a toddler separated from her, in Silver End, Essex. Although he has been happily married for more than forty years and has four children and several grandchildren, the revelation provided a missing piece in the jigsaw of his personality.

As medical advances continued, wives faced the prospect of caring for, and living with, men who had survived unimaginable physical and emotional traumas. Even soldiers who experienced plastic surgery at its most rudimentary, in the First World War, often managed to live long, normal lives. In many cases, such as William Spreckley's, their ravaged flesh seemed to settle into a rugged version of old age that offered no hint of the operations and months spent recuperating with other similarly bandaged soldiers. Harold Gillies continued to develop the practice of plastic surgery, but it was not until the Second World War that a demand re-emerged – this time most often from the terrible burns suffered by RAF pilots. Gillies's cousin, Archibald McIndoe, became the most famous of these surgeons through the help he gave to more than 600 servicemen who, because of the pioneering nature of his surgery, called themselves with typical RAF bravura, 'The Guinea Pig Club'. Perhaps more than Gillies, McIndoe tried to rebuild his patients' confidence and to encourage a belief that they could enjoy a normal life by sending them to the nearby pub and encouraging them to go to parties.

While McIndoe was helping badly burned servicemen, Ludwig Guttmann was setting up a spinal injuries unit at Stoke Mandeville Hospital in Aylesbury, Buckinghamshire. On 29 July 1948, the first day of the London Olympics, Guttmann organised an archery competition for sixteen injured servicemen and women in an event called the Stoke Mandeville Games. Guttmann saw sport as a way of taking his patients' minds off their injuries. This evolved into the International Stoke Mandeville Games and in 1960 became the Paralympics. Although the competition is no longer restricted to servicemen and women, many of the competitors are still veterans who have suffered injuries while serving in the army. The competition, which is now widely televised, has gone a long way towards changing perceptions of what being disabled means and to making wives and their families proud. It now seems unthinkable that a disabled veteran would not be invited to a victory parade, as happened in London after the Falklands War in October 1982.

Likewise, our way of remembering the dead has become more inclusive even than the Tomb of the Unknown Warrior, which came to represent the loss of so many. The National Memorial Arboretum, which was opened in 2001 on 150 acres of old gravel workings at Alrewas, near Lichfield in Staffordshire, continues this spirit but, rather than making a virtue of anonymity, stresses the diversity of the dead. Most of the 300 memorials tell a story through the way the dead are remembered: by a wall, a building, a statue or a plant. You can stroll its wide-open aisles and find the memorial that nourishes your own family story. Far East POWs are remembered in a wooden building with a veranda that is a museum in itself; nearby you can see sleepers from the Death Railway and the original lychgate built by POWs to remember those who died in Changi Jail in Singapore. The brass plaques on the Basra Memorial Wall glisten in the sun; the wall originally stood in Iraq but was taken down and rebuilt in Staffordshire by British soldiers. The memorial to war widows is – perhaps fittingly – low-key by comparison and consists of a wood of native trees interspersed with crocuses and daffodils that visitors are invited to wander through. There is no statue, just a simple grey block.

While such a memorial suggests passive, if still painful, mourning, the bronze monument in London to women who served in the Second World War has an urgency and immediacy. The sculpture in Whitehall shows the uniforms worn in the armed forces, as well as the clothes of those who worked in factories, hospitals, the armed services and farms. The crumpled coats, hats and dungarees look as though they have been hastily thrown on pegs, that at any moment the wearer will return to scramble into them. These are the clothes that women like Renee Boardman wore as she worked in a munitions factory while her husband Tom was held prisoner in the Far East.

Politicians now talk about a 'military covenant' of care for soldiers during and after their time in service. One Conservative MP, himself a former army officer, warned that the proliferation of military funds and charities – one estimate puts the figure at 2,500 organisations – makes it harder for veterans and their families to find the right medical help for physical and psychological problems. Another politician could not resist drawing on her own family experience of life in the army to defend the need to honour this covenant. She also reminded the House of Commons of Queen Elizabeth I's statute of 1593 which provided a weekly parish tax to support disabled army veterans returning to their homes.

But what it means to be a soldier – and by implication to be a soldier's wife – has changed dramatically over the last 200 years. Even in the final few months of completing this book, the list of jobs the army is now expected to tackle has ranged widely over different types of crises. Soldiers with medical training have been on standby to take the place of striking doctors, squaddies have formed lines to bounce sandbags into place against rising floodwater and, most worryingly for army wives, soldiers have been ready to provide the 'boots on the ground' talked about in the parliamentary debate over air strikes against Syria. The British Government has said it wants to end the ban on women taking frontline infantry roles within a few years. If this happens, there will be more army husbands and boyfriends who will face the anxious waiting – a role traditionally held by women.

As terrorism has appeared on European streets, in London, Paris and Brussels, wives who at the start of my research were willing – and often eager – to speak their minds have, for safety's sake, shrunk back into the shadows, afraid to be identified as part of an army family. They are once again as nameless as the ordinary women who travelled to Crimea or who now lie in overgrown graves in India and other parts of the former British Empire.

There is some safety in numbers. Military choirs have continued to flourish; social media provides an anonymity unavailable to earlier generations. It may be that the personal letter – even if it is delivered electronically – will survive longer among army wives than in other parts of society. Or perhaps an army marriage can be more easily summed up by one of the few objects carried faithfully from one posting to another. There may be no clearer way to mark the domestic life of an army wife than in the list of homes on the back of a battered spice rack.

Bibliography

Books

Acton, Carol. *Grief in Wartime: Private Pain, Public Discourse*, Palgrave Macmillan, Basingstoke, 2007.

Adie, Kate. *Fighting on the Home Front: The Legacy of Women in World War One*, Hodder & Stoughton, London, 2014.

Aldrich, Richard J. *Intelligence and the War against Japan: Britain, America and the Politics of Secret Service*, CUP, Cambridge, 2000.

Anglesey, The Marquess of (ed.). *'Little Hodge': being Extracts from the Diaries and Letters of Colonel Edward Cooper Hodge Written During the Crimean War, 1854–1856*, Leo Cooper, London, 1971.

Bainton, Roy. *The Long Patrol: The British in Germany Since 1945*, Mainstream Publishing, Edinburgh, 2003.

Bamfield, Veronica. *On the Strength: The Story of the British Army Wife*, Charles Knight & Co., London and Tonbridge, 1974.

Barham, Peter. *Forgotten Lunatics of the Great War*, Yale University Press, London, 2004.

Barr, Pat and Desmond, Ray. *Simla: A Hill Station in British India*, Scolar Press, London, 1978.

Barrett, Duncan and Calvi, Nuala. *GI Brides: The Wartime Girls Who Crossed the Atlantic for Love*, HarperCollins, London, 2013.

Beckett, I.F.W. *Riflemen Form: A Study of the Rifle Volunteer*

Movement 1859–1908, Pen & Sword Military, Barnsley, 2007.
Bigwood, Rosemary. *The Scottish Family Tree Detective*, Manchester University Press, 2006.
Birch, Dinah and Drabble, Margaret (eds.). *The Oxford Companion to English Literature*, Oxford University Press, Oxford, 2009.
Bishop, Alan and Bostridge, Mark (eds.). *Letters From a Lost Generation: The First World War Letters of Four Friends: Roland Leighton, Edward Brittain, Victor Richardson, Geoffrey Thurlow*, Little, Brown, London, 1998.
Blakeman, Pamela. *The Book of Ely*, Barracuda Books, Buckingham, 1994.
Bostridge, Mark. *Florence Nightingale: The Woman and Her Legend*, Viking, London, 2008.
Bourke, Joanna. *Dismembering the Male: Men's Bodies, Britain and the Great War,* Reaktion Books, London, 1996.
Bowman, Martin W. *Images of War: Norwich Blitz: Rare Photographs from Wartime Archives*, Pen & Sword, Military, Barnsley, 2012.
Boyden, B. *Tommy Atkins' Letters. The History of the British Army Postal Service from 1795*, National Army Museum, London, 1990.
Braithwaite, Brian; Walsh, Noëlle; and Davies, Glyn. *The Home Front: The Best of Good Housekeeping, 1939–45*. Ebury Press, London, 1987.
Brawer, Nicholas A. *British Campaign Furniture: Elegance under Canvas, 1740–1914*, Harry N. Abrams, New York, 2001.
Briggs, Asa. *The History of Broadcasting in the United Kingdom Volume II: The Golden Age of Wireless*, OUP, London, 1965.
Brittain, Vera. *Testament of Youth*, Virago, London, 1978.
Brown, Douglas R. *East Anglia 1942*, Terence Dalton, Lavenham, 1988.
Butler, Elizabeth. *Elizabeth Butler, Battle Artist: Autobiography*, Fisher Press, Sevenoaks, 1993.

Callan, Hilary and Shirley Ardener (eds.). *Incorporated Wife*, Croom Helm in association with the Centre for Cross-Cultural Research on Women, London, c. 1984.

Carpenter, Humphrey. *J.R.R Tolkien: A Biography*, HarperCollins, London, 1995.

Carr, Jean. *Another Story: Women and the Falklands War*, Hamish Hamilton, London, 1984.

Carrington, Hereward. *Psychical Phenomena and the War*, T. Werner Laurie, London, 1918.

Chilvers, I. *The Oxford Dictionary of Art and Artists*, Oxford University Press, Oxford, 2009.

Collingham, Lizzie. *Curry: A Tale of Cooks and Conquerors*, Vintage, London, 2006.

Collingham, Lizzie (EM). *Imperial Bodies: The Physical Experience of the Raj, C.1800–1947*, Polity Press, Cambridge, 2001.

Compton, Piers. *Colonel's Lady & Camp-Follower: The Story of Women in the Crimean War*, Robert Hale & Company, London, 1970.

Connolly, S.J. (ed.). *The Oxford Companion to Irish History*, OUP, Oxford, 2007.

Costello, John. *Love, Sex & War: Changing Values, 1939–45*, Collins, London, 1985.

Cunningham, Hugh. *The Volunteer Force: A Social and Political History 1859–1908*, Croom Helm, London, 1975.

Custance Green, Hilary. *Surviving the Death Railway: A POW's Memoir and Letters from Home*, Pen and Sword Military, Barnsley, 2016.

Dahl, R. *Boy: Tales of Childhood*, Penguin, London, 2001.

Dalrymple, William. *The Last Mughal: The Fall of Delhi, 1857*, Bloomsbury, 2009.

De Courcy, Anne. *The Fishing Fleet: Husband-Hunting in the Raj*, Weidenfeld & Nicolson, London, 2012.

Denby, Elaine. *Grand Hotels: Reality & Illusion: An Architectural and Social History*, Reaktion Books, London, 1998.

Doyle, Peter and Walker, Julian. *Trench Talk: Words of the First World War*, The History Press, Stroud, 2012.

Duberly, Mrs Henry. *Journal Kept During the Russian War, From the Departure of the Army from England in April 1854, to the Fall of Sebastopol*, Longman, London, 1855.

Earle, Rebecca (ed.). *Epistolary Selves, Letters and Letter-Writers, 1600–1945*, Ashgate, Aldershot, 1999.

Emden, Van, Richard. *The Quick and the Dead: Fallen Soldiers and Their Families in the Great War*, Bloomsbury, London, 2012.

Fenton, Roger. *Roger Fenton, Photographer of the 1850s, Hayward Gallery, London, 4 February to 17 April 1988*, South Bank Board, London, 1988.

Figes, Orlando. *Crimea*, Penguin, London, 2010.

Fishman, Sarah. *We Will Wait: Wives of French Prisoners of War, 1940–1945*, Yale University Press, New Haven and London, 1991.

Fleming, G.H. *Victorian 'Sex Goddess', Lady Colin Campbell and the Sensational Divorce Case of 1886*, Oxford University Press, Oxford, 1990.

Fleming, Peter. *The Fate of Admiral Kolchak*, Rupert Hart-Davies, London, 1963.

Fussell, Paul. *Wartime: Understanding and Behavior in the Second World War*, OUP, Oxford, 1989.

Garth, John. *Tolkien and the Great War: The Threshold of Middle Earth*, HarperCollins, London, 2004.

Gilman, Sander L. *Making the Body Beautiful: A Cultural History of Aesthetic Surgery*, Princeton University Press, Woodstock, 2001.

Gillies, Harold. *Plastic Surgery of the Face, Based on Selective Cases of War Injuries of the Face Including Burns*, Hodder & Stoughton, London, 1920.

Gillies, Harold and Millard, Ralph. *The Principles and Art of Plastic Surgery*, vol. 1, Butterworth, London, 1957.

Gillies, Midge. *Amy Johnson: Queen of the Air*, Phoenix, London, 2004.

––– *Waiting for Hitler: Voices from Britain on the Brink of Invasion*, Hodder & Stoughton, London, 2007.

––– *Writing Lives: Literary Biography*, CUP, Cambridge, 2009.

––– *The Barbed-Wire University: The Real Lives of Allied Prisoners of War in the Second World War*, Aurum, London, 2012.

Goodley, Héloïse. *An Officer and a Gentlewoman: The Making of a Female British Army Officer*, Constable, London, 2012.

Gormanston, Eileen. *A little Kept*, Sheed and Ward, London, 1953.

Graves, Robert. *Goodbye To All That*, Penguin Modern Classics, London, 1957.

Greer, Germaine. *The Obstacle Race: The Fortunes of Women Painters and their Work*, Secker and Warburg, London, 1979.

Gregory, Richard L (ed.). *The Oxford Companion to the Mind*, OUP, Oxford, 2004.

Grierson, J.M. *Records of Scottish Volunteer Force 1859–1908*, Edinburgh, 1909.

Haber, L.F. *The Poisonous Cloud: Chemical Warfare in the First World War*, Clarendon Press, Oxford, 1986.

Hamilton, Ian (ed). and Noel-Tod, Jeremy. *The Oxford Companion to Modern Poetry*, Oxford University Press, Oxford, 2013.

Harrington, Peter. *British Artists and War: The Face of Battle in Paintings and Prints, 1700–1914*, Greenhill Books, London and Stackpole Books, Pennysylvania in association with Brown University Library, Rhode Island, 1993.

Haste, Kate. *Rules of Desire: Sex in Britain: World War I To the Present*, Vintage, London, 2002.

Hazelgrove, Jenny. *Spiritualism and British Society between the Wars*, Manchester University Press, Manchester, 2000.

Hemingway, Ernest. *A Moveable Feast*, Vintage Books, London, 2000.

Hennessey, Patrick. *The Junior Officers' Reading Club: Killing Time and Fighting Wars*, Penguin, London, 2010.

Heyman, Charles. *The British Army Guide, 2012–2013*, Pen & Sword Books, Barnsley, 2011.

Hichberger, J.W.M. *Images of the Army: The Military in British Art, 1815–1914*, Manchester University Press, Manchester, 1988.

Holmes, Richard; Singleton, Charles; and Jones, Spencer (eds.). *The Oxford Companion to Military History*, OUP, Oxford, 2001.

Holmes, Richard. *Tommy, The British Soldier on the Western Front 1914–1918*, Harper Perennial, London, 2005.

––– *Sahib: The British Soldier in India, 1750–1914*, Harper Perennial, London, 2006.

––– *Dusty Warriors: Modern Soldiers at War*, Harper Perennial, London, 2007.

––– *Soldiers, Army Lives and Loyalties from Redcoats to Dusty Warriors*, HarperPress, London, 2011.

Holton, Graham and Winch, Jack. *Discover Your Scottish Ancestry: Internet and Traditional Resources:* Edinburgh University Press, Edinburgh, 2009.

Hughes, Kathryn. *The Short Life & Long Times of Mrs Beeton*, Fourth Estate, London, 2004.

Huxley, Gervas. *Lady Denman, GBE, 1884–1954*, Chatto & Windus, London, 1961.

Hyams, Jacky. *Bomb Girls, Britain's Secret Army: The Munitions Women of World War II*, John Blake, London, 2013.

Inglis, Honourable Lady. *The Siege of Lucknow: A Diary*, James R. Osgood, McIlvaine, London, 1892.

Jeffery, Keith. *MI6, The History of the Secret Intelligence Service, 1909–1949*, Bloomsbury, London, 2010.

Jenkins, Roy. *Churchill*, Pan Books, London, 2002.

Jolly, Emma. *My Ancestor Was a Woman at War*, Society of Genealogists, London, 2013.

Jones, Annie. *Gumboots and Pearls: The Life of a Wife of . . .*, Owl Press, Kingston upon Thames, 1990.

Junger, Sebastian. *War*, Fourth Estate, London, 2011.

Kaye, M.M. *The Sun in the Morning*, Penguin, London, 1992.

Kelly, Christine. *Mrs Duberly's War: Journal & Letters from the Crimea*, 1854–56, OUP, Oxford, 2007.

Kennedy, M., Bourne. *The Concise Oxford Dictionary of Music*, Oxford University Press, Oxford, 2007.

Kennet, Lady. *Self-Portrait of an Artist, From the Diaries and Memoirs of Lady Kennet*, John Murray, London, 1949.

Kershaw, Ian. *The End: Hitler's Germany, 1944–45*, Allen Lane, London, 2011.

Khan, Yasmin. *The Raj at War: A People's History of India's Second World War*, Bodley Head, London, 2015.

Kirkby, Mandy (ed.). *Love Letters of the Great War*, Macmillan, London, 2014.

Kollar, Rene. *Searching for Raymond: Anglicanism, Spiritualism and Bereavement Between the Two World Wars*, Lexington Books, Maryland, c. 2000.

Lancaster, Bill. *The Department Store: A Social History*, Leicester University Press, Leicester, 1995.

Langbridge, R.H. *Edwardian Shopping: A Selection from the Army & Navy Stores Catalogues 1898–1913*, David & Charles, Newton Abbot, 1975.

Lee, Laurie. *As I Walked Out One Midsummer Morning*, Penguin Modern Classics, London, 2014.

Leslie, Anita. *Cousin Clare: The Tempestuous Career of Clare Sheridan*, London, Hutchinson, 1976.

Lessing, Doris. *Alfred and Emily*, Fourth Estate, London, 2008.

Lunt, James. *Jai Sixth! The Story of the 6th Queen Elizabeth's Own Gurkha Rifles 1817–1994*, Leo Cooper, London, 1994.

Macfarlane, Robert. *The Old Ways: A Journey on Foot*, Hamish Hamilton, London, 2012.

Mackenzie, John M. (ed.). *Imperialism and Popular Culture*, Manchester University Press, Manchester, 1986.

––– *Popular Imperialism and the Military, 1850–1950*, Manchester University Press, Manchester, 1992.

Macnaghten, Angus. *'Missing': An Account of the Efforts Made to Find an Officer of the Black Watch reported 'missing' on 29th October, 1914, During the First Battle of Ypres*, Dragon Books, Bala, North Wales, 1970.

McCartney, Helen B. *Citizen Soldiers: The Liverpool Territorials in the First World War*, CUP, Cambridge, 2005.

McCourt, Edward. *Remember Butler: The Story of Sir William Butler*, Routledge & Kegan Paul, London, 1967.

Malcolmson, Robert and Searby, Peter (eds.). *Wartime Norfolk: The Diary of Rachel Dhonau, 1941–1942*, Norwich Record Society, Norwich, 2004.

Massie, Alistair and Parton, Frances (in association with the National Army Museum). *Wives and Sweethearts: Love Letters Sent During Wartime*, Simon & Schuster, London, 2014.

Millgate, Helen. D. and Shaw, Maureen. *War's Forgotten Women: British Widows of the Second World War*, The History Press, Stroud, 2011.

Nicholson, Virginia. *Singled Out: How Two Million Women Survived Without Men After the First World War*, Penguin, London, 2008.

––– *Millions Like Us: Women's Lives in War and Peace, 1939–1949*, Viking, London, 2011.

Orwell, George. *Down and Out in Paris and London*, Penguin, London, 1933.

Owen, James. *Commando: Winning World II Behind Enemy Lines*, Abacus, London, 2013.

Pare, Richard. *Roger Fenton, 1819–1869*, Aperture Foundation, New York, 1987.

Parker, Peter. *The Last Veteran: Harry Patch and the Legacy of War*, Bloomsbury, London, 2010.

Parkes, Meg and Gill, Geoff. *Captive Memories: Far East POWs & Liverpool School of Tropical Medicine*, Palatine Books, Lancaster, 2015.

Pound, Reginald. *Gillies: Surgeon Extraordinary: A Biography*, Michael Joseph, London, 1964.

Procida, Mary A. *Married to the Empire: Gender, Politics and Imperialism in India, 1883–1947*, Manchester University Press, Manchester, 2002.

Proud, E.B. *History of the British Army Postal Service*, Proud-Baile, Brighton, 1980.

Rappaport, Helen. *No Place for Ladies: The Untold Story of Women in the Crimean War*, Aurum Press, London, 2007.

Reid, Fiona. *Broken Men, Shell Shock, Treatment and Recovery in Britain 1914–30*, Continuum, London, 2010.

Robinson, Howard. *Britain's Post Office: A History of Development from the Beginnings to the Present Day*, OUP, Oxford, 1953.

Rogerson, Sidney R. *Twelve Days on the Somme: A Memoir of the Trenches, 1916*, Greenhill Books, London, 2006.

Roper, Michael. *The Secret Battle: Emotional Survival in the Great War*, Manchester University Press, Manchester, 2009.

Rowbotham, Sheila. *A Century of Women: The History of Women in Britain and the United States*, Viking, London, 1997.

Sage, Lorna. *Bad Blood*, Fourth Estate, London, 2000.

Shakespear, L.W. *The History of the Assam Rifles*, Macmillan, London, 1929.

Shephard, Ben. *A War of Nerves: Soldiers and Psychiatrists, 1914–1994*, Jonathan Cape, London, 2000.

Sheridan, Clare. *Nuda Veritas*, Thornton Butterworth, London, 1927.

Simpson, Grant S. (ed.). *The Scottish Soldier Abroad, 1247–1967*, John Donald Publishers, Edinburgh, 1992.

Soames, Mary (ed.). *Speaking for Themselves, The Personal Letters of Winston and Clementine Churchill*, Doubleday, London, 1998.

Speller, Elizabeth. *The Sunlight on the Garden: A Memoir of Love, War and Madness*, Granta, London, 2007.

Spencer, William. *Records* of the *Militia and Volunteer Forces, 1757–*

1945: including Records of the Volunteers, Rifle Volunteers, Yeomanry, Imperial Yeomanry, Fencibles, Territorials and the Home Guard, PRO Publications, Richmond, c. 1997.

Spiegelhalter, David. *Sex by Numbers: What Statistics Can Tell Us About Sexual Behaviour*, Profile Books, London, 2015.

Spiers, Edward M. *The Late Victorian Army, 1868–1902*, Manchester University Press, Manchester, 1992.

—— *The Scottish Soldier and Empire*, Edinburgh University Press, Edinburgh, 2006.

Steel, Flora Annie and Gardiner, Grace (eds. Ralph Crane and Anna Johnston). *The Complete Indian Housekeeper and Cook*, OUP, Oxford, 2010.

Stokes, Doris and Dearsley, Linda. *Voices in My Ear – The Autobiography of a Medium*, Aiden Ellis, Henley-on-Thames, 1980.

Stone, David. *Cold War Warriors: The Story of the Duke of Edinburgh's Royal Regiment (Berkshire and Wiltshire) 9th June 1959–27th April 1994*, Leo Cooper, Barnsley, 1998.

Storey, Graham, Tillotson, Kathleen and Easson, Angus (eds.). *The Pilgrim Edition of The Letters of Charles Dickens*, Clarendon Press, Oxford, vol. 7, 1993.

Thompson, Brian. *Keeping Mum: A Wartime Childhood*, Atlantic, London, 2006.

Thorne, Elisabeth. *From Simla to Cambridge: The Journey of My Life*, Paul Barrett Book Production, Cambridge, 2014.

Trollope, Joanna. *Britannia's Daughters: Women of the British Empire*, Hutchinson, London, 1983.

Trustram, Myna. *Women of the Regiment: Marriage and the Victorian Army*, CUP, Cambridge, 1984.

Turner, Barry and Rennell, Tony. *When Daddy Came Home: How War Changed Family Life Forever*, Arrow, London, 2014.

Tytler, Harriet (ed. Anthony Sattin). *An Englishwoman in India: The Memoirs of Harriet Tytler, 1828–1858*, Oxford University Press, Oxford, 1986.

Usherwood, Paul and Spencer-Smith, Jenny. *Lady Butler: Battle Artist, 1846–1933*, Alan Sutton, Gloucester, 1987.

Venning, Annabel. *Following the Drum: The Lives of Army Wives and Daughters, Past and Present*, Headline Review, London, 2006.

Watkins, Carl. *The Undiscovered Country: Journeys Among the Dead*, The Bodley Head, London, 2013.

Weedon, Brenda (and others). *A History of Queen Mary's University Hospital Roehampton*, Richmond, Twickenham & Roehampton Healthcare NHS Trust, 1996.

Whaley, Joachim (ed.). *Mirrors of Mortality: Studies in the Social History of Death*, Europa Publications, London, 1981.

Williams, Mari. A. *A Forgotten Army: Female Munitions Workers of South Wales, 1939–1945*, published on behalf of the History and Law Committee of the Board of Celtic Studies, Cardiff, University of Wales Press, 2002.

Winter, Jay. *Sites of Memory, Sites of Mourning: The Great War in European Cultural History*, CUP, Cambridge, 1995.

Wood, Stephen. *The Scottish Soldier: An Illustrated Social and Military History of Scotland's Fighting Men Through Two Thousand Years*, Archive Publications, Manchester, 1987.

Woodforde, John. *The Strange Story of False Teeth*, Routledge, London, 1968.

Young, Louisa. *A Great Happiness: The Life of Kathleen Scott*, London, Macmillan, 1995.

Miscellaneous

National Army Museum lecture by Rupert Willoughby explains how Jane Austen's novels reveal an intricate grasp both of military technicalities and of contemporary events. Recorded on 8 September 2011.

Researching Far East POW History Group newsletter.

Unpublished Thesis

Makepeace, Clare. *A Pseudo-Soldier's Cross: The Subjectivities of British Prisoners of War Held in Germany and Italy During the Second World War* (Birkbeck College, University of London, 2013).

Articles

Acton, Carol. 'Writing and Waiting: The First World War Correspondence between Vera Brittain and Roland Leighton', *Gender & History*, vol. 11, April 1999, pp. 54–83.

Biernoff, Suzannah. *Social History of Medicine*, vol. 24, no.3, pp. 666–85, 'The Rhetoric of Disfigurement in First World War Britain'.

Evans, Elizabeth. 'A Soldier's Wife in the Crimea' by the narrative of Mrs Elizabeth Evans, late 4th (King's Own) Regiment of Foot, as told to Walter Woods in *The Royal Magazine*, July 1908, pp. 265–72.

Hazelgrove, Jennifer. 'Spiritualism after the Great War', *Twentieth Century British History*, vol. 10, no. 4, 1999, pp. 404–30.

Higgens, Charlotte. 'The Road Home, Review', the *Guardian*, 30 November 2013.

Markovits, Stefanie. 'Rushing into print, "Participatory Journalism" During the Crimean War', *Victorian Studies*, vol. 50. no. 4.

Savage, Gail. 'The Wilful Communication of a Loathsome Disease': Marital Conflict and Venereal Disease in Victorian England, *Victorian Studies*, autumn 1990.

Sokoloff, Sally. '"How are they at home?" community, state and servicemen's wives in England', 1939–45, a University College Northampton publication. Published online: 19 December 2006.

Miscellaneous Fiction

Barker, Pat. *Life Class*, Penguin Books, London, 2008.

Farrell, J. *The Siege of Krishnapur*, Weidenfeld & Nicolson, London, 1996.

Hardy, Thomas. *Far From the Madding Crowd*, Vintage Classics, London, 2015.

Trollope, Joanna. *The Soldier's Wife*, Black Swan, London, 2013.

West, Rebecca. *The Return of the Soldier*, Virago, London, 2010.

Woolf, Virginia. *Mrs Dalloway*, Wordsworth Editions, London, 1996.

Miscellaneous TV and Radio

'Creative Forces', Broadcast on BBC Radio 4, Thursday, 14 November 2013.

'The War Widows of Afghanistan', First broadcast: Wednesday, 23 July 2014, BBC World Service.

'Timeshift: The British Army of the Rhine', first broadcast, BBC Four, 22 October 2012.

'Who Do You Think You Are?', BBC1, First broadcast 2 October 2014.

Archives are cited in the Endnotes (pp. 350–76).

Endnotes

Amounts calculated using Bank of England inflation calculator

Abbreviations

British Library: BL
Frances Janet Wells: FJW
Imperial War Museum: IWM
Margaret Campbell Hannay: MCH

Prologue

Page 4 Barbara Wilton – interview, 23 March 2013 and subsequent email exchanges.

Page 6 '68,000 women' – Soldiers are not obliged to supply information about their marital status. However, a Freedom of Information response shows the number of UK Regular Forces declaring marriage or a civil partnership at 1 November 2014 as 68,210, which represents 43.7 per cent of UK Regular Forces.

Page 6 'the rate is twice as high in the army as in civilian life' – http://www.telegraph.co.uk/news/worldnews/9329265/What-is-life-really-like-for-the-soldier-of-2012.html

Page 6 'In a survey, divorcées . . .' – *Army Families Federation Survey, Divorce Survey 2015.*

Page 7 'In 2015, 7,790 women . . .' – Ministry of Defence's *UK Armed Forces Quarterly Personnel Report*, 1 April 2015.

Page 8 For more information on Dumbarton, see: http://www.valeofleven.org.uk/contributions/dumbartonargylls

Page 8 'curious singing noise' – Graves, Robert. *Goodbye to All That*, p. 82.

Page 9 'Jane Austen's novels show . . .' – National Army Museum lecture by Rupert Willoughby, recorded on 8 September 2011.

Page 10 'The Girl I Left Behind Me' – Spiers, Edward M., *The Scottish Soldier and Empire, 1854–1902*, p. 116 (http://americanart.si.edu/collections/search/artwork/?id=11492).

Page 12 'Groups such as the military' – www.ssafa.org.uk.

Page 12 'Names such as' – www.combatstress.org.uk and www.helpforheroes.org.uk.

Chapter One: Getting There: Packet ships, palanquins and ponies

Page 15 'Tin-lined packing-cases . . .' – Kaye, M.M. *The Sun in the Morning*, p. 105.

Page 16 'I remember clinging . . .' – ibid., p. 305.

Page 17 'Hind-Urdu' – Khan, Dr. Y. *The Raj at War: A People's History of India's Second World War*, p. 73.

Page 17 See http://www.telegraph.co.uk/news/obituaries/1453069/M-M-Kaye.html

Page 18 'They remember taking . . .' – Bamfield, V. *On the Strength – The Story of the British Army Wife*, p. 36.

Page 18 'sea pie' – Tytler, H. *An Englishwoman in India: The Memoirs of Harriet Tytler, 1828–1858*, p. 90.

Page 18 'On another occasion . . .' – ibid., p. 96.

Page 19 'In the early days . . .' – Holmes, R. *Sahib: The British Soldier in India 1750–1914*, p. 92.

Page 20 'Ordinary soldiers were not allowed ashore . . .' – ibid., p. 104.

Page 20 'gained weight' – ibid., p. 113.

Page 20 'beating through a heavy swell' – *The Times*, 8 March 1825.

Page 22 'scarce a rag to cover them' – ibid.

Page 22 'Turkey-red' – For more information about how the *Kent* was remembered in the Turkey Red fabric and for details held in the National Museums Scotland, see http://www.nms.ac.uk/explore/collections-stories/art-and-design/colouring-the-nation/research/styles-and-patterns/figures-and-objects/

Page 22 'cork floating bed' – Brawer, Nicholas A. *British Campaign Furniture*, p. 158.

Page 23 Lady Inglis – Inglis, Lady Julia. *The Siege of Lucknow, A Diary* – all references taken from the online version.

Page 25 'Most had to bed down like animals . . .' – Rappaport, H. *No Place for Ladies: The Untold Story of Women in the Crimean War*, p. 34.

Page 25 'weakened almost to delirium' – Duberly, F. *Journal Kept During the Russian War, From the Departure of the Army from England in April 1854, to the Fall of Sebastopol*, p. 3.

Page 25 'creaking of that windlass!' – ibid., p. 25.

Page 26 'four miles an hour' – Holmes, R. *Sahib: The British Soldier in India 1750–1914*, p. 25.

Page 27 'Thugs' – Tytler, *An Englishwoman in India: The Memoirs of Harriet Tytler, 1828–1858*, p. 24.

Page 27 'I began to think of home . . .' – Camp Sousneer – 2 March, MCH.

Page 27 'I took or rather my Bearers . . .' – Camp Judore, 11 March, MCH.

Page 27 'so dreadful . . .' – Camp Oojain, 8 March, MCH.

Page 28 'At around five feet . . .' – De Courcy, A. *The Fishing Fleet: Husband-Hunting in the Raj*, p. 75.

Page 28 'five days' – ibid., p. 308.

Chapter Two: Accommodation: Barracks, bungalows and bivouacs

Page 29 'Beware Balaclava Road' – Jones, A. *Gumboots and Pearls, The Life of a Wife of . . .*, p. 16.

Page 30 'if an army wife digs up' – Barbara Wilton, email to the author, following interview.

Page 30 'The Scandal of Shoddy Homes for Heroes' – *Daily Mail*, 26 June 2012 http://www.dailymail.co.uk/news/article-2164683/The-scandal-shoddy-homes-heroes-Conditions-undermine-fragile-morale-troops-risk-lives-battle-say-MPs.html

Page 31 'the first purpose-built barracks' – Holmes, R. *Soldiers: Army Lives and Loyalties from Redcoats to Dusty Warriors*, p. 510.

Page 31 'fourteen women to permission for all wives to "live in"'– Trustram, M. *Women of the Regiment: Marriage and the Victorian Army*, p. 34.

Page 31 'Saltaire, Port Sunlight and Bournville' – ibid., p. 70.

Page 32 'typhoid and tuberculosis were rife' – Bamfield, V. *On the Strength: Story of the British Army Wife*, p. 22.

Page 32 'scarlet fever' – ibid., p. 76.

Page 32 'In 1858 the House of Lords' – Holmes, R. *Soldiers: Army Lives and Loyalties from Redcoats to Dusty Warriors*, p. 522.

Page 32 'them "on the strength" of' – ibid., p. 490.

Page 32 'wrens' – ibid., p. 585; Trustram, M. *Women of the Regiment: Marriage and the Victorian Army*, p. 118.

Page 33 'about one quarter of the British Army had VD' – Holmes, R. *Soldiers: Army Lives and Loyalties from Redcoats to Dusty Warriors*, p. 585.

Page 33 'Contagious Diseases Acts' – Connolly, S.J. *The Oxford Companion to Irish History*.

Page 33 'the rates for infection remained high in India' – *ibid.*, p. 585.

Page 33 'In 1800 six women per hundred-men company' – Venning, A. *Following the Drum: The Lives of Army Wives and Daughters*, p. 31.

Page 33 'twelve per hundred-men' – Holmes, R. *Sahib: The British Soldier in India 1750–1914*, p. 490.

Page 33 'To go' or 'Not to go' – Bamfield, V. *On the Strength: Story of the British Army Wife*, p. 41.

Page 33 'to be left' – Venning, A. *Following the Drum: The Lives of Army Wives and Daughters*, p. 30.

Page 34 'cut his throat' – Bamfield, V. *On the Strength: Story of the British Army Wife*, p. 46.

Page 34 'In the latter case' – Venning, A. *Following the Drum: The Lives of Army Wives and Daughters*, p. 33.

Page 34 'The wife of a Rifleman' – Rappaport, H. *No Place for Ladies: The Untold Story of Women in the Crimean War*, p. 18.

Page 34 '2nd Battalion of the Rifle Brigade' – ibid., p. 26.

Page 35 'body-strippers' – http://britishlibrary.typepad.co.uk/untoldlives/2013/07/smiling-with-dead-mens-teeth.html

Page 35 'body-strippers' – Venning, A. *Following the Drum: The Lives of Army Wives and Daughters*, p. 164.

Page 35 'buckles, buttons' – ibid., p. 165.

Page 35 Lieutenant Mathew Anderson – http://www.waterloo200.org/category/waterloo-people/ – accessed 23 October 2014.

Page 35 Obituary: *The Gentleman's Magazine, June 1844, p. 669.*

Page 35 'What would some of your Army women' – 'A Soldier's Wife in the Crimea', the narrative of Mrs Elizabeth Evans, late 4th (King's Own) Regiment of Foot, as told to

Walter Woods, in *The Royal Magazine*, July 1908, p. 265.

Page 36 'three-quarters of the infantry' – Trustram, M. *Women of the Regiment: Marriage and the Victorian Army*, p. 14.

Page 36 'It was tramp, tramp, tramp' – 'A Soldier's Wife in the Crimea', p. 267.

Page 36 'forts such as Fort William' – Holmes, R. *Sahib: The British Soldier in India 1750–1914*, p. 138.

Page 37 'chummeries' – ibid., p. 141.

Page 37 'In 1859 only about a quarter of Indian barracks' – ibid., p. 142.

Page 38 'Cleanliness' – Collingham, E.M. *Imperial Bodies: The Physical Experience of the Raj, c.1800–1947*, pp. 46–8.

Page 40 'a captain could expect one that was 10½ft wide' – Brawer, N.A. *British Campaign Furniture: Elegance under Canvas, 1740–1914*, p. 43.

Page 41 'A Commanding Officer in India' – ibid., p. 49.

Page 41 'and occasionally women' – ibid., p. 158; several women made campaign furniture, e.g. Fanny Heal, Elizabeth Powell and Margaret Tait.

Page 41 'Furniture makers like Chippendale' – ibid., p. 29.

Page 41 'field bed' – ibid., p. 32.

Page 42 'care should be . . .' ibid., p. 40.

Page 42 'an officer in the 19th Bengal Lancers' – ibid., p. 108.

Page 42 'manufacturer of choice' – NAM, CABAL Concise Report, NAM 2001-06-96-1.

Page 42 Captain Benjamin Simner, of the 76th Regiment' – Brawer, N.A. *British Campaign Furniture: Elegance under Canvas, 1740–1914*, p. 41.

Page 43 'It is pleasant to think . . .' – quoted in Brawer, N.A. *British Campaign Furniture: Elegance under Canvas, 1740–1914*, p. 41.

Page 43 'Harrods boasted that it packed for "Head, Mule or Camel Loads"' – ibid., p. 180.

Page 43 '1871 by a small group of officers who needed a wine club' – Lancaster, W. *The Department Store: A Social History*, pp. 24–25.

Page 43 http://www.housefraserarchive.ac.uk/company/?id=c0512

Page 43 decanting wine – introduction, Langbridge, R.H. *Edwardian Shopping: A Selection from the Army & Navy Stores Catalogues 1898–1913*.

Page 43 Campaign furniture remained popular until the end of the nineteenth century when armies needed more lightweight furniture. In the Boer War of 1899–1902 furniture became less domestic and more transient, reflecting the guerrilla strategy. Although Ross ceased trading in 1909, other types of furniture remained popular, many reflecting the campaigns in which they had seen active service: the folding Douro chair, with its padded leather back and straps for arm rests, is named after a Spanish river familiar to soldiers in the Peninsular War; a Roorhkee chair, a more squat, but equally light canvas or leather chair similar to a modern 'Director's chair', recalled the British Army's base of the same name in India. Items of campaign furniture regularly appear at auction today – a testimony to their longevity of construction and design.

Page 44 'wooden palisades and snow screens' – Figes, O. *Crimea*, p. 284.

Page 44 'They were allowed to find their own accommodation' – ibid., p. 283.

Page 45 'Lady Erroll later told a grandchild' – Rappaport, H. *No Place for Ladies: The Untold Story of Women in the Crimean War*, p. 47.

Page 45 'medieval monks' – Compton, P. *Colonel's Lady & Camp-Follower: The Story of Women in the Crimean War*, p. 110.

Page 46 'When Lord Raglan, Commander-in-Chief of the British Expeditionary Army, heard' – ibid., pp, 110–11.

Page 46 'Joseph Paxton' – Figes, O. *Crimea*, p. 469.

Page 46 *Hodge* – Anglesey, The Marquess of, *'Little Hodge'* being extracts from the diaries and letters of Colonel Edward Cooper Hodge written during the Crimean War, 1854–56.

Page 46 'very dowdy' – British Library, MS 47218 A, also quoted in Kelly. C. (ed.). *Mrs Duberly's War: Journal & Letters from the Crimea*, p. 212.

Page 47 'cursed ships' – ibid., p. 151.

Page 48 'crashing and crowding together' – Duberly, F. *Journal Kept During the Russian War, From the Departure of the Army from England in April 1854, to the Fall of Sebastopol*, Longman, p. 132.

Page 48 'anything clever' – BL, MS 47218 A, also quoted in Kelly, C. (ed.). *Mrs Duberly's War: Journal & Letters from the Crimea*, p. 208.

PART ONE: THE IMPERIAL ARMY WIFE

Chapter Three: The Early Anglo-Indian Army Wife: Margaret Campbell Hannay

Page 51 For details of Hannay's later career see the website of the 6th Queen Elizabeth's Own Gurkha Rifles at http://www.6thgurkhas.org/website/regiment-history/1826-1856

Page 52 'Fishing Fleet' – Holmes, R. *Sahib: The British Soldier in India 1750–1914*, pp. 443–446; de Courcy, A. *The Fishing Fleet: Husband-Hunting in the Raj*; Kaye, M.M. *The Sun in the Morning*, p. 68.

Page 52 'Mollie Kaye remembers her mother' – ibid., p. 68.

Page 52 'According to one estimate' – Holmes, R. *Sahib: The British Soldier in India 1750–1914*, p. xxi.

Page 52 'charged a hefty premium' – de Courcy, A. *The Fishing Fleet: Husband-Hunting in the Raj*, p. 4.

Page 53 'At the beginning of the nineteenth century' – Dalrymple, W. *The Last Mughal: The Fall of Delhi, 1857*, p. 9.

Page 53 'or even to run two separate' – Holmes, R. *Sahib: The British Soldier in India 1750–1914*, p. 446.

Page 53 'Between 1780 and 1785 Indian women appear' – Dalrymple, W. *The Last Mughal: The Fall of Delhi, 1857*, p. 73.

Page 53 'had been edited out of the memoirs' – ibid., pp. 9–10.

Page 53 For some ordinary soldiers – Holmes, R. *Sahib: The British Soldier in India 1750–1914*, p. 149.

Page 53 'in Burma' – ibid., p. 447.

Page 53 'In parts of Assam' – Collingham, E.M. *Imperial Bodies: The Physical Experience of the Raj, c.1800–1947*, p. 185.

Page 53 'the beautiful little mosque' – 21 January 1829, MCH.

Page 53 'immense number of Alligators' – 15 February 1829, MCH.

Page 54 'I could not help crying . . .' – 31 January 1829, MCH.

Page 54 'I enjoy a March' – 4 February 1829, MCH.

Page 54 'Every tree and shrub' – 19 January 1829, MCH.

Page 54 'at Mysopoorie I did just as I pleased' – 20 January 1829, MCH.

Page 55 'as if we were beings from a different world' – 21 January 1829, MCH.

Page 55 'not proper for' – ibid.

Page 55 'I like to see everything' – 2 March 1829, MCH.

Page 55 'now so accustomed – Camp Nuryarpore', 7 March 1829, MCH.

Page 55 'so ignorant poor' – 15 February 1829, MCH.

Page 55 'lazy man . . .' – 5 March 1829, MCH.

Pages 55–6 'The truth is Hanny dined' – 27 January 1829, MCH

Page 56 'sent about the orders' – ibid.

Page 56 'I shudder . . . frightful ravines' – 18 February 1829, MCH.

Page 56 'I am obliged' – ibid.

Page 57 '. . . the Officers are all quite disconcerted' – 2 March 1829, MCH.

Page 57 'the old Colonel' – 6 March 1829, MCH.

Page 57 'so attentive . . .' – 20 January 1829, MCH.

Page 57 'chatters and makes' – 21 January 1829, MCH.

Page 57 'a curious Temple' – 23 January 1829, MCH.

Page 57 'one of the prettiest pillars' – ibid.

Page 57 'finest Native garden' – 22 January 1829, MCH.

Page 58 'Mama you know' – 31 January 1827, MCH.

Page 58 'The illness killed more soldiers in India' – Holmes, R. *Sahib: The British Soldier in India 1750–1914*, p. 473.

Page 59 'rude tribes' – BL, India Collection no. 4, 1836–1837. vol. 1582 F4.1582.

Page 59 'I think it right' – ibid.

Page 59 'stiff hand-to-hand fight' – Shakespear, L.W. *History of the Assam Rifles*, p. 9.

Page 59 'beautiful verses' – 31 August 1839, MCH.

Page 59 'jungle warfare' – Lunt, *Jai Sixth! 6th Queen Elizabeth's Own Gurkha Rifles 1817–1994*, p. 4.

Page 60 'Reverend Edward Higgs' – BL, Mss Eur E262/(107a).

Page 60 'roughest of roads, bridlepaths or tracks' – Shakespear, L.W. *History of the Assam Rifles*, p. 3.

Page 61 'sore heart . . . harshness' – 20 August 1839, MCH.

Page 61 '. . . I have a horror of going . . .' – 9 September 1839, MCH.

Page 61 'She makes me laugh' – 18 September 1839, MCH.

Page 62 'It seems impossible to live' – 1 September 1839, MCH.

Page 62 'one of the poor Sepoys is dead' – 8 September 1839, MCH.

Chapter Four: The Crimean Wife: Fanny Duberly, Nell Butler and Elizabeth Evans

Page 63 'two generals who will not fail me' – Figes, O. *Crimea*, p. 255.

Pages 63–64 Nell Butler – 29 June 2001, *The News*; 5 June, 1909, *Hampshire Telegraph*; 3 May 1963, *Portsmouth Evening News*; *Hampshire Magazine*, August 1977.

Page 64 Elizabeth Evans – See 'A Soldier's Wife in the Crimea', the narrative of Mrs Elizabeth Evans, late 4th (King's Own) Regiment of Foot as told to Walter Woods, in *The Royal Magazine*, July 1908 and http://www.kingsownmuseum.plus.com/mrsevans.htm

Page 64 'a hastily abandoned picnic' – Figes, O. *Crimea*, p. 218.

Page 65 'good three-quarters of the army wives' – Rappaport, H. *No Place for Ladies: The Untold Story of Women in the Crimean War*, p. 30.

Page 65 'The British Army permitted six wives' – ibid., p. 23.

Page 65 'Some 400 ships' – ibid., p. 69.

Page 66 'a further 250 travelled to Turkey' – ibid., p. 30.

Page 66 'occasionally referred to the French' – Figes, O. *Crimea*, p. 176.

Page 68 'in which 2,000 British' – ibid., p. 218.

Page 68 'many agonies in the Crimea' – 'A Soldier's Wife in the Crimea' in *The Royal Magazine*, July 1908, pp. 265–72.

Page 68 'it was wonderful' – 'A Soldier's Wife in the Crimea' in *The Royal Magazine*, July 1908, pp. 265–72.

Page 68 'In a photo' – http://www.kingsownmuseum.plus.com/mrsevans.htm

Page 69 *Mrs Duberly's War, Journal & Letters from the Crimea*, edited with an introduction and notes by Christine Kelly, provides a compelling account of Fanny's entire life.

Page 70 'pushing, vulgar' – Kelly, C. (ed.). *Mrs Duberly's War, Journal & Letters from the Crimea*, p. 299.

Page 70 'tremendous woman' – BL, MS 47218 A, also quoted in Kelly, C. (ed.). *Mrs Duberly's War, Journal & Letters from the Crimea*, p. 38.

Page 71 'after waiting some time' – ibid.

Page 71 'broken-winded' – ibid., p. 39.

Page 71 'a few exceptions' – ibid., p. 141.

Page 72 'Private & Confidential' – ibid., p. 46.

Page 73 'this vile diarrhoea' – BL, MS 47218 A, also quoted in Kelly, C. (ed.). *Mrs Duberly's War, Journal & Letters from the Crimea*, p. 199.

Page 73 'Her maid, "poor Mrs Blaydes"' – Duberly, F. *Journal Kept During the Russian War, From the Departure of the Army from England in April 1854, to the Fall of Sebastopol*, Longman, p. 47.

Page 73 broiling conditions – Duberly, F. *Journal Kept During the Russian War, From the Departure of the Army from England in April 1854, to the Fall of Sebastopol*, p. 29.

Page 73 'thirsty horse' – ibid., p. 30.

Page 73 'stale egg and a mouthful of brandy' – ibid., p. 31.

Page 73 'verdant hills' – ibid., p. 32.

Page 74 'terrible distress' – BL, MS 47218 A, also quoted in Kelly, C. (ed.). *Mrs Duberly's War, Journal & Letters from the Crimea*, p. 164.

Page 75 'God help and support her' – Duberly, F. *Journal Kept During the Russian War, From the Departure of the Army from England in April 1854, to the Fall of Sebastopol*, p. 91.

Page 75 'fine healthy strong man' – ibid., p. 211.

Page 75 'frantic frenzy' – BL, MS 47218 B, also quoted in Kelly, C. (ed.). *Mrs Duberly's War, Journal & Letters from the Crimea*, p. 211.

Page 75 'poor servant' – Duberly, F. *Journal Kept During the Russian War, From the Departure of the Army from England in April 1854, to the Fall of Sebastopol*, p. 123.

Page 75 'Alas, poor woman!' – ibid., p. 123.

Page 75 'It is a novel office' – BL, MS 47218 A, also quoted in Kelly, C. (ed.). *Mrs Duberly's War, Journal & Letters from the Crimea*, p. 97.

Page 76 'a very good woman nevertheless' – ibid., p. 152.

Page 77 'fatigue, illness & excitement' – ibid., p. 188.

Page 77 'We were a few minutes late' – Duberly, F. *Journal Kept During the Russian War, From the Departure of the Army from England in April 1854, to the Fall of Sebastopol*, p. 221.

Page 77 'booted & spurred' – BL, MS 47218 A, also quoted in Kelly, C. (ed.). *Mrs Duberly's War, Journal & Letters from the Crimea*, p. 193.

Page 77 'clean over the parapet of a trench' – ibid., p. 195.

Page 78 'I think the impression made' – Duberly, F. *Journal Kept During the Russian War, From the Departure of the Army from England in April 1854, to the Fall of Sebastopol*, p. 285.

Page 78 'sort of Bashi-Basouk' – BL, MS 47218 A, also quoted in Kelly, C. (ed.). *Mrs Duberly's War, Journal & Letters from the Crimea*, p. 137.

Chapter Five: The Changing Image of the Soldier and His Wife

Page 79 'The cannon' – Blakeman, P. *The Book of Ely*, pp 95–96.

Page 79 '"muscular" Christian' – Figes, O. *Crimea*, p. 473.

Page 80 'and hundreds of memorials' – ibid., p. 467.

Page 80 'dead numbered one in three' – ibid., p. 480.

Page 80 '100,000' – ibid., p. xix.

Page 80 'Parents continued to call their . . .' – ibid., p. 479.

Page 80 'Some passers-by' – ibid., p. 468.

Page 81 'salt prints' – *Salt and Silver, Early Photography 1840–1860*, Tate Britain leaflet.

Page 81 'Aimable-Jean-Jacques Pélissier' – http://www.npg.org.uk/collections/search/person/mp03492/aimable-jean-jacques-pelissier-1st-duc-de-malakoff

Page 82 'The people's War' – as Stefanie Markovits points out in 'Rushing into print: "Participatory Journalism" During the Crimean War', *Victorian Studies*, vol. 50. no. 4.

Page 82 'diplomats or army officers' – Figes, O. *Crimea*, p. 305.

Page 82 'first person everyman of a narrator/hero' – Markovits, S. Rushing into print, "Participatory Journalism" During the Crimean War, *Victorian Studies*, vol. 50, no. 4.

Page 83 'although the lamp' – Bostridge, M. *Florence Nightingale: The Woman and Her Legend*, p. 251.

Page 83 '130,700 copies a week' – ibid.

Page 83 'As Nightingale's modern biographer' – ibid., p. 263.

Page 83 'a principle of accountability' – ibid., p. 223.

Page 83 'Nightingale used money' – ibid., p. 228.

Page 84 'Paul Julius Reuters' news agency' – http://thomsonreuters.com/en/about-us/company-history.html

Page 84 'Now the whole army' – Markovits, S. 'Rushing Into Print: "Participatory Journalism" During the Crimean War', *Victorian Studies*, vol. 50, no. 4.

Page 84 'the hard frost in Britain' – Figes, O. *Crimea*, p. 304.

Page 85 'Fanny Duberly produced a stream of letters' – Kelly, C. (ed.). *Mrs Duberly's War: Journal and Letters from the Crimea, 1854–6*, pp. xxxiii and 290.

Page 85 'first published in 1869' – *The Concise Oxford Dictionary of Music (5).*

Page 86 'Before the war' – Figes, O. *Crimea*, p. 47.

Page 86 'Arithmetic on the Frontier' – I. Hamilton and J. Noel-Tod, *The Oxford Companion to Modern Poetry.*

Page 87 'In the period 1815–49' – Hichberger, J.W.M. *Images of the Army: The Military in British Art*, p. 125.

Pages 87–88 'The army, the officers' – ibid., p. 7.

Page 88 'Ruskin' – Harrington, P. *British Artists and War: The Face of Battle in Paintings and Prints, 1700–1914*, p. 153.

Page 88 'He was no longer' – Hichberger, J.W.M. *Images of the Army: The Military in British Art*, pp. 161–2.

Page 88 'Returning from the Fair' – ibid., p. 164.

Page 88 'Home' – ibid., p. 159 and see: http://collection.chrysler.org/emuseum/view/objects/asitem/220/127/title-asc?t:state:flow=f48877dd-b39c-482a-8a92-32db50f1a461

Page 88 'menfolk off to war' – ibid., pp. 168–172.

Page 88 'As Figes points out' – Figes, O. *Crimea*, p. 468.

Chapter Six: The 'Great Sepoy Mutiny': Harriet Tytler, Fanny Wells and Lady Julia Inglis

Page 90 'Tootooing' – Tytler, H. *An English Woman in India: The Memoirs of Harriet Tytler, 1828–1858*, p. 114.

Page 90 '*chapatties*' – ibid., p. 111, Holmes, R. *Sahib: The British Soldier in India, 1750–1914*, p. 73.

Pages 90–91 'Little did we expect' – Tytler, H. *An English Woman in India: The Memoirs of Harriet Tytler, 1828–1858*, p. 115.

Page 91 'raging hot wind' – ibid.

Page 91 'twenty degrees Fahrenheit' – ibid., p. 208.

Page 91 'Sahib, Sahib, the *fauj* (army) has come' – ibid., p. 115.

Page 91 'Madame, this is a *revolution*' – ibid., p. 116.

Page 92 'isolated round tower' – Dalrymple, W. *The Last Mughal: The Fall of Delhi, 1857*, p. 176.

Page 92 '18 feet in diameter' – Tytler, H. *An English Woman in India: The Memoirs of Harriet Tytler, 1828–1858*, p. 208.

Page 92 'many of the woman had been told'– Dalrymple, W. *The Last Mughal: The Fall of Delhi, 1857*, p. 176.

Page 92 'Mamma, will these naughty' – Tytler, H. *An English Woman in India: The Memoirs of Harriet Tytler, 1828–1858*, p. 118.

Page 92 'My poor child' – ibid.

Page 92 'dear Mrs Peile'– ibid., p. 122.

Page 93 'thick brown mass' – ibid.

Page 94 'doctrine of lapse' – Holmes, R. *Sahib: The British Soldier in India, 1750–1914*, p. 70.

Page 95 'Baggage Master to the Field Force' – Tytler, H. *An English Woman in India: The Memoirs of Harriet Tytler, 1828–1858*, p. 177.

Page 96 'The first year of our stay in Barrackpore' – ibid., p. 77.

Page 97 'nervous affection' – FJW, May 1857.

Page 97 'gentlemen innumerable' – ibid.

Page 97 'Oh dear Papa' – ibid.

Page 97 'The nights were very pleasant' – Inglis, J.

Page 98 'took refuge in a small' – ibid.

Page 98 'native gaol' – ibid.

Page 98 'such a Babel' and 'such a smell of smoke' – FJW.

Page 98 'garrison disease' – Captain Birch's narrative in Inglis.

Pages 98–99 'light infantry' – quoted in Holmes, R. *Sahib: The British Soldier in India, 1750–1914*, p. 392.

Page 99 'a "torment"' – Inglis.

Page 99 'Every kind of insect, fleas' – ibid.

Page 99 'The contemplation seemed too dreadful' – ibid.

Page 99 'Do not negotiate' – ibid.

Pages 99–100 'so she has not been of much use' – FJW, Lucknow, December, from Allahabad, 1857.

Page 100 'a most ragged appearance' – Inglis.

Page 100 'great amusement', 'feel the confinement very much' – ibid.

Page 100 'Poor Miss Jennings' – FJW.

Page 101 'wretched face' – ibid.

Page 101 'We are coming to save you' – Inglis.

Page 101 'tremendous cheering' – ibid.

Page 101 'poor little angel' – FJW, 12 December, from The Fort, Allahabad.

Page 102 'In a letter to his father-in-law' – ibid., 18 December 1857.

Page 102 'Those who remember' – 24 April, *Bristol Times*, 1858.

Page 103 'at a terrific pace' – Tytler, H. *An English Woman in India: The Memoirs of Harriet Tytler, 1828–1858*, p. 131.

Page 103 'were worth £20,000' – ibid.

Page 103 'from where we had with difficulty to be extricated' – ibid., p. 134.

Page 105 'swollen by the heat' – ibid., p. 145.

Page 105 'like Lord Roberts and Major Hodson' – ibid., pp. 146, 214 and 215.

Page 105 'with the setting moon' – ibid., p. 147.

Page 106 'the usual aid of a bottle of milk' – ibid., p. 148.

Page 106 'Oh! It is only a shell' – ibid., p. 151.

Page 107 'the glistening of the bayonets' – ibid., p. 153.

Page 108 'In case of a hopeless reverse' – ibid., p. 160.

Page 108 'Plaques and tourist' – Procida, M.A. *Married to the Empire: Gender, Politics and Imperialism in India, 1883–1947*, p. 60.

Page 108 'first images of Delhi' – Dalrymple, W. *The Last Mughal: The Fall of Delhi, 1857*, p. 138.

Page 109 the Residency – http://www.columbia.edu/itc/mealac/pritchett/00routesdata/1800_1899/1857revolt/lucknowresidency/lucknowresidency.html

Page 109 Edward Hopley's 'An Alarm in India' – Harrington, P. *British Artists and War: The Face of Battle in Paintings and Prints, 1700–1914*, p. 161.

Page 109 'Highland Jessie' – http://www.nam.ac.uk/online-collection/detail.php?acc=1975-02-3-1

Page 109 'inspired' – Harrington, P. *British Artists and War: The Face of Battle in Paintings and Prints, 1700–1914*, p. 174.

Page 109 'caught the imagination' – in the British television series *Downton Abbey*, the Dowager Countess, Violet Crawley, tells her granddaughter, 'Remember your great-aunt Roberta. She loaded the guns at Lucknow.' https://uk.news.yahoo.com/love-war-rage-pbs-downton-abbey-returns-202703183.html

Page 110 'the taboo' – Hichberger, *Images of the Army: The Military in British Art, 1815–1914*, p. 60.

Page 110 'horrible Cawnpore pictures' – Harrington, P. *British Artists and War: The Face of Battle in Paintings and Prints, 1700–1914*, p. 166.

Page 110 'Designed to Commemorate' – ibid., p. 167.

Page 110 'who was to do . . .' – 'Up Guards and at them!' by John Springhall, *British imperialism and Popular Art, 1880–1914*, p. 62.

Chapter Seven: The 'Career Wife': Lady Elizabeth Butler

Page 111 'disorderly old billiard room' – Graham Storey, Kathleen Tillotson and Angus Easson (ed.) *The Pilgrim Edition of The Letters of Charles Dickens*, Clarendon Press, Oxford, volume seven, p. 178.

Page 112 'ruckle of bones' – Gormanston, E. *A Little Kept*, p. 22.

Page 112 'Queen Victoria was said' – ibid., p. 23.

Page 112 'quarter-mile-long' – http://www.theguardian.com/artanddesign/2014/aug/21/royal-victoria-hospital-netley-ww1-first-world-war-photographs-documentary-philip-hoare

Page 113 'one plane of action' – Greer, G. *The Obstacle Race: The Fortunes of Women Painters and Their Work*, p. 83.

Page 114 In 1879 Elizabeth failed to win election to become an Associate of the Royal Academy and it was not until 1936 that Laura Knight became the first woman to be elected.

Page 114 'The Roll Call' – Usherwood, P. and Spencer-Smith, J. *Lady Butler: Battle Artist, 1846–1933*, pp. 57–9.

Page 114 Colonel Loyd Lindsay was one of the founders of what became the British Red Cross Society.

Page 114 'I awoke this morning' – Butler, E. *Elizabeth Butler: Battle Artist, Autobiography*, p. 88.

Page 115 'diamond bracelet' – Hichberger, J.W.M, *Images of the Army: The Military in British Art, 1815–1914*, p. 77.

Page 115 'The Roll Call went on tour' – Usherwood, P. and Spencer-Smith, J. *Lady Butler: Battle Artist, 1846–1933*, p. 29.

Page 115 'uneventful' – Butler, E. *Elizabeth Butler: Battle Artist, Autobiography*, p. 16.

Page 115 'Roll Call Thompson' – Usherwood, P. and Spencer-Smith, J. *Lady Butler: Battle Artist, 1846–1933*, p. 31.

Page 115 'bother' – Butler, E. *Elizabeth Butler: Battle Artist, Autobiography*, p. 91.

Page 115 'Nowadays' – ibid., p. 91.

Page 117 'ghosts with agonised faces' – ibid., p. 27.

Page 117 'give the British soldiers a turn' – ibid., p. 78.

Page 117 'Lady Jeune (later, Lady St Hellier)' – Gormanston, E. *A Little Kept*, p. 24.

Page 117 'abject slavery' – ibid., p. 58.

Page 118 'What may you not do' – Usherwood, P. and Spencer-Smith, J. *Lady Butler: Battle Artist, 1846–1933*, p. 69.

Page 118 'sutlers' wars' – McCourt, E. *Remember Butler*, p. 168.

Page 119 'her query about the letters' – Butler, E. *Elizabeth Butler: Battle Artist, Autobiography*, p. 82.

Page 119 'dingy little pawnshop' – ibid., p. 81.

Page 119 'any amount of grey' – ibid., p. 151.

Page 119 'usually that interesting' – ibid., p. 181.

Page 120 'all within fifteen shillings' – Denby, E. *Grand Hotels, Reality & Illusion: An Architectural and Social History*, p. 186.

Page 121 'most trying' – Butler, E. *Elizabeth Butler: Battle Artist, Autobiography*, p. 153.

Page 121 'Whenever I get a whiff' – Gormanston, E. *A Little Kept*, p. 52.

Page 122 'The Fine Art Society paid' – Usherwood, P. and Spencer-Smith, J. *Lady Butler: Battle Artist, 1846–1933*, p. 66.

Pages 122–3 'William's annual salary' – ibid., p. 70.

Page 123 'poor old Arabi' – Butler, E. *Elizabeth Butler: Battle Artist, Autobiography*, p. 153.

Page 123 'fidgety . . . like a good boy' – ibid., p. 154.

Page 123 'going through brown paper' – ibid., p. 153.

Page 124 'One more painting' – MacKenzie, J.M. *Imperialism and Popular Culture*, p. 71.

Page 124 'What is surprising' – Gormanston, E. *A Little Kept*, p. 33.

Page 124 'To me' – ibid., p. 34.

Page 124 'partially deaf' – ibid., p. 53.

Pages 124–5 'a difficult function' – Butler, E. *Elizabeth Butler: Battle Artist, Autobiography*, p. 165.

Page 125 'always found touches' – ibid., p. 166.

Page 125 'most unseemly' – ibid., p. 195.

Page 125 'Every one got jammed' – ibid., p. 195.

Page 125 'seldom up to schedule' – Gormanston, E. *A Little Kept*, p. 53.

Page 125 'terrible tragedy . . . maddening delays at home' –Butler, E. *Elizabeth Butler: Battle Artist, Autobiography*, p. 152.

Page 126 'flood of filth' – *The Times*, 21 December 1886.

Page 126 For a full account of the trial see *Victorian 'Sex Goddess': Lady Colin Campbell and the Sensational Divorce Case of 1886* by G.H. Fleming.

Page 126 'Boldini' – http://www.npg.org.uk

Page 127 'most notorious scandals of the Victorian' – Savage, G. 'The Wilful communication of a loathsome disease: marital conflict and venereal disease in Victorian England', *Victorian Studies*, autumn 1990.

Page 127 'Syphilis was widespread' – Hughes, Kathryn. *The Short Life & Long Times of Mrs Beeton*, pp. 182–3.

Page 130 'The Foreman added' – quoted in Fleming, G.H. *Victorian 'Sex Goddess', Lady Colin Campbell and the Sensational Divorce Case of 1886*, p. 240.

Page 130 '599 lines' – ibid., p. 225.

PART TWO:

LOSS AND THE GREAT WAR

Chapter Eight: The Army Widow: Clare Sheridan and Hazel Macnaghten

Page 135 'The room' – Sheridan, C. *Nuda Veritas*, p. 112.

Page 136 'queer new voice' – ibid.

Page 136 'Oh, darling, my darling' – ibid.

Page 136 'But Wilfred should have known' – ibid.

Page 136 'heaps' – ibid.

Page 137 'prayers for the dead' – Kollar, R. *Searching for Raymond: Anglicanism, Spiritualism, and Bereavement Between the Two World Wars*, p. 17.

Page 138 '4.5 million bereaved' – Reid, F. *Broken Men, Shell Shock, Treatment and Recovery in Britain, 1914–1930*, p. 173.

Page 138 'around 250,000' – Nicholson, V. *Singled Out*, p. 24.

Page 138 'experimental compensations' – Brittain, V. *Testament of Youth*, p. 445.

Page 138 'As always in wartime' – ibid., quoted in Kollar, R. *Searching for Raymond: Anglicanism, Spiritualism, and Bereavement Between the Two World Wars*, p. 8.

Page 138 'The number of societies' – Hazlegrove, J. *Spiritualism and British Society Between the Wars*, p. 3.

Page 138 '100,000 *séance* circles' – ibid.

Page 138 'whisky and cigars' – ibid., p. 25.

Page 138 'had girlfriends' – Watkins, C. *The Undiscovered Country: Journeys Among the Dead*, p. 250.

Page 138 'Oh, how natural' – Carrington, H. *Psychical Phenomena and the War*, p. 260.

Page 139 'the best-looking man of his time' – Leslie, A. *Cousin Clare: Biography of Clare Sheridan*, p. 57.

Page 139 'Clare wore smocks' – ibid, p. 61.

Page 140 'happier and a pleasanter companion' – Sheridan, C. *Nuda Veritas*, p. 105.

Page 140 'Those war days' – ibid., p. 106.

Page 140 'hurried pencil scrawl' – ibid., p. 107.

Page 140 'My Darling' – Soames, M. (ed.). *Speaking for Themselves: The Personal Letters of Winston and Clementine Churchill*, p. 125.

Page 141 'You will only read this' – Sheridan, C. *Nuda Veritas*, p. 108.

Page 141 'another young wife' – Carrington, H. *Psychical Phenomena and the War*, p. 173.

Page 141 'In Lincolnshire' – Hazelgrove, J. *Spiritualism after the Great War, in Twentieth Century British History*, vol.10, no. 4, 1999, pp. 404–30.

Page 142 'the army's Grave Registration Committee . . . "secondary relics"' – Watkins, *The Undiscovered Country: Journeys Among the Dead*, p. 243.

Page 142 'free photos' – Van Emden, R. *The Quick and the Dead: Fallen Families and Their Soldiers in the Great War*, p. 150.

Page 142 'In one extreme case' – Van Emden, R. *The Quick and Dead: Fallen Families and Their Soldiers in the Great War*, p. 156.

Page 142 'Edward Thomas' – Macfarlane, R. *The Old Ways: A Journey on Foot*, pp. 354–55.

Page 142 'A tiny hole below' – Roper, M. *The Secret Battle: Emotional Survival in the Great War*, p. 217.

Page 142 'in a violent hurry' – Brittain, V. *Testament of Youth*, p. 251.

Page 142 'rakishly' – ibid., p. 252.

Page 142 'relics' – ibid., p. 251.

Page 143 'charnel-house smell' – ibid., p. 252.

Page 143 'Ada Deane' – Watkins, *The Undiscovered Country: Journeys Among the Dead*, p. 247.

Page 143 'Among the major combatants' – Winter, J. *Sites of Memory, Sites of Mourning: The Great War in European Cultural History*, p. 2.

Page 143 'language of loss' – ibid., p. 5.

Page 143 'More than 300,000 British' – *Dictionary of National Biography*, entry for the unknown warrior.

Page 144 'Around three million of the nine million who had died left widows' – Winter, J. *Sites of Memory, Sites of Mourning: The Great War in European Cultural History*, p. 46.

Page 144 'their name was last after' – Acton, C. *Grief in Wartime,* p. 45.

Page 144 'Parents usually won these tussles' – Winter, J. *Sites of Memory, Sites of Mourning: The Great War in European Cultural History,* p. 26.

Page 144 'their presence was sometimes pushed' – Roper, M. *The Secret Battle: Emotional Survival in the Great War,* p.225.

Page 144 'Gladstone' – Van Emden, R. *The Quick and the Dead: Fallen Families and Their Soldiers in the Great War,* p. 132

Page 144 http://www.bbc.co.uk/programmes/p023vt6l

Page 144 'nearly half its dead went home; the last in' – Van Emden, R. *The Quick and the Dead: Fallen Families and Their Soldiers in the Great War,* p. 278.

Page 144 'secret exhumations' – ibid., p. 279.

Page 144 'Sir Fabian Ware' – http://www.cwgc.org/about-us/history-of-cwgc.aspx

Page 144 '14 per cent of widows' – Van Emden, R. *The Quick and the Dead: Fallen Families and Their Soldiers in the Great War,* p. 227.

Page 145 Page xx 'Thomas Cook' – ibid., p. 284.

Page 145 '140,000 widows' – Cannadine, D. 'War and Death, Grief and Mourning in Modern Britain', In *Mirrors of Mortality: Studies in the Social History of Death,* p. 231.

Page 145 'Cambridge railway station' – Winter, J. *Sites of Memory, Sites of Mourning: The Great War in European Cultural History,* p. 90.

Page 145 'community in mourning' – ibid., p. 9.

Page 145 For the Unknown Warrior see: *New Dictionary of National Biography;* Watkins, C. *The Undiscovered Country: Journeys Among the Dead;* Van Emden, *The Quick and the Dead: Fallen Families and Their Soldiers in the Great War;* http://www.westminster-abbey.org/our-history/people/unknown-warrior

Page 147 'titled ladies' – Roper, M. *The Secret Battle: Emotional Survival in the Great War,* p. 221.

Page 147 'almost hallucinatory' – Watkins, C. *The Undiscovered Country: Journeys Among the Dead,* p. 240.

Page 148 'unconsecrated . . . taint of a pauper's grave' – ibid., p. 244.

Page 148 'Life expectancy' – Cannadine, D. (Ed. Joachim Whaley). 'War and Death, Grief and Mourning in Modern Britain', in *Mirrors of Mortality: Studies in the Social History of Death,* page 193 (London: Europa Publications, 1981).

Page 148 'The English were less' – ibid., p. 196.

Page 148 'Vera Brittain gathered together the books' – Acton, C. *Grief in Wartime: Private Pain, Public Discourse,* p. 23. See *Testament of Youth,* p. 23.

Pages 148–9 'a mourning engagement ring' – Acton, Carol. 'Writing and Waiting: The First World War Correspondence between Vera Brittain and Roland Leighton', *Gender & History,* vol. 11, no. 1, April 1999, p. 70.

Page 149 'Regret – No Trace' – Bourke, J. *Dismembering the Male: Men's Bodies, Britain and the Great War,* p. 230.

Page 150 'Awful pleased' – Macnaghten, A. *Missing,* p. 9.

Page 150 'red waistcoat' – ibid.

Page 150 'The Germans have been trying' – ibid.

Page 150 'among the most gruesome affairs' – ibid., p. 10.

Page 150 'This life' – ibid., p. 10.

Page 150 'In an account written ten years' – ibid., p. 14.

Page 152 'American Express' https://secure.cmax.americanexpress.com/Internet/GlobalCareers/Staffing/Shared/Files/our_story_3.pdf

Page 152 'Do you know' – Macnaghten, A. *Missing*, p. 42.

Page 153 'I am afraid this leaves' – ibid., p. 55.

Page 154 'One fiancée was given six' – Bourke, J. *Dismembering the Male: Men's Bodies, Britain and the Great War*, p. 128.

Page 154 'Kipling's son' – Cannadine, D. 'War and Death, Grief and Mourning in Modern Britain', in *Mirrors of Mortality: Studies in the Social History of Death*, p. 214.

Page 154 'Of course, we were all there' – Sheridan, C. *Nuda Veritas*, p. 113.

Page 155 'Mummie, Mummie, I can't see you' – ibid., p. 113.

Page 155 'Mummie, I don't like this dark' – ibid., p. 114.

Page 155 'Don't be a fool' – ibid.

Page 156 'between Bulgaria and Trieste' – Macnaghten, A. *Missing*, p. 58.

Chapter Nine: The Letter: Lena Leland, Clementine Churchill and Ethel Cove

Page 157 'by Morse code' – Carpenter, H. *J.R.R. Tolkien: A Biography*, p. 78.

Page 157 'Parting from my wife then . . . it was like a death' – quoted in Garth, J. *Tolkien and the Great War*, p. 138.

Page 158 'a pattern of dots' – ibid., p. 144.

Page 158 'The writer was not supposed' – Bourke, J. *Dismembering the Male: Men's Bodies, Britain and the Great War*, p. 22.

Page 158 IWM, Catalogue number, Documents.6280, Private Papers of Captain H.J.C. Leland DSO.

Page 159 'on literary references' – Van Emden, R. *The Quick and the Dead: Fallen Soldiers and Their Families in the Great War*, p. 35.

Page 159 'According to a grandson' – IWM Sound Archive, Catalogue number 20702, Tom Leland.

Page 162 'Christmas puddings, oranges' – Roper, M. *Secret Battle: Emotional Survival in the Great War*, p. 94.

Page 162 'given command of a battalion' – https://www.nationalchurchillmuseum.org/churchill-in-world-war-i-and-aftermath.html

Page 162 'a boon & a pet' – Soames, *Speaking for Themselves: The Personal Letters of Sir Winston Churchill and Clementine Churchill*, p. 116.

Page 162 'a small box of food' – ibid., p. 116.

Page 162 'more than half my life' – ibid., p. 118.

Page 162 'delightful snap-shot' – ibid., p. 118.

Page 163 'There was a thick fog' – ibid., p. 118.

Page 163 'brandy' – ibid., p. 118.

Page 163 '2 more pairs of thick Jaeger draws' – ibid., p. 120.

Page 163 'I now have to wipe' – ibid., p. 127.

Page 163 'the most divine' – ibid., p. 132.

Page 164 'soldiers and soldiers' wives' – ibid., p. 151.

Page 164 'a telegram with terrible news' – ibid., p. 201.

Page 165 'in *The Secret Battle*, 25 per cent' – Roper, M. *The Secret Battle: Emotional Survival in the Great War*, p. 54.

Page 165 'Before 1795' – Boyden, P.B. *Tommy Atkins' Letters: The History of the British Army Postal Service From 1795*, p. 4,

Page 165 'Act of Parliament' – ibid ., p. 4.

Page 165 'During 1855' – ibid., p. 10.

Page 165 'The war marked the last' – ibid., p. 18.

Page 165 'After 1914 letters home which weighed' – Roper, M. *The Secret Battle: Emotional Survival in the Great War*, p. 28.

Page 165 'By 1917 soldiers on the Western Front – Boyden, P.B. *Tommy Atkins' Letters: The History of the British Army Postal Service From 1795*, p. 28.

Page 166 'expeditionary spelt forty-three' – Robinson, H. *Britain's Post Office: A History of Development from the Beginnings to the Present Day*, p. 237.

Page 166 'The Post Office also delivered £2 million' – http://www.postalheritage.org.uk/explore/history/firstworldwar/

Page 166 'dropped to four' – McCartney, H. *Citizen Soldiers: The Liverpool Territorials in the First World War*, p. 95.

Page 166 'Mesopotamia' – Roper, M. *The Secret Battle: Emotional Survival in the Great War*, p. 52.

Page 166 'Lever Brothers' – McCartney, H. *Citizen Soldiers: The Liverpool Territorials in the First World War*, p. 97.

Page 166 'the 19,000 mailbags' –http://www.postalheritage.org.uk/explore/history/firstworldwar/

Page 166 '*only* five deliveries a day' – Robinson, H. *Britain's Post Office: A History of Development from the Beginnings to the Present Day*, p. 238.

Page 166 'During the Boer War' – Boyden, P.B. *Tommy Atkins' Letters: The History of the British Army Postal Service From 1795*, p. 27.

Page 167 'Field Service Post Cards' – ibid., p. 30.

Page 167 '300 letters' – McCartney, H. *Citizen Soldiers: The Liverpool Territorials in the First World War*, p. 90.

Page 167 Correspondence between Wilfrid, Ethel and Marjorie Cove is part of the Liddle Collection, University of Leeds. Classmark: LIDDLE/WWI/GS/0375

Page 167 'London and Smith's Bank' – http://heritagearchives.rbs.com/companies/list/union-of-london-and-smiths-bank-ltd.html#fl6BPLjdEjwRTrXo.99

Page 170 'embroidered cards' – http://www.libraryofbirmingham.com/silkembroideredpostcards

Page 173 'Bank Clerks' Orphanage' – http://www.rbsremembers.com/aftermath-and-legacy/caring-for-children-of-the-fallen.html

Page 174 'Anthony Buckeridge' – ibid.

Chapter Ten: The Damaged Husband

Page 178 'damaged man' – Petter, Martin. *Aftermath of the Great War: Rank, Status and the Ex-Officer Problem*, Historical Journal vol. 37, no. 1 (March 1994, p. 129).

Page 178 The film of Ladd's studio can be viewed at: https://www.washingtonpost.com/local/an-american-sculptors-masks-restored-french-soldiers-disfigured-in-world-war-i/2014/09/22/4748b8d4-38ec-11e4-9c9f-ebb47272e40e_story.html

Page 178 'brave faceless ones' – http://www.washingtonpost.com/local/an-american-sculptors-masks-restored-french-soldiers-disfigured-in-world-war-i/2014/09/22/4748b8d4-38ec-11e4-9c9f-ebb47272e40e_story.html

Page 178 See: http://webarchive.nationalarchives.gov.uk/+/http://yourarchives.nationalarchives.gov.uk/index.php?title=Wood,_Francis_Derwent_%281871-1926%29_sculptor

Page 178 'as an orderly' – Biernoff, S. 'The Rhetoric of Disfigurement in First World War Britain' *Social History of Medicine*, vol. 24, no. 3, p. 677.

Page 178 See: http://www.npr.org/templates/story/story.php?storyId=7556326

Page 178 'at the 3rd General Hospital in Wandsworth, London' – http://www.iwm.org.uk/collections/item/object/205213406

Page 179 'psychological insight' – https://www.washingtonpost.com/local/an-american-sculptors-masks-restored-french-soldiers-disfigured-in-world-war-i/2014/09/22/4748b8d4-38ec-11e4-9c9f-ebb47272e40e_story.html

Page 179 'the thinness of a visiting card'– http://www.smithsonianmag.com/history/faces-of-war-145799854/

Page 180 'they "passed"' – Gilman, S.L. *Making the Body Beautiful: A Cultural History of Aesthetic Surgery*, p. 158.

Page 180 'repulsive' – https://www.washingtonpost.com/local/an-american-sculptors-masks-restored-french-soldiers-disfigured-in-world-war-i/2014/09/22/4748b8d4-38ec-11e4-9c9f-ebb47272e40e_story.html

Page 180 'greetings' – ibid.

Page 180 'There was always an almost iridescent shiny cast' – Hemmingway, E. *A Moveable Feast*, p. 70.

Page 181 'the problem of "passing"' – Gilman, S.L, *Making the Body Beautiful: A Cultural History of Aesthetic Surgery*, p. 158.

Page 181 'weakness for wounded heroes' – Young, L. *A Great Task of Happiness: The Life of Kathleen Scott*, p. 185.

Page 182 'Bernard "Tiny" Freyberg' – http://www.nzhistory.net.nz/people/bernard-freyberg

Page 182 'five wound bars' – Young, L. *A Great Task of Happiness: The Life of Kathleen Scott*, p. 185.

Page 183 'At the hospital I worked' – ibid., p. 187.

Page 183 'I feel terribly like God' – ibid., p. 187.

Page 183 'These men without noses' – ibid., p. 188.

Page 183 'practical jokes' – Pound, R. *Gillies: Surgeon Extraordinary, a biography*, pp. 84 and 85.

Page 184 'he bought £10 worth' – Gilman, S.L. *Making the Body Beautiful*, p. 159 and Gillies, H.D. and Millard, R. Ralph. *The Principles and Art of Plastic Surgery*, vol. 1, 1957, p. 7.

Page 185 http://www.gilliesarchives.org.uk/

Page 185 'Royal Army Medical College' – Holmes, R. *Tommy: The British Soldier on the Western Front*, p. 466.

Page 185 'Advances in medicine and hygiene' – ibid., p. 483.

Page 185 'Saline drips . . . Thomas splint' – ibid., p. 483.

Page 185 'Only one thing' – Van Emden, R. *The Quick and the Dead: Fallen Soldiers and Their Families in the Great War*, p. 85.

Page 185 'Over 41,000 British soldiers' – Bourke, J. *Dismembering the Male: Men's Bodies, Britain and the Great War*, p. 33.

Page 186 'a full pension' – Biernoff, S. 'The Rhetoric of Disfigurement in First World War Britain', *Social History of Medicine*, vol. 24, no. 3, p. 671.

Page 186 'presentable enough to be a blind man' – Gillies, H.D. and Millard,

D. Ralph. *The Principles and Art of Plastic Surgery*, London: Butterworth 1957, p. 27; Biernoff, S. 'The Rhetoric of Disfigurement in First World War Britain', *Social History of Medicine*, vol. 24, no. 3, p. 681.

Page 186 'children of one veteran fled – Biernoff, S. 'The Rhetoric of Disfigurement in First World War Britain' *Social History of Medicine*, vol. 24, no. 3, pp. 668–667 (footnote 45).

Page 186 'a most extraordinary experience' – Young, L. *A Great Task of Happiness, The Life of Kathleen Scott*, p. 185.

Page 186 'merriest banter' – War Muir, R.A.M.C. *Observations of an Orderly: Some Glimpses of Life and Work in an English War Hospital*, p. 88, quoted in Biernoff, 'The Rhetoric of Disfigurement in First World War Britain', Social History of Medicine, vol. 24, no. 3, p. 671 (footnote 34).

Page 186 'Physical agility' – Biernoff, S. 'The Rhetoric of Disfigurement in First World War Britain' *Social History of Medicine*, vol. 24, no. 3, p. 675.

Page 187 'INDEPENDENT SPINSTER' – February 1919, the same advert appeared in December 1921.

Page 187 'over 11,000 operations' – Pound, R. *Gillies, Surgeon Extraordinary. A Biography*, p.54; p. 88., quoted in Biernoff, S. 'The Rhetoric of Disfigurement in First World War Britain', *Social History of Medicine*, vol. 24, no. 3, p. 671.

Page 188 Gillies' work featured in the Faces of Battle Exhibition, National Army Museum, 14 November 2007. See: http://news.bbc.co.uk/1/shared/spl/hi/picture_gallery/07/magazine_faces_of_battle/html/11.stm

Page 188 'compared to a suitcase handle' – http://www.bbc.co.uk/guides/zxw42hv

Page 189 'When the huge, oedematous forehead' – Gillies, H.D. and Millard, D. Ralph. *The Principles and Art of Plastic Surgery*, London: Butterworth, 1957, p. 41.

Page 190 'phwat an aisy toime' – Gillies, H.D. *Plastic Surgery of the Face*, p. 68.

Page 191 'if we made a poor repair' – Gillies, H.D. and Millard, D. Ralph. *The Principles and Art of Plastic Surgery*, London: Butterworth, 1957, p. 45.

Page 191 'Hardest of all' – ibid., p. 9.

Page 191 'a corporal' – ibid.

Page 191 'I'm not disfigured!' – Gillies H.D. and Millard, D. Ralph. *The Principles and Art of Plastic Surgery*, London: Butterworth, 1957, p. 27.

Chapter Eleven: The Changed Husband

Page 193 'Swiss mercenaries' – Holmes, Singleton and Jones, *The Oxford Companion to Military History*, entry on 'psychiatric casualties'.

Page 193 'Shells used to come bursting' – Graves, Robert. *Goodbye to All That*, p. 235.

Page 194 'five-bob flips' – Gillies, M. *Amy Johnson: Queen of the Air*, p. 22.

Page 194 'like a broken army' – Lee, L. *As I Walked Out One Midsummer Morning*, p. 11; Macfarlane, R. *The Old Ways: A Journey on Foot*, p. 315.

Page 194 'some nervous trouble' – Orwell, G. *Down and Out in Paris and London*, p. 168.

Page 194 'Some of the returning soldiers – Macfarlane, R. *The Old Ways*, p. 21.

Page 196 'urine-drenched socks' – Haber, F. *The Poisonous Cloud: Chemical Warfare in the First World War*, p. 45.

Page 196 'sanitary towels' – Holmes, R. *Tommy: The British Soldier on the Western Front*, p. 421.

Page 196 '*Daily Mail* mounted a campaign' – Haber, F. *The Poisonous Cloud: Chemical Warfare in the First World War*, p. 45.

Page 196 'Black Veil Respirator' – ibid., p. 46.

Page 197 'So there was this load' – Lessing, D. *Alfred and Emily*, p. 172.

Page 197 'Maconochie' – Holmes, R. *Tommy: The British Soldier on the Western Front*, p. 285.

Page 197 'bathmat' – Doyle, P. and Walker, J. *Trench Talk: Words of the First World War*, p. 94.

Page 197 'Ypres became Wipers' – Holmes, R. *Soldiers: Army Lives and Loyalties from Redcoats to Dusty Warriors*, p. 456.

Page 197 'pip-squeak' – Doyle, P. and Walker, J. *Trench Talk: Words of the First World War*, p. 165.

Pages 197–8 'toffee apple'– ibid., p. 173.

Page 198 'flying pig' – ibid., p. 174.

Page 198 'Sir Charles Myers' – Reid, F. *Broken Men: Shell Shock, Treatment and Recovery in Britain, 1914–1930*, p. 26; Shephard, B. *A War of Nerves: Soldiers and Psychiatrists, 1914–1994*, p. 1.

Page 198 'A 1922 War Office committee' – Holmes, Singleton and Jones, *The Oxford Companion to Military History* and Gregory, *The Oxford Companion to the Mind*.

Page 198 '*hystérie de guerre* or *commotion par obus*' – Reid, F. *Broken Men: Shell Shock, Treatment and Recovery in Britain, 1914–1930*, p. 28.

Page 198 'The *Spectator* had pointed out' – Shephard, B. *A War of Nerves: Soldiers and Psychiatrists, 1914–1994*, p. 7.

Page 198 'the bulging eyeballs' – Bourke, J. *Dismembering the Male: Men's Bodies, Britain and the Great War*, p. 108.

Page 198 'Charles Blondin' – Shephard, B. *A War of Nerves: Soldiers and Psychiatrists, 1914–1994*, p. 2.

Page 199 'Rumour had it' – Dahl, R. *Boy: Tales of Childhood*, pp. 108–9.

Page 199 'spoke with a Lancashire' – Shephard, B. *A War of Nerves: Soldiers and Psychiatrists, 1914–1994*, pp. xvii and xviii.

Page 199 'struck dumb' – Reid, F. *Broken Men: Shell Shock, Treatment and Recovery in Britain, 1914–1930*, pp. 18 and 39.

Page 199 'The hair of one patient stood' – Shephard, B. *A War of Nerves: Soldiers and Psychiatrists, 1914–1994*, p. 73.

Page 199 'change in personality' – ibid., p. 56.

Page 199 'paint the house in odd colours' – ibid., p. 251.

Page 199 'One patient was so worried' – Barham, P. *Forgotten Lunatics of the Great War*, p. 250.

Page 199 'wife of a cotton twirler' – ibid., p. 240.

Page 199 'thrash her' – Roper, M. *The Secret Battle: Emotional Survival in the Great War*, p. 6.

Page 200 'jumped from a bridge' – Barham, P. *Forgotten Lunatics of the Great War*, p. 131.

Page 200 'a man threw' – *The Daily Herald*, Friday, 15 October 1920, p. 2.

Page 200 'Private Harry Barrow' – Barham, P. *Forgotten Lunatics of the Great War*, p. 131.

Page 200 'By June 1917, 1,216' – ibid., p. 108.

Page 200 'to wander into No Man's Land' – ibid., p. 128.

Page 200 'a more specialist approach was needed' – Reid, F. *Broken Men: Shell Shock, Treatment and Recovery in Britain, 1914–1930*, p. 29.

Page 200 'In December 1914' – ibid., p. 30.

Pages 200–1 'By the war's close, 80,000 cases' – Bourke, J. *Dismembered the Male: Men's Bodies, Britain and the Great War*, source: Showalter, E. *The Female Malady: Women, Madness and English Culture*, p. 63.

Page 201 'Viscount Knutsford' – Reid, F. *Broken Men: Shell Shock, Treatment and Recovery in Britain, 1914–1930*, p. 32.

Page 201 'It would not be easy' – *The Times*, 18 January 1915.

Page 201 'Quiet, rest, the "home feeling"' – ibid., 25 May 1915.

Page 201 'but very few exceptions all have recovered' – ibid., 26 May 1915.

Page 203 'His daughter' – Blakeway Productions – 'Shell Shock' for Channel 4, IWM 20703.

Page 204 'The number of officers' – Barham, P. *Forgotten Lunatics of the Great War*, pp. 252, 254 and 256.

Page 204 'Treatment varied' – ibid., p. 87; Shephard, B. *A War of Nerves: Soldiers and Psychiatrists, 1914–1994*, p. 74

Page 204 'April 1915 and April 1916' – Reid, F. *Broken Men: Shell Shock, Treatment and Recovery in Britain, 1914–1930*, p. 13.

Page 204 '6,435' – ibid., p. 111.

Page 204 'revealed that nearly 12,000' – Barham, P. *Forgotten Lunatics of the Great War*, p. 231.

Page 204 'pre-war average of 10–11 per cent' – ibid., p. 145.

Page 204 'Scotland' – Reid, F. *Broken Men: Shell Shock, Treatment and Recovery in Britain, 1914–1930*, p. 80.

Page 204 'pension to buy a bike' – Barham, P. *Forgotten Lunatics of the Great War*, p. 346.

Page 205 'at great personal risk' – ibid., pp. 341–42.

Page 205 '18,596 pensions' – Reid, F. *Broken Men: Shell Shock, Treatment and Recovery in Britain, 1914–1930*, p. 10.

Page 205 'According to official figures, in 1937' – Barham, P. *Forgotten Lunatics of the Great War*, p. 4.

Page 205 'The 1930 Mental Treatment Act' – ibid., p. 303.

Page 205 'batman' – Roper, M. *The Secret Battle: Emotional Survival in the Great War*, pp. 137–146.

Page 206 'a pact' – Van Emden, R. *The Quick and the Dead: Fallen Soldiers and Their Families*, p. 104; Acton, C. *Grief in Wartime: Private Pain, Public Discourse*, p. 37.

Page 206 'write to his widow' – Holmes, R. *Tommy: The British Soldier on the Western Front*, p. 361.

Page 206 'memorial book' – Roper, M. *The Secret Battle: Emotional Survival in the Great War*, p. 225.

Page 206 'Lord Peter Wimsey' – Reid, F. *Broken Men: Shell Shock, Treatment and Recovery in Britain, 1914–1930*, p. 21.

Page 206 'any true reconstruction' – Bourke, J. *Dismembering the Male: Men's Bodies, Britain and the Great War*, p. 128.

Page 206 'Sidney Rogerson', *Twelve Days on the Somme: A Memoir of the Trenches*, pp. 60–1, quoted in Holmes, R. *Soldiers: Army Lives and Loyalties from Redcoats to Dusty Warriors*, p. 204.

Page 206 'stay in the ranks' – Holmes, R. *Tommy: The British Soldier on the Western Front*, p. 145.

Page 207 'Stockbrokers' Battalion' – Roper, M. *The Secret Battle: Emotional Survival in the Great War*, p. 243.

Page 207 'nearly 40 per cent of the service' – Bourke, J. *Dismembering the Male: Men's Bodies, Britain and the Great War*, p. 131.

Page 207 'Northumberland Fusiliers' – Roper, M. *The Secret Battle: Emotional Survival in the Great War*, p. 133.

Page 207 'their "wife"' – Bourke, J. *Dismembering the Male: Men's Bodies, Britain and the Great War*, p. 135.

Page 208 'sport moustaches' – Holmes, R. *Tommy: The British Soldier on the Western Fron*, p. 368.

Page 208 'around 417,000 men were admitted' – Holmes, R. *Soldiers: Army Lives and Loyalties from Redcoats to Dusty Warriors*, p. 587; Bourke, J. *Dismembering the Male: Men's Bodies, Britain and the Great War*, p. 161, says 400,000.

Page 208 'self-inflicted wound' – See 'Sex and the Somme: The officially sanctioned brothels on the front line laid bare for the first time' by Clare Makepeace, http://www.dailymail.co.uk/news/article-2054914/Sex-Somme-Officially-sanctioned-WWI-brothels-line.html. see also http://www.bbc.co.uk/news/uk-england-25762151

Page 208 'regimental bazaars' – Holmes, R. *Sahib: The British Soldier in India, 1750–1914* and *Soldiers: Army Lives and Loyalties from Redcoats to Dusty Warriors*, p. 480.

Page 209 'extraordinary baby bubble' – Spiegelhalter, D. *Sex by Numbers: What Statistics Can Tell Us About Sexual Behaviour*, p. 174.

Page 209 'female workforce rose by 50 per cent' – Shephard, B. *A War of Nerves: Soldiers and Psychiatrists, 1914–1994*, p. 147.

Page 209 'all-male shipyards' – Adie, K. *Fighting on the Home Front: The Legacy of Women in World War One*, photo opposite p. 203.

Page 209 'The *Daily Mail*' – Shephard, B. *A War of Nerves: Soldiers and Psychiatrists, 1914–1994*, p. 147.

Page 210 'Eleanore Stephens' – Roper, M. *The Secret Battle: Emotional Survival in the Great War*, pp. 94 and 216 and Massie, A. and Parton, F. *Wives and Sweethearts: Love Letters Sent During Wartime*, pp. 30–41.

Page 211 'three times as many divorces in 1919 as 1913' – Bourke, J. *Dismembering the Male: Men's Bodies, Britain and the Great War*, p. 163.

Page 211 'incurable insanity' – Barham, P. *Forgotten Lunatics of the Great War*, p.188.

Page 211 'In 1912, 2.75 per cent' – Van Emden, R. *The Quick and the Dead: Fallen Soldiers and Their Families*, p. 46.

Page 212 'he leads me such a life' – 23 January 2014, *Independent* and *Guardian*.

Page 212 'Marriages among widows' – Van Emden, R. *The Quick and the Dead: Fallen Soldiers and Their Families*, p. 304.

Page 212 'Harry Patch' – ibid., p. 308.

PART THREE: WORLD WAR TWO

Chapter Twelve: Life on the Home Front: Diana Carnegie, 1940

Page 215 'Bruce Belfrage' – http://www.bbc.co.uk/programmes/p027f6hz

Pages 215–16 Belfrage recreated the moment at http://www.bbc.co.uk/news/uk-22765668

Pages 217–19 Correspondence between Diana and James Carnegie is reproduced by kind permission of Charlotte and Sophie Carnegie.

Page 219 'Officers' Groundsheets' – Costello, J. *Love, Sex and War: Changing Values, 1939–45*, p. 79 and

Haste, C. *Rules of Desire: Sex in Britain: World War I to the Present*, p. 127.

Page 219 'American Tail Supply' – Barrett, D. and Calvi, N. *GI Brides: The War-Time Girls Who Crossed the Atlantic for Love*, p. 23.

Page 219 'the committee found' – Haste, C. *Rules of Desire: Sex in Britain: World War I to the Present*, p. 127.

Chapter Thirteen: Life on the Home Front: Rachel Dhonau, Summer 1941 to December 1942

Page 226 'The thought that Jakob' – 10 August 1941.

Page 226 'I was just going to bed' – 8 August 1941.

Page 227 'It is a funny feeling' – 2 August 1942.

Page 228 'father was born in Aachen' – Malcolmson, R. and Searby, P. (eds.). *Wartime Norfolk: The Diary of Rachel Dhonau 1941–1942*, p. 1.

Page 228 'engaged at least once' – ibid.

Page 228 'in Paris' – ibid., p. 4.

Page 229 'It seems almost like a dream' – 17 July 1941.

Page 229 'No letter from my husband' – 29 July 1941.

Page 230 'It will be like being' – 6 August 1941.

Page 230 'I feel quite nervous' – 13 August 1941.

Page 230 'I didn't listen' – 16 August 1941.

Page 231 'who knows how long?' – 24 August 1941.

Page 231 'I had a letter' – 13 September 1941.

Page 231 'which though a good' – 17 September 1941.

Page 232 'I thought how desolate life' – 19 July 1941.

Page 232 'I miss my husband' – 21 October 1941.

Page 233 'I have seen them in Sheringham' – 17 October 1941.

Page 233 'venereal disease' – Costello, J. *Love, Sex and War: Changing Values, 1939–45*, p. 127.

Page 233 'Paris and Brussels' – ibid., pp. 146–7.

Page 234 'A Defence Regulation' – Haste, C. *Rules of Desire: Sex in Britain: World War I to the Present*, p. 133.

Page 234 'one bishop' – Costello, p. 356.

Page 234 'Nearly a third of all' – Haste, p. 109.

Page 234 'The divorce rate, which had plunged during the economic Depression' – Costello, J. *Love, Sex and War: Changing Values, 1939–45*, p. 13.

Page 234 '1942 rose by 100 per cent rose each year above the 1939–42 average' – ibid., p. 275.

Page 234 'almost no work that day' – 29 September 1941.

Page 235 'She is very young' – 11 October 1941.

Page 235 'If they want to sleep' – 14 October 1941.

Page 235 'Adamson argued' – Hansard Commons Debates, *30 June 1943, Vol. 390 cc1743–52*.

Page 236 'German private' – *The Times*, 29 October 1943.

Page 236 'A British POW, Andrew Hawarden' – IWM, 66/132/1.

Page 236 'An injured GI' – Costello, J. *Love, Sex and War: Changing Values, 1939–45*, p. 349.

Page 237 'which is nice' – 20 December 1941.

Page 239 'dismay and certainly disgust' – 12 February 1942.

Page 239 'public shelters to avoid' – Bowman, M. *Images of War – Norwich Blitz – Rare Photographs from Wartime Archives*, p. 9.

Page 240 '162 people had died' – Brown, R. Douglas. *East Anglia 1942*, p. 61.

Page 240 'She says she feels quite empty' – 4 June 1942.

Page 241 'I shall soon have to' – 8 February 1942.

Page 242 'My aunt always makes' – 22 March 1942.

Page 242 'And I can't see why a soldier's child' – 10 September 1942.

Page 242 'Every time he goes' – 23 August 1942.

Page 243 'earned about five times more' – Barrett, D. and Calvi, N. *GI Brides: The War-Time Girls Who Crossed the Atlantic for Love*, p. 11.

Page 243 'to 419,000' – Haste, C. *Rules of Desire: Sex in Britain: World War I to the Present*, p. 110.

Pages 243–44 'The Soldiers, Sailors and Airmen's Families' ibid., p. 110.

Page 244 'In extreme cases' – Fussell, P. *Wartime Understanding and Behavior in the Second World War*, p. 39.

Page 244 'about 80,000 women' – Haste, C. *Rules of Desire: Sex in Britain: World War I to the Present*, p. 126.

Page 244 'also fathered around 70,000 illegitimate children' – Costello in ibid., p. 126.

Page 244 'months to secure the necessary paperwork' – Barrett, D. and Calvi, N. *GI Brides: The War-Time Girls Who Crossed the Atlantic for Love*, p. 57.

Page 244 'threw him out of a second-storey window' – Costello, J. *Love, Sex and War: Changing Values, 1939–45*, p. 317.

Page 244 '1943, a Canadian was hanged for killing' – ibid., p. 317.

Page 244 'of Launceston' – ibid., p. 318.

Page 245 'I can't imagine why' – 10 October 1942.

Page 246 'No one reading this diary' – 4 November 1942.

Chapter Fourteen: The Prisoner of War's Wife: Renee Boardman, 1942–44

Much of this chapter is based on an interview with Ronald and Tom Boardman, 8 January 2014, and on subsequent email and telephone communication.

Page 247 'Gracie Fields of tomorrow' – *The Journal*, 30 January 1997, and *Daily Dispatch*, 10 December 1931.

Page 249 'soap' – *Researching FEPOW History Group Newsletter*, 8 February 2012.

Page 249 'register at an employment exchange' – Jolly, E. *My Ancestor was a Woman at War*, p. 103; Williams, M.A. *A Forgotten Army: The Female Munitions Workers of South Wales, 1939–1945*, p. 65.

Page 250–51 http://www.bbc.co.uk/history/british/britain_wwtwo/women_at_war_01.shtml

Page 251 'notes of encouragement' – Williams, M.A. *A Forgotten Army: The Female Munitions Workers of South Wales, 1939–1945*, p. 72.

Page 251 'Mary' – ibid.

Page 251 'about 10 shillings a week' – *How Are They at Home?* p. 31. *Women's History Review*, http://www.tandfonline.com/loi/rwhr20

Page 251 '"How are they at home?" community, state and servicemen's wives in England', 1939–45, Sally Sokoloff, University College Northampton. Published online: 19 December 2006.

Page 252 'between £2 and £4 a week' – Hyams, J. *Bomb Girls: Britain's Secret Army: The Munitions Women of World War II*, p. 33.

Page 252 'for example, 2–10 p.m.' – ibid., p. 18.

Page 252 'tetryl, cordite and trinitrotoluene (TNT)' – ibid., p. 80.

Page 252 'jewellery, hair clips and combs' – ibid., p. 76.

Page 252 'boiled sweet' – Hyams, J. *Bomb Girls: Britain's Secret Army: The Munitions Women of World War II*, p. 19.

Page 253 'Just as he was shedding clothes' – Gillies, M. *The Barbed-Wire University: The Real Lives of Prisoners of War in the Second World War.*

Page 253 'Risley' – Working on the Suicide Squad: At Risley Royal Ordnance FactoryArticle ID: A2311507 Contributed on: 18 February 2004; *Sitting on top of a bomb – the unsung heroines of Risley ROF* by Susan Wilkes http://web.archive.org/web/20030511134357/http://www.rof-risley.fsnet.co.uk/bestofbritish/best_of_brit_44.jpg

Page 253 'heat from their fingers' – Sitting on top of a bomb – *the unsung heroines of Risley ROF* by Susan Wilkes

Page 254 'Blowing your nose' – Hyams, J. *Bomb Girls: Britain's Secret Army: The Munitions Women of World War II*, p. 188.

Page 254 'jaundice-coloured sheets' – ibid., p. 60.

Page 254 'canaries' – Williams, *A Forgotten Army: The Female Munitions Workers of South Wales, 1939–1945*, p. 80.

Page 254 'naturally blonde' – Hyams, J. *Bomb Girls: Britain's Secret Army: The Munitions Women of World War II*, p. 60.

Page 254 'the whites of your eyes' – ibid., p. 153.

Page 254 'wear bibs' – ibid., p. 189.

Page 254 'Max Factor "cake" make-up' – ibid., p. 161.

Page 255 'In 1942 the British Red Cross' – Parkes, M. and Gill, G. *Captive Memories: Far East POWs & Liverpool School of Tropical Medicine*, p. 171.

Page 256 '22 per cent of' – ibid., p. 26.

Page 257 'Phyllis Baker' – Green, C. *Surviving the Death Railway: A POW's Memoir and Letters from Home.*

Page 259 'Daisy Duffield' – IWM, Mr D. Duffield, Documents.13502 (05/56/1).

Chapter Fifteen: The End of the War: Surviving the Peace, 1943–45

Page 265 'dropped some 2,452 V-1 pilotless' – http://www.bbc.co.uk/history/worldwars/ww two/ff7_vweapons.shtml

Page 266 'killed over 2,500 Londoners' – ibid.

Page 269 'lonely not knowing' – she later told Tom.

Page 269 'SS *Corfu*' – ibid., p. 76.

Page 270 'a sense of guilt and shame' – Parkes, M. and Gill, G. *Captive Memories: Far East POWs and Liverpool Tropical School of Medicine*, p. 164.

Page 271 'plodding' – interview with the author.

Page 271 'quite romantic' – ibid.

Page 275 'Thousands of children' – For further accounts of the difficulties of returning fathers see, Turner, B. and Rennell, T. *When Daddy Came Home: How War Changed Family Life Forever* and Summers, J. *Stranger in the House.*

Page 275 'domestic drudge' – Sage, L. *Bad Blood: A Memoir*, p. 8.

Page 275 'Like many who'd married' – ibid., p. 112.

Page 275 '"Uncle" or "Mister"' – Turner, B. and Rennell, T. *When Daddy Came Home: How War Changed Family Life Forever*, p. 135.

Page 276 'kissing the photo on the wall goodnight' – ibid., p. 141.

Page 276 'In France' – Fishman, S. *We Will Wait: Wives of French Prisoners of War 1940–1945*, p. 146.

Page 276 'sick down his back' – Sage, L. *Bad Blood: A Memoir*, p. 8.

Page 277 'One hundred and thirty thousand civilians quoted in' – Turner, B. and Rennell, T. *When Daddy Came Home: How War Changed Family Life Forever*, p. 198.

Page 278 'Research that appeared in the 1950s' – ibid., pp. 270–1.

Page 278 'as well as France and the US' – Fishman, S. *We Will Wait: Wives of French Prisoners of War 1940–1945*, p. 147.

PART FOUR: THE MODERN ARMY WIFE

Chapter Sixteen: The Cold War Wife

Page 281 'Unexpected success' – http://www.stripes.com/news/from-dooley-to-jones-bases-in-germany-feed-us-soccer-team-s-multicultural-success-1.257375

Page 281 'One could say' – http://www.psmag.com/navigation/politics-and-law/u-s-military-shaped-american-soccer-82915/

Page 282 'More than 400,000 Germans had been killed' – Kershaw, I. *The End: Hitler's Germany, 1944–1945*, p. 379.

Page 283 *'A Guide for Families in BAOR'* – IWM.

Page 284 'provision of dish cloths' – *Timeshift: The British Army of the Rhine*, first broadcast BBC Four, 22 October 2012.

Page 287 'Sue and Richard Middleton' – interview, 23 March 2013 and subsequent email exchanges with Sue and Richard Middleton.

Page 288 'Jean Metcalfe' – http://news.bbc.co.uk/1/hi/uk/622515.stm

Page 289 'life expectancy at eight hours' –*Time Shift: The British Army of the Rhine*, first broadcast BBC Four, 22 October 2012.

Page 290 'Elizabeth Speller' – various interviews with the author and email exchanges.

Page 291 'solid' – Speller, E. *The Sunlight on the Garden: A Family in Love, War and Madness*, p. 155.

Page 291 'Operation Rocking Horse' – Stone, D. *Cold War Warriors: The Story of the Duke of Edinburgh's Royal Regiment (Berkshire and Wiltshire), 1959–1994*, p. 137 and Speller, E. *The Sunlight on the Garden: A Family in Love, War and Madness*, p. 157.

Page 292 'Carol Armstrong' – interview with the author, 26 March 2013, and subsequent email exchanges.

Page 295 'children of parents in the armed forces' – *Creative Forces*, BBC Radio 4, first broadcast 14 November 2013.

Page 295 'fish in a tank' – interview with retired teacher.

Page 299 'OMO' – Speller, E. *The Sunlight on the Garden: A Family in Love, War and Madness*, p. 164.

Page 299 'series of attacks' – http://www.nytimes.com/1988/05/02/world/3-british-servicemen-are-killed-in-ira-attacks-in-netherlands.html

Chapter Seventeen: The Modern Army Wife

Page 306 'Deployment bonuses' – tweeted by 'Mrs P. (@ARmyWagBlog)

Page 307 'played mind games' – Carr, J. *Another Story: Women and the Falklands War*, p. 38.

Page 307 'Afghanistan Time' – http://www.cafepress.co.uk/+deployment+clocks

Page 308 'speak-your-weight machine' – http://www.theguardian.com/media/2002/feb/25/broadcasting.falklands

Page 308 Reporting of the Falklands War: http://archive.iwm.org.uk/upload/package/29/mediawar/technolfalk.htm

Page 308 'devoid of trees and buildings' – Carr, J. *Another Story: Women and the Falklands*, p. 30.

Page 308 'raised £63,000' – ibid., pp. 28–9.

Page 309 'As Iraq is three hours ahead' – Holmes, R. *Dusty Warriors: Modern Soldiers at War*, p. 160.

Page 310 'windiest place on earth' – ibid., p. 161.

Page 310 'break' and 'over' – Junger, S. *War*, p. 197.

Page 312 'It forces you to literally' – 'Staying in Touch With Home, for Better or Worse', *The New York Times*, 16 February, 2011.

Page 313 Alcoholism: http://www.kcl.ac.uk/kcmhr/publications/assetfiles/2013/Aguirre2013b.pdf

My thanks to Major Jamie Woodfine for decoding some of the terms described in this chapter.

Epilogue: Life After the Army

Page 319 'A soldier aged over forty' – http://www.army.mod.uk/join/Careers-in-the-Army.aspx

Page 321 'In recent years' – MOD press office.

Page 322 'Until 1847 the ordinary soldier enlisted for life' – Trustram, M. *Women of the Regiment: Marriage and the Victorian Army*, p. 18.

Page 322 'officers were not obliged to retire' – Spiers, E.M. *The Late Victorian Army, 1868–1902*, p. 92.

Page 322 'She marched 2,028 miles' – Kelly, C. *Mrs Duberly's War: Journal & Letters from the Crimea, 1854–1856*, p. i.

Page 323 'Andaman Islands' – Tytler, H. *An Englishwoman in India: The Memories of Harriet Tytler, 1828–1858*, p. 178

Page 323 'During his term in office' – ibid.

Page 325 'But the greatest joy of all' – 'A Soldier's Wife in the Crimea' by the narrative of Mrs Elizabeth Evans, late 4th. (King's Own) Regiment of Foot as told to Walter Woods, in *The Royal Magazine*, July 1908, pp. 265–72.

Page 325 'In other accounts widows' – de Courcy, A. *The Fishing Fleet: Husband-Hunting in the Raj*, p. 6.

Page 326 'battled for nearly forty years to secure' – quoted in Rappaport, H. *No Place for Ladies: The Untold Story of Women in the Crimean War*, p. 237.

Page 326 'receiving some kind of pension' – Trustram, M. *Women of the Regiment: Marriage and the Victorian Army*, p. 93.

Page 326 'both on and off the strength' – ibid., p. 175.

Page 326 'in 1881 the Government agreed' – ibid., p. 93.

Page 327 '2,359 widows by the end of 1900' –http://www.nationalarchives.gov.uk/pathways/census/pandp/people/wido.htm

Page 327 'Only widows who were only the strength' – Millgate, H.D. *War's Forgotten Women: British Widows of the Second World War*, p. 22.

Page 327 'Josephine Downey' – http://www.nationalarchives.gov.uk/pathways/census/pandp/people/wido2l.htm

Page 329 'could cry together' – Van Emden, R. *The Quick and the Dead: Fallen Soldiers and Their Families in the Great War*, p. 317.

Page 329 'write to the parents of her fiancé' – Nicholson, V. *Singled Out: How Two Million Women Survived Without Men After the First World War*, p. 309.

Page 329 'gradually it all stopped' – Callan, H. and Ardener, S. (eds.). 'The Incorporated Wife', 1984, p. 96.

Pages 329–30 'Falklands widows were allowed' – Shaw, M. and Millgate, H.D. *War's Forgotten Women: British Widows of the Second World War*, 2011, p. 99.

Page 330 'More than 200 widows' – Shaw, M. and Millgate, H.D. *War's Forgotten Women: British Widows of the Second World War*, 2011, p. 100.

For more information on the Grant-in-aid scheme, see: http://support.britishlegion.org.uk/app/answers/detail/a_id/236/kw/widows%20trips%20to%20far%20east

Page 330 'Some 4,500 widows' – http://www.theguardian.com/uk/2000/nov/08/richardnortontaylor

Page 330 'Since 1967' – Shaw, M. and Millgate, H.D. *War's Forgotten Women: British Widows of the Second World War*, 2011, p. 100.

Page 330 'flag' – Acton, C. *Grief in Wartime: Private Pain, Public Discourse*, p. 3.

Page 330 Recent legal battles over wills – http://www.telegraph.co.uk/news/uknews/law-and-order/11924371/A-battle-of-willsmothers-of-dead-soldiers-taken-to-courtlisa-billing-sharon-leverett.html

Page 331 'someone (same sex or otherwise)' – email exchange with MOD press office.

Page 335 'military covenant': http://www.publications.parliament.uk/pa/cm201516/cmhansrd/cm160107/halltext/160107h0001.htm

Page 335 '2,500 organisations': http://www.johnnyforplymouth.co.uk/wp-content/uploads/2016/01/2016-01-JME-BD01-10.pdf

Page 335 'on her own family experience' – Mrs Anne-Marie Trevelyan (Berwick-upon-Tweed) (Con).

Page 335 http://medicalxpress.com/news/2016-01-highlights-scale-health-military-veterans.html

Page 335 'end the ban on women' – http://www.theguardian.com/uk-news/2014/dec/19/women-combat-roles-british-army-infantry-armoured-units

Acknowledgements

The group of people who most deserve my thanks cannot – for security reasons – be named. Nevertheless, I hope the army wives of serving soldiers realise how grateful I am for their time, their hospitality and their honesty. I would also like to thank the husbands and partners of the wives I interviewed. I realise it cannot have been easy to have had their lives scrutinised.

Thanks to the group of women I affectionately think of as 'my Cold War wives': Barbara Wilton, Sue Middleton, Carol Armstrong and Elizabeth Speller. Husbands Chris Wilton and Richard Middleton deserve an additional mention for their patience and interest. James and Mary Thorne provided further insights and Elisabeth and the late Cornie Thorne answered many questions about army life.

Diana Carnegie burst onto the scene when the letters she wrote during the Second World War appeared at auction and which I bought – blissfully unaware that they were stolen. Getting to know Diana's daughters, Sophie Carnegie and Charlotte Purkis, has been a great pleasure. I am very grateful for their generosity in allowing me to quote from their parents' correspondence so fully and for being helpful in so many other ways.

I was delighted to spend time with Ron and Tom Boardman – which is always a pleasure. Hilary Custance Green allowed me to read a pre-publication version of her book, *Surviving the Death Railway: A POW's Memoir and Letters from Home*. Kevin Morrison once again shared his knowledge of the Second World War and Deborah Arnander led me to Rachel Dhonau.

I enjoyed a fascinating afternoon with 'Michael' Spreckley's granddaughter, Ally White, and am very grateful for her help and to Patrick Hartley for putting me in touch with her in the first place. Andrew Bamji was prompt in replying to my queries about the work of Harold Gillies. I am, grateful, too, to Tom Leland for allowing me to quote from his grandfather's correspondence and to Vanessa Blake for helping me to explore my grandfather's First World War records.

Other army wives appeared only through letters and diaries and I would like to thank the archives and libraries who maintain these treasures: Argyll and Sutherland Highlanders Museum; Army Medical Museum; Berkshire Record Office; Dumbarton Library; the British Library; British Music Hall Society (and its historian, Max Tyler); Cambridge University Library; Commando Veterans' Association; Gonville and Caius College, Cambridge University (with special thanks to M.S. Statham, College Librarian); the Imperial War Museum (with special thanks to Simon Offord); 6th Queen Elizabeth's Own Gurkha Rifles (especially Brian O'Bree); King's College London Archives; Liddle Collection, University of Leeds; National Archives; National Archives of Scotland; the Mass Observation Archive; the National Army Museum; National Memorial Arboretum; Museum of Army Chaplaincy (and in particular, David Blake AMA, Curator); Parliamentary Archives; Portsmouth History Centre; Researching Far East POW History; SSAFA; Silver End Heritage Society; University of Cambridge, Centre of South Asian Studies and the Wellcome Institute.

Darragh McElroy, Chief Communications Officer, Ministry of Defence was very helpful in answering questions and Lou O'Connell explained the particular challenges of life in the modern British Army. Jamie Woodfine decoded some of its jargon. Gillian Richmond, an Army BRAT and author of *The Last Waltz*, a play about two army wives, helpfully highlighted some of the most recent memoirs about service life.

I am grateful for the help and encouragement of friends. Among the writers, I would particularly like to thank Kathryn Hughes, Clare Makepeace and Lizzie Collingham. Clare was kind enough to read a chapter and I value her comments on that section of the book, as well as her many helpful suggestions for further reading.

Veronica Forwood and Roger Browning read a draft of the book and gave me invaluable comments. Andrew Balmford, Sarah Blakeman, Jenny Burgoyne, Adrian and Judith Dunn, Louise Fryer, Paul Horrell, Adrian Leslie, Sarah Mnatzaganian, Meg Parkes, Gavin Perry, Bridie Pritchard and Rosy Thornton were constantly encouraging. My cousin Agnes Henderson answered several questions about our relatives, as did Michael and Bob Kelly on the other side of the family. Jenny Colls was a true friend through some of the hardest months and I also enjoyed talking to her about life in Cold War Germany. Kate Bull offered insight into the paediatric care of young babies.

Researching *Army Wives* coincided with a happy three-year period as Royal Literary Fund Fellow at Magdalene and Wolfson Colleges in Cambridge. I would like to thank the Masters and Fellows at both colleges for making me so welcome and for the Royal Literary Fund for running such a wonderful scheme. I am also, again, indebted to the Society of Authors.

Teaching Creative Writing at Cambridge University's Institute of Continuing Education continues to be a pleasure and an inspiration. I'm grateful to the students who continually challenge and surprise me and to my wonderful colleagues: Jenny Bavidge, Sarah Burton, Lisa Hitch, Christina Koning, Liz Morfoot, Katherine Roddwell, Jem Poster and Elizabeth Speller.

As with my previous book, *The Barbed-Wire University*, the idea for *Army Wives* was Graham Coster's. I am very grateful for his inspiration. Thanks, too, to Melissa Smith for seeing the idea through to publication. Jane Donovan has been a thorough and sensitive copy-editor and I am equally grateful to Caroline Curtis for her skill as a proof-reader. My agent, Faith Evans, has provided her usual attention to detail and support in so many ways.

Authors, perhaps particularly of non-fiction, can be difficult to live with. Our daughter, Rosa, has long since left behind the familiar childhood cry of long journeys, 'Are we nearly there yet?', to replace it with, 'Is the book nearly finished yet?' Finally, the answer is 'Yes!' Thank you, Rosa and Jim, for your patience and love.

My mother, Renee Gillies, was an army wife for a matter of months, although the army's influence on her husband, my father, Donald, hovered over their long marriage. She was a great supporter of each of my books and I'm sorry she didn't live to see the publication of *Army Wives*. When I wrote my first book, she and my father shared the dedication. This book is dedicated solely to her memory.

Permissions

'There's Something About A Soldier'
Words & Music by Noel Gay, © Copyright 1933 Chester Music Limited Trading as Richard Armitage Music.
All Rights Reserved. International Copyright Secured.

Extracts from Margaret Campbell Hannay, Hannay Papers, and Frances Janet Wells, the Berners Papers, including the letters of Mrs. Frances Janet Wells, are both published by kind permission of the University of Cambridge, Centre of South Asian Studies.

Anthony Sattin was kind enough to grant permission for me to quote from *An Englishwoman in India: The Memoirs of Harriet Tytler, 1828–1858*.

I am grateful to Fisher Press for their permission to quote from their new edition of *Elizabeth Butler, Battle Artist, Autobiography*, first published in 1993.

Jonathan Frewin was kind enough to allow me to quote from the literary estate of Clare Sheridan.

I am very grateful to the Trustees of the Imperial War Museum for allowing access to their collections and to copyright holder Tom Leland for permission to quote from his grandfather's papers.

Correspondence between Diana and James Carnegie is reproduced by kind permission of Sophie Carnegie and Charlotte Purkis.

Quotations from Vera Brittain are included by permission of Mark Bostridge and T.J. Brittain-Catlin, Literary Executors for the Estate of Vera Brittain 1970.

Letters of Winston S. Churchill reproduced with permission of Curtis Brown, London, on behalf of The Estate of Winston S. Churchill © The Estate of Winston S. Churchill.

Letters of Clementine Spencer Churchill reproduced with permission of Curtis Brown, London, on behalf of The Master, Fellows and Scholars of Churchill College, Cambridge © The Master, Fellows and Scholars of Churchill College, Cambridge.

Extracts from the diaries of Rachel Dhonau are reproduced with permission of Curtis Brown Group Ltd., London, on behalf of The Trustees of the Mass Observation Archive.

Every effort has been made to trace copyright holders. The publishers will be glad to rectify in future editions any errors or omissions brought to their attention.

Index

1st South Staffordshire Regiment 159
2nd Infantry Brigade 122
3rd Light Cavalry 90
4th Dragoon Guards 76
4th (King's Own) Regiment 68
6th Royal Scots Fusiliers 162
8th Royal Irish Hussars 69, 322, 323
10th Hussars 120
10th Royal Fusiliers 207
11th Native Infantry 90
14th Artillery Brigade 86
18th Division 234, 235, 239
20th Native Infantry 90
31st Regiment 21
32nd Regiment 98
38th Native Infantry 96
50th Native Infantry 51
93rd Regiment 76

abortion 233
'The Absent-Minded Beggar' (Rudyard Kipling) 326-7
Abu Naji 310
accommodation 29-48
- army quarters 29-30, 284
- barracks 31-3, 35, 37
- billeting 31
- bungalows 37-8
- campaign furniture 41-3
- gardens 30, 54, 264
- huts 46-7, 48
- living 'out' 30-1, 302-3
- 'march in'/'march out' 30, 284
- officers 44, 45, 284, 305
- privations 31-2, 37, 45-6
- shoddy 30
- tents 40-1, 44, 45, 46
- unmarried couples 6, 330-1

Adamson, Janet 235-6
adultery 234
Afghanistan 11, 303, 304, 308-9, 311, 312, 314
Agutter, Jenny 295
Air Mail service 28
air-raid shelters 241, 246
Albert, Prince Consort 81, 148
Aldershot 31, 32, 122
Alexandra, Queen 201
Alma, Battle of (1854) 64, 65, 68, 122
'An Alarm in India' (Edward Hopley) 109
Andaman Islands 323
Anderson, Lieutenant Mathew 35
Anderson shelters 241
Arabi Pasha 123
Armistice Day 143, 146, 328-9
Armstrong, Carol 1, 292-5, 296-7, 299
Armstrong, Major Richard 293-4, 295
army
- Cardwell's army reforms 86, 322
- changing public perceptions of soldiers 79, 85-6, 87, 88, 89
- covenant of care 31, 335
- hierarchical nature 242, 296-7, 305

Army Air Corps (AAC) 290, 297, 303
Army Families Federation 12
Army and Navy Stores 43-4
Arras, Battle of (1917) 142

art
soldiers and conflicts, portrayals of 87-9, 109-10, 112-17
see also Butler, Lady Elizabeth
Ashanti campaign 159
Asquith, Herbert 181
Assam Light Infantry 59
asylum patients 204
atomic bomb 269
Attlee, Clement 268
attributes of a soldier 6
Austen, Jane 9
Auxiliary Territorial Service (ATS) 218-19, 233
Ava (steamship), loss of 23-4

Baby Blitz 265
Bad Blood (Lorna Sage) 275
Bahadur Shah 90
Baker, Captain Barton Custance 257
Baker, Sir Herbert 144-5
Baker, Phyllis 1, 257, 258
Balaclava helmet 85
'Balaclava' (Lady Elizabeth Butler) 117
Balaklava 65, 66, 70, 76, 84
Bank Clerks' Orphanage 173-4
Barrackpore 20, 36, 37, 40, 90, 96
barracks 31-3
corner system for women 31-2, 35, 37
married quarters 32, 37
Barrie, J.M. 181
Barrow, Private Harry 200
Basra Memorial Wall 334
bathing 38
batmen 205-6
'Bavarian Artillery Going into Action' (Lady Elizabeth Butler) 117
BBC 215-16
Belfast 299-300
Belfrage, Bruce 215-16
Bengal Army 94
Bennett, Jill 70
Berlin 290-1, 297
Berlin Airlift 290
Berlin Wall 291
Berwick 31
Bevin, Ernest 268
bibis 53
bigamy 211, 232
billeting 31
Birkenhead (troopship), loss of 22-3
birth control 233, 241
birth rates 209
Black, Catherine 191-2
'The Black Brunswicker' (John Millais) 88-9
black soldiers 244-5, 327
Black Watch 149, 151, 182
Blitz 222, 239, 277, 287
Blomfield, Sir Reginald 145
Blondin, Charles 198
Blood, Gertrude *see* Campbell, Lady Gertrude
Blood, Neptune 128-9
Blunt, James 295
Boardman, Irene ('Renee') 1, 247-51, 253, 254, 255-7, 269, 271, 335
Boardman, Tom 247-9, 252, 256-7, 269-70, 271
body strippers 35
Boer War (1899–1902) 125-6, 166-7, 185, 326-7, 331
Boldini, Giovanni 126
Bolst, Clifford Erskine 181-2
Booty, Dolly 1, 259-60
Booty, Private Ernest 259
Box, Rebecca 326
Bridge on the River Kawi (film) 256
British Army of the Rhine (BAOR) 282-3
British Families Education Service 295
British Forces Post Office (BFPO) 310
British Raj *see* India; Indian Mutiny
Brittain, Vera 138, 141, 142-3, 148-9
brothels 72, 208-9
Brown, Jessie 109
Brown, Percival 211-12
Buckeridge, Anthony 174
Buller, General Sir Redvers 118
Burma (Myanmar) 53
Butler, Ellen ('Nell') 1, 64, 66-7, 73, 326
Butler, Lady Elizabeth (Elizabeth Thompson) 1, 111-26, 127, 130-1
Butler, Josephine 33
Butler, Private Michael 66, 67
Butler, Brigadier-General Sir William 111-12, 117-19, 120, 122-4, 125-6, 127, 129-31

'Calling the Roll after an Engagement, Crimea' (Lady Elizabeth Butler) 112-15, 118, 119
Cambridge Military Hospital 184
Camel Corps 119-20
campaign furniture 41-3
Campbell, Lord Colin 108, 127
Campbell, Lady Gertrude (née Blood) 126-30
Campbell v. Campbell 127-30
Canada 112
Captain Philips (film) 318
Cardigan, Lord 46
Career Transition Partnership 321
Carnegie, Diana 1, 216-25, 243, 261-9, 272-5, 331-2
Carnegie, Second Lieutenant James 216-17, 218-25, 261, 264, 265, 266, 267, 272, 273, 331-2
Carrington, Hereward 138
Carroll, Lieutenant 172-3
Carter, Lieutenant Edward August 42
cavalry regiments 69
Cavell, Edith 146
Cawnpore 100, 107-8, 110
Cenotaph 147
Chamberlain, Neville 229
Chambers, Mary 260
Changi Jail 256, 334
chaplains 131, 146
Chaplin, Charlie 329
Charge of the Light Brigade (1854) 35, 75, 76-7
The Charge of the Light Brigade (film) 70
'Charge of the Light Brigade' (Tennyson) 86
Chemin des Dames 151
children
  education 16, 94, 104, 173-5, 296
  fears 314-15
  illegitimate 10, 234, 235, 244, 327
  juvenile crime 278
  letters 170-1, 174-5
  mixed-race 53
  orphans 54, 143, 326
  and returning fathers 274-6
  sibling rivalry 277
  see also education
China 33
Chippendale, Thomas 41
Chivenor Barracks 11
The Choir: Military Wives (BBC TV) 11
choirs, army 11, 306-7, 336
cholera 58-9, 62, 63, 72, 75, 99
Churchill, Clementine 1-2, 140, 162-4, 166
Churchill, Lady Randolph 139
Churchill, Winston 135, 140, 162-4, 268, 273, 329
  Iron Curtain Speech 289
City of London Territorials 139
clairvoyance 154
Clive, Robert 36
clothing 74, 263, 274
Colchester 31
Cold War 281-99
'The Colours: Advance of the Scots Guards at Alma' (Lady Elizabeth Butler) 122
Combat Stress 12
commemoration of the dead 141-2, 144-5
  see also mourning; war memorials
commissions, selling and buying of 86
Commonwealth Graves Commission 144, 330
communications
  communicating bad news 301-2
  e-blueys 310, 311
  instant, drawbacks of 311-12
  social media 309, 311, 312, 336
  see also letters
compassionate leave 243-4
The Complete Indian Housekeeper and Cook (Flora Steel and Grace Gardiner) 38
conscription 139-40
  women 250
Contagious Diseases Acts 33
contraception 233, 241
Cook, Captain 21-2
Cook, Thomas 145
Cooper, Gary 218
Courtneidge, Cicely 4, 6
Cove, Ethel 2, 167-73, 174-5
Cove, Gunner Wilfrid 167-73
Cresswell, Adelaide 2, 70-1, 73
Cresswell, Captain 74-5
Crimean War (1853–56) 34, 36, 44-8, 63-87, 89, 326
  accommodation 44-8

in art 112-15, 119
casualties 80
Charge of the Light Brigade (1854) 33, 75, 76-7
media coverage of 31, 80-5
travelling to 24-5
women on campaign 65-78
Cuban missile crisis (1962) 289-90
Curragh 31, 32
Curragh 'Wrens' 32
Cuttack Legion 52

Dad's Army 275
Dahl, Roald 198-9
Deane, Ada 143
death
anniversaries of 328-9
death certificates 173
distant graves 142, 148, 329-30, 375
domestic shrines to the dead 141, 148-9
and mourning 137-8, 141, 328-9
next-of-kin issues 330-1
next-of-kin notification 308-9
relics 142-3
repatriation of the dead 144, 330
Death Railway 256, 334
'The Defence of Lucknow' (Tennyson) 109
'The Defence of Rorke's Drift' (Lady Elizabeth Butler) 123-4
Delhi 90-3, 95, 104, 105-7, 108-9
Derby Scheme 167
deserters 200
Devonshire Regiment 141
Dhonau, Private Jakob 226, 227, 228, 229-31, 237-8, 240, 242, 245-6, 332
Dhonau, Rachel 2, 226-35, 236-43, 245-6, 332
Dickens, Charles 48, 111, 116
Dickens, Kate 88
diphtheria 32
disabled and maimed soldiers 176-92, 333-4, 335
amputations 185
disability pensions 205
facial disfigurement, fear of 185-6
loss of sight 186
marriage prospects 186-7
masculinity issues 185-6
'passing' problem 180, 181
pensions 186
prosthetic make-up 176-81
reconstructive surgery 181-6, 188-92, 333
stigma of disfigurement 186
disease 32-3, 35
see also individual index entries
divorce 6, 211, 234
Doherty, Pete 295
domesticity in war, male experience of 207
Dover Castle 122
Down and Out in Paris and London (George Orwell) 194
Downey, Josephine 327-8
Doyle, Sir Arthur Conan 137
drinking culture 72, 315-16
Duberly, Fanny 2, 25, 45, 46, 47-8, 69-78, 81-2, 85, 86-7, 322-3
Duberly, Henry 69, 70, 82, 322, 323
Duffield, Daisy 2, 259-60
'Dulce et Decorum Est' (Wilfred Owen) 196
dysentery 72, 105, 159, 322

e-blueys 310, 311
East India Company 36-7, 51, 52, 53, 59, 94
East Indiamen sailing ships 20
Eden, Anthony 256
Edmondson, Ade 295
education
army schools 295
boarding schools 16, 94, 104, 173-5, 296
British Families Education Service 295
Education Act, 1870 165
Edward VII 127, 148
Eisenhower, General 245
Elizabeth, the Queen Mother 147
Ellerman, Sir John 182
Ely Rifle Volunteers 79
enlistment periods 86, 322
entertaining duties 124-5, 297-8, 315
Erroll, Lady Eliza 2, 34, 45, 71-2
Evans, Elizabeth 2, 35, 36, 64, 66, 67-8, 73, 325-6
Evpatoria 74
Ewart, Colonel 103-4
exemptions from military service 211-12

faithless soldier figure 9, 13, 88

Falklands War 307-8, 312, 329-30, 334
media coverage 307-8
Far From the Madding Crowd (Thomas Hardy) 9
The Far Pavilions (M.M. Kaye) 15
Fearon, Colonel 21
Fenton, Roger 80-2
Fields, Gracie 251
Finnegan, Letitia 75-6
'Fishing Fleet' 52
flogging 127
food and clothing parcels 161, 162, 163, 169-70, 210, 311
Forces Free Air Letters (FFAL) 311
foreign correspondents 82-3
Formby, George 247
Forrest, Annie 2, 46-7
Forrest, Major William 46-7
Fraser, Captain Simon 51
Fraser-Tytler, Mary Seton 139
French, Dawn 295
Freyburg, Bernard 182
friendships between soldiers 205-7
funerals 144

Galloway, James 114, 115
gas masks 222
gas warfare 8, 160, 195, 196, 202
gas-gangrene 185
Gaston, Edward Page 152
Gay, Noel 4, 6
George V 146, 147
George VI 147
Germany
Army Wives' clubs 292
Cold War era 282-99
food and food rationing in 284-7, 291
postings to 282-99
postwar devastation 282-3
relations between Germans and the British military 290
Soviet invasion, fear of 291
Gibraltar 159
Gillies, Agnes 2
Gillies, Alexander 8, 9-10, 195, 208
Gillies, Donald (author's father) 8
Gillies, Donald (author's great-grandfather) 7-8, 9-11
Gillies, Harold Delf 183-4, 186, 188, 189, 190-1, 333
Gillies, Rebecca 2, 10, 11
Gillies, Renee 2
Girl Guide Movement 296
'The Girl I Left Behind Me' 10
GIs 233, 242-5
black GIs 244-5
romantic liaisons 243-4
Gladstone, William Ewart 144
Gold Coast Regiment 159
Goodbye to All That (Robert Graves) 193-4
Gordon, General 118, 120, 125
Gordon-Cumming, Roualeyn 71
Grave Registration Committee 142
Graves, Robert 193-4, 208
Gray, Effie 88
Greenaway, Kate 117, 126
Guards Memorial, London 80
'The Guinea Pig Club' 333
Gull, Major Francis 185
Guttman, Ludwig 333

Haig, General 146
'Halt on a Forced March: Retreat to Corunna' (Lady Elizabeth Butler) 119, 121
Hannay, Margaret Campbell 2, 25-7, 40-1, 42, 51-2, 53-62
Hannay, Lieutenant Simon Fraser 51, 52, 55-6, 57, 59-60, 61
Harrods 43, 223
Hartnell, Norman 263
Havelock, General 99, 101
Hawarden, Andrew 236
Hawksmoor, Nicholas 31
Hawley, Captain Robert Beaufoy 70
head of household, women's role as 277
Heal's 43
Help for Heroes 12
Hemingway, Ernest 180
Hepplewhite, George 41
Hicks, John Braxton 129
Hiroshima 269
Hitchcock, Alfred 218
Hodge, Lieutenant-Colonel 46, 47, 76
Home Guard 218
'Home' (John Noel Paton) 88

house moves 5, 6-7, 120, 321
packing 15-16
house purchase, Help to Buy Scheme 321-2
Humperdinck, Engelbert 295
huts 46-7, 48

ill health 58, 62, 68
see also disease
Illustrated London News 48, 83, 109, 116, 123
'In Memoriam: Henry Havelock' (Joseph Noel Paton) 110
Ince, William 41
India 32, 33
Indian Army 15-16, 33, 36-41, 51-62, 93-4, 95-6
insurgents 59, 60
local 'wives' 53
travel in 25-8
Indian Mutiny 53, 90-5, 322, 325
in art and literature 109-10
atrocities 107-8
causes 93-4
public interest in 110-11
siege of Delhi 105-7, 108-9
siege of Lucknow 23, 97-102, 109
infant mortality rates 148
Inglis, Lady Julia 3, 23-4, 97, 98, 99, 100, 324-5
Inglis, Major-General John 98, 99, 324-5
Inkerman, Battle of (1854) 112
Intelligence Corps 227, 229, 332
IRA 299
Iraq 308, 309-10, 334
Ireland 111, 118, 131, 159
see also Troubles, Northern Ireland
Iron Curtain 289
Irving, Washington 88

James, Henry 139, 155
jaundice 73
Jekyll, Gertrude 145
'Jessie's Dream' (Frederick Goodall) 109
Johnson, Eastman 10
Jones, Jermaine 281
journal-keeping 53-8, 62, 86-7, 97
see also Mass Observation diaries
Journey to the North of India (Lieutenant Arthur Connolly) 65
Julien, Louis 69

Kanchanaburi 330
Kaye, Sir Cecil 16-17
Kaye, Daisy 16-17
Kaye, Mollie 3, 15-16, 17, 52
Kelly, Bernard 8
Kelly, Brian 8, 332
Kelly, Peggy 3, 8, 332-3
Kennedy, John F. 289
Kent (troopship) disaster 20-2
Kersham, Nellie 260
khamtis 59, 60
Kilvert, Robert Francis 115
Kipling, Rudyard 86, 145, 154, 326-7
Knutsford, Viscount 201
Kreisler, Fritz 135

Ladd, Anna Coleman 178, 179, 180
Lancashire Fusiliers 157
laundry work 35, 68, 76, 99-100
Lear, Edward 183
leave periods 164, 229-31, 236-8, 242, 265, 304
compassionate leave 243-4
Lee, Laurie 194
Leighton, Roland 142, 148
Leland, Captain Herbert John Collett 158-62, 164, 165, 201-3
Leland Collett, Lena 3, 158-9, 161-2, 202, 203
Lenin, Vladimir Ilyich 329
Leonard, Gladys 137
Lessing, Doris 196, 197
letters 13, 311-12, 336
advice on letter writing 243
censorship 84, 158, 167
children's letters 170-1, 174-5
circulation of 166
coded 157-8
Crimean War 84-5
literacy and 165
to POWs 256-7
Victorian era 17-19, 26, 37-9, 96-7, 101-2
World War One 157-75, 202
World War Two 217, 218-19, 219-20, 221-2, 223-4, 261-9, 272-4, 332
Lewis, Beatrice 52

lice 25, 73, 99, 237
life after the army 318-22
life expectancy 148
literacy 165
literature, soldiers and conflicts in 88, 109
Lloyd George, David 146, 164
Lodge, Sir Oliver 136-7
London Olympics (1948) 333
London Regiment 195
Loos, Battle of (1915) 140
Louise, Princess 122, 127
Loyd-Lindsay, Lieutenant Robert 114, 122
Lucknow 23, 96-102, 109
Lumley, Joanna 295
Lutyens, Sir Edwin 144, 146-7
Lyndoe, Edward 231
Lytton, Lord 108

McDonald, Ian 308
McGonagall, William 22
McIndoe, Archibald 333
Macnaghten, Angus 149-54
Macnaghten, Hazel 3, 149, 150-4, 155-6
Malone, Gareth 11, 306
Manning, Cardinal 117, 118
marching with the regiment 25-7, 36, 40, 51, 54, 67-8, 73, 322
Marlborough, Duke of 128, 129
'Marmion' (Sir Walter Scott) 108
marriage
  advertising for a partner 186-8
  bigamy 211, 232
  by proxy 235-6
  divorce 6, 211, 234
  divorce rate 6
  GI brides 244
  hurried weddings 6, 169, 211, 234-5
  inter-racial 53
  strains on 6-7
  successful 5
  twenty-first century 13-14
  Victorian era 12-13, 32
Marx, Francis 85
Mass Observation diaries 227, 229-30, 231, 232-3, 235, 237, 240-1, 242, 243, 245, 246
Matrimonial Times 186-7
Mayhew, John 41
media coverage 12, 307-9
  Crimean War 31
  Falklands War 307-8
Menin Gate 154, 156
Menshikov, Prince 64
menstrual cycle 219, 229-30, 274
mess functions 315
Metcalfe, Jean 288
Metropolitan Police 332
Meynell, Alice 111, 116, 117, 127
Mhow 51, 54
Michelmore, Cliff 288
Middleton, Captain Richard 287, 290, 319-20
Middleton, Sue 3, 287-90, 289-90, 296, 297, 298, 319-21
Millais, John Everett 87-8, 114
Milner, Sir Alfred 125
missing in action 149-54
moon, universal symbolism of 17, 307
morale 158, 165
morality 31-2, 232, 233, 234, 242-3
  see also sexual behaviour
Mordaunt, Sir Charles 127
Morgan, Fred 172
Morrison shelters 241, 246
mourning 137-8, 141-9, 154-6, 328-9
Mrs Dalloway (Virginia Woolf) 199-200
munitions factories 197, 209, 250-5
Murray, Major James 151
Music While You Work 251
Muybridge, Eadweard 114
Myers, Sir Charles 198
Mysopoorie 54

Nagasaki 269
nannies 264, 273
Napoleon Bonaparte 120
Napoleonic War 19-20, 82, 84
National Army Museum 42
National Memorial Arboretum 334
Neuve Chapelle, Battle of (1915) 210
New South Wales 33
News From Home (John Millais) 87
Nicholas I, Tsar 63
Nightingale, Florence 67, 72, 83, 114, 118
Norwich 239-40, 242-3
nursing 66-7, 83, 191-2

ocean travel 17-24
disasters 20-4
onboard fires 21, 25
privations of 18, 25
troopships 17-23, 47-8
officers' wives
family support role 75, 209-11, 257, 258
socialising duties 124-5, 297-8, 315
status conscious 297, 305
support networks 298
Omar Pasha 81
orphans 54, 143, 326
Owen, Wilfred 196

Paget, Lord George 69-70, 72
Pakistan 28
palanquins 26-7, 55, 58, 323
pals battalions 207, 209-10
Paralympics 333-4
Paris terrorist attacks (2015) 13
Patch, Ada 212
Patch, Harry 212
Paterson, Jackie 248
Paton, Joseph Noel 88, 109-10
Paxton, Joseph 46
pay
officers 123
regular soldiers 242
Separation Allowance 166, 210, 235
women war workers 251-2
see also pensions
Pélissier, Aimable-Jean-Jacques 81
Penelope (wife of Odysseus) 9
Peninsular War (1808–14) 35, 111
Penny Post 165, 166
pensions 173, 186, 195, 200, 203, 205, 236
disability pensions 205
orphans 326
reduced 249
taxation of 328
unmarried couples 330-1
widows 200, 325-6, 327-8
Percival, Lieutenant General 249
pet animals 217-18, 237
Phoney War 220
photography, war 80-2
plastic surgery 181-6, 188-92, 333
poppies 12
Postal Service 165-6
see also letters
Potato Famine 111, 124
prayers for the dead 137
pre-deployment briefings 305-6
pregnancy
fecundity 209, 245
unmarried girls 219, 233, 236
wartime rations 262
women in the armed services 219
Pride and Prejudice (Jane Austen) 9
prisoners of war (POWs)
Boer War 167
camaraderie 331
Far East POWs 235, 249, 252, 253, 255-8, 269-70, 277, 330, 334
postwar payments to 330
postwar traumas 271-2, 277, 331
return home 269-71
wives' support network 257, 258, 259-60
World War One 152, 153, 156, 207
World War Two 8, 236, 249, 252, 253, 255-60, 269, 276
Probyn, Sir Lesley 150
prosthetic make-up 176-81
prostitution 32-3, 72, 76, 161, 208-9
psychical phenomena 141, 143
see also spiritualism

RAF 333
RAF Brize Norton 313
Raglan, Lord 46, 66, 73, 81
rail travel 27-8
Railton, David 146
Ramsden, Staff-Sergeant Major 63
rationing 216, 262, 263, 273
postwar Germany 284-5
Raymond, Or Life and Death (Sir Oliver Lodge) 136-7, 138
The Recruiting Officer (George Farquhar) 9
recruiting officers 86
Red Cross 144, 151, 152, 156, 167, 176, 177, 255-6, 270
Red Cross Military Hospital 200-2, 203
Red Cross Studio of Portrait Masks 178
Red River Expedition (1869) 112
'Red Sea Route' 20
redundancy packages 319

'The Relief of Lucknow' (Thomas Jones Barker) 109
repatriation of the dead 144, 330
resettlement courses 320
retirement 318-22, 318-33
'Retribution' (Edward Armitage) 110
'Return from Inkerman' (Lady Elizabeth Butler) 122
The Return of the Soldier (Rebecca West) 149, 199
'Returning From the Fair' (Thomas Webster) 88
returning soldiers
 children, relationships with 274-6
 euphoric homecoming 313
 home life, adjusting to 194-8, 207, 274-8, 312-14
 impact on family dynamics 197, 276-8, 313
 mental illness 193-4, 198-205
 rituals 313
 see also prisoners of war (POWs)
Reuters' news agency 84
Rheindahlen Garrison 294-5, 299
Rhodes, Cecil 125
Rifle Brigade 140
Rigby, Fusilier Lee 12, 309
rituals and superstitions 307
Roland, Madame 71-2
Ross and Co. 42
Royal Army Medical College 185
Royal Army Medical Corps (RAMC) 178, 184
Royal Army Ordnance Corps (RAOC) 248
Royal Artillery 267
Royal Cambridge Asylum for Soldiers' Widows 326
Royal Corps of Signals 257, 258
Royal Corps of Transport 299
Royal Engineers 284
Royal Munster Fusiliers 159
Royal Ordnance Factory 250-1
Royal Patriotic Fund 325, 326
The Ruby in the Smoke (Philip Pullman) 109
Ruskin, John 87-8, 112, 117, 118
Russell, William 82-3
Ryle, Herbert Edward 146, 147

Sadiya 59
Sage, Lorna 275, 276
Saunders, Jennifer 295
Sayers, Dorothy L. 206, 218
scarlet fever 32
'Scotland for Ever!' (Lady Elizabeth Butler) 119
Scots Guards 122
Scott, Kathleen 181-3, 186
Scott, Robert Falcon 181
scurvy 72, 98
Scutari 45, 65, 67, 83
séances 135-7, 138, 154-5
seasickness 18, 25
The Secret Garden (Frances Hodgson Burnett) 59
Separation Allowance 166, 210, 235
servants 38-9
Sevastopol 65, 68, 75
 siege of (1855) 77, 79
sexual behaviour 219, 233, 268
 see also prostitution
sexual desire 218, 226, 232, 272
Shadow of the Moon (M.M. Kaye) 109
shampoo 38
Shaw, George Bernard 126
Shearer, Thomas 41
shell shock 189, 193-4, 198-205
Shepheard's Hotel, Cairo 120-1
Sheraton, Thomas 41
Sheridan, Clare 3, 135-6, 138-9, 140-1, 149, 154-5, 329
Sheridan, Richard Brinsley 139
Sheridan, Captain Wilfred 135, 136-7, 138-41, 154-5
Sherwood Forresters 188
The Siege of Krishnapur (J.G. Farrell) 100
Siege of Lucknow 23
Simla 15, 27
Simner, Captain Benjamin 42-3
Simner, Mary 42-3
Singapore, fall of (1942) 239, 249, 257
Sir John Ellerman Hospital for Disabled Officers 182-3
Skype 309
slang 197-8, 316-17
smallpox 73, 98
Smith, 'Kokana' 76
soccer 281-2

social media 309, 311, 336
Soviet Union *see* Cold War
Soyer, Alexis 45
Spanish flu 209
Special Air Services (SAS) 308
spectator sport, war as 34-5, 64, 77
Speller, Elizabeth 3, 290-2
spinsters 186-7
spirit photos 143
spiritualism 135-7, 138, 154-5
Spreckley, William Michael 188-90, 333
SSAFA (Soldiers, Sailors, Airmen and Families Association) 12, 243-4, 298
Stephens, Eleanore 3, 210-11
Stephens, Lieutenant-Colonel Reginald 210
Stevenson, Juliet 295
Stoke Mandeville Games 333
stowaways 34, 73
Strachey, Lytton 118
Streatfield, Noel 218
Suez Canal 20
suicides 99, 200, 246
Sullivan, Arthur 126
support networks 5, 11-12, 306-7
  organisational 11-12, 306
  POW wives 257, 258, 259-60
  unofficial 11, 298, 306-7
sutlers 34
syphilis 127, 208

Taj Mahal 57
Taylor, Maik 281-2
Tel-el-Kebir, Battle of (1882) 123
telegraphy 84
Tenniel, John 65
Tennyson, Alfred, Lord 86
tents 40-1, 44, 45, 46
terrorism 13, 299, 335-6
tetanus 185
The Third Man (film) 190
Thomas, Edward 142
Thomas splint 185
Thompson, Thomas 111, 116
Thugee 27
tigers 60
Tikaram, Tanita 295
The Times 82, 84, 114, 124, 130, 201, 236
TNT 254
Tolkien, Edith 3
Tolkien, J.R.R. 157-8
Tolstoy, Leo 86
Tomb of the Unknown Warrior 145-6, 147-8, 334
Tommy Atkins image 85-6, 89
Tonks, Henry 181, 182-3
travel 15-28
  ballots for allocated places 33-4
  marching with the regiment 25-7, 36, 40, 51, 54, 67-8, 73, 322
  ocean travel 17-24
  palanquins 26-7, 55, 58, 323
  rail 27-8
  stowaways 34, 73
  wagons 20
troopships 17-23, 47-8, 73-4
Trotsky, Leon 329
Troubles, Northern Ireland 282, 292, 298, 299-300
tuberculosis 32
Twelve Days on the Somme (Sidney Rogerson) 206
Two-Way Family Favourites 288-9
typhoid 25, 32
Tytler, Harriet 3, 18, 20, 27, 90-3, 94-6, 103-7, 108-9, 323-4
Tytler, Lieutenant John Adams 95
Tytler, Captain Robert 90, 91, 93, 95, 103, 104-5, 106, 323-4

Ulster Defence Regiment 300
Umballa (Ambala) 103-4
underwear 208, 263
United States
  GIs (World War II) 233, 242-5
  see also Cold War
Utility Wear 263

V1 flying bombs (doodlebugs) 265
V2 rockets 265-6
Vanity Fair (William Makepeace Thackeray) 71
Varna 72, 73, 84
venereal disease 33, 127-8, 208, 233-4
Victoria, Queen 85, 86, 95, 112, 114-15, 118, 148
Victoria Cross 89

Vietnam War 330

wanderlust 321
war memorials 80, 140, 145-8, 154, 334-5
War Stores Scandal 126
War Widows' Association 328
Ware, Sir Fabian 144
Waterloo, Battle of (1815) 35, 116-17
Watts, George Frederic 139
wedding presents 42
welfare officers 304, 305-6, 313
Wells, Frances ('Fanny') 3, 17-19, 20, 36, 37-40, 96-7, 98, 99-102
Wells, Walter 17-18, 19, 39-40, 40, 102
West, Rebecca 149
West African Frontier Force 159
West Coast of Africa expedition (1873–74) 112
Wheeler, Sir Hugh 107
Whistler, J.A.M. 126
White, Colonel Adam 59, 61
widows 135-56, 308, 324, 328-30
  loss of social life and support 329
  memorial to 334
  pensions 325-6, 327-8
  remarriage 212, 325, 327
  séances 135-7
  visits to final resting places 329-30, 375
  see also mourning
Wilde, Oscar 126
Wilkinson, Ellen 235, 236
wills, eve-of-battle 330
Wilton, Barbara 3, 4-5, 30, 290, 296, 297-8, 298, 299-300
Wilton, Flight Commander Chris 290, 298, 299-300
'wives' exercises' 315
Wolseley, Sir Garnet 112, 118, 120, 123
women in the armed services 7, 219
  see also Auxiliary Territorial Service (ATS); Women's Royal Army Corps (WRAC)
Women's Institute 320
Women's Royal Army Corps (WRAC) 292-4
Wood, Francis Derwent 178-80
Woolwich 31, 32
Wootton Bassett 12
work
  administrative 232
  armed services 7, 292-3
  artists *see* Butler, Lady Elizabeth (Elizabeth Thompson)
  domestic 34, 35, 44
  factory work 197, 209, 250-5
  independence 197, 277-8
  laundry 35, 68, 76, 99-100
  munitions 197, 209, 250-5
  nursing 66-7
  postal workers 166
  teaching 54, 60
  Women Returning to Work courses 320
  World War One 209, 211
  World War Two 249-51
Workers' Playtime 251
World War One (1914–18) 16, 17, 131, 135-212, 328
  Armistice 16
  battlefield tourism 145
  conscription 139-40
  mourning for the dead 137-8, 141-9, 154-6
  soldiers missing in action 149-54
  specific language of 197-8
  see also disabled and maimed soldiers; prisoners of war (POWs); returning soldiers
World War Two (1939–45) 215-78, 328
  bombing campaigns 222-3, 224, 227, 239-40, 241, 252, 265-6
  cessation of hostilities 267
  demobbing 272
  evacuation programmes 222
  Phoney War 220
  postwar austerity 273
  rationing 216, 262, 263, 273
  threatened invasion of Britain 220
  VE Day 267-9
  VJ Day 269
  see also prisoners of war (POWs); returning soldiers
Wright, Ada 3, 195, 196
Wright, Robert Thomas 195, 196, 207
writing boxes 42
Wyatt, Brigadier-General Louis John 146

Ypres, Second Battle of (1915) 196

Zululand 120